THE LIFE OF

SAMUEL J. TILDEN

WRITTEN BY

JOHN BIGELOW

REVISED AND EDITED BY

NIKKI OLDAKER

"WHEN THE PEOPLE RISE THE SYSTEM GETS CLEANSED"...
—SAMUEL JONES TILDEN

Dedicated To

Public Librarians & History Teachers Worldwide

Acknowledgments

A special thank you to all the National Arts Club Presidents, especially O. Aldon James for preserving the Samuel Tilden historical landmark Gramercy Park home. Also to the Trustees and donors of the New York Public Library for continuing to support Samuel Tilden's gift of the first free public library system in the United States.

CONTENTS

Presidential canvass of 1876 – Assailable points
of Grant administration
Popular majority for Tilden and Hendricks
Inception of the conspiracy to defeat the popular choice
Senator Barnum, John C. Reid, and the "New York Times"
William E. Chandler's break of day dispatches
Troops ordered to Florida
President Grant's dispatch to General Sherman
Foul operations of conspirators in Florida
How reward by President Hayes and General Barlow

The conspirators' operations in Louisiana
William Pitt Kellogg
Visiting statesmen in New Orleans
The composition and operations of the
Louisiana Returning Board
Garfield
Sherman
Anderson
Jewett
Eliza Pinkston
Fraudulent registration
The reward of the conspirators

Lois Blanc's account of his visit to Louis Napoleon when
a prisoner at ham, and the loss and recovery of his voice in
London
The story of General Cavaignac's brother and mother
Tilden's exposure in recrossing the channel
Returns to the United States
The "Indian Corn Speech"

The trials and temptations of a bachelor millionaire
Proposals of marriage in verse and prose

The cipher dispatches
Tilden's address to the people of the United States
in regard to them
His examination by a congressional committee
A calumnious report corrected
Letter to Senator Kernan

Income tax returns
New persecutions by the administration
The capitulation of the administration
The ignominious end of seven years' persecution
Letters of Edwards Pierrepont, special counsel
for the government
SL Woodford, United States District Attorney;
Green B, Raum, United States Commissioner
of Internal Revenue
Charles J. Folger, Secretary of Treasury; and
Benjamin H. Brewster, Attorney General
of the United States

The purchase of Graystone
Dinner to J.S. Morgan
Mr. Tilden rebukes third-term candidates for the Presidency

Tilden withdraws from public life
Letter to Mr. Manning declining the presidential
nomination in 1880
The Cincinnati convention
Tilden urged for a re-nomination in 1884
Tilden's second letter of declension

Tilden's relations to the new President
Senator Garland a suitor
Letters to Manning
Tilden's and Jefferson's views of civil service
Harbor defences
Letter to Carlisle
Tilden's friends proscribed at Washington
Letter to Watterson
George W. Julian
Tilden discourages his nephew and namesake
from embarking in politics
R.B. Minturn
Manning's illness and retirement from the treasury
History of the Monroe Doctrine
The Broadway railroad
Advice to Governor Hill against the proposed
enlargement of the Eric canal
Favors the bill for and international park and
for the protection of the Adirondack forests

Tilden's last days
The books Tilden read
His death
Whittier's elegiac verses
Tilden's funeral
Tilden's Will
The validity of the Tilden will contested
The trustees of the Tilden Trust purchase a half-interest
in the estate

James C. Carter's argument
Provision made by the Legislature and afterwards withdrawn,
for the Tilden Free Library

The Life of

Samuel J. Tilden

Written by John Bigelow

Edited by Nikki Oldaker

CHAPTER I

Presidential canvas of 1876 – Assailable points of Grant administration- Popular majority for Tilden and Hendricks – Inception of the conspiracy to defeat the popular choice – Senator Barnum, John C. Reid, and the "New York Times: - William E. Chandler's break of the day dispatches – Troops ordered to Florida – President Grant's dispatch to General Sherman – Foul operations of conspirators in Florida – How rewarded by President Hayes – General Barlow.

The presidential canvass of 1876 was one of exceptional bitterness. The public officers of the party in control of the federal government had been charged by the press on the platform, by prominent and responsible Republicans as well as by the opposition, not only with gross neglect of official duty, but with official conduct for much of which the laws provided the most degrading penalties. They charged, among other things that during the whole eight years of General Grant's administration the ordinary expenses of the government, exclusive of pensions and interest on the public debt, had been increased at the inordinate rate of $75,000,000 a year.

That its influence had been exerted to procure its insertion on the bill that was to double the President's salary, and, as an inducement for its passage, a provision that the increase of pay which Congress had already awarded the members should date back to the beginning of their term, by which means they were to receive about $1,000,000 of back pay.

That in a single month in 1874 one million gallons of whiskey were sold in St. Louis which has not paid the lawful tax, amounting to

$700,000, through the collusion of officials attached to the Treasury Department, who were tried and convicted of sharing in the plunder. As St. Louis was but one, and by no means the most considerable, of the cities in which large distilleries were in operation, it was estimated and charged that from these frauds alone, which had been going on for many years, the loss to the treasury had been not less than $15,000,000 a year. O. C. Babcock, the President's private secretary, and the one Avery, the chief clerk of the treasury, were both indicted for participating in these robberies. Avery was convicted, but to save the President's private secretary from the State prison, and for other reasons which it is too painful to even suggest, Mr. Henderson, the lawyer selected by the Attorney General for the prosecution of these rogues, was displaced at the special instance of the President, as was publicly charged, and, so far as I know, never denied.

That financial agency of our government abroad was taken from the old and responsible banking-house of the Barings, of London, who had held it through a long succession of administrations, and was given to the house of Clews and Co., of which one partner was an Englishman, but then residing in New York, and the other Swede, who at one time was Swedish consul in New York, form which position he had been relieved at the instance of our government for blockade-running during the war. To secure their appointment it was charged the Clews and Co. agreed, in writing to give a quarter, or some other portion, of their profits to one Cheever, a notorious familiar at the White House; another quarter to one James A. Van Buren, which name subsequently proved to be a pseudonym, and the appropriation to it was understood to represent a gratification to some personage too important to be named; and the eight to a brother-in-law of the President. It is not surprising that, with so many divisions, the dividends of Clews and Co. were disappointing, and that they soon failed and went into bankruptcy, debtors to the government for a large amount.

That the soldiers of the United States were ordered to take possession of the legislative halls of Louisiana in 1874, and drive from the House of Representatives who were opposed to the usurpation of the executive chair by William Pitt Kellogg, the Jonathan Wild of Louisiana politics, who had been placed in it by the aid of a drunken and corrupt judge of the federal court.[1]

That George Williams Curtis was compelled to retire from Civil Service Commission, because "the circumstances under which several important appointments had been made seemed to him to show an abandonment both of the letter and the spirit of civil service regulations," and because "he was unwilling to be held responsible for acts which he considered nothing more nor less than a disregard of public pledges and a mockery of the public faith."

That Mr. Bristow, the Secretary of the Treasury, and Mr. Cox, the Secretary of the Interior, who where the only friends of a reformed civil service in the cabinet, were expelled from it because they were its friends.

That one vice-president, one speaker of the House of Representatives, three senators, and five chairman of congressional committees, all partisans of the executive, dishonored themselves, the government and the nation by marketing their influence as legislators; that a secretary of the treasury did the like by forcing balances in the public accounts; that an attorney general did the like by appropriating public funds to his own use; that a secretary of the navy did the like by enriching himself and his confederates out of percentages levied upon contractors with his department; while secretary of war was impeached for high crimes and misdemeanors.

Then there was the Emma mine swindle, in which one of our ministers to England was understood to be implicated; enormous frauds in the Indian and printing departments and in the New York custom-house; extravagant and corrupt expenditures for post-offices and public structures of various kinds, which, during fifteen years, had amounted to $51,164,978, while for the same purposes during the seventy-two previous years of our national existence the corresponding expenditures had been less than twenty-nine millions. There was the Venezuela scandal, the San Domingo scheme, the Credit Mobilier scandal, and

---

1   The books of the State department show that the indebtedness to the government of Clews, Habicht, & Co. on the 24th of September, 1872, when they went into liquidation amounted to $145,451.47. Up to November 29, 1887, the company had paid off $38,718.77 of this indebtedness. In 1882 the State department comprised with Henry Clews for his individual share of the indebtedness for the $12,500, leaving the sum of $94,232.70 still standing charged to Clews, Habicht, & Co. on the books of the Register of the Treasury.

defalcations of public offers so numerous as almost to constitute the rule rather than the exception in the public service; so numerous, indeed, that the Secretary of the Treasury persistently refused to comply with the law which required him annually to report them to Congress.

Bigelow states, "I will not swell these pages with more of these unsavory charges, which, to be compete and explicit, would alone fill a volume. It will be for the historian, in due time, to deal with this saturnalia of crime and political prostitution, which few Americans even now can recall with a blush.

Most of these charges were established by congressional or by judicial inquiry, many by both. They of course placed many thousands individuals – indeed, it would be no exaggeration to say hundreds of thousands- on the defensive, who, if deprived of the protection of sympathetic administration, would be personally as well as politically ruined. They naturally dreaded the accession of a Democratic administration, from which they could expect little indulgence; but the prospect of having their operations reviewed by an administration Tilden at its head made them desperate. His name had more terrors for them than that of any other man in the Republic, and when his nomination with such practical unanimity by the St. Louis convention transpired, they realized at once that *vae victis* (woe to the vanquished) was to be the battle cry of the campaign, and that Tilden must be beaten or they be ruined. They were in the condition of rats assailed in a room which offered no hole for escape. The situation gave them the courage and the recklessness of despair. They took up the cry of the furious goddess, maddened by the unsuccessfulness of her malice.

"Flectere si nequeo superos Archeronta Movebo"
"If I cannot move heaven I will raise hell."

They did not undertake to defend themselves, for that, they knew, was useless. Their crimes were of record, and suspected, if not known, of all men. Their plan of battle was to assail Tilden with charges bred of their own foul imaginings; in the language of Voltaire, *"faire la guerre des pots de chambre, (English translation - make war with your pots)* , in the hope of persuading the people that he was no better than they, and that they, and that nothing was to be gained by admitting him and his party to power. They denounced him as a railroad wrecker, because he had employed his extraordinary talents as a lawyer and an organizer in rescuing a number of railways from bankruptcy and converting them into productive properties. They charged him with extorting excessive fees for his professional services, though he had never had a bill for services successfully questioned, nor had he ever accepted a contingent fee in his life. They charged him with rebel sympathies during the war, though he was one of the leaders of the revolt against the administration which was proposing to legalize slavery in the free Territories; though he supported Van Buren and Adams for President in 1848-9; thought he refused his consent to repeal the Missouri Compromise in 1854; though he attended and his name figured in the list of officers of the Union meeting held in New York immediately after the attack on Fort Sumter, and also attended another meeting of the bar, held for the same purpose; and though he was during the war in more or less continuous consultation with every member of President Lincoln's cabinet, the only two surviving members of which were then on the stump advocating his election.

They charged him with intending, if elected, to indemnify the South for their losses during the rebellion and to assume the rebel debt – a charge for which there was only the flimsy foundation that the Southern States favored his nomination and were expected to vote for him at the election. Though the prospect of the payment of such losses had not been regarded of sufficient magnitude to deserve the notice of the nomination convention of either party, Mr. Tilden waived his right to disregard the charge, and in reply to a letter from the Honorable A. S. Hewitt, who then represented in Congress the district in which Mr. Tilden resided, gave these charges a most explicit and satisfactory denial. Even the "Tribune," which had already quite forgotten Mr. Tilden's oft-acknowledged claims to its respect as a man, and its admiration as a statesman, confessed that the charge which it had not thought unworthy of the hospitality of its columns had been fully disposed of by this letter.

It was further charged that his health was too feeble to endure the fatigues of the presidential office, especially when increased as they would be enormously by the restoration of a party which had been excluded from the administration of government for some fourteen years, and by such changes of men and measures as would be the inevitable consequences of such restoration.

It was not the Governor's health about which they were solicitous. They could have borne his clinical sufferings and even his demise with Christian fortitude, and aided perhaps in imposing the burden which would have contributed to it.

"If the assassination could trammel up the consequence and catch with his surcease success."

But there was Hendricks quite ready to leap into the saddle. He was no "reformer," it is true, but he was before all things a thorough party man of the most unadulterated strain, who they knew full well would neglect no partisan advantage or leave one stone upon another of the administration party that could be thrown down. There was no alternative left them but to defeat Tilden, and as it could not be done by fair means, it was too late for them to scruple about a resort to foul.

The most unequivocal evidence of their having reached this stage of desperation was exhibited in the report put into circulation soon after the Governor's nomination, that he had failed to make full and fair returns of his income to the tax assessors. Because on one occasion he had received the sum of $20,000 as compensation for professional service which did not seem to correspond with his tax returns for that year, it was assumed that his return was false, concealing or ignoring the fact that the fee in question was his compensation for eight or nine successive years of severe professional toil. I shall have occasion to deal this subject more at length later, when the aid of the federal jurisdiction was invoked to assist, with this weapon in its hands, in defeating his renomination to the presidency in 1880 and in 1884.

But all their efforts proved unavailing. The Governor had lived too long in the public eye; his service had been too considerable; his character had sunk its roots too deep into the confidence of his countrymen, and its branches covered too large a territory to be seriously disturbed by such a storm as could be provoked be the reckless misrepresentations of a crowd of rogues whom the people were bent on haling to judgment.

At the election, on 7th of November, 1876 the total vote for Tilden electors in the United States was, 4,300,316 – for Hayes – 4,036,016 – a majority for Tilden of 264,300 – Tilden's majority over Grant majority in 1872 – 703,574 – Tilden's majority over Grant's majority in 1868 – 1,287,128.

He was the choice of the people and with a larger majority by some 700,000 than had ever been cast by the people of the United States for any other person. But all this majority did not make him President. The Constitution provides that the people of the several States shall choose electors whose votes are to decide to be counted, or for which candidate, are problems which henceforth, as we shall now proceed to demonstrate, there is no calculus of variations that is competent to solve.

As a necessary preliminary to this demonstration the reader is requested to imagine himself in the editorial rooms of the "New York Times" at ten o'clock on the night of the 7th of November; present John Foord, then editor in chief; John C. Reid, editor of the news department; and Charles H. Miller, the present editor of the "Times," but then occupying a subordinate position. Sufficient returns from the election had been received to extinguish all hope of electing Hayes, and to warrant the preparation of an editorial article to that effect which appeared in the first edition of the "Times" on the 8th. The article commences as follows:

The New York Times set to ink this editorial for the morning paper dated November 8, 1876:

"A DOUBTFUL ELECTION"

At the time of going to press the result of the presidential election is still in doubt. Enough has been learned to show that the vote has been unprecedentedly heavy. Both parties have exhausted their full legitimate strength, while the peculiar Democratic policy, for which such extensive preparations were made in the large registry of this city, and in the enormous registry in Brooklyn, have had its effect, *and that in some States where the shotgun and rifle club were relied upon to secure a Democratic victory, there is only too much reason to fear that it has been successful.*

The writer closes his article as follows: "The Democrats, in order to gain the election (New York being conceded), must have carried New Jersey, and in addition either Oregon or Florida. The returns from new Jersey leave the State in doubt. Oregon is not heard from. Florida is claimed by the Democrats."

Between eleven and twelve o'clock, and while the editorial gentlemen above names were assembled together to take some refreshments, a note was received from the chairman of the Democratic National Committee, the United States Senator Barnum, of Connecticut, asking what news the "Times" people had from Louisiana, South Carolina, Oregon and Florida. Mr. Reid, who was an intense partisan, and had been very much cast down by the returns, asked to see the note, read it over carefully, then sprang up and, with a volley of explicatives suited to the message he had to deliver, exclaimed, The Democrats are in doubt over Louisiana, and South Carolina and Florida, and Oregon; it's a close vote; we must stop the press and claim them for Hayes; we must claim as ours everything that the Democrats concede as doubtful." Reid's reading of senator Barnum's mind. And his mode of turning it revelation to account, was approved by his colleagues; and the following editorial, prepared without unnecessary delay, displaced the one that had already gone to press for the county edition.

FROM THE "NEW YORK TIMES," NOV. 8, 1876 (CITY EDITION):

"A DOUBTFUL ELECTION"

At the time of going to press the result of the presidential election is still in doubt. Enough has been learned to show that the vote has been unprecedentedly heavy. Both parties have exhausted their full legitimate strength, while the peculiar Democratic policy, for which such extensive preparations were made in the large registry of this city, and in the enormous registry in Brooklyn, have had its effect.

Conceding New York to Mr. Tilden, he will receive the electoral votes of the following states:

Alabama	10	Arkansas	6	Connecticut	6
Delaware	3	Georgia	11	Indiana	15
Kentucky	12	Maryland	8	Mississippi	8
Missouri	15	New Jersey	9	New York	35
North Carolina	10	Tennessee	12	Texas	8
Virginia	11	West Virginia	5		
		Total	**184**		

"Governor Hayes will receive the votes of the following States:

California	6	Colorado	3	Illinois	21
Iowa	11	Kansas	5	Louisiana	8
Maine	7	Massachusetts	13	Michigan	11
Minnesota	5	Nebraska	3	Nevada	3
New Hampshire	5	Ohio	22	Oregon	3
Pennsylvania	29	Rhode Island	4	Vermont	5
Wisconsin	10	South Carolina	7		
		Total	**181**		

"This leaves Florida *alone* still in doubt. *If the Republicans have carried that State, as they claim, they will have 185 votes – a majority of one.*"

It will be observed that the desponding words which I have italicized in the first article are eliminated from the second, and all the doubtful States, including Florida, claimed for Hayes, assuring him a majority of one in the Electoral College.

What was it in Mr. Reid's mind in setting up a formal claim to all these States, on receiving the impression from Senator Barnum's inquiry that they were "close," we need not speculate about; for we have his own testimony upon the subject.

Not satisfied with the share which William E. Chandler had been appropriating to himself of the credit for securing the election of Hayes, Mr. Reid published in the "Times" of June 15, 1887, an account of what followed the operations in the "Times" office, which have already been disclosed.

Mr. Reid informs us that before daylight on the morning of the day succeeding that of the election, William E. Chandler, a personage who, as my reader of this generation at least are aware, was already renowned beyond the boundaries of his native State of New Hampshire for what the French call les petites politques (small politics) arrived at the Fifth avenue hotel in New York. Soon after his arrival, and between six and half-past six in the morning, Mr. Reid, who in this communication does not give his name, but uniform describes himself as an editor of the "New York Times," also entered the Fifth Avenue hotel. He went at once to the rooms of the national committee, and found them occupied only by a number of servants of the hotel who were in engaged in cleaning and setting the rooms to rights. He was informed that everybody had gone home or to bed a couple hours before. He left the room and started for the clerks' desk to ascertain the number of Mr. Zachariah Chandler's room.[1]

On his way to the office of the hotel he came in collision with a small man wearing an immense pair of goggles, his hat drawn down over his ears, a greatcoat with a heavy military cloak, and carrying a gripsack and a newspaper in his hand. The newspaper was the "New York Tribune." The stranger cried out, "Why Mr. Blank, is that you?" The gentleman knew the voice and said, "Is that you, Mr. Chandler?" He answered, "Yes I have just arrived from New Hampshire by train. Damn the men who have brought this disaster upon the Republican Party!" The gentleman replied, *"The Republican party has sustained no disaster. If you will only keep your heads up here, there is no question of the election of President Hayes*. He has been fairly and honestly elected.

Mr. Reid and Mr. Chandler then proceeded to the latter's room in the hotel.

The visitor went over the ground carefully, State by State, from Maine to Oregon, counting the electoral vote in each State, and showing the vote as it was finally counted for Hayes and Tilden. After he had finished, William E. Chandler said, "Well what do you think should be done?"

The gentleman replied, "Telegraph immediately to leading Republicans, men in authority, in South Carolina, Florida, Louisiana, California, Oregon, and Nevada."

Mr. Chandler made no reply to this proposition, but said, "We must go and see Zach."

After some difficulty, Mr. Reid and William E. Chandler succeeded in finding Zach Chandler's room.

The door was shortly opened, and Mr. Zachariah Chandler was discovered standing in his night-dress. William E. Chandler then said, closing the door," Here is a gentleman who has more news than you have, and he has some suggestions to make."

---

1 Mr. Zachariah Chandler was then a member of the United States Senate form Michigan, and also chairman of the Republican National Committee.

To which Zach Chandler replied, "Yes, I know him. What is it?" with which he seated himself on the edge of the bed.

William E. Chandler then said, "The gentleman will tell you the story himself. He understands it better than I do."

The gentleman then went over the details of the election, and added the recommendations he had made to William E. Chandler. The chairman of the national committee lay down and said, "Very well, go ahead and do what you think necessary."

Mr. Reid and William E. Chandler then rushed in company to the telegraph office in the hotel. It was not yet open for business. It would not be open for an hour or more.

The gentleman said, "I'll have to take these messages to the main office of the Western Union."

Chandler called a servant and directed him to have a carriage brought to the Twenty-third street entrance. Then Chandler said," Well, what do you want to do?"

The gentleman replied, "We'll first telegraph to Governor Chamberlain, of South Carolina." The gentleman dictated the dispatch, as follows; "To D.H. Chamberlain, S.C: Hayes is elected if we have carried South Carolina, Florida and Louisiana. Can you hold your State? Answer immediately."

Mr. Chandler took the dispatch in shorthand, as dictated. The following dispatch was then dictated to S.B. Conover, Tallahassee. Florida, "The presidential election depends on the vote of Florida, and the Democrats will try to wrest it form us. Watch it and hasten returns. Answer immediately. Do not be cheated in returns. Answer when sure."

To S.B. Packard, of Louisiana, the following dispatch was sent: "The presidential election depends on the vote of Louisiana, and the Democrats will try and wrest it from you."

Mr. Reid says dispatches of like import were sent to Oregon and California. He then adds: "William E. Chandler signed with his own name the dispatches to Oregon and to Gorman, of San Francisco. To the dispatches sent to Conver, Packard, and Chamberlain the narrator's recollection is he signed the name of Zachariah Chandler. William E. Chandler at one took the telegraph blanks and wrote from his stenographic notes the dispatches above printed, the gentleman standing by him taking every dispatch as he finished, and carefully reading it.

When the last dispatch was transcribed, Chandler handed it over to the gentleman and said, "Are they all right?" He was informed that they were.

The gentleman jumped into the carriage waiting and told the driver to go to the main office of the Western Union with all possible speed. Probably the quickest time ever made by a carriage from the Fifth Avenue hotel to the Western Union was made that morning. Arriving at the Western Union office, the gentleman went to the receiver's desk and handed in the dispatches. The receiver replied, "The national committee has no account here, and we can't do it. Why not charge them to the New York Times account?"

The gentleman replied, "All right," and the receiver immediately handed them back to him to be countersigned. This was promptly done. The gentleman returned to his carriage and was driven back to the Fifth Avenue hotel. There was still nobody stirring connected with the national committee.

The New York Times has never to this day, June 15, 1887 been reimbursed by the national committee or William E. Chandler; nor has William E. Chandler, or any national committee ever offered to repay the "Times" for the telegraph tolls or for any of the expense incurred on that morning.

Here we have, upon the most authentic possible testimony a quasi official account of the first stage in the erection of the complicated structure of fraud by which the choice of the American people was to be defeated and their executive government delivered over to a usurper.

That the Tilden and Hendricks ticket was entitled to 184 electoral votes was undisputed. That the Hayes and Wheeler ticket was entitled to 165 electoral votes was also undisputed. There were 369 electors in all. The Tilden ticket, therefore with 184 votes, needed by one more to give it the majority required for an election. The Hayes ticket, having only 166 electoral votes assured required 19 more votes to ensure the election.

The four votes of Florida, the eight of Louisiana, and the seven of South Carolina made just nineteen. To get one of these votes was sufficient to elect Tilden and Hendricks. To elect Hayes and Wheeler it was necessary to get the whole nineteen.

The "Times" of the 9th followed up the operations initiated in its columns the previous morning by boldly claiming to have returns which gave the election to Hayes, though it could have had nothing of the kind. If it had any returns of such import, they were of course simply the partisan reverberations of Chandler's dispatches.

THE BATTLE WON
"A REPUBLICAN VICTORY IN THE NATION – GOV. HAYES ELECTED PRESIDENT AND WILLIAM A. WHEELER VICE PRESI-DENT – THE REPUBLICANS CARRY TWENTY-ONE STATES CASTING 185 ELECTORAL VOTES- A REPUBLICAN MAJORITY IN THE NEXT CONGRESS."

The dispatches received since our last issue confirm the reports on which the "Times" yesterday claimed 181 electoral votes for Governor Hayes. On Wednesday the following States were put down as surely Republican: Colorado, California, Illinois, Iowa, Kansas, Maine, Massa-chusetts, Michigan, Minnesota, Nevada, Nebraska, New Hampshire, Oregon, Ohio, Pennsylvania, Rhode Island, Vermont, Wisconsin, Louisiana, and South Carolina. Some of these States were claimed by Democrats; but all intelligence, thus far received, not only shows that the above estimate was correct, but Florida, which was left in doubt, has gone Republican by at least 1,500 majority, - our latest dispatches say 2,000, - and that the two Republican Congressmen are also elected. Encouraging reports were received from Oregon early yesterday morning, and in the afternoon came the decisive news that the Demo-crats conceded the State, which had given a Republican majority of over one thousand, and gained a Republican Congressman. In Nebraska the same condition of affairs was shown. There the Republican majority rose to 8,000. Dispatches from Nevada made it certain that the State had gone for Hayes. The latest news from South Carolina shows a Republican victory, the Democrats conceding the State to Hayes and the Republicans claiming 5,000 majority. Louisiana is one of the States which the Democrats have claimed; but our dispatches, coming from various sources in the State, show that it has gone Republican. The latest intelligence points to the certain election of Gov. Rutherford B. Hayes to the presidency, and a Republican victory in the nation.

In no other newspaper in New York City or elsewhere, I believe, was a serious doubt expressed of Tilden's election. It was conceded in the

"Times" office, and but for the inquiry of Barnum I am assured, upon the best authority, that the question of his election would never have been raised. The evidence which that inquiry furnished of the closeness of the voted operated like an open basement window at night to a burglariously disposed passer-by. If the vote was so close as this inquiry warranted the suspicion that it was, what was easier for the administration, with its control of the army, of all the federal offices, including the judiciary, and with all the patronage of the federal government in reserve, to warp the Tilden vote sufficiently to give Hayes the nineteen votes which he lacked; and how few are active in politics anywhere who are not ready to reason like the tyrant of Thebes:

"Be just, unless a kingdom tempts usurpation; For that, sovereignty only is adequate temptation."

The scheme of the Fifth Avenue conspirators spread through the party as rapidly as the poison from the bite of an adder. Republican leaders all over the country were signaled at once to claim all the disputed States and persist in claiming them. At the same time it was arranged to send men, "who could be depended upon" to each of the States whose electoral vote was to be tampered with; to provide ample means for such contingencies as might arise; and finally to open communication with the President and Secretary of War to secure for the Returning Boards such protection for the work expected of them as they might require. [1]

Senator Zachariah Chandler, chairman of the National Republican Committee, proposed to take charge of Florida, and a credit was opened for him at the Centennial Bank in Philadelphia, whose officers were his friends. William E. Chandler, the man with "the immense pair of goggles" also went to Florida, and the Department of Justice ordered its detectives to report to him in Tallahassee. Thomas J. Brady, with a force of special agents of the Post Office Department, followed the

---

[1] Note: George W. Childs in his Reminiscences reports that a Republican Senator and other leading Republicans were early at his office the day after the election to meet General Grant, who was then at Philadelphia attending the closing exercises of the Centennial Exposition, and the guest of Mr. and Mrs. Childs. These gentlemen insisted that Hayes was elected, "notwithstanding the returns." Mr. Childs tells us that Grant did not agree with them, but contented himself with merely expressing a negative opinion.

Chandler's with money for immediate use. William A. Cook, of Washington, was sent to Columbia, S.C. The election took place on Tuesday, the 7th, and before Thursday night the 9th, these men were all on their way to their posts.

On the same day, or night rather, the following orders were issued to General W. T. Sherman by J.S. Cameron, Secretary of War, all dated from Philadelphia:

10 P.M. "Order four companies of soldiers to Tallahassee, Fla., at once. Take them from the nearest points, not from Louisiana or Mississippi, and direct that they be moved with as little delay as possible.

11 P.M. "In addition to the four companies ordered to Tallahassee, order all troops in Florida to the same point, and if you haven't more than the companies named, draw from Alabama and South Carolina. Advise of the receipt of this and your action.

11:15 P.M. "Telegraph General Ruger to proceed once to Tallahassee, Fla., and upon his arrival there to communicate with Governor Sterns. Say to him to leave affairs in South Carolina in hands of an eminently discreet and reliable officer."

General Grant, who evidently had not yet been let fully into the scheme mapped out in the early morn of the day after the election, and who was satisfied that Tilden had been duly elected, did not quite comprehend the motive for all these military preparations for securing a fair election which had been held three days before. He evidently had suspicions that something was afoot, the nature and purpose of which there was a manifest disposition to disguise, if not altogether to conceal, from him. He concluded therefore, to do a little telegraphing on his own account and without the intermediation of his guileless Secretary of War. Persuaded in his own mind that Tilden and Hendricks were elected, he seems to have been getting suspicious that some of the people about him, with the connivance of Hayes, were plotting something for which he himself did not care to be responsible, and for that reason sent the following telegram to General Sherman, and gave it simultaneously to the press:

"To General W.T. Sherman, Washington, D.C.:
Instruct General Auger, in Louisiana, and General Ruger, in Florida, to be vigilant with the force at their command to preserve peace and good order, and to see that the proper and legal Boards of Canvassers

are unmolested in the performance of their duties. Should there be any grounds of suspicion of fraudulent counting on either side, it should be reported and denounced at once. No man worthy of the office of President would be willing to hold office if counted in, placed their by fraud; either party can afford to be disappointed in the result, but the country cannot afford to have the result tainted by the suspicion of illegal or false returns.   Signed: "U.S. Grant."

Two weeks before the election the federal troops in South Carolina had been increased to thirty-three companies, taking for that purpose every available on the Atlantic seaboard from Fortress Monroe northward.

The President's telegram, whatever the motive that inspired it, was not in accordance with the plans of the conspirators. The direction, "to see that the proper and legal Boards of Canvassers are unmolested in the performance of their duties" was easy to execute, for there was no danger whatever if the Boards of Canvassers being molested in the performance of their duties; and it was entirely within the scope of the executive authority, if lawfully invited, to direct the generals in command in the several States, in the event of an outbreak, to cooperate with the local authorities "to preserve peace and good order." No other interference of federal troops within a State was lawful, nor could even such and order by lawfully enforced until the governors of the respective States had reported that they were unable to preserve the peace, a condition of things which could not have been honestly affirmed to exist in any State of the Union at that time. But how were commanding generals to comply with the second term Grant's last telegram, and see whether there were any grounds for suspicion of fraudulent counting on either side? And to whom were they to report and denounce it? In Louisiana the canvassers all, without exception, were Republicans. And in Florida all but one were Republicans. Was it false counting by his own party the President wished his soldiers to guard against? If so, he did not send enough, or at least enough of the right kind. How, too, could the commanding generals ascertain whether there were any grounds of suspicion of fraudulent counting, unless they had been directed to supervise the reception, as well as the canvassing, of the returns? But this was equivalent to an impeachment of the integrity of the Returning Boards.

Besides, a "fair count of the votes actually cast" was precisely what the conspirators did not want. Two days before President Grant stepped between his Secretary of War and the people, with those memorable dispatches, the polls had been closed, and the returns "of the votes actually cast," save from remote counties and parishes in Florida and Louisiana had been turned in. There was no possibility then of fraudulent counting, except by the Returning Boards. When President Grant sent those dispatches of the 10th of November it is evident that if he really meant what he said he was not aiming his gun at any Democratic influences at work in the disputed States, but at the reckless crowd about him who were tampering with the Returning Boards.

Believing, as we now know he did, that Tilden was elected, he might very naturally have suspected that all the forces of the federal government were being rallied by his political staff for the single purpose of defeating him. Grant, with all his limitations, as a President, is generally believed to have been too direct a man to let fly the Parthian shaft with which he concluded his telegram to Sherman, if he were merely "playing the galleries."

The Returning Boards of South Carolina and Louisiana could be depended upon to return Republican electors, for the character of the Republican officials of those States were known to be equal to the emergency if properly, "protected" and adequately "encouraged." The "encouragement" was on its way, and the action of the Secretary of War left no doubt that the "protection" also was at hand. Of Florida the managers were not so certain, as there were doubts about the powers of the Returning Boards in that State, and also about the degree of dependence to be placed upon its members. W.E. Chandler telegraphed from Tallahassee in cipher on the 13th of November, "Send $2,000 to Centennial Bank of Philadelphia so I can draw for it. Have Arthur send Republicans acting with Democrats." On the 15th he telegraphed again," Florida needs eminent counsel and help. Can you send $3,000 and $2,000, making it $5,000? Danger great here."

Which of these sums was used for counsel and which for help has never transpired.

On the arrival of W.E. Chandler in Tallahassee, the 13th, telegrams were sent to the local Republican managers telling them that the "State is close and you must make an effort to render every possible assistance," and that "funds from Washington would be on hand to meet every requirement."

Chandler's promise that "counsel" and "protection" should not be wanting, and that the "funds" from Washington were on their way, were very well as far as they went; but Chandler was not the candidate for the presidency, and there was no satisfactory evidence that Hayes, if elected, would feel under any obligation to take up Chandler's paper. In fact, the business he was engaged in, and the means by which he and his confederates were carrying it on, were not calculated to inspire the utmost confidence in his promises, nor indeed a sufficient degree of confidence in his promises, nor indeed a sufficient degree of confidence to induce the average politician to disgrace himself for such an indefinite consideration. He felt too, probably, that for the security of his own share in the harvest for which he was ploughing, as well as to strengthen his credit with the Florida officials, he must be able to show the existence of more direct relations between himself and the candidate for whose election he was toiling. For this or some other reason he telegraphed to the private Secretary of Hayes, "to send Stanley Matthews and others of high character."

It so happened that when this note reached Columbus, Stanley Matthews, ex-Governor E.F. Noyes, and Attorney General Little, all of Ohio, Senator John Sherman and James A. Garfield, had already left for New Orleans "to fix" the electors of Louisiana. Chandler's request was promptly forwarded to them, and in response Noyes accompanied by John A. Kasson, of Iowa, and Lew Wallace, of Indiana started forthwith for Tallahassee, where they arrive November 20th. Now the magnetic circuit was complete. Noyes came direct from Hayes, and whatever engagements he endorseds, it was correctly understood that Hayes in the fullness of time would execute. Up to this time Chandler had received $15,000, besides what he took with him. In one of his dispatches November 28th, he asks for "$3,000 in large bills; probably shall not need it, - majority about twenty, - but be ready for any emergency."[1]

---

1 Note: Subsequently Samuel B. McLin, Secretary of State of Florida, and one of the members of the Returning Board, testified before a congressional committee to prevalent opinion amoung the Florida Republicans that Mr. Noyes represented Hayes. He said, "Looking back now to that time (of the canvass) I feel that there was a combination of influences that must have operated most powerfully in blinding my judgment and swaying my action." What the combination of if influences were he in part disclosed. "I was shown numerous telegrams addressed to Governor

With a practically unlimited credit at Washington, and the prospective patronage of the federal government hypothecated to the conspirators, the fate of the electoral vote of Florida was not difficult to forecast.

Those who wish to know in ample detail to what foul uses all these vast and complex resources were devoted for the purpose of wresting from the State of Florida its right to a voice in the choice for the presidency, I must refer to the voluminous records of the forty-fourth and forty-fifth Congresses. Even a concise detail of it would occupy more space that I can venture to devote to the entire career of the most conspicuous individual victim of the conspiracy which is there laid bare. I must content myself with the briefest possible summary of some of the transactions to which the power and dignity of the federal government, and to a large extent the honor of the nation, were deliberately prostituted.

The returns of the county canvassers in Florida when footed up showed a majority for the Tilden electors, - 24,441 votes for Tilden and Hendricks, and 24,350 for Hayes and Wheeler. By the law of Florida and by a decision of its Supreme Court the county returns were final, and the Canvassing Board had merely the ministerial duty of tabu-

---

Sterns and other from the trusted leaders of the Republican party in the North, insisting that the salvation of the country depended upon the vote of Florida being cast for Hayes. These telegrams also gave assurances of the forthcoming of money and troops if necessary in securing the victory for Mr. Hayes. Following these telegrams trusted Northern Republicans, party leaders, and personal friends of Mr. Hayes arrive in Florida as rapidly as the railroads could bring them. I was surrounded by these men, who were ardent Republicans, and especially by friends of Governor Hayes. One gentleman particularly Governor Noyes of Ohio, was understood to represent him and speak with the authority of a warm personal friend, commissioned with power to act in his behalf. These men referred to the general destruction of the country should Mr. Tilden be elected, the intense anxiety of the Republican party of the North, and their full sympathy with us. I cannot say how far my action may have influenced by the intense excitement that prevailed around me, or how far my partisan zeal may have led me into error; neither can I say how far my course was influenced by the promises made by Governor Noyes, that if Mr. Hayes became President I should be rewarded. Certainly their influences must have had a strong control over my judgment and actions."

L.D. Dennis, the Republican boss in Alachua county, also testified that Noyes "often spoke of Mr. Hayes and referred to him as his intimate friend, and gave us assurances of Mr. Hayes fidelity to the Republican cause, and of his special desire to take care of Southern Republicans."

When asked if Noyes was generally regarded by the people there as the personal representative of Hayes, Dennis answered, "We regarded him as such. I cannot state by what means I arrive at that conclusion, but he was regarded by the people there as the special representative of Mr. Hayes. It was generally understood that he was there at the request of.

lating the votes and declaring the result. There was no resource fro the conspirators but to disregard the law and doctor the returns to the extent necessary to meet the emergency. This they unhesitatingly proceeded to do.

The votes of one precinct in Hamilton County, which gave Tilden electors a majority of 31, were all thrown out on the affidavits of two Republican inspectors that they had absented themselves at different times during the day of the election form the polls, and without any pretense of fraud of illegal voting.

The other votes of another precinct of Jackson county, Florida which gave the Tilden electors 291 votes and the Hayes electors 77, were thrown out because the inspectors went to dinner after locking the ballot-box in a secure place and leaving the key with the Republican inspector, who certified to the returns and testified that there was no fraud nor wrong about the election.

The entire votes of Manatee County – 262 for the Tilden electors to 26 for the Hayes electors – were thrown out on the ground that there had been no registration, when the fact was that Governor Stearns would not appoint a county clerk, that there might be no registration in this strong Democratic county. There was no pretense of fraud, or that any illegal vote had been cast. Governor Stearns was rewarded with the appointment of Commissioner of Hot Springs, Arkansas at $10 a day, within thirty days after the Hayes' inauguration.

The votes of Key West – 401 for Tilden and 59 for Hayes – were all rejected because the election officers failed to complete the certificate of their returns on the day of the election, without any imputation or pretense of fraudulent voting. The ballots had been counted after the close of the poll on the night of the election, the result announced, and the certificate partly made out, when a bottle of ink was upset and a new certificate had to be made. This was postponed until the following morning when the ballots were recounted and found to tally exactly with the count of the previous day, except that one more ballot was found for the Republican electors.

While no pretext was too flimsy to procure the rejection of votes for a Democratic elector, no crime was so flagitious as to exclude a vote for a Republican elector. The negro clerk and negro inspector of Alachua County brought with them L.G. Dennis, the Republican boss of that county, a blank for the returns of the election *already signed and sealed,* the figures not yet filled in. When asked by Dennis for the vote of their precinct, they said 178 Republican and 141 Democratic. At this Dennis expressed great indignation and said the business had not been properly managed. The blacks expressed contrition and were sent to an upper room, supplied with printed list of voters of the county, and from this proceeded to add 219 names to the poll list and as many votes for the Republican candidates. Notwithstanding that one of the inspectors made an affidavit that the return was forged and false, it was counted and allowed by State canvassers. Dennis procured one of the Democratic inspectors to corroborate the returns of the negro inspector and clerk by a bribe of $100, and another affidavit of the same character from one Floyd Dukes was procured at the price of $25.

When the *alter ego* of Mr. Hayes, ex-Governor Noyes, to whom was assigned the defense of this fraud before the State canvassers, wanted Dennis subsequently to support the transaction by his testimony before a Congressional committee, Dennis gave him to understand that he did not propose to do any swearing. His own testimony upon this point is worthy of reproduction.

Q.   Did Mr. Noyes ask you to become a witness yourself in regard to the precinct?

A.   Yes, Sir.

Q.   Were you a witness or had you made an affidavit with reference to box No. 2 of Archer precinct which affidavit was to be used before the Returning Board?

A.   No, sir; I never made any statement whatever for that purpose.

Q.   State the conversation which took place between you and Mr. Noyes in regard to your appearing as witness before the Returning Board in reference to box No. 2 at Archer precinct?

A.   He did express that desire several times. I do not know that he ever spoke of it but once as though he intended to put me on the stand, and then I advised him not to do it.

Q.   What did you say to him, and what did he say to you?

A.   I do not recollect the exact words, but I think he said in a familiar sort of way that he should put me on the stand that day. I suggested to him that I should be a detriment to his case if he did, and that I thought he had better not do it.

Q. Can you repeat the exact words which you used in reference to your being a detriment to his case.
A. I cannot, but I made it strong. I may have said that unless he was ready to abandon his case, he had better not put me on the stand. I may have made it as strong as that. I wanted to give him to understand that I did not want to go on the stand to make any statement under oath. I cannot repeat the exact words; but it was said with sufficient force to have the desired effect.
Q. Did Governor Noyes, after you told him in form of words that it would be inconvenient to his case to put you on the stand, ever refer to that refusal on your part to go on the stand in any form of words?
A. I think he jocosely said one day that I was not very forward about swearing, of something of that kind.
Q. Wasn't it something like this: You talk very well enough Dennis, but you don't swear?
A. Something to that effect.

For his services in maintaining the validity of this return, Noyes was rewarded soon after Hayes inauguration, with the mission to France.

The county judge and clerk of the Election Board of the seventh precinct of Jefferson County stole a bundle of one hundred Democratic tickets, which the inspectors had tied up as they were counting the ballots, and left in their place one hundred Republican tickets. The clerk confessed his crime and fled the State to avoid prosecution. Though the facts were all proven before the Returning Board, the return was accepted and counted. The county judge and clerk were rewarded with clerkships in the Land Office at Washington, with a salary of $1,200 each per annum.

In the Monticello precinct of Jefferson County all but five of the Democratic ballots were stolen and Republican ballots substituted and counted.

Joseph Bowes, who was the inspector at Precinct No. 13, Leon County, "procured a lot of small Republican tickets to be printed in very fine type, and on thin paper. These tickets, spoken of in Florida as "little jokers," he had printed at the official Republican printing-office. Before the election he showed them to Mr. McLin, and stated his purpose in using them. The plan was to fold them up inside the ballots that were voted, and have them surreptitiously cast, or otherwise smuggle them into the ballot boxes, which their small size easily admitted of. McLin advised Bowes not to use them. After the election Bowes stated that he had managed to smuggle seventy-three of them into the boxes of his precinct, and he told McLin, after the State had been awarded to the Democrats, and it was known Drew was to be governor, that he was in a scrape on this account, and that he had to clear out for stuffing the boxes.

The evidence establishing this fraud of ballot-box-stuffing was before the Returning Board, but the return for Precinct No.13, Leon County was accepted.

General Francis C. Barlow, ex-Attorney-General of New York, was one of the visiting statesmen who went to Florida at President Grant's request to witness a fair count of the ballots actually cast. Dennis and Chandler soon discovered that Barlow was not the sort of man they required to deal with the Alachua case, and Noyes was assigned in his place. Barlow continued, however, to take an active part in making up the Republican case; but when the returns were all in, he became satisfied that, applying the same tests to the Republican votes as the Republicans insisted upon applying to Democratic votes, the result would be a majority for Tilden. He endeavored to impress this view upon one of the State canvassers, - Cowgill by name, -whom he believed to be an honest man. Why he did not lay it before the Board, unhappily for Barlow, if not for the country, does not appear. Barlow swears that after a full discussion of the case Cowgill said," I agree with you. I cannot conscientiously vote the other way. I cannot conscientiously vote to give the State to the Hayes electors."

Governor Stearns, learning that Cowgill was closeted with Barlow, joined them to learn what might be going on, and was told by Barlow what he had been saying to Cowgill. Cowgill left with Stearns. Barlow and he never met again. Cowgill came to Washington soon after the inauguration, confident of recognition. He had been promised and auditorship in the treasury, was tendered the position of special agent in the internal revenue service. This did not accord with his estimate of his services, and he returned to Florida, a wiser if not a better man.

When McLin, who was Secretary of State of Florida, and ex-officio member of the Returning Board, was subsequently asked by a congressional committee, "what promises these visiting statesmen from the

North made to the Republican leaders and the Returning Board, if the State should go for Mr. Hayes, he replied: "Well General Wallace told me on several occasions that if Mr. Hayes should be elected, that the members of the Returning Board should be taken care of, and no doubt about that; that Governor Noyes represented Mr. Hayes and spoke with him and was in favor of it. Then on one occasion William E. Chandler came to me and stated that he didn't like to say it to me, but he would say it to me, and he spoke for General Wallace, also that if the State went and was canvassed for Mr. Hayes, that the members of the Returning Board, - at least he referred to a majority of the board, - Dr. Cowgill and myself, would be well taken care of, and there would be no doubt of it; he said he was authorized to say that."

McLin further testified that Dr. Cowgill told him that in March 1877, he was in Washington and saw Hayes frequently; that he was received very kindly by the President, and given free admission to the White House at all times, and that he had expressed himself as being under great obligations to him and me in the canvass, and that he felt not only under political obligations, but personal obligations, that he would certainly pay at an early day.

McLin was appointed justice of the Supreme Court of New Mexico *ad interim,* and failed confirmation because Senator Conover, of Florida, opposed it.

F.C. Humphreys, elector at large on the Republican ticket, was appointed collector of customs at Pensacola.

Dennis Eagan, chairman of the Republican State Committee, was appointed collector of internal revenue.

Governor Stearns was appointed commissioner of the Hot Springs, Arkansas.

J.M. Howell, the deputy clerk of Baker county, who assisted the county judge Driggers in getting up the fraudulent return from that county, was appointed collector of customs at Fernandina.

Dennis was appointed to a sinecure position in the supervising architect's office at Washington at a salary of seven dollars a day.

One of the negroes who assisted Dennis in making up the spurious returns for Alachua county, and swore to affidavits for him, was appointed night inspector in the Philadelphia custom house.

The other negro who rendered Dennis the same service was appointed a clerk to the auditor of the treasury of Post-Office Department.

.Joseph Bowes, who had the "little jokers" printed, and voted seventy-three of them himself, and who was one the busiest manufacturers of affidavits, and who had to flee the State to escape the legal penalties of his iniquity, took refuge in Washington, where he was rewarded with a clerkship in the Treasury Department, on a salary of $1,600 per annum.

W.K. Cessna, county judge of Alachua County, who assisted Dennis in procuring Green R. Moore to make his $100 affidavit, was appointed postmaster at Gainesville, Fla.

Lewis A. Barnes, another of Dennis' assistants, was appointed register of the Land Office at Gainesville, Fla.

Moses J. Taylor, the clerk of Jefferson county and inspector of one of the polls of the Monticello precinct, who got away with all but five of the Democratic tickets and substituted Republican tickets was also made a clerk in the General Land Office at Washington.

John Varnum, an affidavit maker and assistant general of militia, was appointed receiver of the United States Land Office.

Manual Govin, a postmaster at Jacksonville, and an assistant affidavit manufacturer, was sent to consul to Leghorn.

M. Martin, acting chairman of the Republican State Committee, was made surveyor-general of Florida.

George H. DeLeon, secretary to Governor Stearns, was appointed a clerk in the Second Auditor's Office at Washington.

George D. Mills, telegrapher at Tallahassee and one of the clerks of the State canvassers was appointed clerk in the Pension Office at Washington.

John A. Kasson, who accompanied Noyes to Florida to vouch for Hayes' gratitude for favors expected, was appointed envoy extraordinary to Austria.

Lew Wallace, for like service, was appointed Governor of New Mexico, declining which, he was sent to Constantinople as minister-resident.

F.N. Wicker, the collector of customs at Key West, upon whose testimony the State canvassers rejected the poll No. 3 of that town, was continued in office.

Thomas J. Brady, Second Assistant Postmaster-General, who carried the money to Chandler, accompanied by H. Clay Hopkins, agent of the postal division of New York city, William T. Henderson, L.L. Tilball, B.H. Camp, Alfred Morton, all post-office inspectors, were retained in office by President Hayes. Tilball was subsequently promoted to the Unites Sates marshalship of Arizona.

William E. Chandler, not receiving a prompt reward for his services, turned upon the chromo President he had hung up in the White House for deserting his Louisiana and South Carolina coefficients, and practically acknowledged that Hayes had never been elected President by the people.

General Barlow, the only one of the visiting statesmen who seems to have believed that Grant and Hayes were in earnest in professing a desire for a fair count, was the only other one of the whole array whom Hayes failed to recognize. He was charged with disloyalty to the party, and put into Coventry, where it has since left him to chew the cud of sweet and bitter fancies. Had he the same duty committed to him again, I venture to doubt whether he would not, by a timely disclosure of his convictions, have assisted Tilden to take the oath of office to which the people had chosen him, instead of permitting that great office to be sequestered to the base uses of a partisan conspiracy by his forbearance.[1]

---

1 It is just to Mr. Barlow to say that his support of Hayes for President, in 1876 was not from any distrust of Mr. Tilden personally, nor from any doubt of his superior fitness for the duties of chief magistrate, but from a distrust of the party which nominated him.

The apprehensions here expressed may have had its weight in determining him to assume the passive attitude which he occupied after he had satisfied himself that the electoral vote of Florida was wrested from Tilden by fraud.

The general here, as Mr. William C. Bryant and many other distinguished patriots had done before him, make the capital mistake of underestimating the numbers and power of the Democratic party who supported the Union during the war, whose sacrifices in its behalf were not made nor to be estimated by any partisan measure. Mr. Lincoln in selecting for his cabinet advisers a majority of life-long Democrats, to say nothing of his generals, of whom by far the larger proportion who distinguished themselves were of the same party, displayed, in my judgment, a wiser appreciation of the political forces upon which he had to depend for the preservation of the Union.

CHAPTER II

The methods by which Hayes electors were secured from Louisiana were, if possible, more shameless and indefensible than those employed for the like purpose in Florida.

William Pitt Kellogg, then Governor of Louisiana by virtue of an illegal order of Judge Durell of the United States District Court, enforced by federal troops under orders from President Grant, enjoys the credit of having concocted the measures by which the people of that State were deprived of their choice of presidential electors. His objective point was a seat in the United States Senate for himself. He had already managed to subject all the elective machinery of the State to his personal control. He had the appointment of the supervisors and assistant supervisors of registration for every parish and ward in the State; he dictated the appointments of all the commissioners of election, the State register of voters and his clerks.

Events subsequently disclosed a deliberate purpose on the part of Kellogg and his Republican confederates to invalidate the election in seven parishes where they found they could not control the negro vote, and by fictitious registration of names to make up whatever number of votes might be needed to secure a majority. To understand how this was to be accomplished it is necessary to notice some of the peculiarities of the Louisiana election laws.

The Returning Board in Louisiana had no power to reject the vote of any precinct unless the certificate from such precinct came to them accompanied by a sworn protest signed by the supervisors, that intimidation had been practiced. The Commissioners of Elections in each parish were required by law to make out their returns on the day of the election, and if anything happened to affect "the purity and freedom" of the election, they were to make a statement thereof under oath and have three citizens vouch for its truth, and forward this statement with their returns, the tally sheets, registration lists, all made out in duplicate, one to the supervisor and one to the clerk of the Parish Court.

These returns from the commissioners the supervisors were required by law to consolidate in duplicate; have them certified as correct by the clerk of the District Court, according to the returns in his office; to deposit one copy of the consolidate statement with the said clerk and "forward the other mail, enclosed in an envelope of strong paper or cloth securely," to the Returning Board, with all the returns made by the commissioners, including their statement, if any, in regard to occurrences affecting the "purity and freedom" of the voting. They had no authority to reject the returns from any poll or to refuse to compile them in their consolidated statements.

When these consolidated returns reached the Retuning Board, its duty was first to compile the vote from those polls where there was presented no evidence that there had not been "fair, free and peaceable registration and election." That done, they were to take up the cases where the commissioners had reported that there had not been a fair, free, and peaceable registration and election.

The law required this Returning Board to meet in New Orleans "within ten days after the closing of the election, to canvass and compile the statements of the votes made by the Commissioners of Election," and to continue in session till "such returns have been compiled." The law also required that this board should consist of "five persons to be elected by the Senate from all political parties." The Senate pretended to have complied with this law by appointing four Republicans and one Democrat. The Democrat that was appointed resigned. The law provided that in case of any vacancy by death, registration, or otherwise, by either of the board, then the vacancy *shall be filled* by the residue of the returning officers." It was very certain that the presence of a Democrat to witness the work they had in hand would prove most inconvenient, and therefore they refused to fill the vacancy.

The scheme upon which Kellogg finally settled for invalidating the election was by alleging intimidation of voters, and upon that pretext throwing out enough Democratic votes to give the electoral vote of the State to Hayes.

During the two weeks succeeding the election, visiting statesmen of both the great political parties had flocked to New Orleans. Several of the more conspicuous representatives of the Democratic party there lost no time in addressing a note to Stanley Matthews, James A. Garfield, John A. Logan, William D. Kelly, John A. Kasson, William M. Evarts, E.W. Stoughton, and John A. Dix, each and all whom claimed to represent either the President *in esse* (In being; actually existing) or the President *in posse* (In potential but not in actuality). In this note they stated that having understood that the gentlemen that they addressed were there at the request of President Grant, to see that the Board of Canvassers make a fair count of the votes actually cast, they invited a conference in order that such influence as they possessed might be "exerted in behalf of such a canvass of the votes actually cast as by its fairness and impartiality shall command the respect and acquiescence of the American people of all parties."

This invitation was declined by the Republican "visiting statesman" on the ground that they were indisposed to reduce the function of the Returning Board "to the mere clerical duty of counting the votes actually cast, irrespective of the question whether they were fraudulently and violently cast or otherwise vitiated." They further stated that, "it is, in our judgment, vital to the preservation of constitutional liberty that the habit of obedience to the forms of law should be sedulously (Persevering and constant in effort or application) inculcated (To teach (others) by frequent instruction or repetition; indoctrinate) and cultivated, and that the resort to extra-constitutional mode of redress (To set right; remedy or rectify), for even actual grievances should be avoided and condemned as revolutionary, disorganizing, and tending to disorder and anarchy."

Such a plea in avoidance might be successfully demurred to in any court of justice of competent jurisdiction. How the habit of obedience

to the forms of law was to be compromised by the proposed conference, even though at the worst it failed to secure concert of action, is
not quite clear. Be that, however, as it may, if "obedience to the forms
of law" was the motive of their long journey to New Orleans and their
protracted detention there, it proved a singular waste of energy, for
every one of the provisions of the election laws we have cited was
systematically and repeatedly violated, not only with the knowledge
of these political purists, with the undisguised cooperation of most of
them. We shall presently see that these traveling statesmen took a very
different view of their duty when canvassing the votes of the States in
the Electoral Commission.

The election was entirely peaceable throughout the state. In the
volumes of testimony subsequently taken by Congress there was not
a particle of evidence that on the day of election there was any riot,
tumult, or intimidation at a single polling place in the State. The election
officers were all Republicans, and in accordance with the programme
of the Fifth-avenue conspirators they had been all given to understand
that their political future depended entirely upon their faithful execution of their party behests.

There were fifty-six parishes, exclusive of New Orleans, in the entire
State, and nearly one thousand polling places. There were seventy-
four supervisors and assistant supervisors or registration, and three
commissioners of election for each poll, all selected by the Republican
managers, practically by Governor Kellogg.[1]

---

1 The nature of these assurances may be gathered from the following circular issued by the Secretary of the Republican State Committee:

HEADQUARTES REPUBLICAN PARTY OF LOUISIANA,
ROOMS JOINT COMMITTEE OF CANVASSING AND REGISTRATION,
MECHANICS' INSTITUTE, Sept. 25, 1876
SUPERVISIOR OF REGISTRATION, PARISH OR ASSUMPTION, LA:

DEAR SIR: It is well known to this committee that, from examination of the census of 1875,
the Republican vote in your parish is 2,200, and the Republican majority is 900.

You are expected to register and vote the full strength of the Republican party in your parish.

Your recognition by the next State administration will depend upon your doing your full
duty on the premises and you will not be held to have done your full duty unless the Republican
registration in your parish reaches 2,200, and the Republican vote is at least 2,100.

All local candidates and committees are directed to aid you to the utmost in obtaining the
result, and every facility is and will be afforded you; but you must obtain the results called for
herein without fail. Once obtained, your recognition will be ample and generous.

Very respectfully, your obedient servant,
D.J. M.A. Jewett, Secretary.

Samuel J. Tilden on the porch at Graystone

And yet when the returns came to the supervisors, were consolidated, and made ready for transmission to the Returning Board, only two supervisors had made any protests affecting the fairness of the registration or the peaceable and honest character of the election. In but one instance was intimidation alleged. The exception was in the eleventh ward of New Orleans, where two custom-house dependants refused to sign the returns, alleging intimidation. This was for disfranchising four hundred and twelve respectable citizens living in the best portion of the residence quarter of the city. The poll was surrounded all day by deputy marshals and metropolitan police, every one a Republican; and the United States supervisor, also a Republican, was present in the room where the votes were received.

Of the two instances in which the returns of the supervisors stated objections to the votes of their parishes in conformity with the law, one affected only the votes for justices of the peace and constables, and the other was a case where the supervisor declined to incorporate the votes of two polls where he had established but one, and the commissioners without authority had established two.

For one entire week after the election the Republican managers in New Orleans were confident that their plans had succeeded, and that they had carried the State. They so assured their friends at Washington. But to make assurance double sure, they instructed their supervisors of registration to send their returns to New Orleans by mail. The law required them to bring their returns in person. As they came in, the supervisors deposited them at the custom-house instead of delivering, as the law required, to the returning officers. Only seventeen supervisors of registration sent their packages, as the law required, by mail; and the registered packages containing these returns, instead of being delivered to the returning officers as the law required, were stopped at the post-office, and retained there or handed over to the Republican managers.

Had there been intimidation, of course it could only been expected from the Democrats; but what had the Democrats to gain by intimidation? They knew that the Returning Board had been established expressly to "annual votes so secured and provide for votes so prevented." They knew, too, that the Returning Board in 1876 consisted of the same white members as in 1874, when in the parish of Rapids, where Wells, the president of the board resided the whole vote of the parish was thrown out and four Republican members of the Legislature seated, upon a secret affidavit of Wells as to occurrences in that parish on the day of the election, *when he was not there.* The members so seated had not claimed to have been elected, and subsequently, upon the recommendation of the congressional committee, were unseated, and the conduct of Wells was officially denounced.

The most and the best the Democrats could hope for was to offer the Returning Board no pretext whatever for setting aside the election because of intimidation, knowing as they did full well by experience that such pretext would be used against them without scruple or remorse.

The Returning Board consisted of J. Madison Wells, chairman, Thomas C, Anderson, Louis M. Kenner, and G. Cassanave, the last two colored.

The Returning Board should have begun their labors by the express terms of the law on the 17th of November, and should have remained in session until the returns had been complied. The first open meeting for business was not held until the 20th. The interval seems to have been industriously utilized in ascertaining how many votes were to be thrown out to save the Hayes electors, and from what parishes the votes should be taken. Hence the direction to the supervisors of registration to bring their returns in person, instead of sending them, as the law required, by mail. The returns were opened and read by Anderson. What had been going on between their delivery and their opening may be inferred from the following incident which occurred at the session on the 25th.[1]:

---

1 Nine years before, General Sheridan had preferred charges against Wells, the president of the board, while he was provisional governor of Louisiana, for dishonesty, and subsequently – 1877 – Wells was indicted with his three colleagues by the grand jury of Louisiana for falsely and feloniously uttering and publishing as true a certain altered and forged and counterfeited public record; to wit, the consolidated statement of votes of the parish of Vernon, made by the supervisor of registration for said parish, whereby falsely and feloniously 178 votes were added to the number of votes actually cast for the Republican electors, and 395 votes were deducted form the number of votes actually cast for the Democratic electors by the voters of said Parish.

Wells took refuge in the swamps of New Orleans to escape arrest; the two negroes were held to bail in $5,000 each; and Anderson was brought to trial, convicted, and sentenced to two years at hard labor in the penitentiary, and to pay the costs of prosecution. An appeal was taken by his counsel to the Supreme Court, where he was finally acquitted, not on the ground that he had not been guilty of all the forgeries and falsifications alleged, but on the technical ground that the consolidated statement "made, such as was required to be made, by a supervisor of registration,

It had been remarked by the Democrats that very few of the returns came by mail, and it was also a subject of complaint that the returns from many parishes had not yet been received. The returns from De Soto, however, had come by mail. Anderson in submitting them to the Returning Board was quite emphatic in stating this fact. He read, "Consolidated statement of votes of the parish of De Soto," and, after a pause, adding, "with any quantity of affidavits attached." It happened that Mr. Burke and Mr. Gloin, members of the bar of Louisiana, and counsel for the Democrats, were in the room at this time, looking over some papers in parishes laid aside as contested. Mr. Burke asked," When was that package mailed?" Anderson replied that it was mailed at Mansfield, La., and received on the 18th. "What is the date of the first affidavit?" asked Burke. Anderson with some hesitation, replied "November 25th" – "How does it happen," asked Mr. Gloin, "that affidavits made on the 25th were in a package mailed on the 18th?" After considerable confusion and hesitation, Abell, the secretary to the Returning Board, bethought him to suggest that there were two packages, one received on the 18th and the other that day; that the first contained the consolidated statement and the other the affidavits. Visiting statesman Stoughton came to Abell's rescue.

Stoughton, "What return is this received today?"

Abell, "The return before the board now. I also received a small package on the 18th, which I presume was a consolidated statement."

Stoughton, "Was the evidence in the package you received today?"

Abell, "Yes, Sir."

Stoughton, "Oh that settles it – merely a clerical error."

It did settle it, for it showed conclusively that the returns had been tampered with; that the package Anderson had opened, and which had been receipted for on the 18th, was one from which he took the consolidated statement, "with any quantity of affidavits attached." The evening before this exposure occurred there had been a meeting of certain persons specially interested in the vote of De Soto and two or three other parishes. Among them were George L. Smith, the candidate for Congress from the De Soto district; the supervisors of De Soto, Bossier, and Webster parishes; and D. D. Smith, the cashier of the

---

was not the election return" contemplated by the Constitution, and therefore its alteration was not the forgery and falsification of "a legal record."

post-office; and D.J.M.A. Jewett, secretary of the Republican committee, who had made himself conspicuous by recommending the Governor to appoint no supervisors of registration in New Orleans, and thus threw out the entire vote on the principal city of the State. At this gathering, the cashier, Smith, unlocked the post-office vault and took out the returns from De Soto, Bossier, Caddo, and Webster. Those from Bossier, Caddo, and Webster had been brought by the supervisors or the parishes respectively, or by some one selected by them for that purpose, and deposited at the post-office for safe keeping until they were "fixed: for the uses of the Returning Board.

The Returns from De Soto, though they had come by mail, instead of going to the Returning Board as they should have done, were also in the post-office vault and under the absolute control of the men most immediately interested in tampering with the vote of that parish. The purpose of this gathering is fully set forth in the following statement made by D.J.M.A. Jewett, one of the witnesses to its proceedings:

C.L. Ferguson, supervisor, mailed his returns per registered package to New Orleans from Mansfield, November 14th; he reached New Orleans in person about the 23rd; on the 24th I received from George L. Smith, in person, or from some person in his interest, a notice that my presence in the private office of the post-office would be desirable about 9 or 10 P.M. that night. On my arrival I found there George L. Smith candidate for Congress, fourth district; D.D. Smith, cashier post-office; C.L. Ferguson, supervisor De Soto parish; T.H. Hutton, supervisor Bosier parish; John S. Morrow, supervisor; Fred E. Heath, candidate for House of Representatives; and Samuel Gardner, citizen of Webster parish, with one or two others, I think, whom I do not now remember. I had detailed Mr. McArdle to attend, and he was there, but on account of objections on the part of George L. Smith he was sent away. The fact whether protest had been made or not, etc., having been considered, D.D, Smith unlocked the post office vault and produced there from the returns of De Soto, Bossier, Caddo, and Webster. Caddo, it was stated, he had brought down himself. Bossier and Webster he had, as I understood. On the De Soto package I noticed the post-mark of Mansfield and that it bore evidence of registration. It was however, already open. It was unrolled and examined by Smith and myself. *It was not possible to create a Republican majority except by throwing out polls, 1, 3, 5, 7 and 8. These were selected for protest, and Ferguson was asked for facts.* I draughted a protest based on such facts as he had knowledge of, either personally or from information received, or as was suggested by George L. Smith, or by the well known conditions of the parish. This Ferguson copied, and was directed to take the same before F.A. Woolfley for administration of the oath.

It was suggested to me, that of course it was not possible to attach this protest and various affidavits in hand affecting the same parish (taken before Commissioner Levissee, in Shreveport) to the consolidated state of votes, this having come forward by mail, and there being a disagreement of dates, but they should be handed or sent in under section 43, as per my circular letter of instructions.

Not withstanding, the unbounded stupidity of somebody rolled these up in the original package, which, restored apparently to its original condition, went forward by carrier to the board, November 25.

Such was Visiting Statesman Stoughton's notion of a *clerical error* which deprived Tilden of his majorities at five different polls in a single parish.

The returns from ten other parishes were doctored at the same time and in like manner.

"The returns from Bossier," say Jewett, "were handed by Captain Hutton, the supervisor, George L. Smith (the aforesaid candidate for Congress) *for safe keeping,* upon his, Hutton's, arrival in the city, and were by Smith placed in the vault of the post-office.

T.H. Hutton had, on November 13 (the day that he started from Bellevue for New Orleans), sworn his consolidated statement of votes (popularly known as the returns) before George B. Abercrombie, clerk of the court, and had deposited with said clerk a copy, as required by law, at the date named, and when the returns were examined by me in the post-office, this document bore in the space for remarks a protest of the Atkins Landing box (No. 1) and no other.

In my presence, in the private office of the post office, the supervisor interpolated in the same space under the protest noted above, and above the jurat, a second protest, affecting the Red Land box (No. 3). There is no question in my mind but that the protest and exclusion of this box was an afterthought which first took shape at this time (November 24)."

F.M. Grant, who brought the returns from Morehouse parish about a week before the 25th of November, to which there was no protest attached, declined, says Jewett, "the solicitations of Blanchard to make one."

Jewett proceeds:

"The evening of that or the following day, at the Governor's request, Blanchard and myself drove him out to the Governor's residence, where we had a conference respecting his parish and testimony. This being without effect, the Governor took him apart, into an adjoining room, and they conferred together some time. The next day he was again interviewed by Kellogg at the custom-house, and was (as I was informed) taken to see the visiting statesmen. Blanchard informed me that Grant was bulldozed by these and other partied for several days before he make the protest which he made November 18.

At this time I purposely avoided even seeing the visiting statesmen except as I met them casually at Kellogg's, and it was arranged between myself and Mr. Blanchard that he should do everything which would require the slightest connection with them.

This was done because it was not proposed that Mr. Blanchard should testify before either committee of Congress when they came, as was expected, and I desired to be, myself, incapable of answering any inconvenient questions which might be propounded to me touching these gentlemen and their connection with out affairs."

Grady, the supervisor of Ouachita parish, was unwilling to protest the election. "I am informed by Blanchard," says Jewett, "that Mr. Grady was bulldozed by Kellogg, Sherman, Garfield, and others for a week before he would sign the protest. He admitted to myself that he could not stand the pressure. I do not charge or believe that any fact stated by Grady was untrue or unknown to him, at least by common report. The evidence was simply obtained in a manner which deprived it of any legal value."

Clover, the supervisor of East Baton Rouge, refused to compile the statements of votes cast at six different polls, through a willful disregard or ignorance of his duty. He was "sustained in his refusal," says Jewett, "by Kellogg, Campbell, and others, to whose advice he would have yielded. Mr. Clover undoubtedly did this with the promise or expectation of reward."

"It may be said," Jewett continues, "that I ought to have corrected him. This it would have been useless for me to do against the influence of those named, and, while Mr. Blanchard and myself were practically in control of the State registrar's office, and while Govern Hahn would have undoubtedly signed an order (drawn by either of us) to Mr. Clover, the law expressly excepted supervisors from obedience to the rulings or orders of the State registrar of voters, who is at the same time deemed their administrative chief."

Similar refusals of the supervisors of Orleans and Lafourche were attended with similar results.

How another *"clerical error"* in East Feliciana was corrected is thus stated by Jewett:

"James E. Anderson, supervisor, refused, upon his arrival in New Orleans, to make any protest, alleging as a reason his fear of being murdered if he did so. This, in his case, I did not believe, having been convinced by his then secret conduct that he was a corrupt scoundrel, who would protest or not, betray one party or the other (he was unquestionably in the employ of both), as he might conceive to be for his interest.

"As Governor Kellogg was responsible for his being in his parish to go through the farce of an election, I abandoned to Governor Kellogg the task of getting him to testify to notorious facts unquestionably within his knowledge, and washed my hands of him and of his affairs. I was present on two occasions at Kellogg's house, when Anderson and the Governor were in conference respecting his testimony.

"On the 10th of November, immediately after his arrival, Anderson had signed a protest drawn by Hugh J. Campbell, which the following day he distinctly repudiated, and which he stated to be at least in part untrue. This protest was not finally accepted by him again until, as I was informed, Anderson had been promised the position of deputy naval officer, or something that should be a full equivalent. Anderson himself informed me while under the influence of liquor (about November 20) that 'he had got what he was after,' by which remark and its context I understood that he had received pledges of reward for his testimony. I have also been informed that Messrs. Sherman and Garfield assisted in bringing Mr. Anderson 'to listen to reason.'"

Jewett says, in conclusion, that "protests and evidence, such as it was, which had been received and filed up to November 27, excluded votes for Packard 1,620 and for Nichols 9,700. leaving Mr. Packard elected by a clear majority, with a Republican majority in the Senate and House, and also elected three Hayes and five Tilden electors."

Jewett adds that, in pursuance of a "conspiracy to which he alleges that J.M. Wells, Thomas C. Anderson, John Sherman, and J.A. Garfield, and others, were parties, polls were excluded in the parishes of Caldwell, Natchitoches, Richland, Catahoula, Iberia, Livingston, and Tangipahoa, with the result, and for the purpose, of the returning as elected five Hayes electors who were otherwise defeated; that the consideration of this conspiracy was the absolute control of the federal patronage within the State of Louisiana by the said Wells and Anderson; that the evidence used to effect the object of the conspiracy was manufactured without regard to actual facts and with the knowledge of the several conspirators and that the consideration to be given to said Wells and Anderson had been delivered up to date."

But the Returning Board did not rely entirely upon the flexible consciences of supervisors. On the 28th of November Eliza Pinkston, a disreputable negress, notorious in three States for mendacity and beastliness, was borne into the presence of the board and of "the distinguished gentlemen of national reputation: who were there helping to cultivate and inculcate the sanctities of the law. She swore that her husband had been taken from his house in the night, shot seven times, run through and through with knives, and mutilated in various ways her child's throat cut while in her arms; that she was twice shot and her person violated more times than she could remember and that all these outrages were committed by young white men of the neighborhood, many whom she professed to know and identify – one of them a well known and highly respected physician. She also admitted that this medical monster came the day following all these outrages, when sent for, and dressed her wounds and ministered to her wants.

There were scores of reputable gentlemen present who could have exposed this preposterous story, but they were not allowed to testify. The story would answer the concoctors of it better as it stood. Eliza Pinkston lived in Ouachita parish, which gave a large Democratic majority. The board wanted a pretext for throwing it out, and here they had it in a dramatic and thrilling piece of evidence to which the telegraph and the press would delight in giving the widest circulation. Absurd as the story was, it was deemed of sufficient importance for a committee of the House of Representatives to be sent down to Louisiana to investigate it. It was ascertained that her statement that her husband had been shot or mutilated was a fabrication; that the throat of her child had not been cut, and that there was no mark of violence on its body except a slight contusion on its head; that the men whom she charged with these outrages could not possibly have been in her neighborhood on the night in question; that she had made an affidavit in Monroe county for use before the Returning Board, in which she charged the crime of murder and other outrages on other persons, which was sent by the supervisor of Ouachita to the Returning Board November 23, but it was suppressed and withdrawn, and the another made in New Orleans, December 2, was substituted for it.

It was also ascertained that the Returning Board had falsified its own record of the receipt of the returns from Ouachita. The secretary announced that they had been received November 24, but when opened, a letter was found addressed to Mr. Abell, saying,

"Enclosed please find an affidavit of Eliza Pinkston, which I received too late to file with my returns. Please see that it is brought in with other evidence filed with my returns."

This letter was dated November 23rd.

The character of this woman whose testimony was invoked "to inculcate and cultivate obedience to law" as thus summarized by the congressional committee:

"The character of Eliza Pinkston, as developed before your subcommittee to the fullest extent, was such as to render her a fit instrument in the hands of designing men. She had been charged with the murder of the child of persons with whom she had but recently quarreled. The child died of poison. Eliza Pinkston, then know as Lizzie Finch, in Morehouse parish, was arrested, and acquitted only because the main witness to the crime was too young to understand the nature of the oath. The general impression was that she was guilty. When residing in Union parish, she had shamefully beaten an old woman living with her, death ensuing in a few days after. She had abandoned one of her young children, leaving it to starve to death in a fence corner. Another she made way with shortly after its birth. She was an habitual abortionist. She was in perpetual quarrel. Her testimony had been so effectually impeached in the counts of Morehouse parish that the Republican district attorney refused to call her as a witness. Everybody who knew her considered her a desperate character. Eye-witnesses proved that she live with her husband on very bad terms. She was about to kill him at one time when she supposed him asleep. Upon another occasion she assaulted him with an axe, intending to kill him. He was in perpetual dread of harm, as witnesses testified. She was ugly, vulgar, indecent, and lewd beyond the worst."

The rest of this description I am obliged to suppress as too indecent for these pages.[1]

According to this poor wretch's story, which Sherman, Garfield, Stoughton, and Matthews professed to believe, as number of malefactors had been guilty of a series of hideous crimes, not only against the laws of the State of Louisiana, but against the laws of the United States. Why were not steps taken by either jurisdiction to arrest or punish any one of the alleged criminals? The arrest, trial, and hanging of a half-dozen of these murderers, if there were any would have been an object-lesson far more efficacious for cultivating and inculcating obedience to law in Louisiana, than employing the testimony of such an outcast to compass the usurpation of the presidency.

Towards the end of November the Returning Board thought they had rid themselves of enough Democratic votes, by the methods of which we have given only a comparatively few examples, to ensure the election of Hayes, of Packard for governor, and a Legislature that would be shameless enough to send Governor Kellogg to the United States Senate. But when they came to figure up the returns they found that they were still astray in their calculations and that guillotine must again be set to work; that they must throw out the polls in nine other parishes, and the entire vote of East Feliciana and Grant parish. They threw out, in addition, sixty-nine polls from twenty-two other parishes, and refused to include the polls which the supervisors of East Baton Rouge, Lafayette, Lafourche, and the assistant supervisors of three wards in New Orleans had, without any warrant of law, wantonly refused to compile.

---

1 Report 156, Part 1 House of Rep. 44th Congress. 2d Sess. Page 45-6 & H.R. Misc. Doc No 34, part 2 44th Congress 2d Sess pp. 790-794

In all, 13,214 Democratic electors were disfranchised and 2,415 Republican. The highest number of votes "actually cast" for a Democratic elector was 83,817, and for a Republican elector, 77,332. Five of the Republican electors' ran behind the vote of their colleagues 1,141. The average majority for the Democratic electors was 7,116.

The extent to which the people of Louisiana were defrauded by the Returning Board and their accomplices can be determined by another and very simple test, which no amount of perjury nor partisanship can assail.

We have seen that the pretext for throwing out the returns from most of the disfranchised parishes was intimidation of the negroes, by which they were prevented from registering and voting. The rejections from other causes were insignificant in number, and, in their influence upon the result, without importance.

The names of the registered voters for the entire State in 1876, according to the statistics of the State's register's office, were 207,622. of which there were of:

Colored – 115,268 – White – 92,354 – with a total of 23,914 colored voters in the majority.

According to the census of 1870, the colored males of twenty-one years and upwards were 86,913, and white makes of like ages, 87,066.

The colored class included Chinese and Indians, who had no votes.

In 1880 the white males of twenty-one years and over numbered – 108,810, Color makes of like age, 107,970 which showed that both classes had increased in about the same proportion, and their relative proportion could not have materially varied in 1876. If from colored makes the Chinese Indians, and foreign-born negroes are deducted, manifestly the colored voters could not have exceeded the white. Professor Chaille', who had made a special study of vital statistics in Louisiana, expressed the opinion that there was a small majority of white voters in the State. But, as we have seen, there were 22,914 more colored than white voters registered in the State in 1876. Five years after, and five years before, the white voters were in an undisputed majority, Where did these 22,914 colored votes come from, and what had become of the army of negroes who were alleged to have been afraid to register? These figures prove beyond a reasonable doubt that the names of over 20,000 names were registered that had only this nominal existence.

Again, by the census of 1870 the white population of the parish of New Orleans was 140,923 – of the negro – 50,456 with Whites over Negroes equaling 90,467.

By the census of 1880 the white population was 158,369 and the negro – 57,619 – with White over colored by 100,750.

When the registration was completed in 1876, the 57,619 negro population was found to yield 23,495 voters, and 140,923 whites, only 34,913 voters.

Again the State census of 1875 gives an excess of 7,210 colored females over colored males in the parish of New Orleans, that is, in all, 36,013 females. Deducting these from the total of 57,619, there remained by 21,597 colored voters in the whole state in 1880. The number was doubtless somewhat less in 1876, and yet here were at least 2,891 more colored names registered that there could have been colored voters in the parish.

But not content with fraudulently registering nearly if not quite three thousand fictitious names, the Kellogg managers deliberately struck off from the registration lists the names of 7,738 white voters. And this was the way it was done:

With the cooperation of Marshall, Pitkin, and the employees in the post-office, some 30,000 circulars were sent out by the letter-carriers, with instructions to return all not personally served. About 11,000 were so returned. The registration lists were then secretly taken to the custom-house, where the supervisors were directed to strike off the names of all not personally served.

Professor Chaille', after a careful study of all available data, has expressed his conviction that an honest and complete registration of the voters of New Orleans would have given about 40,584 white and 13,500 negro voters, instead of 22,495; and allowing for reasonable contingencies, such as absence, sickness, etc., there ought not to have been of these more than 12,000 registered.[1]

But why accumulate further evidence of the nefarious processes by which this foul conspiracy against the rights of a sovereign State were consummated?

---

1 H.R. Misc. Doc No 34, Part 2, 44th Congress 2d Sess. Pp 1031-1032

It is enough to have shown that the Tilden and Hendricks electors were chosen in Louisiana and Florida by large popular majorities.

That many thousands of Democratic voters were fraudulently disfranchised.

That in no single instance had the commissioners of election shown or even alleged intimidation of voters.

That there was not from a single polling-place in the State a statement of the vote returned in the form required by law.

That no one of the supervisors of registration had made objections to the registration of voters for a single voting place in the form required by law, nor had any of them reported intimidation or violence.

That four supervisors had assumed judicial powers, which the law conferred only upon the returning officers, and by refusing to compile had thus rejected the commissioners' returns from twelve polling-places; while three assistant supervisors for wards in New Orleans had illegally refused to consolidate returns from three polls.[1]

The distinguished statesmen who had assisted at this carnival of lawlessness not only found nothing in the proceedings to rebuke, but did not scruple to share in the loot, presumably in proportion to the importance of their respective services securing it.

Senator Sherman was made Secretary of the Treasury, then quite the most important office in the President's gift.

Stanley Matthews was nominated to a seat on the bench of the Supreme Court of the United States. The Senate declined to confirm him. He was renominated, in 1881, by President Garfield, who had been one of his coadjutors in New Orleans, and through the influence common to all new administrations, with all its federal patronage in reserve, the opposition to him in the Senate was overcome, and he was confirmed.

James A. Garfield, who had his headquarters in the custom-house, where the affidavits were manufactured during the sessions of the Returning Board, was elected to the United States Senate by an arrangement with Stanley Matthews, and subsequently succeeded Hayes as the Republican candidate for the presidency.

---

1 Those who may desire to probe this iniquity to it profoundest deep are referred to the investigations made by committee on the 43rd, 44th and 45th Congresses, and to the more convenient compendium of A.M. Gibson, entitled, "A Political Crime," to which I have been greatly indebted in making this synopsis of the evidence submitted to Congress.

William M. Evarts, who in 1875 had denounced the illegal organization for the Louisiana House of Representatives with the aid of the military, and all the proceedings and acts of that body as well as of the Returning Board of 1874, went to New Orleans in 1876, and lent the weight of his personal and professional influence to assist – unconsciously, I fain believe – the men who were harvesting the crop of crime he had denounced the planting. He subsequently was the leading counsel for Hayes before the Electoral Commission. He received the office of Secretary of State.

E.W. Stoughton, who prepared the report to the President justifying the conduct and fulsomely eulogizing the character of the worthless creatures who constituted the Returning Board, was rewarded with the mission to Russia.

It required the disfranchisement of a less number of the citizens of Louisiana to count in Packard as governor than to count Hayes electors; but then a governor has less patronage than a president to bestow, and it became necessary to abandon Packard to secure a sufficient number of Southern Democratic votes in the House of Representatives, to ensure the ratification of the decision of the Electoral Commission, of which I shall have to speak presently. Packard was reconciled to his fate by receiving the consulate at Liverpool, a place which, whether it was worth fifteen or thirty thousand dollars a year, depended mainly upon the character of the man who held it.

Kellogg was rewarded for his services with a seat in the United States Senate, - by what means may be inferred from the fact that of the members of the Legislature who voted for him, eight senators, three officers of the Senate, thirty-two members of the House, and four officers of the House, making forty-seven in all, received lucrative appointments from the federal government, and, curiously enough, all of these patriots received their appointments from the department of which John Sherman was the chief.

If the persons connected with the canvass, election, and negotiations in Louisiana, sixty-nine were appointed to offices, and all but sixteen of these were treasury appointments.

Wells, the president of the Retuning Board, had one son appointed deputy surveyor at New Orleans; another son and son-in-law, to clerkships in the same institution, on salaries ranging from $1,400 to $1,600 per annum.

Anderson, Wells' white colleague on the Returning Board, was made deputy collector of the port of New Orleans; his son, C.B. Anderson, was made a clerk in the custom-house, on a salary of $1,400; his sons father-in-law, auditor, on a salary of $2,500; and his son's brother-in-law, clerk on a salary of $1,200.

Kenner, one of the negroes on the Returning Board, was appointed deputy naval officer of the same port; one of his brothers was appointed to a $1,600 clerkship, and another brother, a laborer, at a salary of $600.

Cassanave, the other colored member of the board, had a brother who was an undertaker appointed to a place in the custom-house. His own expenses, incurred in defending himself and colleagues in New Orleans against criminal charges, were defrayed in part by President Hayes and Secretary Sherman.

Woodward, clerk of the Returning Board, who assisted in falsifying the election returns, was appointed to a $1,400 clerkship, and was subsequently promoted to an assistant deputy surveyorship, at a salary of $1,600.

Abell, the secretary of the Retuning Board, was appointed to a $1,600 clerkship in the custom-house.

Judge G.B. Davis, a clerk of the Returning Board, and another man of equally easy virtue with any of his associates, also found an asylum in the custom-house.

Green, a colored minute clerk of the board, in due time reached the same port, and afterwards was appointed an inspector at $3 per day.

Charles Hill, another clerk of the Returning Board, and therefore possessed of perilous secrets, was appointed store-keeper, at a salary of $1460.

It is a fact not without significance that none of President Hayes cabinet ministers, save his Secretary of the Treasury, availed themselves the privilege of rewarding any of the members of the Returning Board or of their zealous subordinates.

Whether these dignitaries and emoluments were worth what they cost; whether the honors for which they were beholden to the frauds and forgeries of the four pied and speckled knaves who constituted the Louisiana Returning Board in 1876 are such as their offspring and friends will take pride in; and whether their names will be cherished by their countrymen for their active and passive parts in placing a man in the presidential chair who was not elected to the office by the people, - are questions which may be safely left to the final arbitrament of history.

"How far," said the Hon. Clarkson N. Potter, in his admirable and temperate report, - the most admirable because so temperate, - the controlling visiting statesmen like Mr. Sherman really believed there was any justification for the rejection of Democratic votes by the Returning Board, men will never agree. We are apt to believe in the right of what we earnestly desire. Men who thought the welfare of the country depended upon the continuation in power of the Republican party would naturally have been disposed to consider almost anything justified to retain it there. To us it seems impossible that the flagrant and atrocious conduct of the Returning Board was not realized above all by the men of most political experience, or that the most dangerous and outrageous political fraud of the age was not assisted and advised by those who next proceeded to take possession of its best fruits."[1]

---

1 Chairman of the select committee appointed by the House of Representatives, "to inquire into the alleged fraudulent canvass and return of votes at the last presidential election in the States of Louisiana and Florida."

CHAPTER III

At the meeting of Congress in December the absorbing question was the counting of the electoral vote. It had been usual for Congress to define in advance the manner in which this duty should be discharged. In the session of 1864-5 Congress provided that no electoral vote objected to by either House of Congress should be counted except by the concurrent votes of both Houses. This became notorious as "the 22nd rule." It was re-adopted at the three successive electoral counts of 1865,1869, and 1873. This rule, after having been in force for three successive elections, was abandoned by a resolution of the Senate in December 1875, on motion of Senator Edmunds, at whose instance the Senate adopted, "the rules of that body and the joint rules of the two Houses *except the 22nd joint rule heretofore in use.*" The House of Representatives was at this time largely Democratic, and, had the 22nd joint rule continued in force, any electoral votes which it refused to

count would have been rejected. The rule, which was doubtful consti-
tutionality, had been originally adopted, and subsequently renewed,
for partisan ends; for partisan ends it was now dispensed with by the
Senate, thus leaving the two Houses without any rule to govern them
for counting the electoral votes in February, 1877.

Prior to 1865 and before the adoption of the 22nd joint rule above
referred to, it had been the practice of two Houses of Congress, a little
in advance of the day fixed by the Act of 1792 for counting the votes, -
the second Wednesday of February, - to agree upon the place of meeting
for the discharge of this duty and the order of procedure. Various efforts
had been made from time to time, by one House or the other, previous
to the adoption of the 22nds rule, to appropriated to itself the power
to determine the validity of electoral votes; but all had, for one reason
or another, proved abortive. The 22nd joint rule, adopted by the Republicans in 1865, assumed for the first time the right to reject electoral
votes, as the prerogative of either House.

When the certificates of the electors of the several States came to
be opened at Washington in 1877, it appeared that the certificates of
thirty-four States were uncontested, but that the remaining four were
to be contested. These were the certificates from the States of South
Carolina, Florida, Louisiana, and Oregon. The electoral vote of the
uncontested States was so distributed that the fate of the presidential
candidates depended upon the electoral vote of the four contested
States.

Congress having failed to make any provision beforehand, the mode
of procedure in counting the electoral vote was the first question to be
dealt with.

The Republicans had the control of the Senate, the Democrats of
the House. The Constitution provided that "the President of the Senate
shall, in the presence of the Senate and House of Representatives,
open all the certificates, and the votes shall then be counted." Senator
Morton took the ground that the President of the Senate should be
invested with the plenary authority "to determine all disputes relative
to certificates of the electoral votes; to count them and to declare the
result, which declaration was to be accepted as final, conclusive and
irrevocable." The President of the Senate at that time, Thomas W. Ferry,
of Michigan, owed that position to his party subserviency rather than to
his fame as a statesman. The adoption of such a rule would have been

equivalent to pronouncing Hayes President and making the counting of the electoral vote an idle ceremony. To make it such was obviously the motive of those who advocated it.

The Constitution assigned to the President of the Senate no other specific duty but to open the certificates. Beyond that he was but one of three coordinate bodies authorized to count the votes, settle controversies, and declare the result, as had been virtually the unbroken practice from the foundation of the government. A year had not elapsed since the same Senator Norton had introduced an electoral-count bill which required that the affirmative action of both Houses of Congress should be required to reject *any* certificate of electoral votes, and if more than one return was made, only that one should," be counted, which the two Houses, acting separately, shall decide to be the true and valid return." Nothing had occurred to the Constitution which in the spring of 1876 required the concurrence of the two Houses, acting separately, to count an electoral vote, the President of the Senate to the contrary notwithstanding, that in the winter of the same year could transfer this power to the President of the Senate. That is nothing but a presidential election which begat the temptation to strike the House of Representatives with impotence for the purpose of ensuring the success of the Republican candidates, The inconsistency of the positions, and the absurdity of attempting to reconcile the Constitution with two modes of procedure so diametrically opposed to each other, did not prevent Morton's scheme finding favor with his partisans in Congress, who seemed to have reached the conviction that the end of defeating Tilden would sanctify any means necessary to accomplish it, and that the Constitution itself should yield to such an exigency. Such threatening proportions did this scheme assume that Mr. Tilden devoted more than a month to the preparation of a complete history of the electoral counts from the foundation of the government to show it to have been the unbroken usage of Congress, not of the President of the Senate, to count the electoral votes.

With influence, if any, this publication had upon the ultimate abandonment of Senator Morton's scheme it is difficult to say. Probably not much, for it taught the Senators nothing of which they were ignorant; but about this time the leaders of that body became aware that President Grant did not believe that Hayes was elected, and several prominent Republican members of Congress, among them Senator

Conkling, of New York, were under the same impression, and could not be relied upon to assist in upsetting one of the most venerable traditions of the government, nor in becoming accomplices in the fraud to which it was intended to be contributory.

President Grant seems at no time to have any doubt about the electoral vote of Louisiana belonging to Tilden and Hendricks, or if its being so ultimately decided. In some reminiscences of the late George. W. Child's, published first in the "Philadelphia Ledger" in 1885, and subsequently in a vole, that gentleman said,

" Just before General Grant started on his journey around the world, he was spending some days with me, and at dinner with Mr. A.J. Drexel, Col, A.K. McClure, and myself, General Grant reviewed the contest for the creation of the Electoral Commission, and the contest before and in the commission, very fully and with rare candor and the chief significance of his view was in the fact, as he stated it, that he expected from the beginning, until the final judgment, that the electoral vote of Louisiana would be awarded to Tilden. He spoke of South Carolina and Oregon as justly belonging to Hayes; of Florida, as reasonably doubtful and of Louisiana, as for Tilden."[1]

Col. A.K. McClure and the late A.J. Drexel, who were also guest of Mr. Childs on this occasion, have confirmed his report of this conversation.

The plan, therefore of gagging the House of Representatives in the Electoral College received no encouragement from President Grant. Whether he would have ever made any serious opposition to such a consummation, or whether the Senate would have deferred to him if he had, it is now idle to speculate. Another more plausible, if no less unconstitutional, means of accomplishing the same result was devised for them, the authorship of which has been ascribed to President Grant.

---

1 The Presidential Counts; a complete official record of the proceedings at the counting of the electoral votes in all the elections of President and Vice President of the United States; together with all congressional debates incident thereto or to proposed legislation on that subject; with an analytical introduction. New York, D. Appleton & Co., 1877

The first election of George Washington, in 1759, was only an apparent exception. The election was unanimous, the procedure a formality and with debate or deliberation. See Presidential Counts; also D.D. Fields. "The Electoral Vote of '76, pg. 5

On the 14th of December, 1876, the House of Representatives appointed a committee of seven of its members to act in conjunction with any similar committee of the Senate, "to prepare and report without delay a measure for the removal of differences of opinion as to the proper mode of counting the electoral votes for President and Vice President of the United States, and of determining questions which might arise as to the legality and validity of the returns of such votes made by the several States, to the end that the votes should be counted and the result declared *by a tribunal whose authority none can question and whose decision all will accept.*"

Four days later, and on the eighteenth of the same month, the Senate created a special committee of seven Senators with power," to prepare and report without unnecessary delay such a measure either of a legislative or other character as may in their judgment be best calculated to accomplish the lawful counting of the electoral votes and best disposition of all questions connected therewith, and the true declaration of the result, " and also, "to confer and act with the committee of the House of Representatives."

This joint committee consisted of Senators George F. Edmunds, of Vermont; Frederick T. Frelinghuysen, of New Jersey; Roscoe Conkling, of New York; Allen G. Thurman, of Ohio; Thomas F. Bayard, of Delaware; Matthew W. Ransom, of North Carolina; and Oliver P. Morton, of Indiana; and Representatives Henry B. Payne, of Ohio; Eppa Hunton, of Virginia; Abram S. Hewitt, of New York; William M. Springer, of Illinois; George W. McCrary, of Iowa; George F. Hoar, of Massachusetts; and George Willard, of Michigan. On the 18th of January this committee almost unanimously – Senator Morton only dissenting – reported a bill providing for the creation of a tribunal to be composed of five Senators, five Representatives, and five associate justices of the Supreme Court of the United States, four of the latter being designated by their districts in the bill itself, the fifth to be subsequently chosen by these four; to which tribunal should be referred the conflicting certificates and accompanying documents from the contested States, and all questions relating to the powers of Congress in the premises, with the authority to exercise the same powers in ascertaining the legal vote of such States. The bill further provided that the decisions of such tribunal in every case should stand, unless rejected *by the concurrent vote of both Houses.* Also those objections which might be made to any votes from

States no presenting double certificates should be considered, not by the commission, but by the Houses separately, and *unless sustained by both,* should be of no effect.

The bill, after sharply contested debate in both Houses, passed the Senate January 25, and the House of Representatives January 26. In the former the vote was 47 yeas to 17 nays; the Republicans voting 24 yeas to 16 nays, and the Democrats, 23 yeas to 1 nay; absent or not voting, 9 Republicans and 1 Democrat. In the House there were 191 yeas to 86 nays, the Democrats voting 158 yeas to 18 nays, and the Republicans 33 yeas to 68 nays; absent or not voting, 7 Republicans and 7 Democrats.

How so large a number of the Democrats in Congress were induced to supersede the constitutional machinery for counting the electoral votes, for a device not only unknown to the Constitution, but in all its important bearings inconsistent with it, can only be explained as we explain most blunders which are woven into the web of every human life. Some yielded through ignorance, some for the want of reflection, some to quiet a controversy about the result of which they were indifferent or apprehensive, some to serve personal ends at home that seemed more important to them that the presidential issue, while upon others, many, if not all, these considerations may have been not without their influence.

Unfortunately for Mr. Tilden, the Senate swarmed with Democratic aspirants for the presidency; the two on the committee who negotiated the surrender having been strenuous competitors for that honor before the convention which nominated Mr. Tilden. Nor was the House of Representatives lacking in Democratic candidates who had not been able to regard with satisfaction the triumph of a candidate who had not been in the least indebted to Congress for his nomination, nor much for his success at the polls. Then again, there were perhaps no inconsiderable number who indulged the expectation that the proposed tribunal would elect their candidate, which was to them of more concern than the means by which it was accomplished. The latter class was recruited largely from among those who supported Senator Davis, of Illinois, who then occupied a seat on the bench of the Supreme Court, would be selected as the fifth member from that bench, and whose character and moral authority with his colleagues enough was known to quench any suspicion of his lending support to the fraudulent and unconstitutional devices upon which he would have had to sit in judgment.

Those who were seduced by this aleatory device were rewarded as they deserved. Just as the electoral commission bill became a law, the independent Republicans and the Democrats in the Illinois Legislature elected Judge Davis to the United States Senate. This afforded that gentleman an excuse, of which he naturally availed himself with a prompt alacrity, to decline the proffered place on the commission, and gave to the four judges, two selected from each party, the choice of the fifth, which resulted in the selection of Justice Bradley, a New Jersey Republican, and in leaving the rival candidates entirely at the mercy of the Republican party. By whatever motive they were governed, by whatever temptations seduced, it is now but too evident that the representatives of the people in the lower House inexcusably abandoned their coign of vantage and shirked the most solemn and momentous of all their official responsibilities, in a few short weeks to be marched through the Caudine forks and take their seats of humiliation before the inexorable tribunal of history.

It is hardly necessary to say that Mr. Tilden was too large and experienced a statesman to approve of discharging any constitutional duty by any but constitutional methods. As soon as the action of the Returning Boards furnished a suitable provocation for his interference, he urged his friends in leadership of the House to expose and combat in full debate the threatened, unwarranted usurpation by the President of the Senate of the right to count the votes, and to take no further step until *in both Houses* the great but pacific constitutional battle had been fought on that issue. He was ready to accept all responsibility for the outcome. He assured them that if properly resisted the conspiracy must break down; that it must not be encouraged by the least symptom of concession, but fought inch by inch on the floors of Congress, until the real character of the proposed usurpation should become known throughout the country and the nation's opinion of it could reach Washington. Early in the session he prepared two resolutions which raised the issue upon which he wished that battle to be fought, and which, with some slight modifications by the House committee on "the privileges, powers, and duties of the House of Representatives in counting the electoral votes" that received his approval, were adopted by that committee and reported to the House.[1]

Had the course there traced been followed, it is now apparent that the confirmation of Mr. Tilden's election would have been assured beyond a peradventure. The controlling voices of both parties in the Senate had over and over again, and within a few months, asserted and insisted upon the right of the two Houses to count the vote. They all knew, and many had repeatedly assisted in adding to, the imposing line of precedents under which a challenge of any electoral certificate by either House had sufficed to exclude its vote from the count. A challenge of a single one of the nineteen contested votes would have resulted in Tilden's election, either by the concurring vote of the two

---

1 It was supposed by many that Morton and others engineered the selection of Davis with a full knowledge that he would not serve. It is difficult to see why Davis did not serve on the commission in spite of his election to the Senate, unless his absence from the commission was one of the conditions of his election. However this may be, his retreat from the field in the presence of the enemy effectually disposed of whatever expectations of preferment he might have entertained from the Democratic Party.

This committee consisted of Sparks and Burchard, of Illinois; Tucker, of Virginia; Marsh, of Pennsylvania; Seelye, of Massachusetts; Monroe and Lawrence, of Ohio; and D.D. Field, of New York. The resolutions were as follows:

Resolved, First, That the Constitution does not confer upon the President of the Senate the power to examine and ascertain the votes to be counted as the electoral votes for President and Vice-President of the United States.

Second, That the only power which the Constitution of the United States confers upon the President of the Senate in respect to the electoral votes for President and Vice-President of the United States is to receive the sealed lists transmitted to him by the several electoral colleges, to keep the same safely, and to open all the certificates, or those purporting to be such, in the presence of the Senate and House of Representatives.

Third, That the Constitution of the United States does confer upon the Senate and the House of Representatives the power to examine and ascertain the votes to be counted as the electoral votes.

Fourth, That in execution of their power in respect to the counting of the electoral votes, the House of Representatives is at least equal with the Senate.

Fifth, That in the counting of the electoral votes, not vote can be counted against the judgment and determination of the House of Representatives.

Sixth, That the committee have leave to sit again and report hereafter further matter for the consideration of the House.

The Constitution of the United States, Art. 11, Sect. 111, provides: "The person having the greatest number of votes shall be the President, if such number be the majority of the whole number of electors appointed; and if there be more than one who have such majority, and have an equal number of votes, then the House of Representatives shall immediately choose, by ballot, one of them for President; and if no person have a majority, then from the highest on the list the said House shall in like manner choose the President.

Houses, or, they failing to concur, in his election by the House of Representatives, to which the Constitution has confided the choice in such an emergency, and where the Democrats were in the majority, whether voting by themselves or by States.

Happily we do not depend upon rumor nor oral tradition for our knowledge of Mr. Tilden's views of this crisis and the proper mode of dealing with it.. They will be found most carefully and fully stated as early as the 1st of January, 1877, in the inaugural message of Governor Robinson, of which the portion which appears under the rubric of national affairs was written by Mr. Tilden. The forecast and wisdom of this statement, and its direct bearing upon what had occurred and upon what was to occur, time had only made more conspicuous. In the course of this statement he says:

TILDEN'S VIEWS OF THE CONSTITUTIONAL
MODE OF COUNTING ELECTORAL VOTES

NATIONAL AFFAIRS

"The recent presidential election threatens to prove an epoch of solemn portent in our history. For the first time in the twenty-two elections which have been held for President and Vice-President of the United States, the result remains a subject of controversy after the canvass of the votes within the States had been made and announced. The two Houses of Congress have been heretofore repeatedly required to pass upon the authenticity and validity of electoral votes, but in no former instance had the election turned upon the questionable votes. In every former case the result has been determined by electoral votes which were not in controversy. In the present instance one candidate for President and one candidate for Vice-President have received 184 undisputed electoral votes, as well as a popular majority exceeding a quarter of a million. Another candidate for President and another for Vice-President have received 165 undisputed electoral votes. All the votes of three States, - four in Florida, eight in Louisiana, and seven in South Carolina, - making nineteen in all, are still in dispute; also one of the three in Oregon. In all these cases two sets of returns have been transmitted to the seat of government, directed to the President of the

Senate,' to await the action of the two Houses of Congress, whose duty it is to verify, ascertain, and count the electoral votes.

In a situation involving such momentous results as the chief magistracy of this republic, all the baser as well as the better forces of society are naturally embattled to secure the prize. It is in such crises of history that the controlling force of cardinal principles is liable to be weakened, dangerous concessions to be made, perilous precedents established, sacred traditions violated, and the most important bulwarks of constitutional freedom rendered less secure.

In Louisiana we have seen a State government imposed on the people by the military force of the federal executive under color of a pretended order of a federal judge, which order in itself was void, and which led to the resignation of the judge who made it, to escape impeachment. We have seen the government thus imposed by military force condemned as illegal and a mere usurpation, by both Houses of Congress, and the electoral votes given under its auspices rejected in the counting of the presidential votes in 1873 by the concurrent judgment of the same tribunal. We have seen the government so imposed create 'a Retuning Board' practically vested with absolute power to revise and, if they please, to reverse the results of the election by the people of the State, and thus organize a political mechanism under which an oligarchy in temporary possession of the legislative power of a State might perpetuate their ascendancy indefinitely.

"I pause here in this statement to interpose, in behalf of the people of this great Commonwealth, a solemn denial of the power of any State government or of the federal government to vest such powers as are claimed by the Louisiana Returning Board in any Canvassing Board whatever.

"In the first place, such powers in respect to the choice of presidential electors are not warranted by, but are repugnant to, the Constitution on the United States. The provision of section 1 of article 2 of that instrument, 'that each State shall appoint, in such manner as the Legislature thereof may direct, its presidential electors,' does not confer of the Legislation of a State an unlimited power over the subject. No one will pretend that a temporary majority in the Legislature of the State could grant to an individual, or, to a set of individuals, the power to appoint presidential electors; that it could make this grant for a period of years, or indefinitely, or to his or their heirs or assigns.

"What it cannot do in form it cannot do in substance; what it cannot do directly it cannot do indirectly. The choice which a Legislature is authorized to make for a State, in the mode of appointing presidential electors, is limited to a mere selection between certain known forms of action, recognized in the practice of popular government, and consistent with the nature of popular government. It is a choice of modes, but must not change or destroy the essential character of the thing itself. It is subject to the condition that 'the *State* shall appoint' the presidential electors. The State, that is, the political community knows in our jurisprudence and constitutional law by that name must 'appoint,' and in doing so it must act by and through its known and rightful organs. At the time this provision of the federal Constitution was adopted, it was contemplated that the Legislature of a State possessing all the governmental powers not withdrawn by the provisions of the State Constitution, or transferred to the government of the Union, might itself choose the electors. And, indeed, that was the mode at first generally practiced by the States. The State Legislature at that time was regarded as the most natural and the legitimate organ of the State. The power to choose presidential electors might properly be conferred upon the people of the State by a general ticket, the voters throughout the State choosing all the electors; or they might be chosen by the people of the State voting in districts, each district choosing one elector. These were methods consonant with the principles of our system of government, and by either of which it could be properly said that the State did, in fact, 'appoint' the electors.

"It is historically certain that these different modes were in the contemplation of the convention which formed the Constitution. Experiencing some difficulty, however, in imposing this duty upon all the States by any one uniform system, it devolved upon the Legislatures of each State the authority to choose from among these methods, one for the exercise of that power which it granted in declaring that 'each State shall appoint.'

"While the Legislature of a State may provide that presidential electors shall be appointed by an election of the people, it cannot provide that that election shall not be a reality; that it shall be a sham, and that the actual power of determining the choice shall be invested in a packed committee, whether it be called a 'Retuning Board,' or by any other name.

"Neither can it invest a Board of Canvassers with indefinite or with arbitrary powers, nor with any authority which, by the principles and practice of our jurisprudence and the policy of our elective system, is not fairly incident to the function of ascertaining the votes of the people. This seems to me the obvious, the wide interpretation of the Constitution of the United States and of its laws. Any other doctrine will open the way to abuses, frauds, and usurpations, which must end in destroying popular elections. The moment we depart from a strict construction of grants of power in derogation of the integrity and efficiency of the elective system, we shall be able to find no rule that will protect the rights of the people. We shall tempt transient majorities to seek to prolong their power by tampering with the machinery of elections, and the easiest, most convenient, and most effectual method for such a purpose is by the contrivance of Returning Boards, which shall be packed and equipped with powers hitherto unknown to our laws and practically subversive of the will of the people.

"In the particular case of Louisiana, other equally grave illegalities are believed to exist. The powers vested in the Returning Board are inconsistent with the provision in the Constitution of that State, which guarantees the elective franchise to voters, and also with the provision which confers the judicial power upon the courts. It is probable that the powers of this board, by the law of Louisiana, do not apply to presidential electors; that the board itself was not constituted in accordance with the law under which it was created; and finally, that a condition, without which the Returning Board could not get jurisdiction in cases where it assumed to reject votes of whole districts, was not complied with. There is every reason to believe that the authority exercised by that Returning Board could not get jurisdiction in the cases where it assume to reject the votes of whole districts, was not complied with. There is every reason to believe, that the authority exercised by that Returning Board is void, as repugnant to the Constitution of the United States, and also to the Constitution and laws of Louisiana.

"In this state of the law, that Returning Board, according to public statements of conceded facts, by manipulations of the returns, have changed a majority for one set of presidential electors of about 9,000 to a majority for another set of about 4,000, which would be equivalent to a change of over 80,000 votes in the State of New York.

"In Florida we have seen a Board of State Canvassers, solemnly adjudged by the highest court in the State to possess none be ministerial powers, assume the authority to reverse the choice of electors as shown on the face of the returns made by the officers who conducted the elections and received the votes; and to do this in open disobedience and contempt of the judicial tribunal having jurisdiction in such matters, and vested with the right of final judgment.

"In South Carolina we have seen the Board of State Canvassers fabricating a canvass in like disobedience and contempt of the Supreme Court having jurisdiction and the right of final judgment; we have seen federal soldiery take possession of the capitol of the State, and a corporal at the door determining who were the elect of the people, and who were to be permitted to represent them as legislators. Notwithstanding some of these acts have been disavowed by the federal executive, no mark of disapprobation has been put upon the authors of the outrages; the officer in command goes still unrebuked, and when the Returning Board were committed to prison for contempt, by the highest court of the State, a judge of the United States District Court is sent down to South Carolina, and, without jurisdiction in the case, grants a writ of *habeas corpus*, and discharges the offenders.[1]

These proceedings are the more extraordinary and alarming when we consider that such violations of law and of right have been resorted to, to overturn elections, all of the officers conducting which were of the same political party with the candidates in whose favor these acts have been committed; that the elections were held under the surveillance of troops of the United States without any constitutional warrant for their presence, and that the judicial decisions thus set at naught cannot be suspected of any partisan bias, for they were rendered both in Florida and South Carolina by judges, all of whom were of the same political party with the Retuning Board.

"These interferences of the military power have been committed in flagrant violation of the Constitution and laws. They were not provoked by domestic violence; they were not invited in the only way that would have made them constitutional, by the Legislature of the State; and they were continued after the election was over and during all the

---

NOTE: *habeas corpus* - One of a variety of writs that may be issued to bring a party before a court or judge, having as its function the release of the party from unlawful restraint.

subsequent proceeding of the Canvassing Board. Their tendency was to overawe the voters under the pretense of keeping the peace, though by measures in themselves unlawful, and to deliver dishonest officials from the natural sense of responsibility and the natural timidity in regard to the consequences of their acts, which are providential limitations to men's conception of the crimes upon which they venture.

"While these things were going on in the South a member of the cabinet at Washington was acting as chairman of a partisan national committee, and with the cooperation of some of his colleagues in the cabinet, counseling and systematically stimulating these desperate measures.

"The result which these proceedings seem designed to accomplish cannot be secured without one further step in the process of usurpation. The fabrication of electoral votes amounts to nothing unless they can be counted by the tribunal whose constitutional duty it is to verify and authenticate them. That inexorable necessity has given birth to a new device for counting the votes, not only unknown to the Constitution, but in conflict with the construction hitherto always accepted, and with the invariable practice and precedents. That device is for the President of the Senate to usurp the power if determining what votes shall be counted, and what shall not be counted, and to exercise that power in disregard of the orders of the two Houses. It would not be credible that so monstrous a claim as this could be seriously asserted if leading Senators had not publicly avowed it.

"Nothing could be more abhorrent to the spirit of our system of government that such a one-man power. The President of the Senate is elected by the Senators, and they in turn are elected by the State legislators. He is therefore, three removes from the people. If such a power were to have been vested in a single man, a depository would have been chosen not so far removed from popular accountability. But the people of this country will never vest such a power in any one man, however selected. They will never consent to a new construction of the Constitution and laws that bears such fruit. They will stand firmly in the ancient ways, and insist that the electoral votes in this emergency shall be counted as they have always been counted, by the two Houses of Congress, and by nobody else. They will look with just suspicion upon the purposes of any who would propose to depart from the precedents which have been hallowed by time, and the uniform practice of the Republic from its foundation.

REFERENCE U.S. SENATE WEBSITE:

NOTE: **1913:** The Constitution was amended (17th Amendment) to provide for <u>direct popular</u> <u>election of senators</u>, ending the system of election by individual state legislatures. Connecticut's approval gave the Seventeenth Amendment the required three-fourths majority, and it was added to the Constitution in 1913. The following year marked the first time all senatorial elections were held by popular vote.

The Seventeenth Amendment restates the first paragraph of Article I, section 3 of the Constitution and provides for the election of senators by replacing the phrase "chosen by the Legislature thereof" with "elected by the people thereof." In addition, it allows the governor or executive authority of each state, if authorized by that state's legislature, to appoint a senator in the event of a vacancy, until a general election occurs.

The 17th Amendment to the U.S. Constitution:

The Senate of the United States shall be composed of two Senators from each State, elected by the people thereof, for six years; and each Senator shall have one vote. The electors in each State shall have the qualifications requisite for electors of the most numerous branch of the State legislatures.

When vacancies happen in the representation of any State in the Senate, the executive authority of such State shall issue writs of election to fill such vacancies: Provided, That the legislature of any State may empower the executive thereof to make temporary appointments until the people fill the vacancies by election as the legislature may direct.

This amendment shall not be so construed as to affect the election or term of any Senator chosen before it becomes valid as part of the Constitution.

"The Constitution of the United States confers upon the President of the Senate no power whatever in respect to the counting of the electoral votes, except 'in presence of the Senate and House of Representatives,' to 'open' all the certificates which may be transmitted by the college to the seat of government, directed to him.

"The President of the Senate has ever claimed or exercised such a power at any of the twenty-one presidential elections that have occurred under our Constitution.

"The mode of procedure for the counting of electoral votes has been invariably regulated by the two Houses of Congress, by concurrent resolution or standing rules adopted before the count. Those resolutions or rules have prescribed every step in the whole process; every function of the tellers and of the President of the Senate, whenever any additional service, even of the most formal sort, has been required of him.

"In every instance the counting has been conducted in conformity with the procedure thus prescribed by the two Houses; by servants designated by the two Houses under instructions and in the presence of the two Houses, and with the entire concurrence and the implicit of obedience of every President of the Senate who has participated in these ceremonies.

"So often as any question arisen as to the authenticity or validity of an electoral vote, the two Houses have assumed and exercised the exclusive power to act upon and determine that question. They have, in contemplation of law, themselves made every count; they have from the first assumed exclusive jurisdiction to regulate and govern the whole transaction by temporary concurrent orders adopted for the occasion, by standing joint rules, and by the enactment of laws. Such has been the uniform and uninterrupted course of precedents, the invariable practice of the government, and the official exposition of the Constitution, which has been deliberately adopted, invariable acted upon, and universally accepted.

"*No filter repository of all such powers as are vested in or must of necessity be exercised by the government can be found than the two Houses of Congress. They are not only the general agents of the people under our representative system, but in case of the failure of a choice of President and Vice President by the electoral colleges, they are expressly charged by the Constitution with the duty of making the election.*

"*The people of the United States will never consent to have their Representatives in Congress stripped of these powers,* or tolerate this usurpation by a deputy of the Senate, or by any single person, and still less by an officer who is frequently interested as a candidate in the result of the count.

"In this sentiment and purpose the State of New York cordially concurs. Foremost among all our American commonwealths in population, in the variety and extent of her industries and interests, she has in every vicissitude of public affairs put forth all her strength, moral and physical, to maintain the existence and the just authorities of the Union, and she can never consent that the time-consecrated methods of the constitutional government shall be supplanted or overthrown by revolutionary expedients." [1]

---

1 *Additional note: The late James G. Blaine, serving as one of the visitors at the West Point Military Academy, a year or two after the inauguration of Hayes, expressed himself to me as greatly surprised*

Why Mr. Tilden's advice, so simple, so wise, so logical, so sure sooner or later to enlist the sympathies and respect of every law-abiding citizen in the land, was not followed, is a question which I do not feel called to enter upon here. Besides, it involves the discussion of motives which can never be subjected to any undebatable test; and if they could be, the profit of such a discussion now is more than questionable. I shall discharge my duty as his biographer in reporting what Mr. Tilden did to save his party, without dwelling more than is necessary for that purpose upon what others did to wreck it.

The electoral commission scheme was not disclosed to Mr. Tilden until it was too late for any opposition on his part to be effective in prosecuting his method, which was only constitutional method of settling the questions in dispute. How it was first brought to his attention was thus set down in a carefully considered communication addressed by Mr. Manton Marble of the "New York Sun," on the 5th of August 1878. The tenor of this communication, as well as the circumstances under which it appeared, leave little doubt that before it was given to the public it passed under Mr. Tilden's eyes.

"On the evening of Saturday, January 13, the undersigned, calling upon Mr. Tilden, found him in receipt of the McCrary House bill with proposed amendments, and a letter from Mr. Hewitt advertising the Governor that his counsel thereon would be asked the next day. Mr. Tilden invited the undersigned to call on the morrow, when Mr. Hewitt should be there, to consider this bill – the supposed axis on which the deliberations of the House conference committee were revolving.

"The undersigned thus came to be present January 14, the day and date when Mr. Tilden received from Mr. Hewitt's lips his first information that other measures had been abandoned.; that the Senate conference committee had just disclosed to the House conference committee and electoral commission bill it had privately preparing; that the House committee were pressed to accept and adopt the same, and that the subject he wished to confer upon was that.

"Mr. Hewitt explained as the Senate committee's reason for secrecy, that without it they could not carry the bill. It had been adopted by

---

when the Democrats in Congress assented to the plan of the electoral commission. He added that if the Democrats had been firm the Republicans had no alternative but to yield, and such was the result which he had anticipated.

arrangement between the three Democratic and the four Republican members, and was so strictly observed that when Senator Kernan made inquiry of one of the former, he was told that nothing could be disclosed to him without violating an honorable understanding. So well was the secret kept, that Senator Barnum, now chairman of the national committee, passing through New York on Friday, the 12th, has expressed his conviction that a majority of the Senate, as Mr. Tilden's plan anticipated, would concur in denying the right of Ferry to make the count.

"Before he read the new bill, Mr. Tilden was told by Mr. Hewitt that the Democratic members of the Senate committee were already absolutely committed to it, and would concur with their Republican associates in reporting it to the Senate, whether the House committee should concur or not, and whether Mr. Tilden approved of it or not.

"Is it not rather late, then," said Mr. Tilden, "to consult with me?"

"They do not consult you?" replied Mr. Hewitt. "They are public men, and have their own duties and responsibilities. I consult you."

In other words, as Mr. Tilden expressed himself to me at the time, the parents of this measure, "have sent Mr. Hewitt, not to consult with me about it, but to get my approval of it." This Mr. Tilden declined to give, and urged delay. When its friends pretended that time pressed, he told them, "There is time enough. It is a month before the count. It had best be used, all of it, in making the people and their agents fully acquainted with their rights and duties."

To the statement that the Senate committee would not delay for this to present their bill, with the unanimous approval of its three Democratic members, to the Republican Senate, Mr. Tilden replied: "It is a panic of pacificators. They will act in haste and repent at leisure."

To representations of the danger of a collision of force with the executive, Mr. Tilden replied," Nevertheless, this action is too precipitate. The fears of collision are exaggerated. And why surrender now? You can always surrender. That is all you have to do after being beaten. Why surrender before the battle for fear of having to surrender after the battle is over?"[1]

---

1 This recalls the advice which Dr. Franklin gave to his son when Colonial Governor of New Jersey:

"Perhaps they may expect that your resentment of their treatment of me may induce you to resign and save them the shame of depriving you, when they ought to promote you. But this I would not advise you to do,. Let them take your place if they want it, - though in truth it is scarce

Unfortunately, the course of procedure which Mr. Tilden had traced out and urged upon the party was no longer possible. Their line of battle had been broken. The two controlling Democratic Senators on the committee, by their negotiations had practically surrendered the Democratic fortress. The plain, square issue made by Mr. Tilden could not be revived after a willingness to negotiate and make concessions had once been manifested.

Even had it been still possible to defeat the proposed scheme of arbitration, that would not have restored the fortress; it would not have made it any longer practicable to resume Mr. Tilden's plan of battle. To that, as Mr. Marble justly remarks,

"The conditions of success were an indomitable and untied Democracy and an unbroken favoring public opinion. But the mere proposal of the electoral arbitrament, back by great Democratic leaders, cause three illusions to prevail: the illusion that such an arbitrament was the only alternative to civil war; the illusion that such a tribunal must establish the truth in its decision and the people in their rights; the illusion of the business classes, oppressed by long-suffering under ruinous tariffs and fluctuating currencies, that is was the harbinger of new prosperity. So that the rand and file would have been resuming a contest abandoned by their familiar leasers as hopeless, and attempting recurrence to the earlier issue amidst a public opinion now reversed and hostile."

Instead, therefore, of wasting his energies in useless criticism of what had been done, Mr. Tilden directed his attention to such modifications in the structure of this projected court of arbitration as he thought essential.

If an arbitration is to be adopted, he insisted that the members of the tribunal ought to be fixed in the bill itself, not left to chance or intrigue.

---

worth your keeping, - since it has not afforded you sufficient to prevent your running every year behindhand with me. One may make something of an injury, nothing of a resignation."- Bigelow's "Life of Franklin," under date of Feb. 29, 1874.

That the duty of the arbitrators to investigate and decide the case on its merits should be made mandatory, not left to their decision.

"With both these vital points left at loose ends," he said. "You cannot succeed. You cannot afford to concede, and you can exact, *first*, the selection of good men to compose the tribunal, which is the controlling point; and, *second*, define the nature of the function to be performed by the tribunal, which is next in importance.

"Fix these two points, - good men, explicit powers, - and you might possible get through. Leave them doubtful, and it is happy-go-luck, - the shake of the dice-box."

When pressed by suggestions of the improbability of the House insisting upon its independent constitutional rights without the support of the Democratic Senators who were committed to a compromise, he said,

"If you go into a conference with your adversary, and can't break off, because you feel you must agree to something, you cannot negotiate at all. Unless you are able to break off, you are not fit to negotiate. You will be beaten on every detail."

On the 15th of January Mr. Hewitt telegraphed from Washington to his brother-in-law, Edward Cooper, in New York:

"The Senate committee will probably reject five and report six judge plan immediately. Our Senators feel committed to concur. House committee will not concur, and for present will probably not report."

To this suggestion Mr. Tilden said, "I may lost the presidency, but I will not raffle for it.: To Mr. Hewitt he telegraphed through Mr. Cooper:

"Procrastinate to give few days for information and consultation. The six-judge proposition inadmissible."

The next day Mr. Hewitt telegraphed again to Mr. Cooper:

"Washington, Jan. 16, 1877 – After protracted negotiations Senate (committee) receded from six-judge (scheme), declined five-judge, and offered four senior associates justices, who are to choose the fifth judge, excluding chief justice. Our Senate friends earnestly favor acceptance, because they do not believe it possible to pass over. The Democrats on House committee believe this is the last chance of agreement. We cannot postpone beyond 11 tomorrow, and if we decline, Senate committee will report their original plan, to which our friends are committed. Telegraph your advice."

Mr. Tilden sent the following answer:

"New York, January 16. – Be firm and be cool. Four judge plan will not do. Perhaps worse than six. Complaints likely to arise of haste and want of consultation with members, and embarrassment in exercise of their judgment after plan is disclosed, by premature committal of their representatives. There should be more opportunity for deliberation and consultation. Secrecy dangerous. Probably mistake in itself, and if it results in disaster would involve great blame and infinite mischief."

The night of the day that the foregoing telegram was sent, the foregoing telegrams were canvassed by Mr. Tilden in the presence of several of his friends, at the conclusion of which he dictated the following telegram:

"No need of hot haste, but much danger in it. Some days' interval should be taken. The risk of publicity (is) harmless.

"No information here, nor any opportunity to get information which could justify abstinence from condemning such an abandonment of the Constitution and practice of the government, and of the rights of the two Houses and of the people.

"Nothing but great and certain public danger, not to be escaped in any other way, could excuse such a measure. We are over pressed by exaggerated fears, and forget that the other side will have greater troubles than we, unless relieved by some agreement.

"They have no way out but by usurpation; (they) are bullying us with what they dare not do, or will break down in attempting.

"So long as we stand on the Constitution and settle practice, we know where we are. Consequence of new expedient not enough considered.

"Only way of getting accessions in the Senate is by House standing firm. And judicious friends believe in that case we will go safely through. Opportunity to consult such friends should be given, before even tacit acquiescence (by House committee), if that is contemplated, Though details may be properly discussed, final committal by House committee should be firmly withheld."

Before this telegram had reached, or at least been seen by, Mr. Hewitt, the surrender had been consummated.

In no single particular from the beginning to the consummation of the transaction had the advice of Mr. Tilden been acted upon. He advised the House of Representatives, with a majority in sympathy with the majority of the people, to stand upon it constitutional rights, and leave to the Senate, if it dared, the responsibility of violating those rights.

Instead of exercising the rights and discharging the duties imposed upon it in the most unequivocal terms, it accepted a scheme for counting votes which originated with a body having no corresponding contingent authority, and in political sympathy with the majority of a commission recruited from and controlled by a bench every member of which had been appointed by Republican Presidents.

Mr. Tilden had urged publicity and discussion, insisting that secrecy in respect to any plan involving the rights and interests of the whole people was unwise, dangerous, and essentially undemocratic. The scheme adopted was conceived and begotten in a corner, and never exposed to the light of day until it had wrought irremediable mischief; still less was it submitted to such a discussion as befitted a measure involving the chief magistracy of fifty millions of people.

Mr. Tilden advised against the betrayal of any symptoms of a possibility of concession. "You can surrender at any time," he said. "It will be time enough to surrender when you are beaten." They began their deliberations by concession, and surrendered without an engagement, fully a month before the time for discussion and for the arrival of reinforcements of public opinion for their constituencies could have expired. They made indecent hast to precipitate themselves at the feet of their adversaries, as though they supposed their humiliation would be imputed to them for righteousness.

Mr. Tilden advised them to trust the people, to stand by them and the Constitution; and no one American statesman had ever a better right, from experience, to speak dogmatically on the subject.

Instead of trusting the people, they conducted all their negotiations in secret, and suppressed discussion until everything was surrendered worth saving, or that discussion might have saved.

When it was decided to submit the issue to arbitration, Mr. Tilden insisted that the law creating the arbitrators should require them to decide the issue on its merits, and not leave to them the determination of what were to be their duties. Firmness upon this point, to which the Republicans of the Senate, sooner or later, must have yielded, would most certainly have resulted in confirming the election of the candidate of the people's choice.

This wise advice was rejected, and rejected, too, for clowns' swords and Quaker guns. As the Honorable Henry Watterson most fitly said:

"Mr. Tilden was the one man who took in the whole case and provided a plan to compass it. That plan was for the House of Representatives to exercise its constitutional rights to share in the count of the vote, no State to be counted except by the concurrence of both Houses, precisely as had been done in all preceding elections, each State lacking the concurrence of the two Houses to be thrown out; in the event of a failure of either candidate by this process of throwing out to secure a majority of all the votes, the House to elect the President and the Senate to elect the Vice President. That was Mr. Tilden's plan, pure and simple. It sprang directly from the Constitution, the law and the practice. To overreach it, the conspirators much proceed openly to treason and usurpation. In that event, the House still had its right to elect, and, 'if it elects me,' said Mr. Tilden at the time, 'I will go to Washington and take the oath if I am shot for it the next day.'

"Mr. Tilden's plan embraced no shilly-shallying or foolishness. It meant business. He had to move either by force or by law. Force was out of the question. The country was not prepared for war, and the party would not follow him into war. All that a show of fight on his part could do would be to inflame a few excited spirits and play into the hands of the conspirators, who had the tools, and only wanted the pretext to come down upon the unorganized and helpless Democrats. Wisely he declined either to raffle or bluff for the presidency. He proposed to proceed by law, - the law of every preceding electoral count, - and to force the Republicans, if bent upon their work of usurpation, to resort to violence and treason. He believed they would break down before they got through it. Believing in the people, his idea was that the people needed only to be educated in their rights to maintain them. He presented a line of action. He prepared a magazine of instruction. These were set aside, and, in lieu of them, a bridge was constructed, over which the conspirators could, and did, walk in safety."

On the 31st January the commission was elected, - three Republicans and two Democrats being taken, by agreement, from the Senate, and three Democrats and two Republicans from the House.

- Republicans from the Senate:

George F. Edmunds, of Vermont – Frederick T. Frelinghuysen, of New Jersey and Oliver P. Morton, of Indiana.
- Democrats from the Senate:

Allen G. Thurman, of Ohio, and Thomas F. Bayard of Delaware.
- Democrats from the House:

Josiah G. Abbott, of Massachusetts, Henry B. Payne, of Ohio and Eppa Hunton, of Virginia
- Republicans from the House:

James A. Garfield, of Ohio and George F. Hoar, of Massachusetts

The justices of the Supreme Court designated in the bill were:
- Democrats:

Nathan Clifford, of Maine and Stephen J. Field, of California
- Republicans:

Samuel F. Miller, of Iowa and William Strong of Pennsylvania

The fifth justice elected by these was Joseph P. Bradley, of New Jersey.

In all seven Democrats, and eight Republicans.

It was determined by the Republicans in caucus to leave Senator Conkling off the Electoral Commission, though he had been more influential probably than any other Senator in securing the passage of the bill creating it.[1]

Conkling was omitted because he was known to be in accord with the President in thinking that the vote of Louisiana rightfully belonged

---

1 Note: Mr. Childs says, "Grant was the originator of the plan. He sent for Mr. Conkling, and said with deep earnestness: "This matter is a serious one, and the people feel it deeply. I think this Electoral Commission ought to be appointed." Conkling answered: Mr. President, Senator Morton is opposed to it and to your efforts. But if you wish the commission carried, I can do it." He said, "I wish it done."

Tilden's popular majority over Hayes in the State of New York was 32,818, and the largest aggregate vote ever cast up to that time in that State. It exceeded Grant's vote in 1872 by 81,298, and Greeley's of the same year by 134,764.

to Mr. Tilden. He was the only Republican Senator on the committee who was omitted from the commission. Conkling had agreed to address the Electoral Commission in opposition to its counting the electoral vote of Louisiana for Hayes. Various explanations of his failure to do so are in circulation. I have not been able to determine which of them all had the demerit of securing his silence.

On the 6th of December the electors of the State of New York assembled at the capitol at Albany, organized by the election of Horatio Seymour, president of the college, and proceeded to cast the electoral vote of the State of New York for Tilden and Hendricks for Vice President. On taking the chair Mr. Seymour became the interpreter of the profound concern which had been awakened among the people of all parties in Mr. Tilden's native State by the rumors which were coming from the South. Time has given Mr. Seymour's remarks a pertinence and an importance which was hardly accorded to them at the time of their utterance. After referring to the fact that the year in which were about to participate in the election of a new President of the United States was the hundredth anniversary of our existence as an independent people, he continued:

"At this moment of general congratulation the people were startled by the assertion that there had been discovered in remote Southern States the exact number of electoral votes which would be given to and would elect the presidential candidate who was not the choice of the majority of the American people. This surprise was greater because it was one of the charges made by the Republicans in the canvass to excite the minds of the men in the North, that the 'solid South' would support the Democratic ticket. It was also urged that every Southern State had a deep interest in doing this, because they meant to make demands upon the national treasury. While this charge was unjust, no reason can be given why South Carolina, Florida, and Louisiana should not act in accord with the overwhelming majorities of the adjoining States. The public excitement reached the highest point when it was learned that the men who proposed to give these electoral votes to the candidate of the minority had been for years past charged with grave crimes, and that their personal security against legal punishment depended upon their success if falsifying the returns of their States. To them an honest count meant just punishment. I cannot be charged with partisan prejudice for any terms of reproach I may use in regard to the officials of Louisiana. I have no words strong enough to describe their unworthiness as set forth in official reports made by their political friends. I cannot, if I would, paint the aversion shown in the halls of the capitol by honest Republicans, who shunned them as leprous men whose touch and presence was polluting. Yet a few such men, acting solely in reference to their personal interests, and who believe that the blackness of their crimes in strengthens their claims upon the gratitude of their party, have thus put in peril the interests, the honor, and the safety of the American people. We have not the poor satisfaction of feeling that the dangers that threaten us are even invested with the ordinary dignity of danger. The pride of our citizens is humiliated, and their feelings of security under our laws and Constitution are lessened, when they see that the solemn verdict of eight million voters may be reversed by less than eight infamous men – men who have been branded by the leading orators, statesmen, and journals of their own political party as vile and corrupt, in terms more vigorous that I can repeat. If, under our Constitution, the majority of the electoral votes of the States had been fairly given to the Republican candidates, although the popular majority is against them, all would have acquiesced in their election. Such results are to be regretted, as they do not give administrations the moral power they should have for their own dignity and the good of the country. To elect men to govern the Union against the will of the people by unfair methods is revolution. Such plots involve anarchy, distress, and dishonor. Those who engage in them, when they have taken the first steps, must go on at all hazards. They have staked their political fortunes – it may be their lives and liberties-upon success. Fear goads them on to darker acts of treason. The first false steps forced a reluctant South into rebellion. In the same way they now impel desperate politicians who upheld usurpation in Louisiana in the past, to stand by them now, regardless of the honor and safety of the American union. Will a free people trust such men with the reins of power? Will they consent to be dragged into danger and dishonor by men who are goaded on by fears which always haunt the guilty?

"The glory of this centennial year this fades away and darkens into this national shame and reproach. Aroused patriotism can crush resistance to law, but corruption kills honor, virtue, and patriotism, says the foundations of society, and brings down the structure of states and nations in ruin and dishonor.

"While we implore all classes of citizens to enter upon the duty of deciding what shall be done to avert threatened evils, we respectfully appeal to the great Republican party to see if the heaviest responsibility for a just decision does not rest upon them. And we make this appeal with confidence that a great organization, which had its full share of virtue and patriotism, will not, when it calmly reviews the events of the day, fail to do justice to us, to themselves, and to the country. We do not complain that under the excitement of the canvass, or that before the heat of the election should have passed away, you may for a moment grasp eagerly at a victory without seeing that such a victory may prove a curse to you as well as to others. But we beg you will reflect, now that you have had exerted in your behalf, not only the whole power of the national administration with its hosts of officials, but that the execution of all the laws relating to the election of the officers of the general government was entirely in the hands of your partisans. If we look at the provisions of these laws, we find that they contain features of a startling character, as they were framed before the passions excited by civil war had been allayed, and with reference to States still looked upon as hostile to our Union. The judicial officers of every grade who interpret these laws, almost without exception, belong to your party. The marshals who execute them are heated politicians, the very tenure of whose offices depends upon the success of your ticket. They can summon a vast array of deputies, and all of these may make arrests, in some cases without process, and by express enactment are places above the reach of the laws and the judiciary of the States. At the late election Republican officials, at the expense of the general government, could examine every registry in the principal towns and cities. They could and did arrest men for accidental clerical errors of others in giving the name or the number of a house. In only one instance under these laws was there recognition of the party in power. We do not complain of the enforcement of these laws. On the contrary, we point with satisfaction to the fact that they furnished the proof made by their partisan opponents, that the Democratic vote was an honest one. If fraud is suspected, it must be the work of others, not of the Democratic party. Even if these election laws had been in all cases fairly enforced, they still made a vast array of partisan forces and power, supported by the common treasury, but exerted against the party that carried with it a majority of the American people. We hear much of coercion, intimidation, and undue influences, but nothing approaching this in power can exist in any part of our country. There is no organization which could for a moment contend with it, backed up as it has been by the American army.

"We also appeal to the Republicans to see if it is not true that during the late election the officials at Washington overlooked the fact that they were the government of a country, and acted throughout merely as the administration of a party. Has one step been taken, or the army moved, save at the instance of their political friends? Has there been a recognition of or a consultation with a single citizen who was not allied to them in interest and feeling?

"There is a darker phase of the last election. The administration sent our cabinet officer to take charge of the canvass on behalf of the Republican Party. His very position at the head of its managing committee made a forced loan upon neatly one hundred thousand official dependents. It proclaimed to then in louder tones than words, "You must work. You must vote You must pay to aid the election of a candidate who declares himself in favor of civil-service reform." It told them that if, believing and acting upon his assurance, they followed their own convictions and votes for his opponents; they would be punished by the loss of their positions. They were forced, in thousands of cases, to submit to extortion with smiling faces, but with heavy hearts. If a like intimidation had been used in a Southern State, it would have been seized upon by the administration as a reason for declaring martial law, for arresting and imprisoning every suspected citizen. …

"I have too much respect for the characters of Messrs. Hayes and Wheeler to think that they wish to be put at the head of this Union against the declared wishes of a majority of the American people. I do not doubt that if this is to be done by men in Louisiana, of whom they think as ill as we do, that they would feel that the highest offices of state would be for them not positions of honor and dignity, but political pillories, in which they would stand to be pointed at, now and hereafter, as the representatives of a foul fraud. One thing all men see: *The Republican party cannot decide its own case in its own favor against the majority of the American people, upon the certificate of branded men in Louisiana, without making the body of our citizens and the world at large*

feel that it is a corrupt and partisan decision. **Such judgment will not
only destroy our honor and credit for the day, but will be a precedent for wrongdoing in the future. We cannot have Mexican politics
without Mexican finances and Mexican disorders. The business men
of all civilized countries have been taught by recent bankruptcies
and disorders in governments, made unstable by agitations, to be
watchful and distrustful when they see the slightest deviation from
political honor, without which there can be no financial honor.** On
the other hand, let the party now in power yield to the popular will,
demand honest returns in accordance with the Constitution, bow to
the majesty of the law, and then every citizen will feel a renewed confidence in our institutions and the whole world will hold us in higher
respect and honor."

The commission at Washington perfected it organization on the first
day of February, and the same day received the contested certificates of
the State of Florida.

I shall be brief in dealing with the deliberations of the Electoral
Commission, for the simple reason that the Republican members of
that tribunal controlled it; and upon every question, I believe without
a single exception, bearing upon the success of their candidate, voted
with their party. Wherever his success depended upon going behind the
returns, they went behind the returns; and when his success depended
upon treating the returns as sacred and conclusive, they were treated as
sacred and conclusive; and when his success depended upon counting
the vote of a federal office-holder, though disqualified by the Constitution from serving as an elector, his vote was counted. They adopted no
rule of law or constitutional construction which was not compelled to
yield promptly to party exigencies.

The Florida case involved two vital questions:

First, The legality of the proceedings of the Returning Board in
returning as duly chosen, and the Governor of Florida certifying, the
appointment of Republican electors from that State; and,

Second, Was Frederick C. Humphreys, one of the electors so returned
and certified, being at the time holder of an office under the federal
government, eligible under the Constitution, which provides that no
"person holding an office of trust or profit under the United States shall
be appointed an elector"?

The commission disposed of the first question by deciding by a strict party vote, eight to seven, "that it is not competent under the Constitution and the law as they existed at the passage of said act to go into evidence *aliunde* (*Defined:* From another source; from elsewhere; as, a case proved aliunde; evidence aliunde.) the papers opened by the President of the Senate in the presence of the two Houses, to prove that other persons than those regularly certified to by the Governor of the State of Florida, in according to the determination and declaration of their appointment by the Board of State Canvassers of said State prior to the time required for the performance of their duties, had been appointed electors, or by counter-proof to show that they had not; and that all proceedings of the courts or acts of the Legislature or of the executive of Florida, subsequent to the casting of the votes of the electors on the prescribed day, are inadmissible for any such purpose.

Here the rule is formally laid down that the commission has no legal nor constitutional competence to go behind the electoral certificates delivered to and opened by the President of the Senate.

This rule held good only so long as it served the purpose of the majority.

"As to the objection made to the eligibility of Mr. Humphreys, the commission is of the opinion that, without reference to the question of the effect of the vote of an ineligible elector, *the evidence does not show that he held the office of shipping commissioner on the day when the electors were appointed.*"

Here is the distinct admission that they did take evidence *aliunde* (From another source; from elsewhere) the certificates, to prove that Mr. Humphreys was not ineligible.

The reader is requested to note that this decision in Humphrey's case is made "without reference to the question of the effect of the vote of an ineligible elector." They declined to pronounce against the validity of such a vote, for they already had reasons for apprehending that other cases would come before them in which the electors would appear ineligible on the face of the certificates; and as the loss of a single electoral vote would have been fatal to their candidate, they did not mean to commit themselves against counting the vote of an ineligible elector if his vote should prove to be necessary. In other words, they had undertaken to count Mr. Tilden out and their candidate in, and they did not propose to deprive themselves of the liberty of so construing the Constitution as to accomplish their purpose.

When the Louisiana case was reached, it appeared that two of the electors certified by the Returning Board were disqualified by the Constitution of the United States, and four others by the Constitution of Louisiana, which provides that, "no person shall at any time hold more than one office." A.B. Levissee when elected was a United States commissioner, and O.H. Brewster was surveyor of the United States Land Office. They resigned their federal offices temporarily, were substituted for themselves by their colleagues, and voted for Hayes and Wheeler. Both these men were promptly reappointed to their respective federal offices and resumed their duties. When their case was reached by the commission, it was manifest that the majority could not elect their candidate under the rule laid down in the Florida case. Accordingly they held "that it is not competent to prove that any of said persons so appointed electors as aforesaid held an office of trust or profit under the United States at the time when they were appointed, or that they were ineligible under the laws of the State, or any matter offered to be proved *aliunde* the said certificates and papers."[1]

The commission also decided "that the returning officers of elections who canvassed the votes at the election for electors in Louisiana were a legally constituted body, by virtue of a constitutional law, and that a vacancy in said body did not vitiate its proceedings." The constitution of Louisiana, article forty-eight, prescribes who the returning officers of elections shall be; to wit, the officers of elections at the different polling-places throughout the State. Senator Edmunds, on the 16th of March, 1875, declared in the Senate in unequivocal language that the election law creating the Returning Board was in conflict with the constitution of the State. And yet Mr. Commissioner Edmunds,

---

1   Note: During the count of the electoral votes in 1837 the question of the eligibility of the electors was considered by a Senate committee composed of Henry Clay, Silas Wright, and Felix Grundy, who reported that, "The committee are of opinion that the second section of the second article of the Constitution, which declares that 'no Senator or Representative, or person holding an office of trust or profit under the United States, shall be appointed an elector,' ought to be carried in its whole spirit into rigid execution... This provision of the Constitution, it is believed, excludes and disqualifies deputy postmasters from the appointment of electors; and disqualification relates to the time of appointment and that a resignation of the office of deputy postmaster after his appointment as elector would not entitle him to vote as elector, under the Constitution."

on Feb. 16, 1877, voted that the election law of Louisiana creating the Returning Board was not in conflict with the constitution of the State. Representative George F. Hoar made a report to the House of Representatives in 1875; in which he used the following language in regard to the Louisiana Returning Board's conduct in the election of 1874; "We are clearly of the opinion that the Returning Board had no right to do anything except to canvass and compile the returns which were lawfully made to them by the local officers, except in cases where they were accompanied by the certificates of the supervisor or commissioner provided in the third section." How much more grossly had the Returning Board violated the law in 1876 than in 1874; and yet Mr. Commissioner Hoar voted, Feb, 16, 1877, that the presidential electors returned as elected by that Returning Board were legally elected.

When the Oregon contested case came up before the commission, the electoral tribunal did not permit itself to be in the least embarrassed by its previous rulings. By the laws of Oregon its returning officers were the Governor and the Secretary of State. One of the Republican electors was a postmaster, and consequently disqualified by the Constitution for serving as an elector. The Secretary of State, therefore, gave the certificate to his opponent E. A. Cronin, a Democratic elector. Cronin voted for Tilden and Hendricks. One copy of a certificate of his vote as a Tilden elector in due form was forwarded by mail to the President of the Senate, a second was filed with the United States District Judge, and the third was borne by Cronin to himself to Washington and delivered to the President of the Senate. His vote, therefore, for Tilden and Hendricks was legally and regularly before the two Houses of Congress. Cronin had unnecessarily gone through the form of organizing an electoral college which neither the laws nor the Constitution of the United States require, and for that purpose had appointed two persons to act with him. As one vote for Tilden in Oregon would be fatal to Hayes as one in Louisiana and Florida would have been, this vote had to be rescued as a brand from the burning. But how? Here was a Tilden elector regularly certified by the authorized returning officers. To reject him was to elect in his place a man certified to them to have been an officer of the federal government. Was it to be prepared for this emergency that they forbore in the Florida case to decide whether the holding of a federal office disqualified Humphreys as an elector? It was a very aggravating case for the Republican commissioners to deal with, but they rose to the level of the occasion; "the hope was not drunk wherein they had dressed themselves;" they did not weakly let, "I dare not" wait upon "I would," but boldly decided "that the Secretary of State did canvass the returns in the case of before us, and thereby ascertained that J.C. Cartwright, W.H. Odell, and J.W. Watts had a majority of the *votes given for electors*, and had the highest number of votes for that office, and by the express language of the stature are deemed elected." They further held, "that the refusal or failure of the Governor of Oregon to sign the certificate of the election of the persons so elected does not have the effect of defeating their appointment as such electors."

The commissioners made this decision in favor of Watts, the Republican, solely upon the ground that he had "the highest number of votes." But if the highest number of votes was sufficient for an elector in Oregon, why was it not sufficient in Florida where the electoral ticket had an incontestable majority of ninety-one, and in Louisiana where it had an incontestable majority of over 7,000. They altogether suppress the supreme fact that the Secretary of State had certified to the Governor that another person had been elected and that Watts had not been; and the further fact that the Secretary of State and Governor, and no one else, by law constituted the returning officers of Oregon. This suppression was necessary because in Louisiana they had held that an elector is not appointed according to the terms of the Constitution until he has received the certificate of such appointment from the returning officers. Therefore the decision which elected Watts in Oregon should have admitted all the Tilden and Hendricks electors in Louisiana and Florida, and the decisions in Louisiana and Florida should have elected a Tilden elector in Oregon, had the commission attached any importance to the virtue of consistency in their rulings, or felt that their appointment on that commission invested them with any other function or imposed upon them any other duty than to make Hayes President without violating any more nor any less of the ten commandments and the laws of their country than was necessary. Like Cassandra's lover, they adapted the ethics of the Pagan instead of the Christian code for their purpose:

"Mutemus clypeus, Danaumque insignia nobis Aptemus: dolus an Vritus, quis in hoste requirat?"

There were at least nine Republican electors who where disqualified by virtue of their holding offices under the federal government at the time of their election. Only in the cases of Florida, Louisiana, and Oregon, however, could the question of their eligibility be raised before the commission, and in no two of these cases were the decisions the same. And yet the members of this commission were severally sworn as the Holy Evangelists, "to impartially examine and consider all questions submitted,"... "and true judgment give thereon, agreeably to the Constitution and the laws."

It seem not appropriate to insert here an entry which I made in my diary of the 9th of February, 1877.

"On Thursday (the 8th) Tilden told me a man had called to say that commission was for sale. When I expressed an incredulous sort of astonishment, he said that one of the justices (Republican) was ready to give his vote for the Tilden electors for $200,000. I asked which one. He said he thought he would not tell me that at present. I told him it was improbable, for the judges were all well paid and had life terms of their office. He said the justice in question is reported to be embarrassed from old engagements and obligations...Tilden also told me that the Florida Returning Board was offered to him, and for the same money. 'That,' he said, 'seems to be the standard figure,'"

In a notable debate in the House of Representatives in February, 1879, the Hon. A. S. Hewitt, replying to a scurrilous allusion to Mr. Tilden which Mr. Garfield, who had been a member of the Electoral Commission, had been betrayed into making, confirmed the report that the presidency had been in the market. Time has only added significance and gravity to his many expostulation.

"I think, however, that I can account for this extraordinary proceeding. During the progress of this debate, a gallant soldier, an able lawyer who has been an attorney-general of my State, and who is a staunch Republican, General Francis C. Barlow, of New York, had given evidence on the lower floor of the capitol that the votes of the State of Florida had been unjustly counted for Mr. Hayes; the conclusion being that if it had been counted for Mr. Tilden, he to-day would have been occupying the White House instead of it present de facto and not de jure tenant. is an expression that means "based on ", as contrasted with, This evidence must have touched the gentleman from Ohio to the quick; it must have revived the memories of eight to seven; it must have reminded him how, when the electoral bill was pending in this House, for one whole evening he devoted himself to proving that the law creating the commission was unconstitutional, but that if it should be passed it would be the duty of the commission to take evidence of fraud and go behind the returns. And yet when he was made a judge, acting under a law which he had declared to be unconstitutional, and which as he had affirmed, required evidence to be taken; he consented to violate the Constitution and to deny the admission of the evidence which was necessary to arrive at the truth. When the great wrong thus done by the vote of the gentleman from Ohio-for it was his casting vote in every case that excluded the evidence – was thus made manifest by the testimony of General Barlow, did that feeling of remorse which is the attribute of great minds force him to attempt to drown the reproaches of conscience by alleging that the man who to-day is of right President of the United States was the 'author and finisher' of frauds and therefore should be excluded from the high office to which he had been elected by the people?

> 'High minds of native pride and force
> Must deeply feel thy pangs, remorse!
> Fear for their scourge mean villains have;
> Thou art the torturer of the brave.'

"Gentlemen on the other side realize fully that a great wrong cannot be committed in this country without being finally redressed by the voice of the people, for they remember what took place in General Jackson's case in 1828, and they know that the voice of the people is the voice of God, who had declared, 'Vengeance is mine, I will repay, saith the Lord.' They see no refuge from the coming judgment but in destroying the character of the man whom they have robbed. For months an uninterrupted stream of abuse, misrepresentation, and calumny has been poured out upon his devoted head, but the testimony of the last few days has justified the assertion which I have never failed to make when Mr. Tilden's character and integrity have been attacked, that not one particle of dishonest action can be traced to him, but, on the contrary, it is now manifest to all men that he scorned to purchase *the presidency which found a ready market elsewhere."*

Mr. Hewitt has more recently stated at a public meeting in New York that the electoral vote of one of the contested States had been offered to him for a price.

There is one more chapter in the history of this extraordinary tribunal, without which it would be incomplete.

...."Longa est injura, longae ambiges."

When Anderson was selected to bring the certificates of the Louisiana Returning Board to Washington, he handed the package to Ferry, the President of the Senate, of the 24th of December. Instead of accepting it as he should have done, for better or worse, Ferry called Anderson's attention to the fact that the endorsement on the outside, setting forth the contents of each envelope, had not been signed by the electors as the law required, and recommended Anderson to examine the law and see whether the certificate had been made in accordance with it.

It was the duty of the President of the Senate to receive the package, to open it only in the presence of both Houses of Congress, and leave them to decided what to do with it. He had previously received the duplicate of the package handed to him by Anderson; and he knew that the electors were *functus officii* and no more competent to repair any defect of omission or commission in their returns, weeks after their legal existence had ceased, then to recall the cloud which had shaded them the preceding day. Contrary to the Constitution, which required that the election return should be opened by the President of the Senate in the presence of both Houses of Congress, Anderson's package was opened in Washington by parties whose names have not officially transpired, when, to the consternation of the Hayes engineers, it was discovered that the lack of electors' signatures on the envelope was by no means the only, nor the most serious, defect of the return; that instead of voting separate ballots for President and Vice-President, as required by the Constitution, they had voted for both on one ballot, and had failed to make their return of the votes cast for each candidate on distinct lists with separate certificates, also express requirements of the Constitution.

There was but one course left for them to save their candidate. The certificates made out and signed by the electors in triplicate on the 6th of December must be suppressed, and the false ones purporting to comply with the provisions of the Constitution, must be substituted for them. Anderson left Washington the night of the day he reached there, arrived in New Orleans on the morning of December 28th, and repaired at once to the quarters of Governor Kellogg. The Governor sent for his private secretary, Clark, who at once set about the preparation of new certificates. There was no time to waste. The forged certificates must be on their way to Washington at 5:20 p.m. of the next day, - one set by the hand of a messenger, and another set by the mail; - in order to reach Washington within the time fixed by law for their reception, the 3rd of January, 1877.

Kellogg and Clark, however, with the aid of Anderson, proved equal to the occasion. They had certificates printed to correspond – paper and impression – with the certificates of December 6th. The new certificates were spread out on a large table in the third floor of the State House, where they were to be signed. Such of the electors as could be found were taken up to this room, one at a time, in the order in which they had signed the original certificates. Two, Levisee and Joffroin, were away fully three days' journey from New Orleans. Their autograph signatures, therefore, could not be had. But when the electors who had originally signed below the signatures of these absentees, went up to affix their names to the new certificates, they found the names of the absentee electors in their place. Who forged these names is a question now of secondary importance. The accomplices in the fraud did not agree in their testimony as to the actual perpetrator of the forgery, though none pretended that the names had not been forged. It would have been idle to have done so, as the impossibility of either of the two electors being in New Orleans either on the 28th or 29th of December was a matter of common notoriety.

These forges certificates were not sent to Washington this time by Anderson, who had taken the former certificates, but by a clerk in the State auditor's office, named Hill, who on his arrival went first to Zachariah Chandler, the secretary of the treasury, and chairman of the Republican national committee, to whom he bore a letter also from

Governor Kellogg. Chandler read Kellogg's letter, and then directed Hill to go to the capitol and deliver the forged electoral certificates to Mr. Ferry, the President of the Senate. Senator Sherman was invited by Mr. Ferry to come in and witness the delivery and receipt if the package. That ceremony over, Sherman took Hill into the room of the finance committee, and wrote a letter to Kellogg, which he delivered sealed to the messenger to be delivered to Kellogg in person. .

Thus far it seemed as though this *crevesse,* which at first threatened fall their elaborate fabric of iniquity, had been closed up, or at least gotten under control.

It was still necessary, however, to obtain from the United States district judge in New Orleans the electoral certificates which, in accordance with the requirement of law, had been deposited with him on the 6th of December and replace it with one of the certificates forged on the 29th of December. The district judge declined to grant the application for this substitution, on the ground that he was the custodian of the package merely, and without authority to deliver it to any one except upon a requisition from the Speaker of the House. This respect for the law on the part of the judge seemed puerile to the Kellogg "combine," but it was none the less awkward.

When the two Houses of Congress in their call of the States reached Louisiana, Mr. Ferry, the presiding officer, first handed to the tellers the genuine Kellogg certificate, which had come to him by mail. Next the McEnery certificate, which had come to him in duplicate, - one copy by mail and the other by messenger; next the forged Kellogg certificate, of which two copies – one by mail and the other by messenger Hill – had reached him; and finally a certificate signed by John Smith, declaring that the vote of Louisiana had been cast for Peter Cooper.

This burlesque certificate was read as the others had been, but the convention unanimously ordered it to be suppressed and no mention of it made in the record.

It is now generally understood that this burlesque certificate was sent in to create such a diversion of the attention of the convention as to enable the irregularity of the other certificates to escape observation. If so it was a complete success, for not one of the Democratic lawyers, managers, Senators, or Representatives remarked that there was one certificate made by the Republican electors of Louisiana which did not comply with the requirements of the Constitution, and the duplicates of another, from the same electors, which were in proper form, though forged, - a circumstance which could hardly have been possible but for the confusion and distraction which resulted from the reading of Peter Cooper certificate and the discussion which it provoked.

No trace of this paper remained after the recess of the joint convention of the day it was read. It was probably carried off by its author, who no doubt had more serious motives for sending it than to perpetrate a practical joke, and equally good motives for having it disappear when its purpose was accomplished. The papers in the contested case went to the Electoral Commission immediately after the joint convention adjourned. When the secretary began to read them, and before there had been an opportunity for any one to inspect them, one of the Democratic commissioners moved that the reading be dispensed with and the papers printed. The motion was not opposed. Thereupon the Hon. Nathan Clifford marked the certificates severally for identification as follows:

The first certificate of the Kellogg electors which did not meet the constitutional requirements was marked "No. 1 N.C.;" the Democratic certificate which was all right was marked, "No. 2, N.C.;" and the forged certificate was marked "No. 3, N.C." With these marks on the certificates, they were sent to the printer; but not to the public printer, not to the congressional printer, not to the government printer, in accordance with the invariable rule before and after this, but to a private job printer. When they came back printed the distinguishing marks put on them by Judge Clifford were found to have been omitted; and what is even more extraordinary, this job printer, instead of sending back the originals with the printed copies to the secretary of the commission, who was their responsible custodian, sent only the originals to the secretary, and had two of his press boys distribute the printed copies among the members of the commission and the counsel.

It is no longer susceptible of demonstration that his job printer did not distribute copies of the genuine certificate marked, "No. 1, N.C.;" but if they were distributed, it seems unaccountable that neither of the Democratic commissioners, neither the Democratic lawyers, - some of them the ablest in the country, - nor any one of the two hundred Democratic members of Congress, each and every one whom was already sufficiently familiar with the means by which Republican electors had been returned in Louisiana to be misled by no presumptions in favor

Samuel J. Tilden Circa 1874

of anything they did, - it seems, I repeat, unaccountable that none of these gentlemen should have observed that the copies of certificate No. 1 did not correspond with the copies of the forged certificate No. 3.

Had printed copies of the genuine certificate "No. 1, N.C.," been distributed, it was practically impossible that its defective form should have escaped detection. Its comparison with the other forged certificate "No. 3, N.C.," must have been made, and the differences between them have exploded the whole plot. Nothing of this kind happened, however, and we are driven to the conclusion that two copies of the forged certificate were distributed by this job printer, instead of one copy of the genuine and defective certificate, and one copy of the formally correct but forged certificate.

This curious sequence of strange and unforeseen contraries which beset the final action of the Louisiana Returning Board from the day that action was reduced to writing, was destined to acquire additional proportion and consequence at the hands of Senator Morton. When the Electoral Commission had decided, by a strictly party vote of eight to seven, to count the electoral vote of Louisiana for Hayes and Wheeler, the Senator from Indiana was careful in his motion to that effect to specify "the electoral votes in the certificate 'No. 1, N.C.,'" the genuine but constitutionally defective one. This was done, so far as Mr. Morton was concerned, with full knowledge that the other set of electoral certificates from Louisiana, and the only ones made out in the form required by the Constitution, "were not to be depended on."

When later the record of the proceedings in Congress and of the Electoral Commission came to be made up, it was made to appear that there were before Congress and the commission the certificate of the Democratic electors and the genuine but defective certificate of the Republican electors, and no others: whereas there is every reason to believe that Congress and the commission had before them and considered only two copies of the forged certificates and no other Republican certificates, and that they never had an opportunity of considering the defects of the genuine certificate which was put unchallenged upon their record.

The decision of the Electoral Commission in the case of Oregon, the last disputed State, was communicated to the joint convention of the House of Congress on Thursday, the first day of March. The convention then proceeded with the count, which it prosecuted to its completion on the following Friday morning at ten minutes past four, at which hour the President of the Senate, Thomas W. Ferry, of Michigan, announced that Rutherford B. Hayes, of Ohio, had received 185 electoral votes, a majority of the whole number, and had been duly elected President of the United States; and that William A. Wheeler, of New York, had received the like majority, and had been duly elected Vice President of the United States.

There was a ghastly sort of fitness in selecting "hangman's day" on which to stain the annals of the great Republic with this ignominious record.

> "Excidat illa dies aevo, neo postera credant
> Saecula; nos certe tacamus, et obruta multa
> Nocte tegi nostrae patiamur criminis gentis
>
> "May that foul day be blotted in time's flight
> And buried in oblivion's gloom of night
> We will at least forbear the deed to name,
> Nor let posterity believe our shame."

Republican institutions have never received a more serious blow, nor one from which they will be so long in recovering. If we do these things in the green tree, what may we be expected to do in the dry? We may go on for a while, perhaps indefinitely, "grinding on the gudgeons (*Slang.* One who is easily duped) but now to restore the faith in our institutions, once delivered to the fathers?

"I comprehend perfectly," said an eminent French journalist, with as much wit as justice, "how we may depantheonize Marat," but I cannot conceive how you will ever be able to demaratize the Pantheon."

I here dismiss the story of this the most ignominious (Deserving disgrace or shame; despicable) conspiracy of which modern history has preserved any record. I regret, for the readers sake as well as my own, to have felt compelled to dwell upon it as such length, though I have given only an imperfect summary, far from a complete list of the varieties of crime by which it was consummated. If there be any one who care to pursue the investigation further, they are referred to the congressional record of the investigations which those crimes provoked. I have

deemed it my duty to penetrate so far only into these "corners of nasti-
ness" as to satisfy all who may take the trouble to glance through these
pages, that electors favorable to Tilden for President were chosen by the
people of the United States in 1876, and that by a cumulative series
of frauds and crimes, in which leading national statesmen, cabinet
ministers, and persons occupying seats in the highest judicial tribunal
in the land were, some in a greater, some in a lesser degree accomplices,
that choice was defeated and a usurper put in his place. It is due to the
memory of Mr. Tilden that these facts should be so stated that future
historians shall have neither difficulty nor hesitation in taking note of
them.[1]

Why men occupying the most exalted and responsible positions in
the country should have ventured to compromise their reputations by
this deliberate consummation of a series of crimes which struck at the
very foundations of the Republic, is a question which still puzzles many

---

1   On the day previous to the 3rd of March the House of Representatives, by a vote of 137 to 88
adopted a series of preambles introductory to the following resolution:
Resolved by the House of Representatives of the United States, "That it is the duty of the House to
declare, and this House does solemnly declare, that Samuel J. Tilden, of the State of New York,
received 196 electoral votes for the office of President of the United States, all of which votes were
cast and lists thereof signed, certified, and transmitted, to the seat of the government, directed to
the President of the Senate, in conformity with the Constitution and laws of the United States, by
electors legally eligible and qualified as such electors, each of whom had been duly appointed and
elected in the manner directed by the Legislature of the State in and for which he cast his vote as
aforesaid; and that said Samuel J. Tilden having thus received the votes of a majority of the electors
appointed as aforesaid; he was thereby duly elected President of the United States of America, for
the term of four years commencing on the 4th day of March, A.D. 1877; and this House further
declares that Thomas A. Hendricks, having received the same number of electoral votes for the office
of Vice President of the United States that were cast for Samuel J. Tilden for President as aforesaid,
and at the same time and in the manner, it is the opinion of this House that the said Thomas A.
Hendricks, of the State of Indiana, was duly elected Vice President of the United States for the term
of four years commencing on the 4th day of March A.D. 1877"
Note: The Democratic minority of the Electoral Commission directed the Honorable Josiah
Gardner Abbott, one the of their colleagues from Massachusetts, to prepare an address to the
American people, protesting against the decisions of the majority, in which he was to set forth the
reason for their action which, under the laws establishing the commission, they had no opportunity of reporting to Congress. This address is a vigorous and compact statement of the wrongs
with they and the country had sustained at the hands of the majority, but, for reasons which have
not transpired, was never promulgated. It is understood however, that the result would not have
been changed by protesting, and the minority did not wish to further weaken the respect for the
government from which there was no refuge but in revolution. For a copy of this protest, which is
an essential part of the history of the Electoral Commission, See Appendix A.

of all parties who have no charity for the crimes themselves. I have already referred to the terrors and desperation with which the prospect of Tilden's election inspired the great army of office-holders at the close of Grant's administration. That army, numerous and formidable as it was, was comparatively limited. There was a much larger and justly influential class who were apprehensive that the return of the Democratic party to power threatened a reactionary policy at Washington, to the undoing of some or all important results of the war. These apprehensions were inflamed by the party press until they were confined to no class, but more or less pervaded all the Northern States. The election tribunal, consisting of mainly men appointed to their positions by Republican Presidents or elected from strong Republican States, felt the pressure of this feeling, and from motives compounded in more or less varying proportions of dread of the Democrats, personal ambition, zeal for their party, and respect for their constituents, reached the conclusion that the exclusion of Tilden from the White House was an end which justified whatever means were necessary to accomplish it. They regarded it like the emancipation of the slaves as a war measure. In that way they quieted their consciences for a time at least, and found a peace which passeth all understanding, by virtue of a course of reasoning which they might be suspected of having borrowed from one of Mr. Dickens' amiable heroes:

"I am glad to see you have so high a sense of your duties as a son, Sam," said Mr. Pickwick.

"I always had, sir," replied Mr. Weller.

"That's very gratifying reflection, Sam," said Mr. Pickwick approvingly.

"Werry, sir," replied Mr. Weller. "If ever I wanted anything o' my father, I always asked for it in a werry 'spectful and obliging manner. If he didn't give it me, I took it for fear I should be led to do anythin' wrong through not havin' it. I saved him a world o' trouble in that vay, sir."

"That's not precisely what I meant Sam," said Mr. Pickwick, shaking his head with a slight smile.

"All good feelin, sir, the werry best intentions, as the gen'lm'n said ven he run away from his wife 'cos she seemed unhappy with him," replied Mr. Weller.

The President and Vice President declared by the Electoral Commission to have been the choice of the electors were inaugurated on Sunday, the 4th of March. On the following day the Hon. Charles Francis Adams addressed to Mr. Tilden a letter which, though brief, produced a national sensation. It ran as follows:

Boston March 5, 1877
"Honorable S. J. Tilden, *New York:*
My Dear Sir: On this day, when you *ought* to have been the President of these United States, I seize the opportunity to bear my testimony to the calm and dignified manner in which you have passed through this great trial.

It is many years since I ceased to be a party man. Hence I have endeavored to judge of public affairs and men rather by their merits that by the names they take. It is a source of gratification to me to think that I made the right choice in the late election. I could never have been reconciled to the elevation, by the smallest aid of mine, of a person, however respectable in private life, who must forever carry upon his brow the stamp fraud, first triumphant in American history. No subsequent action, however meritorious, can wash away the letters of that record.

Very respectfully yours,
Charles Francis Adams

The formal and public charge from the son of one President, the grandson of another President, himself in one important national crisis a candidate for the vice-presidency, and in another yet graver national crisis our minister to England, that the man who only the day previous had been formerly clothed with the chief magistracy of the nation, "must forever carry upon his brow the stamp of fraud," conveyed with it throughout the land something of the shock of the fire-bell rung in the night. Had such a letter from such a source appeared the day following the inauguration of any previous President of the United States, its author could hardly have expected immunity from personal outrage. The truth of the charge, however, was so indisputable, that, so far as I am aware, no one of Mr. Hayes's friends or partisans ever attempted to deal with its author, as would have been natural had it been questionable.

Among Mr. Tilden's papers the following fragment of what purports to have been intended as a reply to Mr. Adams' letter has been found. Though only a fragment and never communicated to Mr. Adams, it is interesting a revelation of the state of feeling which the letter had awakened, and of Mr. Tilden's deliberate view of the frauds by which the rights of the nation had been violated.

New York, April 1877

"My Dear Sir: The approving judgment expressed in your letter of March 5th is esteemed by me as the best of testimonies. The circumstances you mentioned, which characterize it as a mere judgment, free from bias of partisanship, passion, or interest, enhance its value. So do also, I may be allowed to add, the large experience, long familiarity with and habitual thoughtfulness concerning public affairs, and the high standards of right and duty.

I should have had little excuse for any want of the qualities of personal demeanor which you commend; for I have not been conscience, in the vicissitudes (defined: One of the sudden or unexpected changes or shifts often encountered in one's life, activities, or surroundings) of what you speak of as the 'great trial,' of any feeling of desire or regret, separate from the public cause I have represented.

That cause I do regard as the greatest that can interest the attention of this generation of Americans.

In advocating the creation of the Union, our wise ancestors often predicted that intestine wars – if unhappily we should fall into them – would end in a subversion of constitutional government and civil liberty. Those who thought, as you and I did, that the federal government should be maintained and carried through the armed conflicts in which it had become inevitably involved, did not shut our eyes to the peril that in the process our institutions, in their spirit and practical working, might be greatly and injuriously affected. Changes in the ideal standards that govern men administering the government and limit what they dare or do, and limit also what the people will tolerate; changes in the unwritten laws established by tradition and habit, often more controlling than constitutions and statues; changes in the enormous recent growth of perverting, abusive, and corrupting influences, - these were evil tendencies, full of danger to everything really valuable in our political system.

To curb and correct these evil tendencies; to restore to the barren forms of government a spirit and substance and practice in accord with the best ideals and original models which had been formed under fortunate circumstances of our early history; to remove the fungus over-growths engendered by civil war, while preserving what ever of good it had saved or gained, - this was the first of objects. A general reform of administration, reducing burdens upon the people and facilitating a revival of industries, would attend as incidents. A complete and cordial reconciliation between estranged populations and classes, the removal if unfounded distrust and fear of each other, the inspiration of mutual confidence, was a necessary condition.

Such was the work most needful to our country in its present condi-tion, the most beneficent that could engage the efforts of patriotism or humanity, - such was that work as it appeared previous to the late election. The events which have happened since and to which you allude have added a new element to that work. Or, perhaps, they have disclosed how far we have drifted away in practice from the theory if our government, and shown that we have a more difficult task to get back than had been apparent. The immense powers which the corrupt influence of the government had to perpetuate itself was never so devel-oped as in the late canvass. I was accustomed to say that it was necessary to start in August with a public opinion which would naturally give you two-thirds of the votes in order to receive a majority in November. The civil service was never so audaciously and so unscrupulously used for electioneering purposed as in the late canvass. The whole body of 100,000 office-holders were made to feel their accountability for partisan service, and a large part of them brought into great activity. The money contributions systematically exacted, and the sums drawn from contractors, jobbers, and persons having business relations with the general government, aggregated a large fund, while the machine was openly worked by a cabinet minister acting as the head of a partisan committee.

The army, likewise, was used as an electioneering instrument. In Louisiana, Florida, and South Carolina the carpet-bag governments –their robberies, oppressions, and crimes – had so repelled public opinion, had so antagonized all taxpayers, all men of business, property, social weight, and personal influence, that the element that remained was incapable of any cohesion, or any action on its own motion. The real object of the military display was not to keep up a police, which was unnecessary and was no part of the function of the federal army, but was to act on the imaginations of the ignorant, disintegrated social atoms and enable the agents of the administration to organize and lead them. It was as true as it is confessed now that without its aid added to the other support of the government, no Republican party could exist in those States.

But all these odds were overcome by the mere mortal force of public opinion demanding better government; and a popular majority of 260,000 votes and an electoral majority of twenty-three votes resulted.

This was not withstanding that California was carried by fraud now ascertained, and several of the new States by corrupt means.

Then came the after frauds: the change of the actual result declared at the polls, by governmental influence falsifying the returns of two States and falsifying the count of the electoral votes."

I was at Mr. Tilden's house when the news of his exclusion from the presidency was announced to him, and also on the 4th of March, when Mr. Hayes was inaugurated. I venture to quote the following contemporaneous entry from my diary, relating to his bearing on that occasion.

"It was impossible to remark any change in his manner, except, perhaps, that he was less absorbed than usual and more interested in current affairs. I spent a week at this time a guest in his house, and I could not see that he was much disappointed as most of the people about him. He had not been so cheerful at any time in the last three years as since the 4th inst. My explanation of this is satisfactory to me. His notion of being President meant a life of care, responsibility, and effort such as none of his predecessors ever encountered. He never contemplated the presidency except as a fearful struggle. When his election was out of the question he was naturally more sensible of his escape from the giants which he had seen in his path than of the honors which might have been his, but were to be worn by another.

This sense of relief and the opportunity it offers of looking after his health, which is daily improving in consequence, have rather made him happier otherwise. When the giants shall have entirely disappeared, and his freedom from care and anxiety become familiar to him, it is probable that he will feel more keenly the loss he has sustained, He regards Thurman and Bayard as chiefly responsible for his miscarriage."

There have been occasional criticisms of Mr. Tilden, not only by those who wished an excuse for their own disloyalty to their party or for their personal pusillanimity (cowardice), but also by some of his faithful friends, that he did not take the oath of office and go on to Washington and claim the presidency at all hazard and regardless of the title conferred by congressional authority upon another. I believe Mr. Charles O'Connor was one of these friends, and I also remember how signally I failed in the effort of 1877 to make Victor Hugo comprehend Mr. Tilden's submission to the decision of the electoral tribunal. He shook his head at the close of my exposition, as if to say, "That is not the way we do things here in France," which was very true. But Charles O'Connor, with all his prodigious (astonishing) abilities as a jurist, was never successful in forming or leading a political party that embraced more than one person; and Victor Hugo resigned his seat in the only deliberative political assembly to which he was ever chosen by his countrymen, from sheer reluctance to prolong the exhibition to the world of his utter impotence and insignificant in a council of statesman. Mr. Tilden had frequent applications from all parts of the country, mainly from friends, for information about his plans; which he had done what he proposed to do, and what he expected his friends to do towards reclaiming the office which had been wrongfully wrested from him. These letters were, I believe, uniformly referred to me, and I answered such as seemed entitles to an answer. A few days before the fourth of March, when the new President was to be inaugurated, a communication appeared in one of the morning papers, "The World," I believe, - affirming, upon the alleged authority of General Woodford, the United States District Attorney for the Southern District of New York, that Mr. Tilden was about to take the oath of office as President in New York, and then to proclaim himself President of the United States. A representative of one of the daily journals called upon me to ascertain the truth of that statement. As the criticisms of Mr. Tilden's behavior, after the members of his own party had, with comparative unanimity and against his judgment, consented to refer the counting of the electoral vote to a special commission, still occasionally reappear where they can be made to palliate or excuse other people's shortcomings, I will here cite the substance of my reply to the inquires of the reporter, in which is embraced all, I think, that needs further to be said on that subject. After disposing of a few topics pertinent, I said:

"There were two contingencies in which it would have been lawful and obligatory for Mr. Tilden to have taken the official oath as President.

"*First,* if Congress had performed its constitutional duty of counting the electoral votes and had declared that Mr. Tilden was chosen by the electoral colleges.

"The two Houses of Congress have all the powers for verifying the electoral votes which the Constitution of the laws confer or allow. Nobody else in the federal government has any such powers. This exclusive jurisdiction of the two Houses has been exercised without interruption from the beginning of the government. It is known to all those who came in contact with Mr. Tilden at this period that he concurred in this view of the powers and duties of the two Houses of Congress exclusively to count the electoral vote. He was perfectly free and unreserved in the expression of his opinions on this subject.

"This contingency, however, never presented itself. Congress, before the time fixed by the law for counting electoral votes, passed the electoral bill, wherein it substantially abdicated its powers and enacted that the Electoral Commission should, in the first instance, make a count, and that its count should stand unless overruled *by the concurrent action of the two Houses.* The electoral tribunal counted Mr. Tilden out, and counted in a man who was not elected. Congress did not overrule their count; consequently the false count stood as law under the act of Congress.

"*Secondly,* The other contingency, in which it would have been lawful and obligatory on Mr. Tilden to have taken the oath of office, was that House of Representatives on the failure of a choice of President by the electoral colleges had itself proceeded to make the election, voting by States in the manner prescribed by the Constitution.

"This contingency, like the first one, never occurred.

"The House of Representatives is required, by the express language of the Constitution, to elect the President when neither of the candidates can command a majority of the electoral votes.

"The right of the two Houses to count the electoral votes and to declare that any person has a majority is a matter of implication, precedent, and practice. But the right of the House of Representatives to supply the failure of a choice is a positive constitutional command. It is not only a right, but a duty. The provision is mandatory. The House is a witness at the opening of the certificates; it is an actor in counting the votes by its own tellers and in its own presence.

"Having such and the best means of knowing whether a choice has been made by the elector colleges, it is also expressly vested with a power and duty to act exclusively and conclusively in the event that no person proves to have been chosen by a majority of the votes of those colleges. The House acquires jurisdiction by that fact. The assent of the Senate to the existence of that fact is nowhere prescribed or required. No judgment, certification, or act of any official body is interposed as a condition the assuming or jurisdiction by the House. When the House has once acted in such a case, no review of its action nor any appeal from its decision is provided for in the Constitution. It is difficult to see why the House in such a case, like all tribunals of original jurisdiction and subject to no appeal, did not insist upon its rights as the exclusive judge of the fact and the law from which it acquired jurisdiction. It was, I am told, a fear that the Senate might lead a resistance to the rightful judgment of the House, and that General Grant would sustain such a revolutionary policy with the army and navy and the militia of the great States in which the Republicans had possession of the governments, that deterred the House of Representatives from the assertion of its rights and induced it to abdicate in favor of the Electoral Commission.

"But without speculating upon causes or motives, one thing is certain: the House of Representatives did not elect Mr. Tilden in the manner prescribed by the Constitution. On the other hand, it did concur with the Senate in anticipating and preventing the contingency in which it might have compelled to act, thus providing an expedient which disarmed it. It adopted the electoral law and went through all the forms required for the execution of the electoral scheme. True, it afterwards, passed a declaratory resolution condemning the action of that tribunal and asserting that Mr. Tilden had been duly elected; but the Constitution had not provided that a man should or could take office as President on a declaratory resolution of the House of Representatives merely. If that resolution could have had full effect to abrogate the electoral law which the House had assisted to enact, it would have created no warrant of authority to Mr. Tilden to take the oath of office. A vote by States that he should be the next President of the United States was still necessary to give Mr. Tilden any more title to the secession than General Grant, and that vote the House of Representatives never gave him.

"I might have disposed of your question more briefly by simply saying that no contingency provided by the Constitution ever existed in which Mr. Tilden could have lawfully or properly take the oath of office as President. I have dwelt upon the matter at some length because of its future as well as past importance. The idea that Mr. Tilden ever thought of taking the oath of office illegally is in my judgment quite preposterous as is the other idea that he would have omitted to take it if any contingency had arisen in which it was his right or duty to take it, or that any menace would have had the slightest influence in preventing his performing his whole obligation to the people. I will venture to say that if it had been his right and duty to take the oath he would not have done so at the City Hall in New York, surrounded by the forces which, according to Mr. Mines, General Woodford pictured to his imagination, but at the federal capitol, even though he had know that he would be kidnapped or subjected to a drumhead court martial five minutes afterwards. It is doubtless true that revolutionary ideas were entertained by the hierarchy of office-holders in possession of the government. General Grant did utter menaces in published interviews and did make a display of military force in Washington to overawe Congress. I presume this was a part of the system of intimidation for which he allowed himself to be used by the office-holders, and which he intended to act upon public opinion through the fear of disturbance, as well as upon Congress. But it is safe to say that what-ever the effects they produced, they did not prevent Mr. Tilden from taking the oath of office. The fear that he would do so, which induced the Republicans to swear their candidate into office privately on the Saturday previous to the commencement of his term of office, besides repeating the ceremony at the inauguration, was born of that consciousness which causes the wicked to flee when no man pursueth. I was aware that about that time Mr. Tilden's house was besieged by emissaries of the press and the telegraph to know if the rumors to that effect which prevailed in Washington were true. This was a species of curiosity which I believe Mr. Tilden did not consider it any part of his duty to relieve."

The following lines from the austere muse of J. Russell Lowell in the satire entitled "Tempora Mutantur" were widely quoted in the columns of the Massachusetts press during the campaign of 1876:

> The Ten Commandments had a meaning then,
> Felt in their bones by least considerate men,
> Because behind them in public consciences stood,
> And without wincing made their mandates good,
> But now that statesmanship is just a way,
> To dodge the primal curse, and make it pay;
>
> Since the office means a kind of patent drill,
> To force an entrance to the nation's till;
> And peculation something rather less
> Risky than if you spelt it with an S;
> Now that to steal by law is grown an art,
> Whom rogues our sires, their milder sons call 'smart.'
>
> "The public servant who has stolen or lied,
> If called on may resign with honest pride.
> An unjust favor put him in, why doubt
> Disfavor as unjust has put him out?
> Even if indicted, what is that but fudge,
> To him who counted in the election judge"
> Whitewashed, he quits the politician's strife,
> At ease in mind, with pockets filled for life."[1]

---

1 Note: President would not rhyme with "fudge."

In a letter to Leslie Stephen, written December 4, and nearly a month after the presidential election, Mr. Lowell thus excuses himself for casting his electoral vote for Hayes.

"There was a rumor, it seems, that I was going to vote for Tilden. But in my own judgment I have no choice, and am bound in honor to vote for Hayes, as the people who chose me expected me to do. They did not choose me because they had confidence in my judgment, but because they knew what that judgment would be. If I had told them that I should vote for Tilden They would

Mr. Lowell was one of the Republican presidential electors of Massachusetts, and from the lofty moral standard by which he had been in
the habit of judging public men, the suspicion obtained the currency
among his friends in the press that he would refuse to cast his vote for
Hayes, which would have resulted in electing Tilden.

The frauds disclosed after the election, by which a majority of the
electors was secured for Hayes, did not, however, prevent Mr. Lowell's
acceptance of the mission to Spain at the hand of President Hayes; to
prove, perhaps, that the allegation of his muse,

"That statesmanship is just a way
To dodge the primal curse, and make it pay,"
has its honorable exceptions.

In further justice to Mr. Lowell it deserves to be recorded that he
has a very respectable precedent for lending his name and reputation
to bolster the administration of the only spurious President in our
annals.

In an old life of Charles James Fox I have read the following entry:

"1781, June 20. Sold by auction, the library of Charles James Fox,
which had been taken in execution. Amongst the books was Mr.
Gibbon's first volume of Roman History, which appeared, by title-
page, to have been given by the author to Mr. Fox, who had written
the following anecdote:

"The author (Gibbon), at Brooke's, said there was no salvation for
this country till six heads of the principal persons in the administration
were laid on the table. Eleven days after, this gentleman accepted the
place of Lord of Trade under those very ministers, and has acted with
them ever since."

If fame for its own sake, if live long in the memory of man, be an
end in itself worth toiling for, Tilden was to be congratulated upon
the decision of the Electoral Commission, for it was the means of
conferring upon him an historic prominence which the most successful
administrations of the presidential office could not have assured him.

---

never have nominated me. It is a plain question of trust. The provoking part of it is that I tried to
escape nomination all I could, and only did not decline because I thought it would be making
too much fuss over a trifle." "Letters of James Russell Lowell.

The poet Martial tells us that the name of Mucius Scaevola, who had thrust his right arm in the fire to punish it for having taken the life of another by mistake for that of the royal invader of his country, would have found its way to the "wallet in which Time carries, on his back, alms for oblivion," had the avenging dagger reached the heart of King Porsenna, for whom it was intended.

> "Major deceptae fama est et gloria dextrae
> Si non errasesett, fecerat illa minus.

So the action of the Electoral Commission has conferred upon Mr. Tilden the unique distinction of being the first – let us hope the last – President elect of the United States feloniously excluded from the chief magistracy; a distinction which like the banishment of Aristides, the assassinations of Caesar, of Henry IV. Of France, of Lincoln, and of Carnot, makes it one of the conspicuous and indestructible landmarks of history.

> "Greater the glory and eke the fame
> Of Scaevola's hand deceived,
> Had it not missed it patriot aim,
> The less it had achieved."

CHAPTER IV

Revisits Europe – Blarney Castle – St. Patrick's Cathedral – Tom Moore's birthplace – The cabman's criticism – Lord Houghton's story – General Grant's reception in London – Elected honorary member of the Cobden Club – Visits the home of his ancestry – Arrives in Paris – Attends the funeral of Theirs – Talk Gambetta – Louis Blanc's account of his visit to Louis Napoleon when a prisoner of Ham, and of the loss and recovery of his voice in London – The story of General Cavaignac's brother and mother – Tilden's exposure in recrossing the channel - Returns to the United States – The "Indian Corn Speech."

During the spring of '77 Mr. Tilden began to feel serious concern about his health. The continued strain to which his energies had been subjected for five or six years, and especially during the preceding six or eight months, had told severely upon his constitution. Arthritic symptoms had begun to manifest themselves to such an extent as to deprive him almost entirely of the use of his left hand, and already slight indications were exhibited of the *paralysis agitans,* popularly known as numb palsy, which was destine to afflict him increasingly for the remainder of his days. His medical advisers counselled abstinence from all serious cares, with rest and recreation. As it was practically impossible to secure either of these advantages in his own country, after much deliberation he decided to try the efficacy of a sea-voyage and a few months' sojourn in Europe.

He made it one of the conditions of his going that I should accompany him.

We sailed in the steamer "Scythia" on Wednesday, the 18th of July, landed at Queenstown on the morning of the 27th, and slept that night at the Imperial Hotel in Cork, but not until we had visited the castle and groves of Blarney. The following day we left for Killarney. On our way we passed near to what, for Ireland, was something of a mountain, the top of which a young Scotchman, riding in the same car with us, quoted the following lines which he said were current in his country:

> "On Tinto's top there is a mist,
> And in that mist there is a kist,
> And in that kist there is a drap,
> And everyone must taste of that."

"Tinto" was the name of a mountain; "kist," of a chest; "drap," a tear drop, a sorrow.

The moral that we extracted from these lines, in which Tilden might have found some consolation, was that there is no position in this world so exalted as to be exempt from tribulation and sorrow, and the higher the elevation the greater was apt to be the tribulation.

We reached Killarney about noon. After lunch we started for Dunlo gap and the lakes. As we approached the gap we were obliged to do homage to a saucy creature who claimed to be a granddaughter of the famous Kate Kearney, whose charms were sung so sweetly by Tom Moore. Whatever had been the charms of the original Kate, it was very clear that none of them had descended to the granddaughter.

Our carriage was equipped with a guide, whom they called a "bugler." Soon after entering the pass he got down and played two or three airs to awaken the echoes in which Moore found the presage in "The answering future" of his own enduring fame.

> " 'Twas one of those dreams that by music are brought ,
> Like a bright summer haze, o'er the poet's warm thought.
>
> "He listened – while high o'er the eagle's rude nest
> The lingering sounds on their way loved to rest;
> And the echoes sung back from their full mountain quire,

As if loath to let song so enchanting expire.

"Oh, forgive, if, while list'ning to music whose breath
Seem'd to circle his name with a charm against death
He should feel proud spirit within him proclaim,
'Even so shalt thou live in the echoes of fame.

" 'Even so, tho' they mem'ry should now die away,
'Twill be caught up again in some happier day,
And the hearts and the voices of Erin prolong,
Through the answering future, thy name and thy song.' "

It was a while passing through the pass of Dunlo that our attention was directed to a lake about one hundred and fifty yards long, into which, we were assured by our bugler (as I suppose thousands had been assured before), St. Patrick had drowned all the snakes in Ireland, and did his work so thoroughly, that "divil a snake had been seen in the country since."

We were left to infer that the water-snake had not been evolved in St. Patrick's time, for there is no tradition, I believe of a water-snake being drowned.

We passed two other points which Moore's verse has made familiar and famous. One was, "The meeting of the waters," where for a hundred feet or so the water falls from one lake into another, through a narrow channel beautifully shaded, and deep enough to admit of the passage of a large boat. The other was, "The fairy isle of Innisfallen."

We arrived in Dublin in the afternoon of Monday, the 30th of July.

On the following morning we sallied forth at an early hour to see what we could of the metropolis of Ireland in a single day, for social engagements, already contracted by telegraph, required us to set our faces towards London the day following. Our first visit, of course, was to St. Patrick's Cathedral – which proved in some sense, a disappointment. We were expecting to see a venerable, mediaeval pile, eloquent if age and historic suggestion. Instead of which we found, it is true, a fine structure; but to all appearance it might have been finished the day before we visited. The stones were freshly cut. To our expressions of surprise at it modern appearance, the verger informed us that the cathedral had been entirely renovated recently by Guinness, the world-renowned brewer of Dublin, at an expense to him, personally, of over £ 150,000. He had left scarcely a trace, inside or out, to remind one of the church commenced A.D. 1190, in which Dr. Swift used to preach his "dearly beloved Roger." Even the places in which the mortal remains of the dean and Stella reposed, had succumbed to the fiend of renovation. The verger pointed to the place where he said their remains were laid, but it is possible that to the next visitor he named some other place. There was no mark or sign to limit his choice. A stone pavement covered the entire floor of the cathedral, bearing no record whatever of anything that lay beneath it. When asked how this came about, the verger said, with a shrug of the shoulders: "Oh, great folks will have their own way." No marks were allowed anywhere on the floor to show were people have been buried.

Upon the walls, but so high that the inscriptions were scarcely legible, were cenotaphs to Swift and Stella placed side by side. While the verger was enlarging to us upon the extent of the renovations, Tilden remarked to me, "It is the old story of the jack-knife: it has had two new blades and three new handles, but it is the same old jack-knife."

From the cathedral we drove to No. 12 Angier street, near by, the birthplace of Tom Moore. It was a plain, three-story brick building. As we descended from our carriage a young man, apparently about thirty years of age, came to the door and said, with a smile, "I suppose you would like to look at the chamber in which Tom Moore was born." We gave him to understand that such was our errand. We saw at once that we were about to enter a drinking saloon, or what is more commonly and fitly denominated a gin-mill. In the course of our visit we learned from our cicerone that such was the business which had been carried on there by Moore's father, and that such was the business which had been carried on their ever since.

The young man conducted us through the front room, which was disorderly and dirty, into and through a middle room, to which there was an entrance from a side street or alley. This room was divided by partitions into stalls like a stable, so that a person could approach the bar, and get what he or she could pay for, in comparative privacy. There were two or three haggish-looking women availing themselves of the privileges of these pens as we passed. They were converged with rags, filthy, and in the last stages of brutal degradation.

We were then conducted upstairs and into the front room or the third story, where we were told the poet was born, and thence to the attic, where he began his career as a writer. It was a low, dark room about eleven by fourteen feet in size, with one window. There was no part of the house, save the front rooms in the second and third storied, that was not reeking with dirt and suspicious odors.

The proprietor was neatly enough dressed, - which made the filth, confusion, and disorder around him seem to us the more surprising. We did not ask him for an explanation, but I incline to suspect that it was not to be found in mere carelessness or indifference to order and neatness. Would not neatness and order have affected and order have affected his patrons unfavorably, and driven them to places more in harmony with their own condition? Outwardly the house looked well and was in good condition; but inwardly it seemed to be full of dead men's bones. We could with difficulty realize that a poet of Moore's genius and refinement could have reared in such a hell as this. And yet, was not the poet's career a more or less logical sequence of his youthful environment? He was not responsible for his father's-dram shop, but did he not become the concocter and dispenser of more subtle and more destructive poisons?

Our driver affected not to know where the poet was born, and when mildly rebuked for his ignorance, said that "Irish people do not care where Moore was born. English and Americans go to see the house; we Irish never take the trouble." When asked for the cause of this indifference he said, "Moore never wrote anything for the people. He liked to live with and to please the great people in England. He did not, like Burns, write for his own country people."

Manifestly the poet's popularity in England was his real offense in the eyes of our Jehu, who probably did not know how to read at all; and if he did, the fact that Moore was as much the national bard of Ireland as Burns was the national bard of Scotland, or Béranger of France, would not in the least have extenuated his crime of trying to please and be popular on the other side of the channel. Be this as it may, it was very clear that here was one at least of the voices of Erin not disposed to prolong

"Through the answering future Moore's name and his song."

On the front wall of the house, between the first and second story, a piece of white marble was let into the wall, upon which was this inscription:

"In this house, on the 28th of May,
1778, was born a poet
Thomas Moore."

Some two weeks after our visit in Dublin, Mr. Tilden and I were guests of the late Lord Houghton one evening at the Cosmopolitan Club, in London. While most of the guests were gone to the refreshment-room, Houghton sat down by my side on a sofa and made a few inquires about what we had been doing. I spoke casually of my visit to the birthplace of Tom Moore; he interrupted me, "Let me tell you something." He then went on to say that in the early part of this century one of the most eminent surgeons in Dublin was sent for to come in great haste to attend a young woman who was supposed to be dying. Putting everything aside, he jumped into a cab and hastened to the place, of which the address had been given him. Beside the young woman for whose injuries he had been called stood a young man with the face expressing the greatest anxiety and distress. He was alternately denouncing himself for what had occurred, loudly invoking the Divine forgiveness, and begging the doctor to spare no effort or expense to save the young woman's life. The doctor found, upon examination, that though somewhat bruised she was not dangerously injured. After doing what for her what seemed in his judgment to be required, he turned to the young man to know what had occurred, and why he held himself responsible for it. The young man proceeded at once to confide to him the story. In brief, the young woman was an actress, then playing minor parts at one of the Dublin theatres; he became enamored of her, and in a moment of passionate recklessness presumed upon her amiability grant. He pressed his suit so pertinaciously that at last she threatened that if he did not desist she would throw herself out if the window.

The very extravagance of her threat rather encouraged than discouraged her admirer, for it never entered his mind that she could be so rash as to execute it, and to threaten it implied to him that she was not more than half in earnest in her resistance.

He persisted with his importunities. True to her word, she sprang through the window, and was soon taken up senseless from the pavement.

Thus far to the doctor Lord Houghton went on to say that the young man was so shocked by the immediate consequences of his misconduct, and so impressed by the virtuous firmness of the young girl, that as soon as she was sufficiently recovered to entertain such proposals, he asked he hand in marriage and was accepted. They were shortly after married, and the young woman became Mrs. Tom Moore.

I asked Lord Houghton if he considered that story as entirely authentic. He said, "Certainly, the facts are well known to many people still living in Dublin."

We afterwards visited the whilom residence of Daniel O'Connell, the birthplace of the Duke of Wellington, and the old Parliament House – the part in which the Commons sat being then occupied as a banking-house. The Lords sat in a smaller room, the furniture of which we found substantially unchanged. A remarkably fine bust of Curran in this room specially engaged Mr. Tilden's attention.

We left Dublin early on the morning of the 1st of August for England, and after a flying visit to Eton hall and the Chester Cathedral, pushed on to London, where on the 3d we found ourselves comfortably installed at the Buckingham Palace Hotel. Here for the succeeding eight or ten days we were obliged to devote ourselves pretty constantly to social engagements, most of which had been contracted for us before our arrival. We, of course, embraced the earliest convenient opportunity of waiting upon Mr. Pierrepoint, then our representative at the English court. In the course of our visit he found occasion to give us at some length the history of the measures he took to secure for General Grant a reception in England such as had never before been accorded to any American. He said that he remembered being in London in 1854 or 1855 when ex-President Van Buren was there and Mr. McLane was minister. Both were invited to a dinner at Lord Clarendon's, then prime-minister. When Van Buren arrived, Clarendon occupied himself with other guests, overlooking Van Buren, who, when dinner was announced, found himself relegated to the foot of the table. McLane complained of this in official quarters on the following day, and the reply was, "You give your ex-Presidents no official rank: how can we?" Van Buren declined all further invitations.

Remembering this incident, Pierrepont said that when he received from Grant the letter announcing his intention to visit England, he promptly sought an interview with Lord Derby, then minister of foreign affairs, to ascertain how the ex-President would be received by the English authorities. He received substantially the same reply that was given to the expostulation of McLane. Pierrepont quoted the case of the ex-Emperor Napoleon III., who had then recently come to England without rank or title, but had been received as a member of a royal or imperial family. The like courtesy was extended to his son. Lord Derby said there might be something in that, and asked Pierrepont to put his wishes in writing, and meantime promised to confer with some of his colleagues. Pierrepont did as requested, and in a day or two waited upon Lord Derby with his programme. Derby said there would be no difficulty so far as the cabinet was concerned, but intimated that he might have difficulty in persuading the ambassadors to yield their precedence to a man without any official character or rank. Pierrepont invited three or four of the ambassadors to meet with him to consider the matter. Count Munster, the German ambassador, insisted that he had no right or power, whatever might be his disposition, to yield precedence to General Grant. Pierrepont argued the question at length; said that he should yield the precedence himself, and he hoped they would see no impropriety in yielding it to an ex-President. The first state dinner to which Grant was invited in London was given by the Duke of Wellington. Count Munster suggested that Pierrepont should make out a plan of the table and arrangement of the guests, which was done. The programme was accepted substantially as made; precisely how, he did not make entirely intelligible. He said that he also insisted that Grant should not make any calls except upon the royal family, and at all entertainments should rank next the Prince of Wales, his precedence being conceded, however, as a courtesy, rather that as a right.

Two or three days after this conversation with Pierrepont, we joined the Right Hon. W.E. Forster at lunch, when Grant's reception became the subject of conversation. He said quite openly, and in the hearing of the whole table, that he did not think Pierrepont had accomplished any desirable result by his stand for Grant; that it was a rather undignified strife on the part of an American ex-President who stood in no need of any homage from the English people which would not have been cordially accorded. He also remarked that the Duke of Wellington was not the kind of man at whose table either Grant or Pierrepont could afford to strive for precedence. Foster at the time recited a letter which he heard had been received by Pierrepont from the duke, and which ran substantially as follows: "That it would gratify him if the greatest general of the United States would give the son of the Duke of Wellington the privilege of entertaining him first at dinner in London." Foster laughed over this as if he thought it the invention of a wag; others regarded it as genuine.

I heard the opinion expressed, by some whose opinions were entitled to respect, that the "London Times" had a great deal more to do with the attentions paid to General Grant than Mr. Pierrepont had; a desire to repair some of the unpleasant impressions made in America by the English government during the war being its ruling motive. I presume the honors were easy.

Though Mr. Tilden's health had apparently been improved by his voyage and practical release from political cares, he was still condemned to a very regular and almost ascetic life, and compelled to decline all hospitalities which were showered upon him, except such as were tendered by old friends and acquaintances. It was impossible for him to accommodate his hours of eating and rest to those of London society. His admirers in England who were thus deprived of the privileges of meeting him socially testified their respect for him by extending to him promptly upon his arrival the privileges of the Athenæum and Reform Clubs, for which however, he had little use. The desire to avoid attentions, which it became occasionally difficult to decline, induced Mr. Tilden to leave London for Scotland somewhat precipitately.

We reached Edinburgh on the 12th of August. We spent ten days visiting scenes and places of greatest interest to us in Scotland, returning to London on the 22nd.

Among the letters awaiting him at his hotel was one advising him of his election as an honorary member of the Cobden Club, to which he sent the following reply:

"BUCKINGHAM PALACE HOTEL, Aug. 23, 1877

DEAR SIR: On my return from Scotland yesterday I had the honor to receive your favor of the 8th inst. advising me of my election as an honorary member of the Cobden Club. I hasten to assure you that

I highly appreciate this courtesy, and that I am most happy to have my name associated in any way with that of the illustrious statesman, the usefulness of whose life it is the worthy purpose of your club to prolong.

"Yours very respectfully,
"S.J. Tilden.

"HON. THOMAS BAYLEY POTTER,
"Honorary Secretary of the Cobden Club."
Vol. II.-9

On the 23rd we left for Canterbury, where Mr. Tilden spent a few days making the acquaintance of his kindred, whose names figure conspicuously in most of the parish registers of that county for many centuries. From the beginning the family appeared to have made its career in the army or in the church; and of the descendants of whom he made the acquaintance while here, pretty much all had followed the traditions of the elders. They were all cultivated and refined people with moderate incomes, buy enjoying in a high degree the respect and confidence of the community to which they belonged.

I am glad to be able to give here extracts from some of the very few letters which Mr. Tilden wrote to his family during his stay in Europe. Never much given to letter-writing, the difficulty and discomfort which he already experienced in handling a pen prevented his writing at all to any but his family, and rarely to them.

To Mrs. Augusta Pelton, the wife of his nephew, he wrote from Canterbury, Aug. 8, 1877:

"We came here Friday evening. On Saturday we passed the morning in the cathedral, which is in many respects the most interesting of any in England. In the afternoon we went out six miles to call on a Mrs. Tylden, the widow of the late Vicar of Chilham. She had two weeks ago written inviting me to call, and lunch at her house. Her husband was by right the head of the Milsted branch of the family, about which you will read in Burke's "Landed Gentry," under that name. By some arrangement of the grandfather, with the consent of the eldest son, the landed estate had gone to the second son by a later marriage, Sir John Maxell Tylden; a result no doubt induced by the imprudence of the father. Her son of nineteen has just entered the artillery as a lieutenant. Her daughter of twenty-one is the flower of the Tyldens here; that is to say, a girl of nice manners, and by much the fairest complexion we have seen. Yesterday in their company we went to Milsted, and saw several members of the family which succeeded to that place, though not living there at present. Gen. William Burton Tilden, who died in the Crimean war, and who was the third brother, left three sons. The youngest, now in Oxford University, Richard by name, came to us with his step-mother, the widow of the general. As the place was rented, we met at the residence of the Vicar of Milsted. He is Mr. Hilton, a genial and cultivated person, with a wife and three maiden daughters, who, with one of his four sons, were at home. And we all sat down to a very nice lunch; visited the manor-house and the church, and then went to a neighboring church at Worm's Hill, which was an earlier seat of the same family.

"A special interest was added to this occasion by the circumstance that Milsted is off from all railroads, and in a purely rural district. We saw the form of English life in the middle class, well to do and cultivated, and in the depths of the country.

I must break off, for it is growing late, and we start early in the morning for Tenterden. I am conscience that I am writing too hastily to do justice to the picture as it exists in our minds, and as I would paint it to yours."

Mr. Tilden returned to London on the 30th of August, and on the 31st left for Lowestoft, on the east coast of England, for the purpose of consulting Dr. Garrod, who had been recommended to him as specially qualified to deal with troubles like those with which he was contending.

The following letter was addressed to his sister, Mrs. Pelton, from Lowestoft:

"LOWESTOFT, Sept. 3, 1877.

"DEAR MARY: This is a sea-shore place, on the eastern coast of England, washed by what is called the German ocean. It is rather a select spot, ten miles south of the larger town, Yarmouth. The house in which I am is within two hundred feet of the water, and my room, a little one in the fourth story, fronts upon the sea. Of course, the fullness of the house has elevated me to such a place. We left Canterbury on the evening of Friday, slept in London, and at twelve the next morning I started for this place, one hundred and seventeen miles from London.

"Mr. Bigelow went the same afternoon to see some friends in Surrey, and is expected here this evening – for it is now six, of a rainy day, and I can scarcely see to write.

"The motive of my coming here is not for the public, but may be mentioned to the family. Dr. Garrod, who is, no doubt, the best man on gout, rheumatism, and the peculiar malady (arthritis) which affects a joint of my first and second fingers of the left hand, whom I had one consultation with in London, has come here for two months of recreation, extending to October 1. It is difficult to see much of him in London, but he consented to see me here, where he is perfectly at leisure. It was a special opportunity for him to learn all possible of my case, and for me to draw from him the results of all the knowledge, reflection, and experience he is capable of applying to it. So I thought at this stage of my journeyings, to discard everything else and come here, and stay as long as I can to contribute to that object...

"He has a nice family, with whom I have become quite well acquainted. He appears to take a special and personal interest in me, and I have come to a clear conclusion that he has more knowledge, experience, reflection, and judgment on such cases – very far more – than any man I have known. As I have the opinion that the malady, though specially affecting only two small joints, is, in all probability, the result of a general cause, and the improvement would affect the general health, and the deterioration would be likely to touch other joints and probably many, besides injuring the general constitution – if I can get real benefit from this gentleman, it is the most important thing that concerns me – altogether out of the dimensions of mere ordinary travel.

"So I have thought it best to come here now, and stay as long as seems useful, and then go on my way, returning to London early October – say a week or ten days before I sail – to take a final observation of the condition of things.

"This statement is very long, and seems tedious, but perhaps you may like to know all about the matter.

"My general health is improving all the time. I can take more exercise, and am growing stronger. The tendency is for the physical discomforts which attend such a malady, and which, between us – I don't say that except to very few – rob existence of almost every recreation and capacity of a pleasurable nature, to diminish slowly, by irregular steps, in which you sometimes doubt all real improvement, but which yet, measure at intervals, show some decided progress. The opinion has been growing upon me that I shall find it expedient to keep from everything which interferes, and to continue the process for a year or more. I must remember that is now but two months since I began the measures which looked to bettering my condition at Sea Girt.

"Resuming my letter this morning (September 4), I have crowded the rest of the topic on the last sheet and begin anew...

"I gave – in a letter to Augusta, I think – some account, hurried and imperfect, of our visit to Milsted, and of the people we saw there. I intended to make a better sketch, but it is not easy to return to a topic once passed, or to turn from what follows it in the current of events.

"On Wednesday, I believe it was, we made an excursion to Tenterden – Mr. Bigelow, Mrs. Tylden, and her son, the young lieutenant of the artillery. The young lady was detained at home by some visitors.

"Passing from Canterbury to Ashford, some sixteen miles, by rail, we took a landau at the latter place for Tenterden. Our ride was through a beautiful country, perfectly rural, and having in it all the elements of picturesque loveliness.

"The fields as you know, are generally separated by hedges; the moisture of the climate preserves and renews the verdure, and the cloudy film that nearly always veils the sun, and softens the light, lends an aspect to nature like that you will see in twilights under our skies or objects under shadow.

"We stopped at the White Lion, a quaint old tavern, that would at once pulled down our country as being a century or two behind the times, but which was interesting as a relic of the past. We visited the church and its yard before lunch. Mr. Bigelow reclined upon the grass and read, while the rest of us ascended the narrow, spiral, stone staircase of the steeple. I will hear record that the platform is reached at one hundred and twenty-two feet by one hundred and forty steps. From it, the view on every side was fine...

"The town is antique, mostly in one street, the houses of brick and the roofs of tiles, with everywhere an appearance of age. It is in a sequestered, agricultural region, not much invaded by modern inventions...

"By the aid of the ordnance map, which is on a very large scale (twenty four inches to the mile), I was able to select the place most worthy of being looked at; and went to see a large and ancient farm-house close to what is called on the map Tilden's Gill. That is a depression on which water runs, except when the period is dry. It is wooded in a narrow strip. The farm is called the Belgar farm, and was sold in 1873 or 4. It contains about one hundred and forty acres. The portions of the land sold are described in the advertisement and conveyances as Tilden's Gill, and embrace the most opulent part of the area called by that name. The farm-house also seems to have a geographical relation to the Gill, to make it more probable than any other place that it was residence of the man from whom the Gill took its designation. The house is a large and old structure, of an apparent age corresponding with this theory. It is of brick, or mainly so, with some accessories of plaster. My recollection is that the will of Nathanial Tilden in 1641, an extract from which is found in Dean's "History of Scituate," speaks of the house as stone; but it said that brick houses are sometimes in the local usage spoken of as stone, and that there are, strictly speaking, no stone houses, that material not being used...

"In the main room of the house, in which we were most of the time, the beams stood out from the ceiling and were numerous and uncased, and at the large windows were propped by an iron standard. A part of the house was neat and comfortable, while some was used for inferior purposes. There is a nice garden and flowers, and a pear-tree trained against one of the walls, large, full of fruit, and vines were abundant. The house is quite a distance from the public road, being reached by a lane.

"The occupant is Thomas Coveney, who is recently upon the place – a respectable, middle aged farmer...

"He had quite a hunt for a map on which the names of the tracts composing the farm were expected to be found, and at length discovered the advertisement and the accompanying map for the recent sale of the property. That map he insisted on leaving out and giving me, negating my inquiry whether it might not sometime be found useful to them...

"I will add that the farm of which I have been writing was bought at the recent sale by F.T. Carey, Esq., Stanbrook Villa, Gravesend, Kent.

"On the whole it is probably, but not certain, the house I saw was the house of our family before 1634, or two hundred and forty-three years ago.

"I must close, for I have scribbled over the last of the six sheets to which the varieties if the Canterbury imprints are limited. Much affectionate regards for Willie, Gussie, Laura, yourself, and all.

"I am truly yours,
"S.J. Tilden"

While at Lowestoft, and on the 5th of September, the news reached us of the death of M. Thiers. On the following day we left for London, and the 7th for Paris, where we took rooms at the Westminster Hotel in the Rue de la Paix. Early on the following morning, and while we were breakfasting, my old and valued friend, the late William H. Huntington, called to say that Mr. Smalley, the London representative of the "Tribune," was in town and had secured a capacious carriage for the purpose of witnessing the funeral solemnities of the illustrious French statesman of the Place St. George, and if it would be agreeable to us, he would be glad to have us join him. Mr. Smalley was good enough to call for us about eleven. Our party was fortunate in being promptly recognized by one of the gentlemen who during our Civil war had been, and still continued to be, attached to ministry of foreign affairs. He gave us tickets which entitled us to all the privileges of the Diplomatic Corps.

After the religious ceremonies at the church we resumed our seats in our carriage; and when the cortège began to move were rather surprised to find ourselves placed among the chief mourners, and our carriage next but one to the hearse – where by virtue of our position we became objects of the sympathy of the largest crowd of people I ever saw in one day. For several miles on our journey to Père la Chaise, every window, balcony, roof, pavement, indeed every standing place commanding a view of the procession, was beaming with faces; even the street was solid with people almost up the wheels of our carriage, leaving scant room for the police to walk their patrol. We could not get within fifty feet of the tomb, and of course heard little of the discourses, which were delivered in conversational tones by speakers invisible to any who were more than twenty feet distant.

The question whether the mortal remains of the wily old politician belonged to the Republicans or to the McMahon administration was settled by the demonstration we had witnessed. There could be no mistaking the political significance of the vast but orderly, respectful, and sympathetic crowd which lined the way of the dead statesman on his last journey, and which had been gathered without the aid or apparent sympathy of a single government drum or place man. It was a spontaneous and eloquent admission that in his death France had lost what Paris at least regarded as her most important, if not her most illustrious citizen.

On the 12th of September Mr. Tilden and I called upon Mr. Gambetta, with whom I had a slight acquaintance, contracted before he had become one of the controlling forces in French politics. He had been condemned, only the day before our visit, by one of the tribunals, to fine or imprisonment for some act of omission or commission, the nature of which I cannot recall. In reply to our inquires about it he gave us to understand that there was more politics than law in the judgment.; that it gave him the least possible concern; that "judicial delays" would throw the final decision of the questions at issue over the election, then close at hand, when his parliamentary privileges would protect him from arrest. He took his election for granted, which, as events proved, he was entitled to do. To the question whether the new assembly would meet soon enough to clothe him with parliamentary privileges, he replied that the legislative bodies would meet immediately after the election under a new law, enacted since the organization of the provisional government and for the sole purpose of embarrassing the Republicans, but which seemed destined, he said, to be useful to the Republicans only.

In reply to an inquiry of Mr. Tilden, Mr. Gambetta said that the Republican voters in France numbered a little less than five million, and their opponents a little less than two millions; that the Republicans consisted in large proportion, of the *ouvriers*, or wage earning class, and of the very large and more intelligent class of people with their *pécule* or small capital who work on their own account – that is, are not salaried, but to a great extent independent of masters or capitalists. This class he regarded as made up of the most independent voters in France.

He described them as *patentés*, or men who had licenses to pursue their respective trades or businesses on their own account. The third quotum were acquisitions, not very numerous, from the other parties. The whole number of registered voters was about eleven millions. The officers of the civil service, exclusive of the army, navy, he estimated at about three hundred thousand, who, until recently had been named by the government. They were now, he said, elected by the cantons, but the necessity of having men for these places possessed of some official experience and cultivation forbade rapid changes; consequently popular influence was not yet much felt by them, though it was gradually penetrating their circle. He thought there were many Democrats among the lower clergy.

As our interview was in the editorial rooms of the journal, of which he was editor and proprietor, our conversation naturally drifted toward the press. Among other things he said that the circulation of the newspaper press in France had decupled in ten years. This extraordinary statement, which there is no reason to suppose exaggerated, is rather an illustration of the restriction and oppression which weighted upon the press under the Empire, than of the multiplication of readers, though their numbers, of course, had been steadily on the increase.

Mr. Gambetta professed to have no apprehension of the army; he said it was now thoroughly national in its feelings and sympathies; it understood and kept posted on the various political problems of the day, and he was persuaded that it could not be used for mischief. In this respect he said the army now very much changed from what it was under the Empire: it is animated by fresh and more elevated purposes. He exhibited the utmost confidence in the future of the Republic, and made light of the opposition, from whatever source it came.

Such was the substance of an interview which lasted about an hour. Gambetta had become quite fleshy, and I was told could not be persuaded to take exercise. It was manifest even then, through riches and honor might be, length of days was *not* in store for him.

On the 17th Louis Blanc was one of our guests at dinner, in the course of which he gave an interesting account of his acquaintance with Louis Napoleon, which, as I have never seen it in print, I am sure I need make no apology for setting down here. He said that in consequence of Louis' attempt to escape from his prison in Boulogne, he was tried, condemned to imprisonment at Ham. On this occasion he was treated, not only by the press, but by the senators and peers of France who tried him, with great severity; the vilest epithets and grossest indignities were showered upon him. Louis Blanc, who was then proprietor of a journal in Paris, wrote an article expostulating with his uncharitable colleagues, closing with the remark, in substance, "That many of those who now abused the prisoner would, had he been successful, have cheerfully licked his boots." Napoleon, who was allowed every comfort and even luxury at Ham, addressed a letter to Louis Blanc, thanking him for the article, and asking him to come and spend a few days with him at Ham. Louis Blanc wrote in reply that could not associate himself in any way or degree with the august prisoner's schemes of ambition, past or future, but he would come to him with pleasures as to a fellow citizen in trouble. He went accordingly and spent three days, shut up with him in the prison, where they had no resource but conversation, which Louis Blanc spoke of as something of a hardship, inasmuch as Napoleon was not fluent of speech. "He seemed ever to be seeking the word to express his idea, that did not come. This made conversation with him tedious."

Napoleon spoke at great length of his political plans, and while he professed to be a friend of universal suffrage, and ready to do whatever the people of France desired their ruler to do, when asked by Louis Blanc in what direction and to what ends he would use his influence to bend or direct the national will, whether he would strive to give it a Democratic or a despotic tendency, Louis Blanc said he could never get from him a reply. He repeatedly tried him on this subject, but always without success.

Louis Blanc had been addressing some of his constituents during the afternoon, and he amused us by enumerating some of the points of his speech which had proved most successful. The one he made upon President McMahon, he said, was applauded with frenzy. He told the story of one of the first Napoleon's generals addressing his soldiers on the eve of an election. "Soldiers," he said, "you will vote as you please; you are perfectly free to act according to your convictions; but if any man does not vote this ticket, I will run my saber through him." The story had at least the merit of antiquity, and with the audience he was addressing his version probably did not seriously compromise his credit as an historian.

During his exile in London, after the falloff the government in '48, and after he had acquired a tolerable command of the English language, Louis Blanc said he was invited to deliver a lecture for the first time in English. He was to dine that day with Edward Dixon, then editor of the "London Athenæum." The prospect of meeting a distinguished London audience, and attempting to talk to them in what to him was a foreign tongue, made him very nervous; and the more he heard about the audience, the more nervous he became. During the dinner he suddenly lost his voice, and found himself incapable of uttering a word in a tome above a whisper. He was in despair. What was to be done? Who was to do it? There seemed to be but one course to pursue, and that was to tell the truth and dismiss the audience; but it was well known that the audience was to consist of everything most distinguished in London society, where Louis Blanc has become already a great favorite. The more they told him of the audience, the worse he felt and the more feeble became his voice. Finally it was decided that he and Dixon should show themselves on the stage and let the audience see, if they could not hear, that he was unable to speak audibly. They accordingly ascended the stage together. Dixon proceeded to make Louis Blanc's excuses, and, when he had done, Louis Blanc stepped forward to verify his friend's statements. Dixon's remarks had been received with sympathetic applause by the entire audience, but when Louis Blanc appeared, the applause was deafening. When it had subsided sufficiently, he attempted to say a few words, mainly for the purpose of showing his dephonetized condition, when to his utter surprise his voice sounded clearer and louder than ever before a public assembly. He said he was never able to speak more effectively, and went on for two whole hours with the slightest inconvenience. Evidently the applause with which he was received cured the nervousness which alone was responsible for his temporary aphony.

Of the mode in which the Church influenced the politics of France in those days Louis Blanc told a curious story. The brother of General Cavaignac was a *libre-penseur,* as well as a very intimate friend of Louis Blanc, in whose arms, in fact, he died. He came one day to consult Louis Blanc about what he characterized, properly enough, as a most delicate matter. He said that his mother for the past two weeks had been pressing him every day to go to the priest and confess himself. It was no use to tell her, he said, that he did not believe in a priest pardoning sins; that he did not wish to act like a hypocrite by pretending to. These protestations only redoubled her pertinacity and anxiety. She asked if he was willing to embitter her remaining days, not only by refusing her request and the assurance of his salvation, but was intent upon persisting in a course which assured her of his damnation. This, with sobs and weeping and tearing of hair and getting upon the knees to him, had been his daily discipline for more than a fortnight. He begged his friend to tell him what he ought to do. Louis Blanc replied to him that the question he had asked him was one which he must decide for himself, and declined to accept the responsibility of advising him. Two days later Louis Blanc heard that he had been to the confessional; and the clerical journals immediately after his decease had a general glorification over his "conversion," and his experiences in the presence of death, especially of the consolation which the Church only could provide, and of which Cavaignac had till then always made light. It is in this way, he said, that the priests retain their power through the women, through the mothers and the sisters of the men, that no man had more often dwelt upon this fact than Cavaignac himself.

We left Paris, and returned to London on the 8th of October. In crossing the channel we found the sea very rough. When about half the way over, a sea struck our steamer with such a violence as to carry away one of the davits and the boat suspended on it, and deluged the deck and Mr. Tilden as well. He was obliged to sit in his wet clothes, not only until we arrived at Dover, but in the cars during the rest of our journey to London; in all more than four hours. It was a fearful exposure for a person in his condition, and filled me with alarm. He arrived at his hotel in London chilled through and almost insensible. After a warm bath and some supper he felt somewhat refreshed; about a half-past ten, however, and immediately after he retired to his bed, he had a chill, which was soon followed by a fever. I sent for Dr. Garrod, who was then in London, and who prescribed for him. He said the lower tips of Mr. Tilden's lungs were congested, and that he must remain in bed for a day or two. For two days we were in doubt whether he would be well enough to sail for home in the "Scythia," in which we had taken passage for the 12th. Happily, however, he continued to improve, and we were enabled to reach Liverpool in time to sail as had been arranged, arriving in New York on the 25th.

On the evening of the 27th Mr. Tilden was serenaded at his residence in Gramercy Park by the Young Men's Democratic Club, whose presence, of course, attracted a crowd. In reply to a few words of welcome from the late Augustus Schell, Mr. Tilden made a short speech which because of his allusions to our great national staple, came to be known as the Indian Corn Speech. In the course of it he said:

"I predict a great increase in the consumption of our corn by Great Britain over 60,000,000 bushels which it reached last year. It is the most natural and spontaneous of our cereal products. Our present crop ought to be 1,500,000,000 bushels against 300,000,000 of wheat. It is but little inferior to wheat in nutritive power. It costs less than one –half of the seaboard, and much less than one-half on the farm. It can be cooked, by those who consent to learn how, into many delicious forms of human food. Why should not British workmen have cheaper food? Why should not our farmers have a great market? Why should not our carriers have the transportation?

"Let us remember that commercial exchanges must have some element of mutuality. Whoever obstructs the means of payment obstructs also the facilities of sale. We must relax our barbarous revenue system so as not unnecessarily to retard the natural process of trade. We must no longer legislate again the wants of humanity and the benefi-cence of God. [Applause.]

He also referred to what he termed "the greatest political crime in our history" in impressive terms.

"In the canvass of 1876 the federal government embarked in the contest with unscrupulous activity. A member of the cabinet was the head of a partisan committee. Agents stood at the doors of the pay offices to exact contributions from official subordinates. The whole office-holding class were made to exhaust their power. Even the army, for the first time, to the disgust of the soldiers and many of the officers, was moved about the country as electioneering instrument. All this was done under the eye of the beneficiary of it, who was making the air vocal with professions of civil war reform, to be begun after he had himself exhausted all the immoral advantages of civil service abuses.

"The step from an extreme degree of corrupt abuses in the elections to a subversion of the elective system itself is natural. No sooner was the election over that the whole power of the office-holding class, led by a cabinet minister, was exerted to procure, and did procure, from the

State canvassers of two States, illegal and fraudulent certificates which were made a pretext for a false count of the electoral votes. To enable these officers to exercise the immoral courage necessary to the parts assigned to them and to relieve them from the timidity which God has implanted in the human bosom as a limit to a criminal audacity, detachments of the army were sent to afford them shelter.

"The expedients by which the votes of the electors chosen by the people of these two States were rejected, and the votes of the electors having the illegal and fraudulent certificates were counted, and the menaced enforcement of his pretended authority by the army and navy, the terrorism of the business classes, and the kindred measures by which false count was consummated, are known.

"The magnitude of a political crime must be measured by its natural and necessary consequences. Our great Republic has been the only example in the world of a regular and orderly transfer of governmental succession by the elective system. To destroy the habit of traditionary respect for the will of the people, as declared through the electoral forms, and to exhibit our institutions as a failure, is the greatest possible wrong to our own country. The American people will not condone it under any pretext or for any purpose.

"Young men, in the order of nature we who have guarded the sacred traditions of our free government will soon leave that work to you. Within the life of most who hear me our Republic will embrace a hundred millions of people. Whether its institutions shall be preserved in substance and in spirit, as well as in barren forms, and will continue to be a blessing to the toiling millions here and a good example to mankind, now everywhere seeking a larger share in the management of their own affairs, will depend on you.

"I avail myself of the occasion to thank you, and to thank all in our State and country who have accorded to me their support, not personal to myself, but for the cause I have represented, and which has embraced the largest and holiest interests of humanity."[1]

---

1 "Writings and Speeches," Vol II. P 486

The Tilden homestead, New Lebanon, NY.

CHAPTER V

The trials and temptations of a bachelor millionaire – Proposals of marriage in verse and prose.

MR. TILDEN'S political opponents gave an involuntary but unequivocal recognition of his singularly unassailable public and private character by their exaggeration of his wealth, and by their misrepresentations of the use he made of it. Failing to find any political doctrine that could be successfully challenged on moral grounds, or any personal infirmities or delinquencies upon which they could make a combined attack, they condescended to appeal to one of the basest sentiments of our unregenerate nature by making a party shibboleth of "old Tilden's barrel." This gave great notoriety to his wealth and a proportionate annoyance to himself, for every mail brought him proffers of assistance in distributing it, not only from all parts of his own country, but, not infrequently, from foreign lands.

Of the number and variety of these communications only men of large wealth are apt to have any idea, nor they, unless their stores have had the factitious advertising which the Republican press and touters gave to Mr. Tilden's accumulations. Churches wanted their debts paid; parents wanted children adopted, or educated, or established in business; debtors wanted their farms cleared of mortgages; unsuccessful speculators wished help to try their luck again; inventors appealed to him to buy an interest in their patents; mothers invited him to marry their daughters; gentle maidens of marriageable age asked for his photograph in exchange for their own, and the honor of a correspondence with him; cranks wished him to let them cure him; promoters wanted, some to have him join them in great mining enterprises, others in draining swamps, and others in cornering the timber of the country. The largest number of applications came from men and women wishing to market their political influence for his.

The late George Bancroft is reported to have said that his experience in teaching the Round Hill Academy at North Hampton removed whatever doubt he had ever entertained of the total depravity of human nature. But neither priest nor pedagogue are often, if ever, forced into such a disgusting familiarity with the morbid anatomy of human society as a notoriously wealthy and successful candidate for popular favor. In this respect Mr. Tilden's experience was unique, for he was the first candidate for the chief magistrate of the United States whose wealth was sufficient to attract public attention, and whose heart and hand were unappropriated. There were times when, had Mr. Tilden listened to all the appeals that were made to him, with all his wealth, he would have been a beggar at the end of any week. To comprehend the nature and extent of this species of annoyance, I will give a few specimens of such appeals as were made by post, and were most readily disposed of; though personal appeals were nearly numerous, and, unless made by absolute strangers, usually consumed more time and therefore proved more serious interruptions. The names and addresses of the writers are of course suppressed.

A Kentuckian, who, though blessed with a large family, thought he was poor, wrote:

"I am a poor man with a large family and am not able to bring them up as I would like. My three youngest are girls aged respectively about thirteen (13), ten (10), and eight (8) years old; I am anxious that they be decently brought up and respectably educated. How would you like to take charge of the education and rearing? And if you should be so disposed, I will give you full charge of them… I know this proposition sounds cruel and unparental, but, sir, it is my overpowering anxiety about them and their future that induces me to write to you."

One of the F. F. V's wrote:

"HONORED SIR: In these times of unusual exigency unusual expediency suggests itself, and the train runs not with extremity. Your own high and unquestionable position is such as to bear the light of a mid-day sun, but the same elevation weakens, sometimes, your best purposes by exposing to your adversary the very movement made with the best intent. To meet this emergency, do you not want a secret emissary who can go from point to point at a moments notice to convey and secure information – one who can accomplish diplomatic interviews without being suspected as your representative, and who can contrive movements without their being heralded to the reading and gossiping world? I am a woman old enough to be discreet, ugly enough not to be noticed, intelligent enough to sift, compare and reason wit enough to evade, wise enough to be silent, and ready enough to report, and if you can or will employ me in this official capacity, you will find me *faithful, trustworthy, and efficient.* I can give you the best reference in the city and in any part of the country, especially in the South. I am a Southern-born woman, familiar with all Southern born influences, especially acquainted with carpet-bag rule, having been a victim of their oppression in taxation. I am personally acquainted with politicians in both parties; and having the entrance to all circles, I have an advantage not usual. I have lived in a political atmosphere all my life, but have now no family ties to restrict my movements, or to give my confidence. My large landed estate in the South is now almost worthless ruins, owing to the working of the new régime; consequently I would seek employment of a remunerative kind – not extravagantly so, but sufficient to my simple needs. The employment I suggest would be congenial to my taste; and in peace or war I am sure that I can be useful. The times are portentous of discord; and if strife should prevail, such service as I could render I know will be in demand. If you will entertain the proposition, I will call to see you at any time. The very proposition *is a secret with myself,* and I hope you will respect it in any event. I only purpose to be in town a day or two."

A widow from Illinois, with four children, two boys and two girls, wrote:

"I cannot keep my children in school and give them food and clothing; therefore I write. I beg you to adopt one of my fatherless children, a boy thirteen year of age, the boy, change his name to Samuel J. Tilden, place him in one of the best schools, watch his progress in his studies, and your generosity shall be remembered for years and years. Please write me when you come or send to this city for the boy."

A hoosier from Indiana wrote:

"...If you will send me some money ill help you along with a grate many more votes as there is a grate maney around here that will sell there votes fore anything then if send; Express to Brownsville Union Co. Indiana."

Another hoosier, who may be presumed to have passed the early part of his life in the land o' cakes, wrote:
"i have written you three letters and i think you election is very dootful in the Western States i have traveled threw indiania Illinois, masura, iway cansas peter cooper and hayes and you name is scarcely mentien and you haf to do something soon or you air beet i can sell you twenty eighty hondred votse for eight hundred dolars myself if you air willen to hep you self i Will hep you i have pledge myself to the people that i Woold give four hundred dolars porvided you would give me four hondred dolars i think that is the best i cando for you now jus send me the for hundred dollars if you think best to do so and if you send it i Will use it fur your lection. if you send it you had better send it in a register letter they air all watching me at the expres ofis and Peter Cooper friends has ofered me thousand dolars to throw my influence to him and I wouldent noy axsept it."

A man who was not all proud wrote from Yankeetown:

"As you are a man that goes in the best and highest of society you must have a great many old clothes that is good but out of fashion and you cant ware them in High Society. i wish that you would send them to me as im have a hard time to git along and winter is adrawing neare...all the way that i can pay you is at the November election that is the ticket i have voted the last 20 years."

An assiduous member of a Tilden and Hendricks club wrote:

"I have been out every night and I am out of work and cannot get any. my shoes are all worn out carrying the Tilden banner and I cannot carry it any longer unless you will send me a new pair."

A Kentuckian who adds Rev. to his name, but whose early education had hardly been what is should have been for one of his profession, wrote:

" As i antisipate a Short tower through the mountains of Ky and should like to have from five to seven hundred dollars more than i have i will therefore ask you to send it to me forthwith By adams express and if i don't make a show of the same i will double the same five times. If convenient Send Silver fore it looks Quite pleasant all is Rite here. you shall hear from me Soon after the election. your. O.B.T.

A Pennsylvanian who was "anxious to free our government from a mass of corruption," and "is foreman of a factory of 37 men which are Republicans," wrote:

"I am prepared to buy their votes at $5 each. If you can remit me the required amount my influence is at your command and the rights of our country."

A Jersey patriot of a frugal mind, but trusting he was honest, and who believed in fighting fire with fire, knew "of over one hundred persons in Trenton who will vote for Hays because they will get 1 dollar a piece for doing so. there never was a time when such a little money could get so many votes. I am a poor man, yet I trust I am honest, yet, I cannot see ware it is wrong to give a man a dollar to vote for the one he wishes to get in when if he dose not do so, the other party will give him the money and get his vote."

"A friend and a brother" of a negro wrote:

"MR. TILDEN:

"SIR: I wish you to send mez as much as $5. to Buye Whiskey to get all the colored votes I can for you."

"A friend of the laboring man from New York writes that he "is president of a secret society which cast more than 13,000 votes in 1874, and almost 17,000 in 1875." He rebukes Mr. Tilden for not having responded to his application for $2,395.20 to save himself and party from defeat.

"Our votes," he says, "will be cast in view of resulting benefits to labor and to securing legislation in that direction rather than from the ordinary motives of party men. If in the end you and the party which has put up your nomination are defeated by us, you must remember that the work was entirely your own, and that we gave you a fair opportunity to have avoided that result."

A patriot from Minnesota wrote:

"I feel very confident that with $10,000 I can get seven thousand votes."

Another patriot from Ohio informs Mr. Tilden that two of the "electoral commissioners" are relations of his, one a school-mate, and all three Republicans; that he asked them privately what they would take to throw their influence for Mr. Tilden; that they answered him confidentially if he would give them $5,000 each they would give their vote all the time for his man. Mr. _____ proposes to give $5,000 out of his own pocket if Mr. Tilden would give the other $10,000 in greenbacks, not in checks, as they might create suspicion.

An editor writes that he publishes a religious paper in Virginia, which is burdened with debt of $500. "It did all a religious paper could do to promote Mr. Tilden's election."

A gentleman who had spent $100 on the election asks Mr. Tilden "to palliate his temporary difficulties with a remittance, which he promises to return in six months."

A New Yorker asks for the loan of some money with which to purchase bees from Brazil.

A modest mamma from Missouri named her third daughter, who was born in 1876, Maggie Tilden _____. "You would admire her, " she writes: "she is an interesting child and in possession of more than ordinary talent; and in order to cultivate her mind, I make a special request of you, and that is to make her a present. You will confer a very great favor upon on our little daughter. You are in possession of millions of dollars and would never miss, say $10,000; in fact any you may wish to give. You are a bachelor and should render assistance."

Another Missourian, a confederate, but with more zeal than discretion, says he met with a man in Douglass county who claimed that Hayes was elected President. The confederate claimed that Tilden was elected. The Douglass county man said, "The Republicans have had the reins of govt. too long in their hands to give it up to a Rebel like you. So," adds the confederate, "I giv him a billet of wood; he soon recovered and come at me for a tussel and the result was I left a blind man forever. "

"You can see from my picture which I send you in this letter, the condition my eyes are in. If you are willing to help me I would be very glad."

His statements were fortified by four certificates as to their truth, all apparently in the same handwriting.

A man from Alabama, of literary aspirations, desires to dramatize, "The Great Crime" by which Mr. Tilden was defrauded of the presidency and ask him, "if not too inconvenient" to furnish a history of the whole affair, as well as the names of the conspirators, for that purpose.

A political enthusiast wrote, "Fifty thousand dollars will carry the State of New York for Mr. Tilden," and asks to have the money sent "with a wrapper round it as you would a newspaper. roll up the ends."

A New Yorker, who admired a cheerful giver, wrote:

"If you would give of the millions of which God has made you the Steward, but two to the cause, New York and Victory would be ours, and Right would prevail... I have a right I repeat to ask this when one poor man draws $56. his all from the Savings Bank and sends it; when one family are going without tea and coffee for a year, to help that much to the right; when my sister and I give what was to have given us a long dreamed of pleasure-trip; when my bothers go to shabby and are pinched and poor but give far more than they can spare to help Hancock. I know you will give most freely but I want you to give as we poor people have, so as it will hurt. Can you see those pitiful sums published and still keep back that hand that is growing old and can hold what the Lord has given it bit a few years longer."

A Missourian damsel, whole moral development seemed to have hardly kept pace with her physical, having received a circular in regard to the Royal Havanna lottery, invites Mr. Tilden to procure one of the circulars, and see if there would be any chance for one of the prizes, and if so to select for her "a ticket that will be sure to draw a prize," and send it to her, and she will send him the money. She kindly adds; "If I draw a good prize they can use my name. It might be, if they knew my condition that they would sell you a ticket that they knew would draw a good prize."

Another Missourian informs Mr. Tilden that his "letter declining a renomination has been read by thousands in the West with sorrow," and that he has several valuable inventions in which he will give Mr. Tilden a half interest if he will aid him in putting them on the market.

A New Yorker "knows how the third party in the field could be withdrawn, and will meet Mr. T's agent to make a satisfactory arrangement. "

Another New Yorker asks Mr. Tilden to return to him the axe which he presented to him in the canvass of '76 that he might present it to General Hancock, as Mr. Tilden had retired to private life. The writer of this letter was notified that he could have the axe by calling for it.

"Joanne of Arc" sends Mr. Tilden a magic ring. "Put it on your finger immediately, and do not remove it. It conveys to you a healing power from God. When taking it from my finger I saw a bright star over it."

A West Virginia lady desires to open an acquaintance by correspondence; had three relatives in Congress, and "will patiently look forward with expectations of receiving a little 'billet-doux.'"

M.M., of Ohio, informs Mr. Tilden that with $1,500 or $2,000 he can secure the votes of 3,000 miners in his district.

A Republican from Ohio, having lost $1,000 through the failure of a friend, will give Mr. Tilden his influence this fall if he will accommodate him with a loan of $1,000.

Another Ohioan will work for Mr. Tilden if he will give him a land warrant for sixty acres of land.

A lumber man from Michigan wrote:

"SIR, If you want to doo anney thing in the pine woods of Michigan you will have to send some money. This stump speeking dos for some folks but not for the Boys in the whoods. They whant a more excitement then that. I have no money and we air all poor but we have a vote just the same. I can do more on the day of election with some monney then all the stumping your great men can do in a year."

Another man from Michigan informed Mr. Tilden that if he will be so kind as to give him a deed of a quarter section of land in the Northwest he will vote for him. "I have always voted Demicratic ticket; now, if you can't give that lot, I cant vote for you; but if you will give me the lot I will send you a certificate from the Co. Clerk that I cast my vote for you."

A Tennesseean informs Mr. Tilden that he is working hard for his election and would he be pleased to receive a suit of clothes as a birthday present.

A friend of Senator Voorhees, of Indiana, informs Mr. Tilden that the certainty of his being President of the United States is greatly due to the untiring determination of his friends, and therefore he says, "As I am very fond of a good horse and one that can trot some, I ask you to say you will present me with one of that kind after you are declared elected. To-morrow we make a *grand rally* to hear Hon. Daniel Vorrhees."

U.U.. of Missouri, says, I have bet everything I have in this world on your being elected. Beat thim if you can is my best wishes."

A New Yorker wrote:

"MR TILDEN, DEAR SIR, I thought I would Rite you to let you know How we are situated. On this Campain we have used up all our money in working for you and we Have mad promised that we can't foolfil on this campaign and hope that you Will Oblige us by sending us some money We want to use some on Musick Band and also we have promised sic cags of Bear after the closing of the Pols. Also other items that we want Paid this time also We Have Never asked anything of you before and am sorry to ask you know But the way we are fixed we cant Help it. We are doing all that Lays in Our Power for you in

Our town we Have Bought over Three Hundred persons On our side and we can more by working hard for them and Our money Has give out and we Hope that you will oblige us By sending us some. This is from _____ and _____ and also we are well know Through this county Rocklane.

"Please answer this soon as you receive this
            "With Out fail"

A fire-insurance agent wrote:

"TILDEN, Will you please give me your opinion as to your prospects for election? this state being pretty well supplied with Rads and some of them anxious to bet on Hayes. I want to make some paupers among them if there is a strong probability of your election. I need some of their money in my biz, and can get it, provided I will put up.

"Assuring you that I am an ardent supporter of yours, I hope you will write me an opinion."

A patriot form Ohio informs Mr. Tilden that

"what is needed now is not the speaking to influence public sentiment, but the almighty dollar to draw the mass of voters with us.

"In this free country it is not expected to carry the day, per-vim to drag men to the election house, but to persuade their minds, and this can be done with them by simply buying them. Send us money to the amount at least 2,000 and we will see what we can do.

A New York Republican, "but not a bigoted one," informs Mr. Tilden that he and nine of his comrades had always had always voted the Republicans ticket, but this year, he writes, "If you think worth while to buy our votes we will go Democratic - $50 apiece is the price. If you will send to my address before election $500 you will receive in return ten sound votes."

A laborer in Ohio, who thought he was worthy of his hire, wrote that:

"the lawyers and doctors get paid mighty big for making speeches and i think i can make votes as some of them and get nothing for it i think i ort to have something for my work i have worked every election yet and i never got anything i think i am working for a good cause and i would like to here from you i think i ort to have something."

Such are types of a class of letters which reached Mr. Tilden by every mail, from his own sex mostly. The imaginations of the other sex seem to have been equally, if not more, inflamed by the report of Mr. Tilden's great wealth, with neither wife nor chick to help him spend or enjoy it.

Mr. Tilden never married. His early associations and delicate health seem to have conspired together to dedicate him to the public service, which became the most constant and engrossing subject of his study and of his mediations from early youth to the very close of his life. He occasionally laid himself open to the suspicion of entertaining matrimonial intentions, by the frequency of his visits to houses where the attractions were such as to warrant such suspicions; but on the occasions of his visits he usually became so much absorbed in talking politics with the senior members of the family that the neglected juniors were apt to retire to rest long before their turn had come. He cared less for the society women than any gentleman possessed of anything like corresponding powers of entertainment I have ever known, and he never seemed to miss such companionship until during the later years of his life, when his infirmities had rendered him comparatively helpless. His sister, Mrs. Pelton, presided over his household until her granddaughter married, when he provided them with an elegant home in New York and an income suited to their needs and station. In his sister's place he invited two of his maiden nieces, daughters of his brother Henry, to live with him, which they continued to do until his death.

When Mr. Tilden was nominated for the presidency he was sixty-two years of age – a period if life when bachelors have generally abandoned all thoughts of matrimony. His wealth and rank and prospects, however, caused him to be regarded by the other sex more than ever in the light of matrimonial speculation. There were multitude of the daughters of Eve who would cheerfully and alas! in many instances might advantageously have accepted the hand and shared the society of a man of his wealth and position, to whatever extent he might be weighed down by age or infirmity. At least Tilden could hardly have failed to reach this conclusion. Nor will the reader be surprised if he did, when he reads a few of the letters which I proposed to cite as specimens of the weapons by which his domestic solitude was assailed.

A widow from Michigan wrote:

"DEAR SIR: I trust you will excuse me for writing to you, a stranger, but having been so greatly interested in your success a few years ago, I have so often thought of you since, that to me you seem more like a dear friend and acquaintance, though I have never had the pleasure of meeting you. I wish you (not your secretary) would write to me just once in answer to this request. I should like to make my home in New York or near there, in the capacity of book-keeper or private secretary, where, if agreeable to my employer, I could remain several years, having little ones to educate. I cannot marry again, but must work if I can. My little boy is bright little fellow of nine years. I wish him to enjoy the advantages of good schools and training. That he may have these with kind treatment, I have decided to remain single the rest of my life – though now but twenty-nine – that I may earn the means to accomplish this purpose. Now that I have confided to you my greatest wish, will you tell me of some one that is, or give me directions that will enable me to obtain permanent work of this kind in a place suitable for a lady? I cannot give references for competency, having never worked, but think I can prove it by trying. Can give best of reference in regards to respectability and honesty, and I will try to improve in writing."

A Virginian writes:

"I see from the 'Cincinnati Gazette' you are a bachelor and one most anxious to marry, and will give to your wife the amount of $500 in money per week. I write, not to make a proposition of marriage, but one which will no doubt meet with much greater favor in your kind and generous heart; which, if acceded to, will procure for you the love, not only of all the single ladies, but the love of all the married ladies as well, of _____congregation."

The way all this was to be accomplished was to give five or six hundred dollars of his pin-money to pay off the debts of the church. The writer adds:

"If you should visit ____I promise you shall see many of its fair beauties. You might gain the affection of some beauty for a wife, and you know the Virginia girls make noted wives."

A damsel from California writes, on a sheet illustrated with the portrait of a dove carrying a billet-doux in its mouth:

"MY DEAR SIR: Allthough in the past the pleasure and honor of your personal acquaintance have been denied to Mama and I, yet we have heard of your noble qualities of mind and heart, and I can assure you, Mr. Tilden, the only wish of my heart is to see you. I would highly appreciate your visit and warmly Thank you for it. The magnificent and beautiful residence which you have erected and which would be an ornament to any city in the world, so successfully brought to completion by means the most commendable, stand forth as enduring energy and indefatigable zeal will perpetuate your memory and transmit your name to generations to come.

"Mr. Tilden, in regard to my reputation would respectfully refer you to Bishop ____, Ex Governor ____ and Senator ___. Mr. Tilden, I would dearly love to be able to see you, though distance separated us; yet in my prayers I always think of you. Accept these slight expressions of regard, and be assured of our good wishes and Prayers that your years may be many Peaceful and happy. I cannot allow this Christmas to pass without wishing you a very merry Christmas and many Happy New Years. Hoping you will receive this with the same intention that I have intended, I shall feel grateful for any kindly consideration you may be pleased to accord to this, my letter. Accept this with my highest regards and everlasting friendship."

A young lady from Michigan pours forth her soul in verse. Her communication was accompanied with the photograph of a face of rare beauty.

"HON SIR:

"Inclosed please find a photograph
Of one who comes to make you laugh
For this is the year accorded by law
For 'maids to propose in, and 'baches' to jaw
And shoot the stout hearts of the Lords of Creation,
And claimed, in spite of money's sway,
The Democrats would gain the day,

"No, no,' I cried, 'it can't be true;
For during my life, one score and two,
There's not been a Democrat president;
But we've bent to Republicans quite content.'
And when it was said, 'In spite of pelf
Cleveland will get it,' I said to myself,
'If Cleveland get this fall's election,
I'll propose to S. Tilden and meet with rejection,'

"Wouldn't it be a joke to the nation?
Wouldn't it cause a great sensation?
When I think of it, sir, I almost wish
I had not set to fry so big a fish.
It is one thing to talk and another to do,
        And I almost lack courage to carry it through.
I live so much within myself,
That none would believe it, except yourself.

" I only can offer my heart and my hand.
A heart, none more tender in the land.
A hand that ne'er lifted itself to do wrong;
But has done all it could to help mankind along.
Only these, yet a man like yourself
Would look more to virtue than worldly pelf.
I refer you to any one here you may find,
Who will say aught about me, 'cept which is kind.

"I trust you, sir, as a Democrat,
That you'll not take advantage of that;
But my letter and picture will never show,

So no one but you and I shall know.
Now ponder well and study my face.
Can you not ever bit of my of my character trace?
Would it not be bliss, by you fireside
To claim it original as your bride?

"Sweet pleasure to me to be the wife
Of a noble man in the eve of his life,
All passions subdued, at peace with the world,
Obliged not to be into politics hurled.
Has not this life seemed vacant to you
With no loving wife, and no fond children too?
O what would you give, had you only a son
To bear your own name when your work here has been done?
This world indeed is bleak and drear,
If we have none to us most dear,
Whom we know love us for our very self,
And not what we have of paltry pelf."

"I hold the respect of all who know me: am a worthy graduate, and pride myself on my good character; so, though you would not get a wealthy bride, you would get one who care not for the world, who is not tainted with the vices of society, and whose whole soul will be wrapt up in the interests of her husband and home. I anxiously wait the issues of my strong fancy. Should you favor it, let me know, and I will send my right name, and any credentials you desire. If you decline, I trust you will send back my letter and picture, with your best wishes for a simple girl."

A Pennsylvania maiden wrote:

"MY DEAR SIR: I am making a silk quilt (where is the lady who is not?) and write to solicit a piece of you necktie. It matters not if it is plain and black (I fancy that's the kind you wear), so it comes from you.

"Each lady thinks her quilt, like each mother her baby, is the prettiest in existence. I am no exception to that rule. My aim is to make my quilt as rich in it's associations as I am trying to make it beautiful in design. This being my object, you will, I trust, excuse my request.

"I want a piece of your tie, not because you are a millionaire, not because you excelled as a corporation lawyer, not because you stand deservedly high as a political leader, nor yet because you were elected President of the United States, but because, though a bachelor, you have always, both in private (so I am informed) and in public utterances, paid woman the tribute she ought to have. A man who does that has a clean mind.

"I am, my dear sir, etc."

A lady of certain age proffers marriages, in a letter with a postage stamp enclosed, presumably to encourage a prompt and favorable reply.

"DEAR SIR: I take the liberty of addressing you on a delicate subject, though one of the utmost importance, as it engrosses the mid and attention of the majority of the human race, as some time, either in your youth, middle age, or later in life. This subject is matrimony. I think we may find, by observation, that marriages contracted later in life are often a source of greater happiness and usefulness than those entered into earlier in life. We know that it is the first advances, thought it merely a matter of custom, sanctioned by the usages of society. If it were the custom for ladies to make the first advances, it would seem just as perfectly right and proper for a true, virtuous woman to offer a proposition of marriage to an honorable man. There are many who have done this. For instance, we have the example of Queen Victoria, who proposed to Prince Albert, and lived a very happy matrimonial life. I suppose it will be necessary for me to give you a description of myself. I have dark brown hair and eyes, dark complexion, good features, am considered good-looking. Medium height, good form – neither thin nor too fleshy. Thirty-three years of age, though look much younger; am taken to be not over twenty-five. Am even-tempered, warm hearted, and affectionate. I am a lady of refinement and education. Am of a good family, and well connected. Have a sister, married to a lawyer in ____, whose father is one of the wealthiest men in ____. Also have a brother in ___, who is also a wealthy man in ____. I can give the best of references and letters of introduction from the most respected, influential citizens. I have had good offers of marriage, but prefer to choose my own husband. The young men have too many 'wild oats' to sow, and are apt to be unsettled. There are exceptions to this, as well as to every other rule. Still I would much rather marry an elderly gentleman, one who is true and honorable. I am naturally intelligent and well informed, especially in regard to politics and business matters. As a wife, I feel that I could be a great help to a husband, by making his interest my own, in regard to any thing or object he most desired to accomplish. As you are a gentleman in public life, I have heard and read so much about you that I have almost felt acquainted; at least have felt that you were perfectly upright and honorable; a gentleman in every sense of the word, and one who would be a loyal husband. I have felt that I could love such a character with a true devotion, so have thought that I would take advantage of leap year following Queen Victoria's example and say, 'Will you marry me?' Now a housekeeper, or relations, however desirable, cannot fill the place of a wife. And in sickness and old age, who will care for a husband so tenderly as a loving, devoted wife? The Bible says, 'It is not good for man to be alone,' and 'Whoso findeth a wife, findeth a good thing, and obtaineth favor of the Lord.' Now, in regard to myself, you do not need to take my word alone, but you have the privilege of becoming acquainted with me, and judging for yourself. As I wish to visit my sister in Chicago you can meet me there if you choose, or any other place you might name. And now I am perfectly sincere and in earnest about this matter. I submit this matter to you for your perusal and thoughtful attention. Hoping my suit will meet with favor, and a reply,

"I remain yours very respectfully."

A young lady from Indiana who weighs about one hundred and twenty-five pounds, and is a detester of dudes, wrote:

"DEAR SIR: You are, I've no doubt, surprised to get a letter from a village in the Hoosier State…

"As it is Leap Year, and the ladies have the privilege of proposing marriage, I have come to you. Unmaidenly; did I hear you say: Well, I suppose it is, but when I tell you it is *unsophisticated love* that prompts me to write this I hope for your forgiveness.

"Since quite a child I have been a great admirer of yours. During the time that you were candidate for President I was very anxious that you would be elected.

"I have never seen you, but having heard such glowing accounts of your generosity and good worth, how can I help but admire you? Please be generous to me and give me a favorable reply.

"I do not want a husband I cannot admire and be proud of; if there is any one thing I do detest it is a Dude. It has always been my ambition to marry some great statesman or a man of unusual intellect and culture. Now, my dear Mr. Tilden, will you be my husband? I assure you, you will never regret it, for I will do everything in my power to make you perfectly happy.

"You perhaps, would like to know who I am and what I am. My name is ____. I weigh about one hundred and twenty five pounds, have dark-blue eyes, fair complexion, and dark-brown hair. I suppose I am a brunette. I do not know exactly how tall I am, but a little below the medium height, and was twenty years old last March. Don't say too young for me: you know it is better to be petted by a young girl, that to be fussed at by an old woman, or worse, a society belle.

"If I had a photograph of myself I would send it to you, but if you get a good profile of ____, the actress, that will do as well, for everyone says I am her perfect facsimile. So if you are an admirer of ____that will be a great deal in my favor.

"My family are highly respectable. My Papa and Mama are both living and I am an only child.

If you are favorably impressed with this letter please let me know as soon as possible as it is a matter of great importance to me."

A young lady from Missouri asks for his hand and "pfotos."

"MY DEAR FRIEND: I send you a few lines as it affords me pleasure in doing so and at the same time hoping to find you enjoying the fruits of health and Happiness I am a young lady of twenty-two summers and hearing so much talk about you and to see if it is all true I thought I would write and see if it was as the parties stated will you please state if you ever engaged yourself to some St. Louis Belles and they refused you many think if very imprudent but they tell every body that and if it is not so I would let them know about it. Dear Sir, as I am an admirer of beautiful pictures will you please do me the honor of presenting me with on of your pfotos. as I am going to the store, I will bring this note to the Post Office. Hoping this will reach you and hoping to get an answer I remain,

"P.S. Direct my answer to the Post Office or to ___ Street, if directed to the P.O. the full name and if at ____the first name.

Yours Respect?

"Please answer as soon as possible.

"Were you a flower,
And I a bee;
A honied kiss
I'd steel from thee.
Fresh as the morn
Bright as the sun
To me you are
The sweetest one."

A staunch little Democrat from Georgia wrote:

"DEAR SIR: If you pardon the liberty I take in so addressing you, you will pardon one among many of human weaknesses.

"This letter is from one of the stanchest little democrats in dresses in the land. A southern girl, who during the eventful time of your candidacy for President, almost 'laid down her arms' and dug for you. I was but a child, and last year it so happened that I wrote for a juvenile paper here, in which I mentioned my 'wild eventful Tilden days,' which were much enjoyed.

"In my own heart today you are the same dear Mr. Tilden, who grew dearer to me, as I grew older, and read of your noble qualties.

"I was disappointed that you did not come south. Mr. Hendricks came, and I enjoyed a most delightful chat with him. He still has a sacred spot in all our hearts. I told him my love for Tilden and Hendricks; only ripened as they grew older.

"Ah well, I doubt your patience with girls, especially left handed ones, whose writing one cannot readily decipher.

"My request is simple. (Please give your Sec'ty a few moments recess) I only ask you to send me something that you consider trivial, for a souvenir of one I love and admire most dearly. I care not what it may be, so it belongs to you. Enclose within a word or two so that I may know my missive is not in vain.

"It's awful for a democrat to feel badly, and as I am such a persistent one, I shall feel like poor Blaine (?) if I do not hear from you. Trusting all reporters are at Salt Lake and cannot spy this

"Yours in all respect and sincerity."

A miss from Kentucky, with a red head, and weighing 136 pounds, wrote:

"MR. TILDEN: While sitting all alone this evening, having just written all my friends, I concluded to write to you. I heard that you said the first lady that addressed you, you would send her a present. I hope the present will be a photograph, as I would like to see it very much. Pap came from Virginia, and he has often told me what a clever man you was. I heard that you was a batchelor and intended to live a different life; I thought you ment a married life; I would like to correspond with you very much. I have fair complexion, black eyes, and a red head. I am18 years old, and I weigh 136 pounds.

"If my letter is accepted write me a answer in return. I am tired of writing so I will close by saying give my love to your sister.

"Remember me when far away and thinking of the past, remember I am a friend of yours that will last forever. Write soon."

A young lady from Illinois sent Mr. Tilden a proffer of marriage, with a lock of her hair and an eloquent analysis of her charms. She handed her letter to her younger sister to enclose in an envelope and post. The younger sister, thinking Mr. Tilden might perhaps prefer a younger bride – she was about nineteen, and the elder twenty-three – or prefer a lighter shade of hair, enclosed a lock of her own hair, with a note imparting her willingness to share his bed and board in case her sister could not.

Another had wrote that her parents had been unfortunate, had lost their money, and requested Mr. Tilden to send the $25,000 to reëstablish themselves.

Another, from North Carolina, sent a bedspread, the work of her own hands, and warranted to last thirty years.

Another, from Michigan, proposes he should adopt the child of a virtuous widow in the neighborhood, and marry her when she is fifteen years old. Meantime employing the mother at monthly wages, who is to die after four years of a broken heart.

Another, had heard of a generous wedding present Mr. Tilden had made one of her cousins, and wishes him to buy of her a silver salver and goblets to match, which, if she were wealthy, she not take $2,000 for, but which Mr. Tilden might have for $1,000. She adds:

"You go out of town ever summer. It would give me pleasure to invite you to spend three or four weeks or more with me, but I cannot afford it. If you will come and give me remuneration sufficient to cover expenses, I will do everything in my power to make your stay enjoyable. Shall I bring the silver salver to you or send it by express, C.O. D.?"

She proposes also to invite several young ladies to meet him if he visits her, and gives him a catalogue of their charms.

Mr. Tilden rarely paid any attention to missives of the character here cited – never unless he chanced to know something of the writer or her kindred. Those who called in person – as many did who had failed to get satisfactory responses to their communications – were pretty uniformly disappointed. The pleasure of receiving them was generally given to one of his clerks attendants. He had the least possible taste for gallantries with any class; but he was far too wise and prudent to give to any woman a pretext for speculating upon her intimacy with him.

The volume of this kind of predatory correspondence was almost incredible. That he passed through this epoch of peculiar temptation without provoking a breath of scandal was a distinction which, unfortunately, can be claimed for few men in public life of equal eminence, in this or any other country.

CHAPTER VI

MR. TILDEN did not realize all the advantages to his health from his European trip that he had hoped for. His adventures in crossing the English channel undid much of the very considerable benefit which he seemed to have derived from it. While his general condition was improved, he could not disguise from himself the fact that his tremulousness was increasing, that his vocal organs were losing their flexibility, and that his left arm and hand were less useful to him than when he left his home. Though his health had now become a somewhat more serious preoccupation than formerly, he did not yet regard it as entitled to interfere materially with his future plans or customary occupations. His renomination for the presidency in 1880 was regarded as a matter of course by both parties, not only because he was immeasurable the most capable and popular candidate his party could present, but because he was the only candidate his party could present, but because he was the only one candidate through whose election the nation could properly resent the wrong it had sustained at the hands of the Electoral Commission in 1877. He was now regarded by the administration, not only as a more formidable candidate than in 1876, but the consequences of his election now were regarded as

more alarming than in 1876, especially to those who had participated
in the frauds which put Hayes into the presidency. He was treated,
therefore, from the very beginning of the Hayes administration as the
one man in the nation who, at all hazards, must be destroyed. This
could not be accomplished by assailing his public life, his opinions,
or his public teachings. That had already been tried pretty faithfully
and had proved unsuccessful. A second attempt was certain to prove
even less successful. There was one course left. The Potter investigation had satisfied the nation that Hayes had not been elected by the
people, and that the majority of electors for him had been secured by
fraud. To this there was no longer any defence, not even the benefit of
a doubt. The only thing to do under those circumstances was, not to
attempt to justify the installation of Hayes, but to persist in efforts to
leave upon the public mind and impression which should stay there
until after the next election at least, that Tilden and his party were just
as bad as Hayes and his party, plus the risk of Tilden's being overruled
by his party, and that the people had nothing to gain by a change of
dynasty. As the administration had control of all the judicial, civil, and
military forces of the government, and necessarily exerted a prodigious
influence over all the organs of public opinion, this did not seem at
the time a hopeless endeavor.

It is no exaggeration to say that the administration used all these
forces with the energy and recklessness of despair.

I am aware that this is a grave allegation – quite too grave to rest
upon the unsupported *dictum* of any individual. I do not propose to
leave it thus unsupported, but to produce such evidence as will, I think,
bear conviction to any unprejudiced reader, that during the whole four
years of Hayes's administration, and regardless of Mr. Tilden's age, his
physical infirmities, his priceless public services, and the place which
he occupied in the hearts of his countrymen, he was pursued by the
agents of that administration with a cruelty, a vindictiveness, an insen-
sibility to all the promptings of Christian charity, which men are rarely
accustomed to exhibit except in their dealing with wild beasts.

Early in the month of October of 1878 a series of telegraphic
despatches in cipher, purporting to have been addressed to well-
known partisans of Mr. Tilden during the electoral crisis of November
and December, 1876, appeared with translations in the "New York
Tribune." These despatches conveyed the impression that persons

holding more or less familiar, not to say confidential, relations with Mr. Tilden had been entertaining propositions for the purchase of the electoral vote of one or more of the contested States. The fact that the votes of many of the electors were notoriously in the market at prices which would scarcely have been a month's income to Mr. Tilden, and that he needed but a single one of them to secure the presidency, helped to give currency to this abominable suspicion, which received additional aliment from the appearance of the name of his sister's son, who with his wife and child was a guest with her in Tilden's house at the time, among the alleged negotiators.

To show the motive which animated the parties through whose agency these despatches – legally as well as morally, in the strictest sense of the word, confidential – came to be public property, it is necessary to go back about two years and trace their history from the time their hallowed privacy was first violated, until they were spread out in the columns of an intensely partisan journal.

On the 23rd and 24th of January, 1877, certain telegraphic despatches relating to the election in Louisiana were delivered to a committee of the House of Representatives, of which Mr. Morrison, a Democrat, was chairman, and certain other telegraphic despatches relating to the election in Oregon were delivered to a committee of the Senate, of which Mr. Morton, a Republican, was chairman.

Pursuant to the direction of Mr. Sargent, chairman of the sub-committee of the Morton committee, on the 25th day of January, about thirty thousand telegraphic despatches, purporting to be all the reside of despatches relating to the election in the possession of the Western Union Telegraph Company, were delivered to Mr. Burbank, a brother-in-law of Mr. Morton, and also the clerk of his committee, or to his temporary substitute.

Mr. Orton, the president of the Western Union Company, whom Mr. Tilden did not hesitate to characterize as an unscrupulous Republican partisan, had previously permitted his party friends to withdraw some of the despatches, and appears to have facilitated the surrender of the rest to the control of the chairman of the Republican senatorial committee, thereby practically excluding everybody else from the privilege of inspecting them. The particular despatches, sent to Morrison committee, were returned. The other despatches were retained by the officers of the Morton committee until some time after the inauguration of Mr. Hayes, and were then, except such as in the meantime had been abstracted, returned to the telegraph company, and afterwards burned by its order.

Some of the despatches which had been abstracted were, more than a year afterwards, in the possession of one George Edward Bullock, of Indiana, who had been a messenger of the senatorial committee, and was a protégé of its chairman, Mr. Morton. This Mr. Bullock obtained from Mr. Hayes the appointment of consul at Cologne, upon the recommendation, among others, of Thomas J. Brady, of Indiana, the Second Assistant Postmaster-General, afterwards so notorious as the head of the fraudulent Star Route ring. Upon the eve of his departure, and after the appointment by the House of Representatives of the committee of investigation into the election frauds in Louisiana and Florida, of which Mr. Clarkson N. Potter was chairman, Mr. Bullock passed over to Mr. Brady – who, while Second Assistant Postmaster-General, had, with three special agents of the Post Office Department, attended the canvass in Florida, and must have been acquainted with everything done there – such of the abstracted despatches as had not been destroyed, and such others as they did not prefer to suppress.

The facts developed subsequently to the inauguration of Mr. Hayes – viz: 1st. The acknowledgment by the administration of Mr. Hayes that the Democratic State officers in Louisiana, Florida, and South Carolina had been legally elected, although In the two former States they received fewer votes than were given to the electoral ticket of Tilden and Hendrick's; 2d, The appointment by Mr. Hayes, to most important offices, of the members of the Returning Boards of Louisiana and Florida, and all of the persons who had been actors and instruments in the frauds perpetrated by those boards, including the two electors whose names were forged in the corrected electoral votes of Louisiana, and the persons who were privy to those foreign forgeries – led to a new investigation by a committee of the House of Representatives, of which Mr. Clarkson N. Potter, of New York, was chairman.

After this committee had been some six months pursuing its investigation, and had developed facts which carried conviction to the minds of fair men of all parties as to the gross nature of the frauds which were made the basis of a false count by the Electoral Commission, it was manifest that something had to be done, and at once, to counteract the moral effect upon the country of these disclosures. The publication of some and the suppression of the rest of these despatches proved to be the only weapon within their reach and ignominious and lawless as they knew such a violation of private correspondence to be, they did not shrink from resorting to it.

The despatches that were published show, what was confirmed by the uncontradicted testimony of the witnesses examined before the Potter committee, that unequivocal offers were made by persons representing, with every appearance of authority, the Returning Board of South Carolina, and a majority of the State canvassers of Florida, to give the Democratic candidates for presidential electors, official certificates that they were duly appointed, for money considerations to be paid after the delivery of such certificates. It was proved that the agent of the South Carolina Returning Board, after his offer was rejected, went to the city of New York to repeat and press his offer, and stayed there several days in the vain endeavor to have his offer accepted. It was also proved, by unimpeachable testimony, that the offer in behalf of certain of the State canvassers of Florida as repeatedly made through various persons. It was further proved that similar offers in behalf of the Returning Board of Louisiana were made to Mr. Hewitt, chairman of the National Democratic Committee, and to others. These offers were prefaced by statements that, if not accepted, pending transactions with the Republicans would be consummated, although involving more risk, because in that case the certificates would be contrary to truth.

All the power of the Hayes administration, vainly struggling to justify it own existence, and all its means of influencing the press, were exerted to create a suspicion against Mr. Tilden that in some instance he had entertained or given countenance, directly or indirectly, to such negotiations.

These efforts totally failed. They were not only destitute of the slightest foundation, but they were so contradicted by every intrinsic probability as to be absurd. Besides, they were disproved by the concurrent testimony of every witness who was examined. Their only pretext was, that the South Carolina and Florida offers had been communicated to one of the nephews of Mr. Tilden, though the fact had been kept secret from Mr. Tilden.

How far that gentleman was led into this indiscretion by a desire to learn the tactics of the adversary, or to gain time and means to prove and to defeat their strategy when it should be completely developed, or to secure the opportunity of submitting the matter to members of the Democratic National Committee, whenever it should assume a definite form, does not clearly appear. It is certain, however, that he took no second step, and all negotiations of this character were rejected and abandoned.

The great controlling fact stands, that none of these offers were accepted, nor their conditions complied with, by any of Mr. Tilden's friends, nor were the certificates of any of the Returning Boards or State canvassers given to the Democratic electors, to whom they rightfully belonged. On the other hand, those certificates were all given to the Republican electors, although at the expense of numerous frauds in the canvasses, false authentications by the governors of three States, and the forging of the signatures of two electors.

Whether for these felonious transactions bribes in money were paid according to the offers which the actors in them professed to have received, has not been proved. But that bribes in the more effectual form of appointments to lucrative offices were actually given to all the felons is now a matter of authentic history. Mr. Potter, in his report, made the following sagacious remarks: "If a man be bribed by a sum down, he may lose it or waste it, and then the control it gave him will be gone. But in an office which he holds at the pleasure of the person who appointed him, he is under continuing control."

When the first publication was made, about October 7, I went to see Mr. Tilden. I found him very much affected. He was very indignant that the existence of such compromising communications should have been kept from him so long. He begged me to stay with him a few days. He was completely overcome than I had ever seen him before.

He regarded these despatches as I did, as the reply of the administration at Washington to the Potter investigation. It having been established by the Potter committee to the conviction of the whole nation that Hayes was not elected, the administration, instead of continuing the defence of Hayes' title, determined to show, if they could, that Tilden was bad enough to have been elected by the same means that Hayes had been. Fortunately, the facts that were no longer in dispute protected Tilden's character.

1) Only one vote was required to elect Tilden. It was in proof that the votes of three States were in the market, and at a price which would have been but a trifle to Tilden.

2) Tilden did not get that vote. Nor was there a particle of evidence that any money was ever furnished to any one by Tilden, or any one else on his account, to secure the one needed vote.

3) Hayes needed all the votes of the three States. All were for sale. Hayes got them all and was elected, and within six months after his inauguration every person known to have been concerned in securing or giving those notes, from the highest to the lowest, received an office or an offer of one.

The position in which Mr. Tilden found himself placed by the publication of these telegrams subjected him to the humiliating necessity, for the first time in his life, of making a public defence of his personal character. He lost no time in preparing and sending the following statement to the press:

"New York, Oct. 16, 1878.

"TO THE EDITOR OF THE HERALD:'

"SIR: I have read the publications in the 'Tribune' of the 8th instant, purporting to be translations of cipher telegrams relating to the canvass of votes in Florida at the presidential election of 1876, and have looked over those printed in the 'Tribune' of this morning relating to the canvass in South Carolina. I have no knowledge of the existence of these telegrams, nor any information about them, except what has been derived from or since the publications of the 'Tribune.'"

"So much for these telegrams generally. I shall speak yet more specifically as to some of them.

"1. Those which relate to an offer purporting to have been made in behalf of some member of the State Board of Canvassers of Florida, to give, for a pecuniary compensation, certificates to the Democratic electors who had been actually chosen.

"None of these telegrams, nor any telegram communicating such an offer, or answering such an offer, or relating to such an offer, was seen by me, translated to me, or the contents of it in any manner made known to me. I had no knowledge of the existence or purport of any telegram relating to that subject. Nor did I learn the fact that such and offer of Florida certificates had been made until long after the 6th of December, at which time the certificates were delivered and the electoral votes cast; and when the information casually reached me, as of a past event, it was accompanied by the statement that the offer had been rejected.

"2. As to the publications in the 'Tribune' of this morning, purporting to be translations of cipher telegrams relating to the canvass of votes in South Carolina in 1876, which I have seen since I wrote the foregoing, I can speak of them no less definitely and positively. No one of such telegrams, either in cipher or translated, was ever shown to or its contents made known to me. No offer or negotiation in behalf of the State canvassers of South Carolina, or any of them, or any dealing with any of them in respect to the certificates to the electors, was ever authorized or sanctioned in any manner by me directly or through any other person.

"I will add that no offer to give the certificates of any returning board or State canvassers of any State to Democratic electors in consideration of office or money or property; no negotiation of that nature in behalf of any member of such board or with any such member; no attempt to influence the action of any elector of President and Vice-President by such motives – was ever entertained, considered, or tolerated by me or by anybody within my influence by my consent, or with my knowledge or acquiescence. No such contemplated transaction could at any time have come within the range of my power without that power being instantly exerted to crush it out.

"A belief was doubtless current that certificates from the State of Florida, conforming to the actual vote of the people were in the market. 'I have not the slightest doubt in the world,' said Mr. Saltonstall, who was in Florida at the time, in a recent interview with the 'Herald' correspondent,' that that [Florida] vote could have been bought, if Mr. Tilden had been dishonorable enough to desire it done, for a great deal less than fifty thousand dollars or twenty thousand dollars.' It was known that either one of the two members who composed a majority of the Florida State canvassers could control its action and give the certificates to the Democrats. Either one of them could settle the presidential controversy in favor of the Democratic candidates, who lacked but one vote.

"How accessible to venal inducements they were, is shown by the testimony of McLin, the chairman of the Board of State Canvassers, in his examination, before the Potter committee in June last. He admitted that the true vote of the people of Florida was in favor of the Democratic electors, and that the fact even appeared on the face of the county returns, including among them the true return from Baker county, notwithstanding the great frauds against the Democrats in some of the county returns. He also confessed that in voting to give the certificates to the Republican electors he acted under the influence of promises that he should be rewarded in case, 'Mr. Hayes became President;' adding that 'certainly these promises must have had a strong control over my judgment and action.'

"After the certificates of the Louisiana Returning Board had been repeatedly offered to Mr. Hewitt and others for money, they were given in favor of the Republican electors, who had been rejected by a large majority of the voters; and the members of this Returning Board now possess the most important federal offices in that State. The pregnant fact always remains that none of these corrupt boards gave their certificates to the Democratic electors, but they all did give them to the Republican electors.

"I had perfectly fixed the purpose, from which I never deviated in a word or act – a purpose which was known to or assumed by all with whom I was in habitual communication – if the presidency of the United States was to be disposed of by certificates to be won from corrupt returning boards by any form of venal inducements, whether of offices or money, I was resolved to take no part in the shameful competition, and I took none.

"The main interest of the victory which resulted in my election was the expectation that through the chief magistracy a system of reforms, similar to that which had been accomplished in our metropolis and in our State administration, would be achieved in the federal government. For this object it was necessary that I should be untrammeled by any commitment in the choice of men to execute the official trusts of the government, and untrammeled by any obligations to special interests. I had been nominated and I was elected without one limitation of my perfect independence. To have surrendered or compromised the advantages of this position by a degrading competition for returning-board certificates would have been to abandon all that made victory desirable, everything which could have sustained me in the larger struggle that victory would have imposed upon me. I was resolved to go into the presidential chair in full command of all my resources for usefulness, or not at all.

"While thus abstaining from an ignominious competition for such certificates, I saw these certificates obtained for the Republican electors, who had not been chosen by the people. These false and fraudulent certificates, now confessed and proved to have been obtained by corrupt inducements, were afterward made the pretexts for taking from the people their rightful choice for the presidency and vice presidency. These certificates were declared by the tribunal to which Congress had abdicated the function of deciding the count of disputed electoral votes to be the absolute and indisputable conveyance of title to the chief magistracy of the nation.

"The State of Florida, which had united all her executive, legislative, and judicial powers to testify to Congress, long before the count, who were the genuine agents, which had by statue caused a re-canvass, the issue of new certificates, and a formal sovereign authentication of the right of the true electors to deposit the votes entitled to be counted, was held to be incapable of communicating to Congress a fact which everybody then knew and which cannot now be disputed.

"Congress, though vested by the Constitution with the authority to count the electoral votes; though unrestricted either as to time when it should receive evidence, or as to the nature of that evidence; and though subject to no appeal from its decision – was declared to have no power to guide its own count by any information it could obtain, or by any authority which it might accept from the wronged and betrayed State whose vote was about to be falsified.

"The monstrous conclusion was thus reached that the act of one man, holding the deciding vote in a board of State canvassers (for without his concurrence the frauds of the other ruling boards would have failed), in giving certificates known at the time, and now by himself confessed to have been obtained by the promise of office – certificates whose character was known months before Congress could begin the count – must prevail over all the remedies powers of the State of Florida and of the Congress of the United States combined, and must dispose of the chief magistracy of this Republic.

"S. J. Tilden."

Not content with this formal disavowal of any knowledge or partici-pation in any negotiations for the exercise of any improper influence over the Returning Boards, Mr. Tilden addressed a sub-committee of the Potter committee, then sitting in New York, the following note:

"15 Gramercy Park, Feb. 7, 1879.

'TO THE CHAIRMAN OF THE CONGRESSIONAL COMMITTEE:
"DEAR SIR: I learn from the public press that it is the desire of your committee to terminate its session in this city during the current week. I take the liberty of requesting that before you leave an opportunity be permitted me to appear before you to submit some testimony which I deem pertinent to the inquiry with which you are charged.
"Very respectfully,
"S. J. Tilden."

The sub-committee consisted of Hunton, of Virginia, the chairman; Springer, of Illinois, Stenger, of Pennsylvania; Hiscock, of New York; and Reed, of Maine – the first three Democrats and the last two Republicans. On Saturday, the 9th of February, by special arrangement Mr. Tilden appeared before the committee.

It was a fearful ordeal. He was very feeble. His voice was scarcely audible above a whisper. By the treachery of political foes and the folly of political allies he had been suddenly cast down from a popular eminence rarely attained by any American, to the degrading abyss of a quarter sessions criminal, with the popular sentiment of the nation more or less infected by the poisonous breath of hostile partisan press. The situation was enough to have paralyzed and crushed a man of less nerve, less conscious of his ability to demonstrate the factious motives which had placed him in that position, and with less conscious of his ability to demonstrate the factious motives which had placed him in that position, and with less faith than his in the ultimate triumph of innocence and justice. The audience chamber was crowded almost to suffocation. Since the examination of Dr. Franklin by the Privy Council in London, in 1774, there has been no public hearing, I believe, in which there have been such vast and grave interests at stake upon the testimony of a single individual. The occasion was one of unusual impressiveness, especially when the cross-examination commenced. It soon became apparent that the Republican examiners were in the hands of their master. Before they had finished, Tilden had changed places with them, and put them on the stand in defence of the administration. The following graphic account of the scene appeared in the "New York Herald' of the following morning:

"At half-past eleven o'clock Mr. Tilden appeared, in company with his brother, Henry A. Tilden, and ex-Secretary of State Bigelow. Mr. Tilden was dressed in black, and had an air of great solemnity on his face, which looked as imperturbable and sphinx-like as ever. Since his last public appearance he seemed to have aged considerably, and yesterday he looked quite ill and feeble. As he afterward explained, he was suffering from a severe cold. It was, indeed, quite a painful spectacle to see the slow, halting, lame walk with which he passed the table and reached his seat. His figure was stiffly drawn up and seemed incapable of bending, as though he were suffering from a paralytic contraction of the limbs. As he entered, every eye was curiously turned upon him. Not a muscle of his face relaxed with animation or expression as he stiffly extended his hand to Mr. Reed, of Maine, who received the salutation with something like a profound bow. Then Mr. Tilden gave his hand to Mr. Hiscock, the other Republican cross-examiner, and after saluting the Democratic members took off his elegant, silk-lined overcoat, stiffly turned round and seated himself at the table, while settling at the same time a large handkerchief in his break pocket.

"Ex-Governor Tilden sat erect in his chair for over two hours and a half, and during the greater portion of this time he gave his testimony in that calm, quiet imperturbable manner peculiar to him, and without hardly moving a muscle or changing the expression of his countenance. His voice, which was hoarse, started very feebly, almost inaudibly. But as Mr. Tilden came to the corrupt negotiations alluded to in the cipher despatches, his hoarse voice rose suddenly to a pitch of loudness, vehemence, and dramatic intensity hardly ever observed in the ex-Governor during the most exciting periods of his life. During these portions of Mr. Tilden's evidence there was a flush of deep feeling over his face, and the mental excitement had such mastery over him that his lips twitched, and one of his hands, said to be smitten with paralysis, trembled in a most painful manner.

"And when Governor Tilden dramatically called on heaven and earth to witness the protestation of his innocence of all knowledge of the ciphers, bringing his clenched fist heavily down upon the table, there was a sympathizing outburst of applause. There was only one relieving glimpse of humor during the entire examination lasting over two hours and a half; namely when Mr. Reed, of Maine, questioned him about 'corrupt attempts,' and the Governor returned dryly, 'Attempts to sell or buy, which?' at which there was some laughter. When the cross-examination had been concluded Governor Tilden held quite a whispered conversation with Mr. Hiscock. The moment Tilden withdrew, which he did in the same slow, halting, imperturbable manner in which he entered, the interest of the day seem to have ended, and the audience thinned out within a few minutes."

The official report of his examination was as follows:

TESTIMONY OF MR. TILDEN BEFORE A SELECT COMMITTEE OF CONGRESS IN RELATION TO THE CIPHER DESPATCHES.

"After Mr. Tilden had been sworn, the chairman of the committee said: Governor Tilden, we received your note requesting permission to appear before this committee and testify. And we shall be glad to hear anything you have to say upon the subject of these cipher telegrams, subject to cross-examination when you are through.

"MR. TILDEN – I have not had an opportunity to see the lithographic copies of the cipher telegrams.

"THE CHAIRMAN – Will you be kind enough, Governor Tilden, to speak a little louder?

"THE WITNESS (AKA GOVERNOR TILDEN) – If you will excuse me, I have a slight cold; but I will speak as loud as I can. Upon publication of the cipher telegrams in the 'New York Tribune' – those relating to South Carolina, on the 16th of October, 1878; those relating to Florida on the 8th of October, 1878 – I read those translations; I did not recognize among them a single one that I had ever seen in cipher or translation, or the contents of which had in any way been made known to me. With respect to those of them that relate to negotiations to induce members of the Canvassing Boards of South Carolina and Florida to give the Democratic electors their certificates, I swear positively that I never saw one of those telegrams, either in cipher or translation the contents of no one of them, nor the purport of any one of them, was communicated to me in any manner whatever.

"I had no knowledge, no information, no suspicion that such a correspondence, had existed until their publication was announced in the 'New York Tribune,' followed by the publication a few days later. No offer, no negotiation in behalf of any member of the Returning Board of South Carolina, of the Board of State Canvassers of Florida, or of any State, was ever entertained by me or by my authority or with my sanction; no negotiations with them, no dealing with them, no dealing with any one of them was ever authorized or sanctioned by me in any manner whatsoever.

"The first information I ever received that any such negotiation had ever existed between any Democrat and any member of the Board of State Canvassers of South Carolina to give their certificates to the Democratic electors was on the 20th day of November, 1876. I am not able to fix that day positively by my own recollection, but I fix it by circumstances. It was the day that Colonel Pelton was in Baltimore. I remember the fact, and fix the date from the circumstances that have appeared during this investigation. On the morning of the 20th of November, 1876, Mrs. Colonel Pelton mentioned in my presence that her husband had gone to Philadelphia. It was a casual mention. I did not know that he was going to leave the city, or that he had left the city until she mentioned it; and her mention of it was so casual as not to attract any attention. A little later in the morning –

"THE CHAIRMAN – Do you mean Philadelphia?

"THE WITNESS – Philadelphia. A little later in the same morning I was called on by the treasurer of the National Democratic Committee, Mr. Edward Cooper, apparently on his way down town. He told me that Colonel Pelton was in Baltimore. He told me that Colonel Pelton had received, or was receiving, an offer in behalf of somebody representing, or claiming to represent, the canvassers of the State of South Carolina to give their certificate to the Democratic electors for a sum of money. I immediately said that no such offer should be entertained; that no negotiations of that nature should be tolerated; that not a cent of money should be furnished for any such purpose; and that Colonel Pelton must be immediately telegraphed to return to New York.

"I did not at that time know that Mr. Smith M. Weed had gone to South Carolina, or that he was there, or that he had been there at any time. I had not seen him after the election, and had no information of his whereabouts at that time.

"The conversation with Mr. Cooper was very brief. The whole matter was disposed of within five to ten minutes. I made no inquiry into details, and there was no discussion between us. Mr. Cooper concurred with me entirely in the measures to be taken; and although I took it for granted that he would make every necessary communication on that subject, I did not leave it to that. I obtained from him Colonel Pelton's address in Baltimore, and caused him to be immediately telegraphed to in a peremptory manner to return to New York. My dispatch was in ordinary language. I had no cipher; I could not read a cipher; I could not translate into a cipher. It never occurred to me that there was any reason for any concealment. My belief is that the dispatch as sent in my own name. I think it was sent within ten minutes after Mr. Cooper's communication to me. Colonel Pelton returned that night to New York.

"With respect to Florida, I never saw any one of the Florida telegrams either in cipher or in translation. The contents of no one of them, so far as I know, were ever communicated to me – I mean the telegrams relating to this subject; and I do not think that the contents of those relating to the course of the controversy down there were communicated to me. I am not able, in looking them over, to recall any one of them that I have ever seen. I did not know – I was not informed – that there had been any offer from anybody claiming to represent the Florida board or any member of it to give their certificates to the Democratic electors, until after the certificates had been delivered and a vote of the electors deposited for transmission to Washington.

"My first information on the subject was subsequent to that – after the 6th day of December, 1876. Some time after Mr. Marble returned – I do not know when, whether it was before I went to England or not – he mentioned to me one day, as a bygone affair, that the vote of Florida was offered, or rather the certificates that would yield us the vote; but he said that the offer had been declined. Some time last summer, about the time that the letter of Mr. Marble on the Electoral Commission appeared, I made a remark about the matter – I spoke to Colonel Pelton about this offer from Florida,. He answered in a single sentence, that all offers had been declined. That is all the knowledge I had on the subject until the publication of these despatches.

"With respect to Oregon, I never saw any one of those despatches. I now refer to despatches that are contained in the 'Tribune' Extra, No. 44.

"MR. SPRINGER – This pamphlet?

"GOVERNOR TILDEN – Yes, sir. I never saw any one of those despatches in cipher or translation. The substance of no one of them was ever communicated to me, except a despatch from Governor Grover stating that he would give the certificate to the Democratic electors. The substance of that despatch was communicated to me by somebody. I did not know that it came in cipher until after it appeared in the examination by Mr. Morton's committee; and in what form that communication was made, I cannot now state, but I was aware of the fact.

"Some of the telegrams appear to have been addressed to Colonel Pelton at No. 15 Gramercy park, which is my residence. I asked one of my young men to look them over and tell me how many there were. I think he told me there were fifteen of the Florida despatches so addressed, chiefly sent from Mr. Marble. So far as I know or believe, none of those despatches were ever delivered to my house.

"MR. STENGER – Do you say chiefly sent to Mr. Marble?

"THE CHAIRMAN – He's says chiefly sent from Mr. Marble.

"THE WITNESS – Chiefly sent by Mr. Marble. So far as I know, none of these were ever delivered at my house. Colonel Pelton's habits and hours and my own were entirely different. I was still Governor of New York, and had many executive duties to perform. I was burdened by the daily reception of people coming from all parts of the United States. From three to five hours a day were, I think usually devoted to these receptions by me. Colonel Pelton seldom came into the house until after I had been long in bed. He was very busy at the committee-rooms, and I saw very little of him. I think if any considerable number of telegrams had come to the house, I should have found it out in some way. I do not believe that any of these cipher telegrams ever came into my house. At any rate, they never met my eye or came within my knowledge.

"Now, one word as to the gentleman who went to the South, to the disputed States, to watch and guard the canvass in behalf of the Democratic party. That measure originated with either Mr. Hewitt or General Grant. Within a day or two after the election, I think, General Grant wrote a letter in which he proposed such an expedient. Mr. Hewitt either had started it before, or embraced it immediately after. I did not select or send the gentleman who went to those States. With few exceptions, they were not selected or sent after consultation with me. I did not attempt to supervise their action. I did not communicate with them. In no instance during the whole of that time did I ever communicate, directly or indirectly, with any gentleman who was in the South on that business; I never received any communication from any of them, except one, signed by Mr. Randall, Mr. Ottendorfer, Mr. Larmar, and Mr. Watterson, suggesting that some kind of a proposition should be made by me to Mr. Hayes. I never answered that despatch except verbally to Mr. Ottendorfer, after he returned and called on me. I was very busy all that time. I took it for granted that these gentlemen understood their business, and I did not undertake to direct them. The idea that they were my personal agents in any sense has no foundation in fact. They were representatives and delegates of the Democratic party, chosen generally by its organization. No man, so far as I know, ever went to any of those States with any commission, authority, or any contemplation to do anything that a gentleman ought not to do, or to do anything but defend the interests of the Democratic party, and to watch and guard those interests against apprehended fraud.

"During the whole time, from the 7th day of November, 1876 which was the day of the election, until the 6th day of December the same year, which was the day on which the electors met and deposited their votes for transmission to Washington, I maintained a uniform attitude. My purpose was under no circumstances to enter any competition to obtain votes, the certificates of the Canvassing Boards of the disputed States, even those to which I believed we were entitled, except by discussion, argument, reason, truth, justice. There never was a time- not a moment, not and instant – in which I ever entertained any idea of seeking to obtain those certificates by any venal inducements, any promise of money or of office to men who had them to grant or dispose of. My purpose on that subject was perfectly distinct, invariable; and it was generally assumed by all my friends without discussion. It may have been sometimes expressed, and whenever the slightest occasion arose for it to be discussed it was expressed. It was never deviated from in word or act.

"To the people who, as I believe, elected me President of the United States, to the four millions and a quarter of citizens who gave me their suffrages, I owed duty, service, and every honorable sacrifice; but not a surrender of one jot or tittle of my sense of right or personal self-respect.

"Whatever disappointment to those who voted for me; whatever the public consequences of suffering a subversion of the elective system, by which alone free government – self-government –can be carried on; by whatever casuistry, a different course might have been advocated or defended – I was resolved that if there was to be an auction of the chief magistracy of my country, I would not be among the bidders. [Applause]

"THE CHAIRMAN – The room will be cleared if this applause does not cease. It is expressly understood that there is to be no manifestation of approbation or disapprobation on either side.

"THE WITNESS (continuing) – I was determined in such an event, or in the apprehension of such an event, that I would meet such a degraded condition of public affairs, not by sharing it in any degree, not by acquiescence, not by toleration, but by an unqualified and perpetual protest, appealing to the people to reassert and reëstablish their great right – the greatest of their rights, the right without which all others are worthless – their right to elective self-government. I have done so.

"*The Cross-examination.*

"THE CHAIRMAN (to Messrs. Reed and Hiscock) – Will you ask Governor Tilden any questions?

"The cross examination was begun by Mr. Reed.

"MR. REED – Governor Tilden, who was your private secretary at the time of these transactions?

"TILDEN – George Smith. Do you mean my private secretary personally or as governor?

"MR. REED – Personally.

"TILDEN – George W. Smith.

"MR. REED – I find among these telegrams in the 'Tribune' one. No. 40, addressed to George W. Smith, No. 15 Grammercy park, in the cipher which was used in these incriminating despatches. It relates to a suggestion in regard to Oregon, and was transmitted by Mr. Manton

Marble to George W. Smith, No. 15 Gramercy park. Did you ever see that despatch?

"TILDEN – I do remember having seen it.

"MR. REED – Have you any impression in regard to it – whether you did receive it or not? Will you kindly look at the translation of the original?

"TILDEN – I have no doubt Mr. Smith can tell. He is here. He has been summoned by the committee.

"MR. REED – Well sir, can you?

"TILDEN – I have no recollection of it.

"MR. REED – None whatever?

"TILDEN – (reading) 'The Governor suggested' –

"MR. REED – The translation follows it. Will you look over the translation and see if that recalls to your mind having received that despatch?

"TILDEN – Mr. Smith may have shown it to me. He will no doubt tell himself; I have no recollection of it.

"MR. REED – Doesn't that suggestion in it about O'Conor's opinion recall anything to your mind?

"TILDEN – I do not remember that Mr. O'Conor was ever applied to for an opinion on that subject.

"MR. REED – Or that any suggestion was made that Mr. O'Conor's opinion should be obtained on the subject.

"TILDEN – I do not remember; it might have been made.

"MR. REED – You have read these various publications in reference to these despatches?

"TILDEN – I read them immediately on their publication.

"MR. REED – Do you recollect one despatch in this same cipher from Louisiana which began, 'Bigler to Russia,' and was translated Bigler to Tilden – do you recollect that?

"TILDEN – I do not remember it.

"MR. REED – Do you remember that which was also sent to George W. Smith, your private secretary – do you remember if that despatch was submitted to you?

"TILDEN – I should think it likely that if Mr. Smith received the despatch; he would have submitted it to me.

"MR. REED – He was your private secretary, and if he had received either of these despatches, it would have been his duty to submit them to you?

"TILDEN – I think so.

"MR. REED – Have you any doubt that he did?

"TILDEN – He was my personal secretary.

"MR. REED – Your personal secretary, precisely; that is what I mean.

"TILDEN – Mr. Charles Sebbens was my secretary as governor.

"MR. REED – It would have been Mr. Smith's duty to have submitted then to you. Have you any doubt that he did submit them?

"TILDEN – I do not know anything about the existence of such a despatch; I have no recollection about it.

"MR. REED – It would seem Governor Tilden, that your personal secretary had this cipher. Do you know whether he did or did not have it, of your own knowledge?

"MR. TILDEN – I do not think that he did have it.

"MR. REED – How then, were these despatches translated if he not have the cipher.

"MR. TILDEN – He may not have been able to translate them. He may have had to get somebody else to do it.

"MR. REED – What do you know about this cipher?

"TILDEN – I do not know anything about it.

"MR. REED – You never had it?

"TILDEN – I never had it.

"MR. REED – And you do not know what it was?

"TILDEN – I could not have put any message into cipher if I had tried; I could not have got any one out of it.

"MR. REED – I am merely suggesting that these despatches seem to indicate that your personal private secretary had this same cipher which has been used in this incriminating despatches in order to give you an opportunity to state any facts in connection with them which will throw light upon that circumstance which seems to be indicated by these despatches. Have you any facts with which you can assist us?

"TILDEN – He is here. He has been summoned by the committee.

"MR. REED – Well, I want to know whether you ever knew that he had it?

"TILDEN – I do not think he had the cipher at all – the cipher that was used at the Everett House. [1]

"MR. REED – When Colonel Pelton returned from Baltimore, did you have an interview with him?

"TILDEN – I suppose I did.

"MR. REED – Do you recollect whether you did or not?

"TILDEN – No doubt I did.

"MR. REED – Will you be kind enough to state what that interview was?

"TILDEN – I cannot recall it in detail. I have no doubt I expressed impatience.

"MR. REED – Will you give your best recollection as to the substance of that interview? Of course I am not expecting you to repeat words, because none of us can do that; but will you give us the substance of what you said to him, and what he said to you?

"TILDEN – I do not think he said anything to me. I think it was a mere outburst of impatience and displeasure that he had had anything to do with the Baltimore transaction.

"MR. REED – To which he made no reply?

"TILDEN – I think he made no reply.

"MR. SPRINGER – I did not hear what you said Mr. Tilden.

"TILDEN – I said my impression was that it was a mere outburst of displeasure and impatience on my part that he had anything to do with the transaction.

"MR. REED – You knew, Governor Tilden, the position which Colonel Pelton occupied in relation to the Democratic National Committee?

"TILDEN – I suppose so; yes, sir.

"MR. REED – You knew he was acting secretary, and that these telegrams in large numbers were coming to him, did you not?

"TILDEN – I knew that a great many telegrams were coming to him.

"MR. REED – He was residing then at your house?

"TILDEN – He was.

---

1 NOTE: Mr. George Smith afterwards testified that he never received this despatch; that he never knew of its existence, or anything about it, except that he had seem it in publication in the hands of the committee, and in the regular issue of the "New York Tribune."

"MR. REED – Did you, after this Baltimore transaction came to your knowledge, make any effort or suggestion that he should be removed from the position in which you knew he was?

"TILDEN – I don't think I did.

"MR. REED – Why not?

"TILDEN – In the first place, I did not know of the Baltimore transaction, except to the extent, that he had been receiving an offer there. I did not know that he had made any negotiations or given any encouragement. I did not acquire any knowledge that these despatches had passed backward and forward until their publication. In the conversation with Mr. Cooper I did not acquire any information on the subject, except in a general way. I thought the best way to deal with the thing was to stop it; and I did stop it, and stopped it effectually. I did not believe it possible that any such transactions could be afterward renewed. Besides, I knew that Colonel Pelton had no power. He was sometimes called acting secretary, but he had command of no money. He had no actual power; he was not able to do anything without the concurrence of other men. I did not imagine he would attempt to do anything of the sort again.

"MR. REED- Did not the fact that he had once attempted to do it give you an idea that he would be likely to do it again?

"TILDEN – I did not suppose that he had attempted to do anything; I simply supposed he had received an offer.

"MR. REED – Will you be kind enough to give us the conversation you had with Mr. Edward Cooper, as nearly as you can recall it?

"TILDEN – I have given it to you in a general way.

"MR. REED – I should like to press the question. I should like to have it as fully as you can give it; and if you will be kind enough to put it in the form of what he said, and what you said, I shall be obliged.

"TILDEN – The conversation with Mr. Cooper did not occupy more than five or ten minutes.

"MR. REED – Did he begin the conversation?

"TILDEN – He began the conversation.

"MR. REED – What did he say? Or if you cannot give that, what was the substance of his opening remark?

"TILDEN – He communicated to me the fact that Colonel Pelton was in Baltimore; the fact that Colonel Pelton was receiving an offer of this nature.

"MR. REED – Did he tell you the amount of the proposition?

"TILDEN – I think he probably gave it.

"MR. REED – Did he tell you the he had received a telegram from Colonel Pelton asking for money?

"TILDEN – I do not know whether he told me that or not; he may have done so.

"MR. REED – What further conversation took place?

"TILDEN – The substance of the conversation was that Pelton was in Baltimore, and that the certificates of the canvassers of the State of South Carolina were offered, and that he was down there doing something – dealing with them, or looking into it in some way.

"MR. REED – Did he tell you anything about Colonel Pelton's having cautioned him not to tell you?

"TILDEN – No.

"MR. REED – Nothing of that sort was mentioned.

"TILDEN – No, he did not mention that he had seen him the night before.

"MR. REED – Where were you the night before?

"TILDEN – I don't remember.

"MR. REED – Do you remember whether you were in New York or not?

"TILDEN – I think I was; I did not know that Colonel Pelton was going away.

"MR. REED – When did you next hear of corrupt attempts, after this, in any of the States?

"TILDEN – What do you mean by corrupt attempts?

"MR. REED – I mean these corrupt transactions that are depicted here.

"TILDEN: Do you mean attempts to sell, or attempts to buy?

"MR. REED – Both, Governor, or either.

"TILDEN – I never heard of any attempt on the part of our people to buy; the atmosphere was full of rumors.

"MR. REED – Have you not read these Smith-Weed despatches, and the whole account which your nephew gives them? And after that do you say that you never heard of any attempt to buy? Do you mean to say that?

"TILDEN – I mean to say that I did not hear at that time.

"MR. REED – Will you say that you have never heard of any attempts to buy?

"TILDEN – I meant up to the time of the publication of these despatches.

"MR. REED – But since then you have heard of it?

"TILDEN – I regard those as attempts to sell rather than attempts to buy.

"MR. REED – It is a distinction which you, of course, have a right to make. With regard to these attempts to sell, when did you first hear of corrupt attempts to sell, subsequent to this Baltimore transaction?

"TILDEN – I cannot say; the atmosphere was full of rumors.

"MR. REED – At what time did you become conscious of this full-ness of the atmosphere, Governor Tilden?

"TILDEN – There were rumors at the investigation before Field's committee about cases of that kind. I met, last summer, a gentleman in the cars-

"MR. REED- Well, I am not after this. I think I expressed it clearly – these criminal attempts either to buy or sell, which are mentioned here in the "Tribune' Extra; when did you first hear of them after the Baltimore experience?

"TILDEN – I did not hear anything more about Baltimore or about South Carolina. That was the end of that. I did not hear anything about Florida till after the vote was given.

"MR. REED – Who first told you of the Florida performance? I will use a neutral term.

"TILDEN – I cannot remember; I first heard of if after the gentleman that went to Florida had returned.

"MR. REED – Did Mr. Marble tell you?

"TILDEN – Mr. Marble told me some time; I think it was later.

"MR. REED – Are you aware that Mr. Marble has testified that he never told you of it?

"MR. STENGER – He cannot be aware of that because Mr. Marble did not so testify.

"MR. REED – I understood him so.

"MR. STENGER – I think you are mistaken.

"MR. TILDEN – I said I do not know whether it was before I went to England or not. Mr. Marble mentioned to me, some time, that the certificate of Florida was offered.

"MR. REED – Was it before what is called the 'Ark and Shekinah' letter?

"TILDEN – Yes, sir.

"MR. REED – Did he tell you the particulars of the transmission of those despatches?

"TILDEN – He did not.

"MR. REED – Did he make any talk to you about this being a danger-signal that he transmitted?

"TILDEN – He did not.

"MR. REED- He never alluded to it in those words or anything like it?

"TILDEN – He merely mentioned the circumstance.

"MR. REED – How did he mention it?

"TILDEN – He mentioned it as a past transaction.

"MR. REED – In what terms, as nearly as you can recollect? Will you give us the conversation?

"TILDEN – He said the Florida certificates were for sale. I did not inquire into the particulars, for several reasons. In the first place, it was long past, and he mentioned it like any other fact in bygone history.

"MR. REED – He did not give you details, and you did not ask for them?

"TILDEN – I did not make any inquiry.

"MR. REED – Did you make any inquiries of your nephew as to the particulars of this South Carolina matter?

"TILDEN – I did not.

"MR. REED – Why not?

"TILDEN – I did not think it was necessary.

"MR. REED – Did you not feel any interest in it?

"TILDEN – I only felt an interest in stopping it.

"MR. REED – Then you did not regard that as a danger-signal?

"TILDEN – Regard what as a danger signal?

"MR. REED – The transmission of the propositions in any way?

"TILDEN – Are you speaking of South Carolina?

"MR. REED – Yes, sir.

"MR. SPRINGER – Mr. Marble's despatch was with reference to Florida.

"TILDEN – I do not know what you mean by danger-signals.

"MR. REED – Would it occur to you that the transmission of a proposition to sell would be a danger signal?

"TILDEN – I should think that a man who had the power to sell, and made the proposition, wanted to sell.

"MR. REED – And the man who transmitted it would transmit it rather for the purpose of purchase than as a danger-signal?

"TILDEN – That would depend on the motives of the man who transmitted it.

"MR. REED – Colonel Pelton is a nephew of yours?

"TILDEN – Yes, sir.

"MR. REED – When did he first begin to reside in your house?

"TILDEN – About nine years ago, I think.

"MR. REED – When did he cease his residence there?

"TILDEN – About the 1st of July.

"MR. REED – He had been your military secretary while you were governor, and was at the time of these transactions your military secretary?

"TILDEN – He was.

"MR. REED – And with your knowledge and consent was the acting secretary of the Democratic National Committee?

"TILDEN – He was not with my consent, though he was with my knowledge.

"MR. REED – You knew it?

"TILDEN – I knew he called himself acting secretary.

"MR. REED – You knew he was really acting secretary?

"TILDEN – I knew he was very active in the business.

"MR. REED – And that he was really acting secretary?

"TILDEN – I came down from Albany in the latter part – the third or fourth week – of September. The canvass was two-thirds completed while I was in Albany. When I came down here I found Colonel Pelton acting as secretary.

"MR. REED – Did you make any objection to his acting as secretary?

"TILDEN – I did.

"MR. REED – To whom?

"TILDEN – To several gentlemen of the committee.

"MR. REED – Will you kindly name them?

"TILDEN – I cannot now.

"MR. REED – Cannot you name any of them?

"TILDEN – No

"MR. REED – Did you make any objection to him, and request him to cease acting in that capacity?

"TILDEN – I did not request him to cease, but I was not pleased with it, for several reasons.

"MR. REED – Did you manifest your displeasure to him?

"TILDEN – I manifested my regret.

"MR. REED- To whom?

"TILDEN – To him.

"MR. REED – What did he say?

"TILDEN – I cannot tell you.

"MR. REED – But you did not go to the extent of insisting on his ceasing to act in that capacity?

"TILDEN – I did not. I have no hesitation in stating to you all about it.

"MR. REED – Of course I cannot go into the whole matter; I only want to go into certain aspects of it. Did you know Mr. Smith M. Weed?

"TILDEN – Yes, sir.

"MR. REED –How long have you known him?

"TILDEN – I cannot say; some years.

"MR. REED – Has he been in confidential relations with you?

"TILDEN – No more than many prominent Democrats.

"MR. REED – But as much as other prominent Democrats?

"TILDEN – As much as some and less than others.

"MR. REED – When did you first know he was in South Carolina?

"TILDEN – Not till after he came back.

"MR. REED – Was it concealed from you?

"TILDEN – I do not know. No, I guess not.

"MR. REED – How did it happen that you did not know he was there?

"TILDEN – Because I did not undertake to know all that was being done by the committee.

"MR. REED – Did you not undertake to keep the general run of it, and of what was going on in the South?

"TILDEN – Not a very close run.

"MR. REED- Well, you undertook to keep the run of it, didn't you?

"TILDEN – When the legal proceedings in Florida were in agitation I gave particular attention to them. I did not undertake to keep much run of these visiting statesmen.

"MR. REED – Not even to know their names?

"TILDEN – I knew their names when I heard them through the public journals.

"MR. REED – And you say now you knew nothing of Mr. Smith Weed's presence in South Carolina until after his return?

"TILDEN – I say so positively.

"MR. REED – Did you have any talk with Mr. Weed about his transmittal of this proposition?

"TILDEN – I presume I did.

"MR. REED – Well, sir, state it.

"TILDEN – In which I took him to task for taking part in such transactions? I did not feel particularly responsible for Mr. Weed.

"MR. REED – At the time was the Oregon affair published, Governor Tilden?

"TILDEN – Published as the result of an investigation by a subcommittee of the Senate.

"MR. REED – About what time?

"TILDEN – I cannot tell you the date.

"MR. REED – About what time? Tell as nearly as you can.

"TILDEN – In the winter of 1877.

"MR. REED – Mr. Pelton remained in your house during that time until July, after the publication of the Oregon despatches.

"TILDEN – He did.

"MR. REED – Mr. Manton Marble occupied confidential relations with you, didn't he?

"TILDEN – He occupied relations with me which to a certain extent were confidential.

"MR. REED – He stopped to bid you good-by before he started to Florida. Do you remember that interview?

"TILDEN – I recollect seeing him before he went to Florida.

"MR. REED – What transpired at the interview?

"TILDEN – Nothing more than leave-taking. I gave him no instructions as to what he should do – no suggestions.

"MR. REED – You say you did not keep a very close run, and did not pay much attention to what the visiting statesmen were doing there, if I understand you right, in South Carolina and Florida. Do I?

"TILDEN – Yes.

"MR. REED – Did you have any purpose in not doing that?

"TILDEN – I had not; I supposed they had been selected by the committee of the Democratic party to do a particular duty, and were competent to do it, and I did not undertake to supervise or direct them. I did not give any human being any advice or instructions in that connection.

"MR. REED – Did Mr. Edward Cooper, when he told you of that South Carolina proposition, inform you that he had given your nephew any encouragement that he would furnish the money?

"TILDEN – He did not.

"MR. REED – Did he make any suggestion of any kind which conveyed that idea in any way to your mind?

"TILDEN – He did not. As I before said, the conversation was very brief. It opened by a mere statement of facts, and I responded so quickly that there was no chance for any discussion. I was irritated at the idea of Pelton mixing himself up in any such transaction. If I had felt disposed to engage in such a transaction, Pelton would have been the last man in the United States that I would have commissioned to have anything to do with it, or allowed to have anything to do with it. I considered his interference to be a piece of officious meddling.

"MR. REED – You published a card on or about October 18, relating to these despatches, did you not?

"TILDEN – I did.

"MR. REED – In that card you made no allusion to these particulars of your knowledge of the transaction which failed at Baltimore, did you?

"TILDEN – I did not.

"MR. REED – Why not?

"TILDEN – There was no occasion to do it.

"MR. REED – I ask the question – why you did not state in this card of explanation to the public, the particulars that you did know of this Baltimore transaction?

"TILDEN – Because it was not pertinent to what I was stating.

"MR. REED – In one paragraph in the letter you say, 'I have no knowledge of the existence of these telegrams, nor any information about them, except what has been derived from or since the publications of the "Tribune."'

"TILDEN – That is true.

"MR. REED – Yes, sir; but were you not aware at the time that that would convey, and did you not intend it to convey, the impression to the public that you knew nothing about these transactions until the publication of the despatches in the 'Tribune'?

"TILDEN – I did not intend to convey anything of the kind.

"MR. REED – Do not you see that it does convey that?

"TILDEN – No; I do not.

"MR. REED- I mean to a reader who does not know as much as you do?

"TILDEN – Read the phraseology, and you will find it as I say.

"MR. REED – I have no knowledge of the existence of these telegrams, nor any information about them, except what has been derived from or since the publications of the "Tribune."' That is literally true you say?

"TILDEN – Certainly.

"MR. REED – You say it is literally true; but don't you see that it conveys, and did you not intend it to convey, to the public, at the time, the impression that you knew absolutely nothing about the transactions themselves?

"TILDEN – No; I did not.

"MR. REED – You at least concealed the fact, or at least you did not make public the fact, that you had information with regard to the transactions themselves?

"TILDEN – Will you be good enough to read the next sentence?

"MR. REED – So much of these telegrams generally' – but then you proceed to speak of Florida; I am confining myself to the South Carolina ones. You can see the letter; I want to be perfectly frank with you.

"TILDEN – You will observe that the two States of Florida and South Carolina are treated separately for this publication. The paragraph immediately following deals in detail with South Carolina.

"MR. REED – Oh, no; it deals with the Board of Canvassers of Florida.

"TILDEN – No; it deals with South Carolina.

"MR. REED – It does in the copy I have.

"TILDEN – Read the next paragraph under 'secondly.'

"MR. REED – Very well, I will call your attention to that. You say; 'Secondly, as to the publications in the "Tribune" purporting to be translations of cipher telegrams relating to the canvass of votes in South Carolina, I can speak of them no less definitely and positively. None of such telegrams, either in cipher or translated, was ever shown to me, or its contents made known to me.' There you confine your denial that you knew anything about it to the telegrams, and do not deny the fact that you knew of the transaction.

"TILDEN – Well?

"MR. REED – Well, now, does it not strike you, and did it not at the time, that that was calculated to convey to the public the impression that you not only knew nothing of the telegrams, and their contents as such, but also that you knew nothing of the transaction?

"TILDEN – No.

"MR. REED – Will you look at it and see if that would not be the natural conclusion from that?

"TILDEN – The question was what I knew about these telegrams. I knew nothing about them.

"MR. REED – Was not the ultimate question what you knew about the transaction?

"TILDEN – That was a separate question.

"MR. REED – Was not the question which you were replying to before the public?

"TILDEN – I will deal with that in a moment. If you observe, my language is different in the case of South Carolina, and of Florida.

"MR. REED – But it is a difference that one would not notice until after this discussion?

"TILDEN – I cannot help your understanding of the language. The language is used with perfect accuracy and perfect truth. The proposition was this: I could not say I knew nothing about any negotiation in South Carolina, for I knew very little. I knew nothing that was contained in any of these telegrams; I knew no details of any of these negotiations; but I did know there had been an offer, and I knew the offer had been refused through my intervention. That is all I knew. I did not know that there had any further negotiations that to receive the offer and finally to refuse it. I did not know that there had been any offer in Florida; so the language of the statement had to be different.

"MR. REED – That is, you were avoiding a misstatement on account of certain facts which you knew, and which at the same time you knew the public did not know. Isn't that true?

"TILDEN – Certainly.

"MR. REED – And so you made your denial in such shape and form that it would avoid this fact when it became known, did you?

"TILDEN – I made my denial-

"MR. REED – (Interrupting) Consistent with this fact when it should become known?

"TILDEN – Strictly consistent with the truth.

"MR. REED – But you say, 'No one of such telegrams, either in cipher or translated, as ever shown to me, or its contents made known to me.' Were you not conscious, then, at that time that that matter which you were explaining to the public was not the telegrams after all, but the negotiations?

"TILDEN – I cover that in my next sentence.

"MR. REED – But you don't cover it in this?

"TILDEN – I did not do everything in one sentence. Be good enough to read the next sentence.

"MR. REED – Yes, I am very familiar with it. Why did you, Governor Tilden, when you came to make this answer to the public, say frankly that you knew of the transaction, so far as you did know of it, and that you then stamped it out instead of using language, which, as you see, might convey to the public the impression that you not only knew nothing about the telegrams, but nothing about the transaction itself?

"TILDEN – I do not see anything of the kind. On the contrary, any intelligent man understands the English language would understand that.

"MR. REED – In the light of the present testimony, do you mean?

"TILDEN – Without reference to that.

"MR. REED- Would anybody infer from this letter that you had any information with regard to the transaction at all.

"TILDEN – No man would infer that I had no knowledge of the offers. There might have been a thousand offers made without my knowledge.

"MR. REED – Did you intend to convey the impression that no offers had been made to you?

"TILDEN – I did not; I intended to avoid that assumption.

"MR. REED – Then why did you not frankly state what was the fact?

"TILDEN – Because, if there had been a hundred men talking to me about such transactions, suggesting and advising them, I was under no obligation, and had no occasion, to state it to the public.

"MR. REED – But there were not a hundred men; there was one particular transaction to which your attention had been directed by the 'Tribune' disclosure. Why did not you mention that one transaction? If you intended to deal frankly with the public, why did you not mention that one transaction?

"TILDEN – I had not seen any of these parties, and did not know whether the despatches were true or not. I did not know anything about them. When I drew this card I had not seen a human being with regard to them. I had not seen Mr. Weed; I had not seen Mr. Pelton. I was not going to inculpate them on subjects which I did not know anything about.

"MR. REED – But at that time you did not know that Mr. Pelton had gone to Baltimore to engage in a transaction of that kind?

"TILDEN – I did not say that.

"MR. REED – Why did you conceal from the public your knowledge of that fact?

"TILDEN – I knew only that Mr. Pelton had gone there to receive a proposition.

"MR. REED – Why did you keep that fact from the public? That would not incriminate anybody except those whom you knew deserved to be incriminated.

"TILDEN – I did not know that.

"MR. REED – Why did you not state that?

"TILDEN – It was not necessary; it was not pertinent.

"MR. REED – Was it not necessary for the information of the community? You undertook to inform the community as to what you knew about this matter. Now, undertaking to inform them by sitting down and writing that letter on the subject, how did it happen that you omitted this fact, of which you knew? That is what I want to get at.

"TILDEN – Because that fact was not pertinent to my discussion.

"MR. REED – Was it not pertinent to the information which you were giving to the public as to your knowledge of this subject?

"TILDEN – It was not pertinent to the things I undertook to the state.

"MR. REED – That is, among the things you undertook to state this was not?

"TILDEN – No.

"MR. REED – You say that the transaction of the Board of Canvassers to Florida was mentioned to you casually, as a past event, accompanied by the statement that the offer had been rejected.

"TILDEN – Yes.

"MR. REED – By whom was that made?

"TILDEN – By Mr. Marble.

"MR. REED – Why did you not, in your card, inform the public who stated that to you?

"TILDEN – It was not necessary.

"MR. REED – Did the non-necessity of withholding that information arise from the fact that on the face of those despatches Mr. Marble was very severely incriminated, and your own statement that he had mentioned it to you would tend to confirm the public impression of that transaction?

"TILDEN – Not at least; I should not have hesitated to put his name in.

"MR. REED – You cannot state why you did not?

"TILDEN – No.

"MR. REED – Why was it omitted? It looks to me as if it had been studiously omitted. What have you to say with regard to that?

"TILDEN – It was not.

"MR. REED – You did not keep it out on purpose, or in furtherance of any design that you then had in your own mind?

"TILDEN – No.

"MR. REED – Nor did you keep out this Baltimore transaction in furtherance of any design that you had in your own mind?

"TILDEN – The Baltimore transaction stands on a different basis, and it was not consummated.

"MR. REED- That you did intentionally keep it out?

"TILDEN – I did not intentionally keep it out; I had no intention of putting it in.

"MR. REED – Did you not very carefully draw these sentences so as to avoid coming in conflict with that fact after it came out, if it should come out?

"TIDLEN – No; I drew these sentences very carefully so as to conform the exact truth.

"MR. REED – Not only to the exact truth so far as the public knew it, but also to the exact truth so far as you knew it?

"TILDEN – Yes.

"MR. REED – Did you have any interview with Mr. Weed before he left for South Carolina?

"TILDEN – I did not; I never saw him after the election until after he got back from South Carolina.

"MR. REED – Do you remember having an interview with him at any bank?

"TILDEN – I do not.

"MR. REED – Nor any conversation with him at any bank?

"TILDEN – I do not.

"MR. REED – Do you recollect the bank that was named in connection with the Oregon affair?

"TILDEN – The Third National?

"MR. REED – I think that is it; Mr. Jordon's bank; the bank that kindly advanced, on the suggestion of Colonel Pelton, or of somebody else, eight thousand dollars for legitimate legal expenses in Oregon. Did you have an interview with him at that bank?

"TILDEN – I do not think I did; I do not remember any.

"MR. REED – Can you tell us whether you did or did not?

"TILDEN – You mean at what time?

"MR. REED – With Mr. Smith Weed, prior to his departure to Florida after the election.

"TILDEN – I do not think I did.

"MR. REED – Can you not put it any stronger than that you do not think you did?

"TILDEN – I do not believe that I did.

"MR. REED – Don't you know whether you did or did not? Be frank with us.

"TILDEN – I am perfectly frank with you, sir; I have no recollection or belief of any such interview.

"MR. REED – Did you ever see him there?

"TILDEN – I do not recollect; I may have seen him there.

"MR. REED – Do I understand you to say that you have no recollection, distinct and positive, of meeting him there at any particular time?

"TILDEN – I do not remember meeting him there at any particular time.

"MR. REED – Do you remember meeting him there at all, at any time?

"TILDEN – I have no distinct recollection of it, though very possible I may have met him there at some time.

"MR. REED – Did you not have a long conversation with him prior to his departure for Florida, at the Third National Bank?

"TILDEN – Florida?

"MR. REED – North Carolina or South Carolina?

"TILDEN – I don't think I did.

"MR. REED – Can you not state it more positively than that?

"TILDEN – I feel sure that I did not see him at all.

"MR. REED – You feel sure that you did not see him and did not have the conversation with him to which I alluded?

"TILDEN – Yes.

"MR. REED – Did I understand you to say that as to Florida you did not know that there had been an offer?

"TILDEN – Until after the 6th of December.

"MR. REED – About what time was it that Mr. Marble communicated this fact to you?

"TILDEN – I cannot state definitely.

"MR. REED – But I understood you to say that it was before the publication of his 'Ark and Shekinah' letter?

"TILDEN – Yes.

"MR. REED – Did Mr. Marble consult you with regard to the publication of that celebrated piece of rhetoric?

"TILDEN – He probably talked to me on the subject.

"MR. REED – Did he read to you any of the sentences in it?

"TILDEN – I think very likely he may have done so.

"MR. REED – The publication was with your assent?

"TILDEN – Not with my assent, nor with my disapproval.

"MR. REED – Did you make any comments, after your knowledge of the Baltimore transaction, that it was rather a harsh sort of letter for him to write?

"TILDEN – I did not.

"MR. REED – Nor any suggestion that there was anything hypocritical about it?

"TILDEN – No, sir; there was not, so far as I knew.

"MR. REED – You had not arrived at that full knowledge which you possess since the publication of the 'Tribune' despatches?

"TILDEN – No.

"MR. HISCOCK – Do I understand you to say that you saw the telegram to George W. Smith, dated November 27, from Tallahassee?

"TILDEN – I do not remember anything about it.

"MR. REED – Have you any doubt that you did see it, it having been addressed to your private secretary at Gramercy park?

"TILDEN – I do not know that any such telegram existed or was ever received; I don't remember anything about it.

"MR. HISCOCK – Do you remember the contents of it as it has been read to you here by Mr. Reed?

"TILDEN – I remember seeing it here.

"MR. HISCOCK – (reading) – It has been suggested from here to Governor of Oregon to refrain from issuing certificate in favor of ineligible elector until advised thereon. Why not obtain and telegraph him O'Conor's opinion? See my despatch to Spain. Have you no recollections of seeing that at all?

"TILDEN – I have not; I may have seen it.

"MR. HISCOCK – Have you any doubt that a despatch of that kind addressed to your private secretary, was shown to you?

"TILDEN – I think if he had received it he probably showed it to me.

"MR. HISCOCK – In that despatch occurs this phrase: 'See my despatch to Spain.' If you saw that despatch, would not the phrase have attracted your attention?

"TILDEN – It might.

"MR. HISCOCK – Have you any doubt that it would?

"TILDEN – It may have done so.

"MR. HISCOCK – I ask you whether the phrase in that despatch, 'See my despatch to Spain,' would not have attracted your attention?

"TILDEN – Perhaps it would, and perhaps it would not.

"MR. HISCOCK – You felt intensely interested over the result in Florida?

"TILDEN – I felt interested, of course; not intensely.

"MR. HISCOCK – You felt interested as a presidential candidate and as the representative of your party, did you not?

"TILDEN – I did.

"MR. HISCOCK – And you were watching the proceedings in those States with very great interest?

"TILDEN – I was watching the proceedings with a certain amount of interest.

"MR. HISCOCK – Do I infer from that that you were watching the proceedings with indifference?

"TILDEN – Not absolute indifference.

"MR. HISCOCK – Did not you keep yourself advised, so far as you were able, as to the steps that were being taken there?

"TILDEN – I did not occupy myself about things which I knew I could not control.

"MR. HISCOCK – Were you not sufficiently interested to keep yourself advised as to what was going on and the steps that were being taken there?

"TILDEN – Not very fully.

"MR. HISCOCK- If a despatch were shown you containing the phrase, 'See my despatch to Spain,' would not the very language of the phrase and the words that were employed in connection with it, one of them being a cipher word, have attracted your attention?

"TILDEN – It might have done so.

"MR. HISCOCK – And especially a despatch of that kind, coming from such a discreet, trusted, and influential member of the party as Manton Marble. Have you any doubt that it would have attracted your attention, coming from him?

"TILDEN – I do not think it all certain I should have paid much attention to it.

"MR. HISCOCK – Now, preceding that despatch and the one to which it must refer is this despatch; 'You are imperiling result here by causing divided counsels and neglecting to answer telegrams. I advise that you find one person to trust, and then trust him for at least one calendar week – possibly two. I will stand in nobody's way, and do my best to transfer to him authority. About one hundred majority on certified copies; Republicans claim same upon returns. Rome needless now; should be recalled."

"TILDEN – Whom does Rome mean?

"MR. HISCOCK – I do not know.

"TILDEN – You ought to know.

"MR. HISCOCK - - continues to read; Rome needless now; should be recalled. Parris and detectives always useless; ditto Wooley, here as in Louisiana a nuisance and impediment, trusted by nobody. I decline to commit Tilden with men so indiscreet. Smith concurs in all aforesaid. Session begun. To Tilden, 'have you recollection of having ever seen that despatch?

"TILDEN – I know that I never did.

"MR. HISCOCK – Have you at any time during the progress of the contest in Florida understood that upon certified copies of the returns the Democrats had, or that you had, one hundred majority for your election?

"TILDEN – A Ninety-three or ninety-five.

"MR. HISCOCK – Then you did understand at one time that upon certified copies of the returns the Democrats had the majority on the Tilden electoral ticket from ninety-three to one hundred.

"TILDEN – Including Baker county, undoubtedly.

"MR. HISCOCK- Do you know how that information was conveyed here?

"TILDEN – I do not; I think I saw it in the newspapers.

"MR. HISCOCK- Do you mean to say that you had no earlier information than that which appeared in the newspapers upon that subject?

"TILDEN – I do not believe that I had.

"MR. HISCOCK – And this despatch you are entirely confidant that you never saw, although it was a despatch sent to Gramercy park?

"TILDEN – I know that I never saw it.

"MR. HISCOCK – And do you believe that none of your friends at that time would have taken the liberty of intercepting any despatches which were sent to Gramercy park, and upon a subject on which you were certainly as vitally interested as any one else?

"TILDEN – The despatch was not addressed to me.

"MR. HISCOCK – No, it was addressed to you; but it, or one other, is the despatch which is referred of November 27, which was addressed to George W. Smith.

"TILDEN – I understand that the despatches addressed to Colonel Pelton at the house in Gramercy park, were delivered by the telegraph people, by standing order, at the committee rooms.

"MR. HISCOCK- I understand that either this or a subsequent despatch which I will soon read, is the one referred to in the phrase, 'See my despatch to Spain." This is the one. There is a despatch, which I have been calling your attention to, addressed to George W. Smith, which has in it the phrase, 'See my despatch to Spain.'

"TILDEN – What despatch is that?

"MR. HISCOCK – The one which I have been reading, or one other which I will read, must be that despatch. I will now read the second one to which that phrase may refer:

"TO COLONEL PELTON, NO. 15 Gramercy Park, New York:

"Please yourself about economies suggested; Coyle exceedingly useful hith-erto. You did not answer my inquiry about Paris, and only mention him at this late date; that promotes unity of action, I suppose. Mention names of Florida friends when you wish to learn how much weight their several requests deserve. Fox impedes daily; it is no relief that you assume responsibility for difficulties he makes. Do not fail to read message to Smith, 15 and 20 cipher. M.M.

"MR. HISCOCK – Did you see that despatch?

"TILDEN – No, I did not.

"MR. HISCOCK – You never saw that despatch?

"TILDEN – No, sir.

"MR. HISCOCK – Then, if I understand you, you took no steps to see the despatch which is described in this phrase, 'See my despatch which is described in this phrase, 'See my despatch to Spain,' and you have no recollection of its ever having been shown to you, although the despatch referring to it was directed to your own private secretary?

"TILDEN – I have no recollection of taking any steps to see any of these other despatches, if I saw this one.

"MR. HISCOCK – How old a person was George W. Smith?

"TILDEN – About twenty-five or thirty.

"MR. HISCOCK – You have no idea that he would have taken the responsibility of intercepting or failing to exhibit to you any despatch which he received?

"TILDEN – No.

"MR. HISCOCK – You have no idea of that kind?

"TILDEN – No.

"MR. HISCOCK – You have no idea but that a despatch which was sent to him in cipher, and which he could not understand, or which he could not read, if he had procured it to be translated, that he would have furnished you the translation?

"TILDEN – I should think he would.

"MR. HISCOCK – He resided in New York city at this time, as I understand?

"TILDEN – Yes he was my personal secretary.

"MR. HISCOCK – Is he now?

"TILDEN – He is now, at this time.

"MR. HISCOCK – Do I understand you to say that the first intimation that you had of the closeness of the contest in Florida was through the newspapers?

"TILDEN – I do not remember what my first information was.

"MR. HISCOCK – You have no recollection upon that subject?

"TILDEN – I think if you will look at the newspapers of the same date as the despatch, you will find the same information. The newspapers generally get ahead of private despatches.

"MR. HISCOCK – I find this despatch sent from New York to both Colonel Woolley and Mr. Manton Marble, directed to them both at Tallahassee: 'Reported here that board have given us one vote.' Do you remember hearing that?

"TILDEN – I do not.

"MR. HISCOCK – Do you remember hearing any rumor of that kind?

"TILDEN – I do not.

"MR. HISCOCK – This is a despatch which was sent by Colonel Pelton to both of these gentlemen as to a rumor which had reached New York, and which they had received, that your electoral ticket had received one vote; and you never heard that? – that one of your electors was elected.

"TILDEN – I do not remember ever hearing that.

"MR. HISCOCK – Do you remember ever having heard it even suggested?

"TILDEN – No. You mention; Mr. Woolley; I had no knowledge of information of his having been there.

"MR. HISCOCK – I am only examining you now upon the question of whether so important a fact as that contained in a despatch requiring an answer, addressed to two gentlemen in Florida, that it was rumored here in New York that one of Mr. Tilden's electors was elected – whether you did not learn that?

"TILDEN – I think I did not, as far as I remember.

"MR. HISCOCK – Can you say that you did not learn it, or do you say that it is very likely that you have forgotten it, if you did not know it?

"TILDEN – I say that I have not the slightest recollection of ever hearing it.

"MR. HISCOCK – There was this despatch, dated December 4, of which I have only read a part. I will read the whole despatch:

"Reported here that board have given us one vote. If so, you will not need to use acceptance. Advise fully."

You never heard of any such despatch as that having been sent to these men?

"TILDEN – I never did.

"MR. HISCOCK – During this canvass, who here in New York did you understand were in consultation with these gentlemen in South Carolina and Florida by telegraph?

"TILDEN – I suppose the committee or some of their agents.

"MR. HISCOCK – Didn't you advise yourself on the subject?

"TILDEN – I did not particularly.

"MR. HISCOCK – Did you not learn the fact – was it not communicated to you – who it was at this end of the line that was in consultation with the gentlemen who were sent to South Carolina and Florida?

"TILDEN – I did not consider that anybody was there especially in consultation.

"MR. HISCOCK – What Democratic gentlemen were there here in New York that you understood that the visiting statesmen in South Carolina and Florida were in communication with?

"TILDEN – I assumed that they were in communication with the National Democratic Committee, or with their subordinates.

"MR. HISCOCK – That is, you assumed that the Democratic National Committee, or some members of it, were here in New York, and in consultation with and being advised of the steps which were being taken by these gentlemen in South Carolina?

"TILDEN – I supposed that some consultations and communications existed; I did not suppose an extensive consultation did exist or could exist.

"MR. HISCOCK – Did you understand at any time that legal proceedings were being taken in South Carolina to restrain the Returning Board in South Carolina?

"TILDEN – I did.

"MR. HISCOCK- Who communicated that fact to you?

"TILDEN – I do not remember.

"MR. HISCOCK – Do you remember whether it was communicated in cipher?

"TILDEN – Not to me in cipher. Nothing was ever communicated to me in cipher.

"MR. HISCOCK – Did you understand during the progress of this canvass that proceedings were being instituted (and successfully instituted), restraining the Governor of Florida from undertaking this canvass?

"TILDEN – I had general information on that subject; I do not know that I had anything more than I got from the newspapers. That proceeding was not dictated from New York, so far as I know; certainly not to me.

"MR. HISCOCK – Did you understand that that was advised by the visiting statesmen to the South, who were in Florida at that time?

"TILDEN – I think it was very likely done by local lawyers.

"MR. HISCOCK – Did you not understand that there was a strong array of counsel from the North to in the South?

"TILDEN – Yes.

"MR. HISCOCK – On both sides?

"TILDEN – Yes, sir.

"MR. HISCOCK – From who did you understand that fact?

"TILDEN – I understood that George W. Biddle, one of the first lawyers in the United States, was there; and Mr. David Sellers, of Philadelphia, Mr. Malcolm Hay, and others.

"MR. HISCOCK – Did you not understand that there were a large array of counsel from outside of the State who were in charge of the scheme of procuring returns from the different canvassing boards scattered throughout the State of Florida; and that there was some confusion existing with reference to Louisiana and South Carolina; and that these three Southern States at that time were supposed to be very poor indeed, and the Democratic party very poor; and did you not understand that there was somebody here in New York who was looking after expenses of the gentlemen who were sent there, and after the expense of sending out the gentlemen to get in these returns?

"TILDEN – I understood nothing about it; I supposed that the committee would take care of their expenses.

"MR. HISCOCK – But you did not trouble yourself to inquire what members of the committee, if any, were here?

"TILDEN – I did not; they changed from day to day.

"MR. HISCOCK - Did you understand at the time that substantially the responsible head of the committee – that is, the one who seemed to act for the committee – was Colonel Pelton?

"TILDEN – I do not know how that is.

"MR. HISCOCK – Did you ever investigate that question?

"TILDEN – I never did.

"MR. HISCOCK – So far as Mr. Marble was concerned, instead of communicating with Mr. Hewitt or Mr. Cooper, he addressed his despatches to Colonel Pelton?

"TILDEN – Mr. Marble is one man.

"MR. HISCOCK – Did you not understand that all the gentlemen in Florida addressed their dispatches to Colonel Pelton?

"TILDEN – I never knew to whom they addressed their dispatches.

"MR. HISCOCK – Did you not understand the fact to be that all the despatches sent by them from South Carolina were sent to Colonel Pelton?

"TILDEN – I knew nothing about it until their publication.

"MR. HISCOCK – Does it not strike you now as singular, with all the light you now have, as remarkable circumstances, that all of these visiting statesmen held communication with New York through despatches addressed to Colonel Pelton, and to him only?

"TILDEN – I do not know that that is a fact.

"MR. HISCOCK – Do you know that that is not the fact?

"TILDEN – I do not; Mr. Hewitt was the chairman of the committee, and they had an executive committee, and some of the members of the committee were there almost every day.

"MR. HISCOCK – Do you know that fact, or is that simply what you understood?

"TILDEN – That is simply what I understood.

"MR. HISCOCK – Did you make inquiry?

"TILDEN – I don't believe I did; I think the information came to me casually.

"MR. HISCOCK – When Colonel Pelton returned from Baltimore I suppose that you saw him immediately?

"TILDEN – I saw him the next day.

"MR. HISCOCK – He had been to some extent dependent upon you, I suppose; that is, as a member of your family, and to some extent provided with a position for the support and maintenance of himself? In other words, you were a patron of his?

"TILDEN – To some extent; he had a business of his own, but was unfortunate in it.

"MR. HISCOCK – You learned from Mr. Cooper, and you could have learned from Colonel Pelton, that he had been to Baltimore for the purpose of consummating a plan for a purchase, by the action of the Canvassing Board of South Carolina, which would ensure the election of the Tilden electors in that State. Did it not occur to you, upon that being communicated to you, that you ought immediately to find out in what relation he stood to the Democratic National Executive Committee?

"TILDEN – Your question assumes more than is true. I did not hear that he had gone to consummate an arrangement; I only heard that he had gone there to receive an offer.

"MR. HISCOCK – Is there any difference between the way that you state it and the way that I stated it?

"TILDEN – Considerable.

"MR. HISCOCK – Would you not infer from his having communicated to Mr. Edward Cooper that he would probably draw upon him the next day for from sixty thousand to eighty thousand dollars, and that he had gone to Baltimore to meet Mr. Smith M. Weed and another gentleman, who had come from South Carolina to meet him there – would you not fairly infer from that that he had gone there to consummate a purchase?

"TILDEN – I did not understand that he said he would draw.

"MR. HISCOCK – Did you understand from Mr. Cooper the sum of money which he stated?

"TILDEN – I presume I did.

"MR. HISCOCK – Do you recollect the amount?

"TILDEN – I do not know that I do; I understood that he had gone there in order to receive or to look into a proposition.

"MR. HISCOCK – Now, understanding that he had been indiscreet enough to go to Baltimore even to look into a proposition for the sale of the certificate to the electors of that State, did you not think that you were called upon to ascertain his relations to the national committee, and to ascertain how far he was committing that body, and how far he was committing himself?

"TILDEN – I thought the best way to deal with such a transaction was to stop it; not only to have nothing to do with it myself, but to stop everybody else from having anything to do with it. I think the same thing in Florida would have been better than what was done. I think instead of appointing Mr. Noyes, who did not stop it, minister to France, and McLin who did it –

"MR. HISCOCK – Don't let us go off on to that question.

"TILDEN – Let me illustrate it. [After a pause.] Mr. Hiscock is evidently trying to probe and search my moral standard.

"MR. HISCOCK – No, I am not addressing myself to that at all; I am only investigating the relations which existed between you and Colonel Pelton, so far as you were committed by his action.

"TILDEN – The object is to impute to me some failure of duty. If I answer that question, I propose to answer it fully; I propose to raise the standard as high as I can, and we will see whether the other gentlemen adopt it.

"MR. HISCOCK – It seems to me that, in this examination, the true way to answer a question is to answer it, so far as you can, directly, and not to seek to answer it by assailing any one else.

"TILDEN – I do not desire to assail anybody; but when a sublimated standard of morals is set up, I propose to analyze it, and to see whether the party that set it up stands up to it.

"MR. HISCOCK – Well, now I will call your attention to another answer you have made here. You have said that if you had entertained any idea – I'm am giving your idea as conveyed by your answer, and not your words, that if you had conceived the idea of influencing these boards venally, or by venal considerations, the last person in the world that you would have chosen for that mission would have been Colonel Pelton. Now I ask you to bear that answer in mind for a moment, and then to state why, after you learned of his visit to Baltimore, you did not deem it proper, and perhaps your duty, to call the attention of Mr. Edward Cooper or of Mr. Hewitt (both of them distinguished and very able men) to the fact that they must take charge of this matter; that Colonel Pelton must be left out of the correspondence; and that they must give it their personal attention, lest you and the Democratic party should be embarrassed, and perhaps scandalized, by the action of Colonel Pelton.

"TILDEN – In the first place, I supposed that those gentlemen were giving it their personal attention. Those gentlemen had the real power, and Pelton had not; they were able to supervise and control it whenever they chose. Mr. Cooper, in particular, had custody of the money, without which Pelton could not involve the committee in the expenditure of a cent. In the next place, Mr. Cooper was the gentleman from whom I derived my information of what was done in Baltimore, and from him exclusively. Mr. Hewitt was his brother-in-law. I did not think that they needed any warning on the subject. In the third place, I regarded the Baltimore thing as very foolish and very wrong, but still as an inchoate transaction. By my intervention it was stopped while there was a *locus penitentiæ*. Now, the civil law does not recognize purposed until they embody themselves in action; the church punishes those purposes merely as sinful thoughts. Pelton had not, so far as I knew, done anything except to receive a proposition from a set of Republican electors to sell the certificates. There was no consummation of the plan; the thing perished in embryo; and it did not strike me as being of such enormous importance as it would, had there been any possibility of the thing succeeding, or of any similar transaction succeeding. I say this without meaning in the least to excuse Pelton, for I do not mean to excuse him. The atmosphere at that time was filled with rumors and assertions of the venality and fraud of these returning boards in those three States and of their offers. I declare before God and my country that it is my entire belief that the votes and certificates of Florida and Louisiana were bought and that the presidency was controlled by their purchase. Pelton, seeing that condition of things, committed a fault; he committed an error; he committed a wrong; he adopted the idea that it was justifiable to fight fire with fire; he adopted the idea, when he saw the presidency being taken away from the man who had been elected by the people and according to the law and the fact, that it was legitimate to defeat the crime by the means he took; he was inexcusable.

"I adopted and entirely different system – an entirely different code of ethics. I scorned to defend my righteous title by such means as were employed to acquire a felonious possession.

"Pelton did not act rightly. He may be tried; he may be condemned; public opinion may punish him. At the same time, even that fault is to be judged according to the facts, according to the times, according to what was being done and what was done. His act was an inchoate offence. On the other side, the act that was done was a completed and consummated offense; it built up a possession of the presidency of the United States in the man who was not elected. And the representatives and champions of that condition of things are the men whose consciences are troubled with the inchoate wrong doing of Pelton, which I stopped and crushed out in the bud!

"MR. HISCOCK – Now, Governor, you will state upon what information you based that belief; and in giving your information you will please give the name of the party communicating it to you.

"TILDEN – I have no private information on the subject; I believe it on evidence before this committee, which is accessible to the public.

"MR. HISCOCK – Do you mean to say that there is any evidence before this committee that either of these returning boards was bought?

"TILDEN – I think so.

"MR. HISCOCK – Will you do me the kindness to point out the witnesses who testified to it, and the evidence to that effect?

"TILDEN - McLin testified that he held the casting vote of the State of Florida; he testified that he gave a false certificate; contrary to fact, and contrary to law. The whole matter is in a nutshell and easily discovered.

"MR. HISCOCK – You are mistaken; McLin has sworn nothing of the kind.

"TILDEN – I think I am not mistaken. McLin said further that his mind was probably influenced by the promise of office. He was immediately afterward appointed to a judgeship in New Mexico; and Mr. Noyes, who was down there, but did not stop the transaction, was appointed to minister to Paris.

"MR. HISCOCK – Are you entirely clear that McLin swore that he was influenced by the hope of being appointed to office.

"TILDEN – I think he said so.

"MR. HISCOCK- Do you swear that he said so?

"TILDEN – I swear that it is my recollection that he substantially said so. Have you the record? That will show. [The committee refers to the record.] Now, gentlemen, I believe that I am competent to be the custodian of my own honor. I do not think that my virtue is of so delicate a texture that it needs that I should practice any brutality toward anybody. I may err in judgment or in conduct; but I think that in all my dealings with Mr. Pelton I have been able, and shall be able, to do about what is right – to protect everybody from any wrong so far as I have any control and at the same time to be just. You have been pursuing a course of examination, the object of which was to ascribe to me some failure of duty, and you have intruded yourself into my domestic and family relations.

"MR. HISCOCK – If you had any information at that time that either the Returning Board of South Carolina or the Returning Board in Florida was being corrupted by the Republicans, or being influenced in their official action by venal considerations, you will state from whom you received that information.

"TILDEN – I had no personal information.

"MR. HISCOCK – You cannot give me the name of any man?

"TILDEN – No; I stated my belief, and I state it on evidence; that, in my judgment, would convict anybody before a common jury.

"MR. HISCOCK – You state it upon evidence, as I understand you, that would convict any one before a common jury. Will you give me now again the name of the person who conveyed that evidence to you?

"TILDEN – The evidence is public.

"MR. HISCOCK – Oh, it is public! Then you mean to say that you have made that serious charge against these returning boards upon what you saw in the papers and upon public rumor?

"TILDEN – No, not upon public rumor.

"MR. HISCOCK – Upon what you saw in the papers?

"TILDEN – I make that charge upon the fact and evidence before your committee and other committees.

"MR. HISCOCK – Now I ask you again to give me any evidence which you had that those boards were being corrupted by the Republicans, outside of rumors that you head on the street or assertions which you saw in the newspapers?

"TILDEN – Those two boards did not act until two weeks afterward.

"MR. HISCOCK – No, they did not; but I said about the time.

"TILDEN – They had not made their decision or given their certificate.

"MR. HISCOCK – Very well; I will accept that as the fact. I will make my question more specific than that. Up to the time of the final announcement of the decision by those two boards respectively, please communicate to this board any evidence which you have that they were corruptly influenced by Republicans, besides the rumors which you heard in the streets and the facts which you saw alleged in the newspapers.

"TILDEN – You will find it in the Field committee –

"MR. HISCOCK – I am not speaking of that time; I am not speaking of so late a period as the Field committee. I am limiting you to the time of their final action.

"TILDEN – That is, up to the 6th of December?

"MR. HISCOCK – Yes, we are not after any congressional investigation. That will speak for itself.

"TILDEN – I have no proof up to that time.

"MR. HISCOCK – You have no evidence up to December 6, 1876. Have you any evidence except what you saw in the newspapers? Did you see any evidence except what you saw in the newspapers?

"TILDEN – I did not personally.

"MR. HISCOCK – Do you know of anybody who did have at that time any evidence? And if so, give his name.

"TILDEN – The testimony before the Field committee discloses.

"MR. HISCOCK – So that all that you know of it you subsequently learned by the investigation before the Field committee? Then, as I understand it, at the time when Colonel Pelton when to Baltimore for the purpose if hearing a proposition on the part of the Returning Board of South Carolina to sell themselves or to give a certificate to the Tilden electors of that State – up to that time you had no information except the rumors which you saw in the newspapers that they were being venally influenced by Republicans?

"TILDEN – I had no proof.

"MR. HISCOCK – You had no evidence except what you saw in the newspapers? – that is my question. Did you have anything except what you saw in the newspapers?

"TILDEN – Up to the 6th of December?

"MR. HISCOCK – Yes, sir.

"TILDEN - I do not think that I had.

"MR. HISCOCK – Then you had nothing except newspaper reports at the time when Mr. Pelton went there for that purpose? Then in your mind you must withdraw, as a justification for Pelton's conduct at that time, the statement that he was ransoming goods from thieves, or that he was fighting fire with fire?

"TILDEN – I did not say that he was justified, but that he thought he was.

"MR. HISCOCK – And that was predicted upon rumors in the newspapers?

"TILDEN – He was perhaps acting upon a belief in his own mind which subsequently proved to be true. I did not say that I defended his position.

"MR. HISCOCK – I did not understand you to say that you defended his position, but I understood in part your answer to be an apology for his position?

"TILDEN – No; an alleviation.

"MR. HISCOCK – My word was 'apology.'

MR. HUNTON – The only difference about that is that he is testifying and you are not.

"TILDEN – (continuing) – The danger of tolerating a wrong on either side is its tendency to grow. One man does a thing because another man does it. By action and reaction abuses and wrongs grow until they become a common practice. That was one of the reasons that impelled me to put my foot down against every approach to anything of this kind.

"MR. HISCOCK – Now I desire to call your attention to one other despatch in this case, which came from Mr. Marble. It is on page 17, No. 34, addressed to Colonel Pelton, No. 15 Gramercy park.

"Woolley asks me to say, Let forces be got together immediately, in readiness for contingencies either here or in Louisiana. Why do you not answer?

Did you ever see that despatch before it was published?
"TILDEN – I never did.
"MR. HISCOCK – Of that are you clear?
"TILDEN – Positive.
"MR. HISCOCK – If you had seen it, the phrase 'let forces be got together immediately for contingencies either here or in Louisiana' would have attracted your attention?
"TILDEN – It might have done so.
"MR. HISCOCK – Have you any doubt that it would?
"TILDEN – I do not understand what it means.
"MR. HISCOCK – I will ask you this question in that connection – If you know or have heard that about that time any considerable sum of money was raised by anybody connected with the National Democratic Committee?
"TILDEN – I have not.
"MR. HISCOCK – Have you known, or have you leaned since, that at any time after the election any considerable sum of money was raised by any Democratic parties here in the city of New York or elsewhere which might be used in those States for political purposes?
"TILDEN – Of that I have no personal knowledge.
"MR. HISCOCK – Have you ever heard so?
"TILDEN – I cannot say that I have.
"MR. HISCOCK – Has any communication of that kind been made to you ever – that any considerable sum of money was raised by Democratic parties which might be used for political purposes? I am now speaking of the time after the election was over.
"MR. SPRINGER - Are you referring to the despatches developed in the 'Tribune'?

"MR. HISCOCK – I have said distinctly, after the election was over.

"TILDEN – I cannot undertake to say, because the committee may have been in debt.

"MR. HISCOCK – I speak with reference to money which was raised by any one.

"TILDEN – I think the committee was pretty largely in debt.

"MR. HISCOCK – You think it was in debt? Is that what I understand you to say?

"TILDEN – Yes; I think it was more or less in debt for a year.

"MR. HISCOCK – My question was, whether you knew of any moneys having been raised which might have been used in those States?

"TILDEN – I do not.

"MR. HISCOCK – Or of any moneys having been raised during the period of time when this correspondence was going on?

"TILDEN – I cannot say whether that was so or not; I cannot tell you.

"MR. HISCOCK – Does that mean to imply that you have heard something of the kind?

"TILDEN – It means I did not keep track of the committee.

"MR. HISCOCK – Will you be kind enough to look on page 28 of the 'Tribune' Extra, No. 44? The last telegram here you will see if from 'Denmark [Pelton] to Smith Weed:

"*Last telegram here. There is undoubtedly good ground, upon which favorable decision could be had; but to be consistent and sustainable, it would and should involve electing Hampton, or else it would be involved in inconsistencies impossible to sustain.*

"TILDEN – Well?

"MR. HISCOCK – Did you ever see that telegram?

"TILDEN – I never did.

"MR. HISCOCK – That sentence that I have read to you is rather in the nature of a legal opinion, is it not?

"TILDEN – It appears to be.

"MR. HISCOCK – Did you ever communicate that legal opinion to Colonel Pelton?

"TILDEN – I don't think I did.

"MR. HISCOCK – Do you not think you did? Is that as strong as you want to put it? I call your attention to the fact that you simply say, "I don't think I did."

"TILDEN – I have no recollection or belief that I did.

"MR. HISCOCK – Do you know with whom Colonel Pelton did advise as to legal questions of that sort?

"TILDEN – I do not.

"MR. HISCOCK – Did he ever advise with you as to these legal questions?

"TILDEN – I have no recollection of his ever doing it.

"MR. HISCOCK – You knew all this time that Colonel Pelton was in direct communication with these gentlemen, did you not?

"TILDEN – What time? What gentlemen?

"MR. HISCOCK – At the time with these gentlemen in Florida and South Carolina.

"TILDEN – I do not think that I knew he was in any special communication with them.

"MR. HISCOCK – Did you not know he was receiving numerous telegrams from the visiting statesmen?

"TILDEN – I did not.

"MR. HISCOCK – Not when he was living at your house, and they are directed to your house?

"TILDEN – They were not directed to my house.

"MR. HISCOCK – They were directed to your house.

"TILDEN – No, sir; only the fifteen Florida ones.

"MR. HISCOCK – Did you not know that others were sent there?

"TILDEN – Sent where?

"MR. HISCOCK – Sent to your house.

"TILDEN – I do not think they were ever sent there.

"MR. HISCOCK – What makes you think they were not?

"TILDEN – I think I should have heard of it if they had been. I have already told you those telegrams were not delivered to my house, according to the best of my knowledge and belief.

"MR. HISCOCK – How do you know?

"TILDEN – I live there, and it would sometimes happen that a telegram would have come within my knowledge.

"MR. HISCOCK – But none of them ever did?

"TILDEN – None of them ever did so far as I recollect or believe.

"MR. HISCOCK – Does it not impair your certainty on that subject that you cannot tell whether or not certain telegrams were received by your private secretary which obviously came there? Might not you have had a similar lapse of memory as to these as to those directed to your private secretary?

"TILDEN – It might have been so as to one telegram; but I do not think a large number of telegrams could have come there without my knowing it.

"MR. HISCOCK – What were Colonel Pelton's hours? What time did he spend at your house?

"TILDEN – He generally came in after I was abed and asleep, and generally went out before seeing me in the morning.

"MR. HISCOCK – Generally before?

"TILDEN – Not always before.

"MR. HISCOCK – Late to bed, and early to rise?

"TILDEN – Not always before; he was hardly ever at breakfast.

"Question by Mr. REED – I will ask one other question: Did there a great many telegrams come to your house, Governor Tilden?

"TILDEN – I cannot say.

"MR. HISCOCK – Did a great many telegrams come to your house at Gramercy park during these days?

"TILDEN – My impression would be there were not a great many.

"MR. HISCOCK – Do not you know there were a great many messengers arriving constantly from the Western Union Company at your house?

"TILDEN – I cannot remember. My impression is there did not a great many arrive. Messages to me would generally come there; messages to Pelton were not delivered there, but went to the national committee room. Of course I cannot undertake to say none came to him there. I should think on election night there came a good many.

"MR. HUNTON – I should like to ask Governor Tilden a question. Telegram 34, on page 17, purports to be from Marble to Colonel Pelton. According to the 'Tribune' translation this telegram is:

"Woolley asks me to say, Let forces be got together immediately in readiness for contingencies either here or in Louisiana. Why do you not answer?
                                        "Marble.

Do you know of any forces, in the sense of military forces or otherwise, that were being used, or that were ready to be used, or that there was any intention at that time to use?

"TILDEN – No, sir, I do not.

"MR. HISCOCK – You knew nothing about forces in that sense?

"TILDEN – No, sir; I thought it meant influence, friends.

"MR. HISCOCK – You state your belief that the returning boards in one or more States were purchased. You had information that led you to believe, and if true would convince you, that at least one of those boards offered itself for sale to the Democratic side.

"TILDEN – It was not sold to the Democratic side; and is not the conclusion legitimate and proper that if not purchased by one side it was by the other?

"MR. REED – Oh! Oh! Oh! I'll ask for the ruling of the chairman on that question.

"TILDEN – It is a matter of logic.

"THE CHAIRMAN (laughingly to Mr. Reed). – Do you expect the Chair to rule out a question he has himself asked?

"MR. REED – Yes, sir; that one, with confidence.

"THE CHAIRMAN – Well, he said, it is a question of logic; and as that is not a matter of investigation, I will rule out both question and answer. That is all, Governor Tilden. "

At the conclusion of Mr. Tilden's examination, the committee went into executive session, when they decided to adjourn and return that evening to Washington.

This proved to be practically the end of the cipher despatch explosion. The men who plotted it had succeeded in disturbing the peace and domestic relations of an infirm old man for several months; they had sent forth reports vitally compromising the private as well as public character of the most eminent statesman of the country, which reports would leave their impression upon the minds of millions of whom the evidence of his innocence would reach only thousands and an impartial posterity, to whose judgment, however, they were indifferent. Their object was accomplished. They had impaired Mr. Tilden's health; they had persuaded many that he was as unscrupulous in his political methods as Mr. Hayes had been, and to that extent fancied they had rendered him less formidable as a candidate for the presidency.

Dante, who had been one of the prior or six first men of Florence, was summoned to answer a malicious charge of peculation; he was not allowed sufficient time to appear and defend himself; was condemned, as contumacious, to a heavy fine, and banished forever from his native city upon which he had conferred its greatest glory. In such company political persecution confers distinction.

I will venture to close what it has seemed proper for me to say of the barbarous effort to degrade Mr. Tilden in the estimation of the world, with an entry made in my diary on Thursday the 13th of February, and four days after the examination of the Fifth Avenue hotel.

"Went around yesterday to Tilden's and found him in a state of unusual irritability. He had heard that Ellis, the president of the Third National Bank, had said that Tilden and Smith Weed passed an hour in close conversation at their bank between ten and one o'clock of the day previous to Weed's departure for the South. This, if true, would convict both Tilden and Weed of perjury, for both had sworn that did not see each other between the day before the election and some time after Weed's return from the South. Weed was sent for, and this morning I met him there. Meantime the papers of the day in question were looked over and both the 'World' and 'Herald' show that Tilden did not go down town that day, by accounting for all his time elsewhere. Weed also had documents to show that it was impossible for Ellis to be correct. After getting these proofs arranged and the papers marked, Tilden got into his coupé and went down to the bank. He returned about 4:30 p.m. to get me to go with him to an art reception given by the late William H. Vanderbilt, and on our way told me that if he had been a half-hour later Ellis would have been gone; that when shown the papers Ellis decided to write to Cox that he had been mistaken, and that he had since been satisfied that neither Mr. Tilden nor Mr. Weed were in the bank that day. Tilden saw that letter and then came off.

"It is curious what devices are resorted to, to destroy this poor man's character. I was thinking this morning that no one but a man of large fortune ought to think of running for the presidency as an independent man. Had Tilden been a man of moderate means he would have been ruined in character long ago. But for his having files of all the daily papers for years back, and clerks to assist in searching them, he would not have been able to collect the proofs of his whereabouts on the days in question in time to stop Ellis going on to Washington; still less the wider range of proof requisite to undo Ellis' erroneous testimony after it had been given.

"The whole of Tilden's time, and the services of several eminent and costly lawyers and a number of clerks, have been constantly required by him since the election to defend him against the prosecutions and the persecutions of the administration. There is no prominent candidate for the presidency at present, nor ever was there one, whose income is or ever was sufficient to provide for these expenses alone.

"The men who will 'run with the machine,' who will for combinations with rings and treat with the baser elements of society, have no such friction to contend with. Those baser elements stand ready to provide all the means necessary for their instruments. But when a man antagonizes rings, refused to make bargains or to give promises, provokes the hostility of all the selfish interests which thrive under a corrupt government only, he has to contend with an amount of feebleness and acquiescence on the part of the class who profess to desire good government and a hostility from those who prefer a bad one, which will crush any one who cannot a moment's notice put his hand upon almost unlimited resources."

Early in 1877 a report was put into circulation in Washington that Mr. Tilden or his friends had been negotiating for the exemption of his bank account from inspection by the Investigating Committee of Congress. Justly indignant at such an imputation, he addressed the following letter to Senator Kernan, the last sentence of which betrays the perfidious origin of the report:

GOVERNOR TILDEN TO SENATOR KERNAN

"NEW YORK, FEB. 21, 1877.

"THE HONORABLE FRANCIS KERNAN, *WASHINGTON, D.C.*:

"A telegram to the Associated Press, published this morning, states that a harmonious agreement had been brought about between the

Senate committee, of which you are a member, and a committee of the House, by which it has been decided not to go into an examination of my back account on the one hand, or the accounts of the chairman of the Republican National Committee on the other hand.

"I repudiate any such agreement, and disclaim any such immunity, protection, or benefit from it. I reject the utterly false imputation that my private bank account contains anything whatever that needs to be concealed. Under the pretence of looking for payment in December, the demand was for all payments after May and all deposits during the nine months.

"The bank was repeatedly menaced with the removal of its officers and books to Washington.

"A transcript of entries of private business, trusts, and charities, containing everything but what the committee was commissioned to investigate, but nothing which it was commissioned to investigate, because nothing of that sort existed, has been taken, with my knowledge, to Washington. Of course there is no item in it relating to anything in Oregon, for I never made, authorized, or knew of any expenditure in relation to the election in that State or the resulting controversies, or any promise or obligation on the subject.

"Mr. Ellis, the acting president of the bank, himself a Republican, some time ago told the chairman of the committee and several of its members, that there is nothing in the account capable of furthering any just object of the investigation. I am also informed that a resolution was passed to summon me as a witness, but have received no subpoena. I had written before this telegram appeared, requesting you to say to the committee that it would be more agreeable to me not to visit Washington if the committee would send a sub-committee or hold session here, but that otherwise I should attend under the subpoena. *As to this arrangement now reported, I have only to say that I can accept decorum and decency, but not a fictitious equivalent for a mantle of secrecy to anybody else.*

"S. J. TILDEN."

CHAPTER VII

Income-tax-returns – New persecutions by the administration – The capitulation of the administration – The ignominious end of seven years' persecution – Letters of Edwards Pierrepont, special counsel for the government; S.L. Woodford, United States District Attorney; Green R. Raum, United States Commissioner of Internal Revenue; Charles J. Folger, Secretary of the Treasury; and Benjamin H. Brewster, Attorney-General of the United States.

THE INCOME – TAX SUIT

The administration at Washington, not content with violating the sanctity of private correspondence for material with which to discredit the candidate of the Democratic party, did not scruple to avail itself of other resources exclusively within its own control, and with despotic recklessness.

In the latter part of August, 1876, an article appeared in the "New York Times," the favorite New York organ of the administration, charging Mr. Tilden with having sworn to false returns of his income; and giving various specious statements of his sources of income purporting to show a substantial discrepancy between its amount and the amount which Mr. Tilden returned. The time selected for this assault betrayed the unworthy motives which inspired it. It was in the high noon of the presidential canvass, in which, of course, all of Mr.

Tilden's energies were enlisted; his bother Moses was lying on what week or two provided to be his death-bed; Mr. Tilden had not found time to complete his letter accepting the nomination of the St. Louis convention, to which his spare moments, usually taken from hours that should have been given to repose, were devoted. It was under these peculiarly trying conditions that he was suddenly and altogether unexpectedly called upon to review the history of transactions already fourteen years old, of which he had preserved scarcely a scrap of memoranda. More than six years had elapsed since he had retire from the active practice of his profession, subsequently to which he had rarely visited his office even for matters of private concern. Add to all these embarrassments, the ruthless hand of one of the same cabinet ministers who subsequently engineered the electoral frauds in Florida and Louisiana was here visibly directing the blow that was aimed at his honor through the columns of the "Times."

Of course such a charge with what appeared to be official specifications, including a facsimile of Mr. Tilden's income tax return, which could only have come from the Department of the Interior, of which Zachariah Chandler was the official head, produced a profound sensation throughout the country. Mr. Tilden's character was of more importance to him than the presidency, and inconvenient and laborious as it was, he felt himself competed to devote several weeks, with the aide of three or four clerks, to evoke from the scattered records of the past, evidence of the false and malicious character of these imputations. With the aid of Judge Sinnott, who had been his confidential law clerk during the period covered by the "Times," he prepared a statement which was published on the 20th of September. The "Nation: of the 28th of that month summoned up the whole case, so far as the main charge of making a false return, perjury, etc., was concerned, in the following table:

"TIMES" CHARGE		TILDEN'S ANSWER		"TIMES" REPLY
1. Fee 2. Fees, etc. 3. Fee 4. Fee 5. Fees 6. Fee 7. Fee	$5,000 2,000 5,000 2,500 4,500 5,000 5,000	1. No such fee ever received 2. No such charge ever made work done by another man. 3 – 6. No such charge ever made, services ended before 1862. No services in 1862	1 thru 6. 7.	No proof. Items declared to have been made up by affixing to the titles of "certain instruments" certain charges "believed to have been approximately correct." No. 2 "withdrawn." No proof; defence irrelevant because offered by a man "well disposed to take refuge in a suggested falsehood."
8. Fee 9. Fee 10. Fees 11. Fees 12.Share of Bonds for services. 13. Salary	10,000 10,000 20,0000 15,000 25,000 1,000	No services in 1862 No services in 1862 No services in 1862 Never received; the company not a client of Mr. Tilden's No bonds retained for services in 1862. Services rendered included in return. Correct except as to date.	8. 9. 10. 11. 12. 13.	No proof; one item of $10,000 "withdrawn." No proof No proof; answer admitted to be conclusive; charge "withdrawn." No proof. Charge "reiterated with renewed emphasis." No proof. Charge repeated. Whole answer pronounced "disingenuous" and characteristic of its author," but total amount of "true income" cut down to $76,000, or $5,882 less than the amount originally said to be "fraudulently concealed."
Total 14. "Obviously false" return for 1863 15. Omission to make returns in subsequent years.	108,000	14. No Answer 15. Permitted by law.	14. 15.	No proof No proof of illegality

For the period subsequent to that covered by this table the "Times" had charged Mr. Tilden with allowing the income-tax-assessor to assess his income at less than its value. The absurdity of this charge leaped to the eyes of every reader. In the first place, not only in New York, but in every State of the Union, property is assessed for taxation by an official assessor, and the taxpayer is never required to make a statement of the amount or value of his property except in pleading for a reduction of his assessment. In the second place, the income tax-law expressly provided that in case the taxpayer omitted to make a return of his income, it should be assessed by the assessor. It was so assessed and paid. The terms of the law had been compiled with, and, as Mr. Tilden confidently affirmed, he paid more those years than would have been required had he made his own returns, which he neglected to do only because the difference was not worth the time and trouble it would have cost him, to apportion to each year the precise amount saved during that period, in litigations covering a series of years.

Mr. Tilden's answer effectually disposed, for the time being, of these charges, which in the somewhat emphatic language of a journal of the period "can be characterized in no milder terms than a vicious lie, a base slander, and a diabolical calumny." The assault had utterly failed of its purpose so far as any effect upon the election was concerned, upon which, if it had any, it seems to have been a favorable one; but the extra toil and worry to which it subjected Mr. Tilden for several weeks during the hottest season of the year, told seriously upon his health and no doubt contributed to shorten his days, in that respect serving the purpose of his tormentors by contributing to disqualify him for the duties of the chief magistracy four years later, to which, had his health permitted, he would have unquestionably have been chosen.

Unhappily for Mr. Tilden's peace, he was still too formidable a political force to be neglected. He was regarded by his party, with practical unanimity, as its inevitable candidate for the presidency in 1880. Thought the assault upon his character had thus far ignominiously failed, the resources of the administration's arsenal of defamation had not yet been exhausted. It had charged Mr. Tilden with making false returns of his income. He had denied it, and the public had accepted his denial, but the administration had prosecuting attorneys and a judiciary all of its own appointment; why not institute proceedings for the money of which it was alleged the government had been defrauded?

That course would at least vindicate in a measure the part which the administration had had in promulgating the original calumnies; it would keep the question of Mr. Tilden's innocence measurably open for partisan uses; it would worry and wear upon their victim, who had no health to spare for litigation; it would induce some who wished to be confirmed in their fanatical hostility to the Democratic party, to believe that where there was so much smoke there must be some fire, and that by wily procrastination, of which the law officers of the federal government have almost unlimited control, the innocence of Mr. Tilden could not be established until after the suspicions thus propagated of his guilt might have accomplished their perfect work. Accordingly a suit was instituted at the instigation of the Hayes government against Mr. Tilden, shortly after the election in 1876, to establish what subsequently was admitted to have been a purely imaginary liability for unpaid income tax. The commencement of this suit was duly heralded through the press. Several months elapsed before Mr. Tilden was furnished with any statement of the grounds of the government's claims. No serious attempt was ever made to bring the case to a hearing, but it was nursed along to be used as convenient means of presenting Mr. Tilden to the country from time to time in the attitude of a culprit. These knavish tactics were pursued throughout the term of the Hayes administration. When the suit had been pending for a year or more the government was forced to admit that it was not in possession of any evidence upon which to sustain its suit, and then had the effrontery to file a bill of discovery to compel Mr. Tilden himself to furnish evidence upon which their prosecution could be sustained. To this Mr. Tilden of course demurred, regarding it as practically an admission that the government had no cause of action. Judge Blatchford, who was sometimes a judge and always a politician, decided against the demurrer.

Pending the litigation over these proceedings, President Hayes and his associate beneficiaries of the frauds by which he had been installed in the presidency were dismissed from the public service, and a new government replaced them. Meantime Mr. Tilden's health had been steadily declining. He had ceased to be regarded as a candidate for the presidency, and there was no longer, therefore, any motive, if there had been any disposition on the part of the new administration, to persecute or defame him. The question now was how to rid of the suit without compromising those who instituted it. That story may be best told in the language of the parties who conducted the retreat. We will commence with the following memorandum of facts prepared for the counsel by Mr. Tilden himself:

TILDEN'S MEMORANDA FOR COUNSEL.

"In compliance with your request a memorandum of certain facts involved in the income-tax-case, discussed in our recent conversations, is furnished.

"1. The action against me is, so far as is known or can be ascertained, the only suit of this nature which has been instituted and prosecuted.

"The suit against Mr. Hazard was for taxes accruing during a portion of the period when the income tax existed. The amount claimed was over one hundred and fifty thousand dollars, and the interest enlarged the claim to at least two hundred and fifty thousand dollars. In the settlement, the United States amended its declaration so as to embrace the whole ten years of the income tax, and to fix the judgment, including principal and interest, at one thousand dollars. Judgment was taken by consent, and the appeal was waived. Mr. Hazard told me that he settled it because it was cheaper to pay such a judgment that the cost of counsel fees.

"(See the letter of Hon. Charles Bradley, Mr. Hazard's counsel Points for Defendant, page 21.)

"The allegation on which the United States rely in the action against me is merely that the assessor did not make the assessment large enough. That naked proposition is aided by no other statement whatsoever.

"The claim as stated in the declaration applies equally in the years in which I made a return and in the years in which I omitted to make a return. No distinction is intimated whether the taxpayer makes a return or leaved the ascertainment exclusively to the assessor.

"The consequence is that the pretensions in behalf of the United States, to review by a court and jury the action of the assessor, extends to every case in which assessment was made during the whole ten years. Mr. Harland, who is familiar with such subjects, estimates that there were some four or five millions of assessments. In every one of them, on the theory of this suit, and action could be brought, treating the assessment as a nullity, and making a new assessment by a court and jury.

"As there is no limitation against the United States of the time for bringing an action, every citizen once liable to the income tax remains exposed to such an action as long as he lives, and his property remains subject to it as long as anything of his estate can be traced.

"Other grave questions arise. For instance, the Statue of 1864 expressly declares that 'the amount due shall be a lien in favor of the United States from the time it was due until paid,' and the lien follows the property into and through the hands of innocent third persons.

"3. By section 3214 of the United States Revised Statues such an action could not be 'commenced' unless the commissioner of internal revenue authorized or sanctioned the proceedings.

"The letter of Commissioner Raum, giving his formal approval of the action against me, was dated January 25, 1877. The *capias*, unaccompanied by any declaration, was issued January 22, 1877, and served on the 27th.

"It is noteworthy in this connection that under date of January 3, 1877, Commissioner Raum had addressed to Mark Bangs, United States District Attorney at Chicago, in answer to a letter dated October 27th previous, an elaborate opinion that the decision of the assessor, 'when an assessment is in the scope of his jurisdiction, cannot be questioned collaterally.'

"You will find the whole opinion on pages 17 – 22 of Defendant's Points.

"The commissioner thus appears as having authorized this suit nineteen days after he had given formal official opinion that such a suit is not maintainable in law. His opinion is published in the 'Internal Revenue Record' of January 8, 1877, and was assessable to the district attorney more than two weeks before the suit commenced.

"4. Not only did the district attorney who brought the suit action, and the commissioner of internal revenue who authorized the action, know at the time, by such high and, to them, conclusive authority, that there was no basis in law for the action, but they were equally destitute of any evidence in their possession to constitute a basis of fact on which to justify the action if it had been maintainable in law. They had nothing but newspaper fabrications, got up in August, September, and October, 1876, during the presidential canvass, ever item of which on being analyzed fails to be probable cause or was disproved at the time.

"I will not go over these in detail. One illustration will suffice. The main attack was made on my return for 1862. The only tangible fact alleged was that in one case I had collected during that year sums for compensation and disbursements which has accrued wholly, or almost wholly, during previous years beginning as far back as 1857. Now, I happen to have in my possession the identical copy of Boutwell's 'Manual,' used by my managing clerk in making out the return for 1862, and it contains an express decision of the commissioner of internal revenue, announced in May, 1863, that the earnings of a lawyer during the previous years are to be excluded from the return, although collected during the year for which the return was made.

"Mr. Harland, at the time he put in a plea forming an issue of law in the case, mentioned to me that Mr. Sherman said to him that if he had had the management of the defence, he should have waived the issue of law and gone to trial, because the district attorney's office had no evidence to sustain the action.

"5. The capias was issued by District Attorney Bliss two days before his successor, District Attorney Woodford, was sworn in. It was served on the 27th. It claimed the round and exact sum of one hundred and fifty thousand dollars as taxes and penalties; it was unaccompanied by any declaration specifying details of which the claim was composed. The complaint was filed on the 14th of April, or about three months later. It aimed to make up the gross claim state in the capias, by alleging an income sufficient to produce the tax. It alleged $2,703,600 of income over and above all on which taxes had been paid, and over and above all lawful deductions. It distributed this immense sum over the tens years, except $100,000, which it claimed for 1861 when there was no tax. It made this distribution on conjecture or arbitrarily. To 1865, which was a year of universal disaster, following the fall of gold and collapse of values resulting form the close of the war, and a year in which unquestionably my income was less then the sum I paid on, it absurdly assigned $333,000 of the excess of income.

"This immense pretended excess of income is a mere myth. For 1862 and 1863 I submitted returns. They were carefully made out by my chief managing clerk, who was a counsellor-at-law, and the habitual expert of the office on questions under the revenue laws. He had access to every source and means of information, and no instructions except a caution against assuming any doubtful question for me to verify. He has now no doubt that the returns were correct, except that they leaned towards the government. Nor have I.

"In the years when no return was made, I do not feel responsible for the assessment of the assessor. It is the universal practice of the State of New York for State, county, and city taxes to be computed on assessments made by the public officers on their own information and judgment. The citizen has a statutory privilege to interfere for the purpose of obtaining a reduction of the assessment; but never interferes for any other purpose. I never heard it suggested, even if the assessment were less than the real value of the subject of taxation (such assessment being made by the assessor on his own information and judgment without interference by the taxpayer), that the taxpayer would be held to be morally culpable. I never heard it suggested that the State, country, or city could afterwards sue the taxpayer for a larger sum than that which it had so assessed and collected by its own officers. The United States income law expressly provided the alternative for the taxpayer, if he chose to leave the assessment to the public officers, and to accept the enhancement of the assessment as a consequence of making no return. It was the policy of the revenue law to make the discretion of the assessor supreme and conclusive. Even if returns were made, the assessor had the power to add to return or to disregard it, and generally to make his own assessment from such information as he might choose to rely on, and to be governed absolutely by his own judgment.

"I discontinued making returns in 1864 because of the total impossibility of solving questions of law which they involved, and at the time when I believed I would pay, and did pay, under the fiat of the assessor, a larger tax that I was properly liable to pay.

"In point of fact, however, I generally paid a larger tax that I ought, and probably did so in every year, unless that result should be changed by eccentric constructions of the law.

"It is my belief that during every one of the ten years I was holding railroad bonds and stocks and other securities, on which the tax was deducted from the interest and withheld before the income reached me, to so large an amount that the income thus taxed was a greater sum that my whole real income from investments.

"In other words, the interest paid out by me was always larger than the income from that portion of my investments on which the tax was not collected by the government through the corporation that issued the securities.

"During the eight years, 1864 to 1871 inclusive, the average amount imposed by the assessor, including his additions for the omission to return, was about $27,000. I estimate the aggregate amount of office expenses which come out of the gross receipts before the net income is ascertained, and of taxes and interest paid out, which are lawful deductions from income, could not be less than $30,000 a year. I estimate that the amount of income on which the tax was collected through corporations issuing securities ranged between $20,000 and $100,000, and could not be less on the average than something between $40,000 and $50,000 a year. That would make the gross receipts over $100,000 a year, and the income-paying tax between $70,000 and $75,000 a year.

"Growth of values of property not sold, whether real of personal, is not income. Gains from real estate converted, unless the real estate has been purchased within two years, were excluded by statutory definition. Accretions from the conversions of bonds and stocks, unless they were bought within the same year, were deemed not to be taxable by the Supreme Court of the United States in Gray v. Darlington, 15 Wallace. Excluding those three classes alone (and there are other classes of exemptions from tax), I believe the growth of all my property during the eight years did not make good the actual realized losses incident to the unsound finance of the time, and furnished the amount on which I paid the income tax, less the cost of living.

"The Parthian arrow of the retiring district attorney was aimed at his successor, and was so understood by Mr. Woodford. It had the additional purpose of lending an appearance of reality and consistency to the electioneering devices used during the canvas of 1876.

"6. As early as the last of August, 1876, and then district attorney indulged in an interview menacing the suit, and later during the canvass he published a report to the commissioner of internal revenue on the subject. Those officers freely used and abused their official characters and official functions to give credit to the electioneering falsehoods of the canvass.

"7. After the amazing decision of Judge Blatchford was rendered, - that in every case whatsoever where there was a return and where there was no return the United States may at any indefinite time afterwards impeach the *quasi* judicial decision of its own assessor, set it aside on the naked allegation that the assessment was not large enough, and re-try the questions of the amount of a man's income by a court and jury, involving countless issues of fact and of law, - my counsel sought the speediest review of his decision by the Supreme Court of the United States. The technical difficulty was interposed that an appeal could not be had except after a judgment. To obviate that, my counsel offered the district attorney to let judgment be taken on the last count, which was for one hundred thousand dollars of income that never existed; providing by stipulation that the action might be renewed as to the other counts, and that the United States might take testimony *de bene esse* as its option.

"They were not able to obtain this arrangement or any arrangement without allowing a judgment to be taken on an enormous amount of fictitious income. The government and defendant are therefore brought to confront a hypothetical trial in a case where it is believed that there is no legal ground of action, even if the government could prove its allegations of fact. That hypothetical trial involves every transaction during a period of ten years, every item of income, and every item of deduction for expenses, for taxes, for interest, for losses by bad debts, by bad investments. It is claimed that such and impalpable element as the increased value of the assets of a company which never made a dividend during the ten years, nor was ever able to collect enough of its means to pay its debts till the last year, is to be counted as income of an individual stockholder, estimating his share in the ratio of his stock. That item alone would involve all the transactions of a mining company for eight years. I mention this as an illustration to what interminable collateral inquires and controversies such a suit so carried on may lead if the plaintiff chooses to give it that character.

"8. It is impossible to conceive of a case in which every reasonable consideration is more urgent than in the present, in favor of settling the questions of law in advance of the trial of the questions of fact.

"In the first place, it must be admitted that there is an extreme improbability that the Supreme Court of the United States would sustain the decision of Judge Blatchford, and overrule the immense series of cases in the courts of the Untied States, of the different States, and of England, establishing the principle that the quasi judicial decision of the assessors and similar officers is conclusive. I cannot suppose that the attorney-general, still less that such a jurist as Mr. Evarts, would have any doubt upon the subject.

"In the second place, a rule which subjects every citizen of the United States liable to the income tax in any one of the ten years to have his tax reopened by a suit, which continues that exposure indefinitely, cannot but be considered a question of great public importance to the mass of taxpayers as well as of great interest to the government. Such a question ought to be settled at the earliest moment by the highest tribunal, and put forever at rest. The offer of my counsel was immediately to carry a judgment to that tribunal, and to unite with the attorney-general in an application for an immediate argument, which would no doubt be granted on motion of the attorney-general. As the United States were not ready at the December term, and recently intimated in court that they would probably not be ready for the February term, no loss of time would result.

"In the third place, there would be a great convenience to the United States and the court in avoiding a hypothetical trial. The case has uniformly been spoken of by the district attorney and by Judge Choate as 'a long case.' How long it will be will depend on the district attorney.

It is quite capable of being ramified to take a whole term or a great many terms. The pretension was set up by the Marquette testimony that the defendant's income should involve, not the dividends declared, not the profits ascertained or adjudged by a corporate act, but the unrealized constructive profits of a company that had at no time been able to pay dividends. That one item would bring into the case all the corporate books for eight years, and more issues of fact than would be comprised in fifty ordinary lawsuits. On such a system, a case which includes all the transactions of ten years ought to take a lifetime. The very existence of such a case illustrates the utter absurdity of the notion that assessment of income is a thing fit to be done by a court and jury.

"In the fourth place, to insist on a hypothetical trial because of the technical difficulty of appeal, or to impose onerous or impracticable conditions not necessary to the interests of the United States, indicates a purpose to conduct the suit merely in such a manner as to harass,

oppress, and defame the defendant. The case has been suspended over
the defendant for two years. It is noticed for each successive term, but
the United States is never ready. The defendant returned from Europe
in October, 1877, influenced largely by necessity of attending to and
the expectation of disposing of this case. He will some time or other
want to be liberated from the necessity of being in attendance at each
successive term. The expenses and other burdens of such a controversy,
with roaming commissions such as those at Boston, Pittsburg, Chicago,
and Marquette, ought not to be imposed upon a citizen unless the
action is sustamable in law.

"9. The attorney-general, in section 362, United States Revised
Statues, is commanded to exercise a general superintendence and
direction over the district attorney. The function of the commissioner
of internal revenue is limited to an asset to the bringing of a suit.
After the suit is brought, the power and responsibility belong to the
attorney-general. Nor can it be doubted that all questions as to the
legal rights of government and its public policy are within the domain
of the attorney-general.

"10. Such a case ought to be acted on with reference to general
considerations of public policy. If the millions of cases in which an
income tax was paid are all open to review as a matter of law, and
it is wise and right and conformable to public policy to undertake a
revision of them, there ought to be a systematic inquiry by competent machinery applying alike to all citizens. The whole action of the
government ought not to be descend into a mere raid of one citizen.

A few days before the meeting of the first Congress after the acces-
sion of Garfield to the presidency, the following letter was addressed by
Vanderpoel, Green and Cuming, of counsel for Mr. Tilden, to the Hon.
Edwards Pierrepont, special counsel of the Untied States:

"VANDERPOLE, GREEN, AND CUMING,
No. 2 WALL STREET,
"NEW YORK, Dec. 3, 1881.

'HON. EDWARDS PIERREPONT, *Special Counsel:*
"SIR: In reference to the case of the United States against Tilden,
while believing that the action must result unfavorable to the United
States, upon the law, if ever the case can reach the Supreme Court,

and upon the facts, whenever a trial shall be had, I recently expressed to you my conviction that the United States ought now to be willing to discontinue the action on their own motion, but that I could yet understand that some embarrassment might exist by reason of expenses for which the United States may become liable relating to the future as well as past conduct of the case.

"I have considered the very great burden to both parties of a futile trial, in a case which theoretically involves an inquiry into ever transaction of an active professional and business life, during the ten years ago, - a futile trial which would swamp a court and jury for an indefinite period, unless the controversy should be limited by the inability of the United States to produce evidence except as to a very small; fraction of the things they draw in question by their claims, as asserted in their complaint.

"I have considered, also that next month it will be five years since this action was commenced; that, as I suppose, at no time have the United States been really ready for trial; that when the present district attorney inherited this action, he found in his office no facts or evidence by which to frame a complaint; that two years later the United States, in a bill of discovery, placed on the files of the court an avowal that they then had no evidence on which they could safely proceed to trial; that at the present time, I believe the United States have not at all improved their condition in this respect; that, nevertheless, the defendant may be subjected, for years to come to the necessity of preparation for each successive term, while totally unable to obtain a final termination of the trial; and that the defendant has been frequently compelled , at great expense and inconvenience, to send counsel five hundred or a thousand or fifteen hundred miles to attend upon fishing excursions in the form of commissions to take testimony *de bene esse,* in which the commissioners could not exclude, but which are not admissible as evidence in the case.

"I have also considered that, not withstanding the inexpediency of subjecting either party or the court to trouble or costs of a hypo-thetical trial, in a case in which there is every probability the Supreme Court will hold as matter of law that there is no cause of action, every expedient for first presenting the question of law to that tribunal has failed; that, notwithstanding the concurrence of all the leading cases in England, in the several States and in the United States, that the *quasi* judicial judgment of a taxing officer fixing the amount of the tax is conclusive upon the government, as well as upon the citizen, and an elaborate opinion of the commissioner of internal revenue, dated January 3, 1877, to the same effect, the interlocutory ruling of the district judge on the demurrer in the case debars an appeal to the Supreme Court until after final judgment at the trial; that, in the ordinary course of things, it would probably take from three to five years to obtain a decision of the Supreme Court on the case, - and that could be obtained only in the contingency that a judgment should be rendered for the United States.

"Considering all these matters, I repeat the suggestion made to you that the United States proceed to discontinue their action, and that they be relieved, by arrangement with me, from the expenses, including counsel fees, which the Untied States have incurred or become liable for; the amount of such expenses, whatever they are, cannot but be small compared with those which each party must here-after incur, if the case goes on.

"Very respectfully yours, etc.,

"(Signed)   A. J. VANERPOEL."

The successive stages of the government's capitulation will be found set forth with sufficient detail in the several communications following:

Edwards Pierrepont, Special Counsel for the United States, to the acting Attorney-General of the United States.

"THE HON. SAMUEL F. PHILLIPS, *Acting Attorney-General of the United States:*

"In the suit of the United States against Samuel J. Tilden to recover income tax, I have the honor to report that after my retainer, on the 8th of March, 1880, I devoted most of my time for an entire month to the investigation of the statues, the judicial decisions, the very long depositions, the examination of witnesses, the laws relating to the admissions of evidence in the case, and to very many consultations with the United States attorney, General Woodford, and his assistant, Mr. Clarke, aided by Mr. Webster, of the internal revenue service, to whose intelligent activity and zeal is largely due the discovery of the more valuable evidence in the case.

"The matter is complicated, and the difficulties of reaching a satisfactory conclusion are increased by the great lapse of time.

"Mr. Tilden's first return for the year 1862.

"BRIEF HISTORY OF THE CASE.

"After Mr. Tilden was nominated for the presidency by the Democratic convention June, 1876, this action was commenced. Up to that time no charge had been made by any officer of the government that the defendant was in default.

"The summons was served under the order of the last district attorney just before he went out of office, and the suit came by inheritance to General Woodford, the present district attorney, who prepared the complaint.

"The complaint contains twelve counts, and demands judgment against the defendant for $128,442, besides interest for many years, and costs of the action.

"Prior to my retainer in the case, in March, 1880, the district attorney, General Woodford, having collected and examined all the evidence within his reach to warrant him in proceeding to trail, accordingly filed a very long bill of discovery against the defendant, as the only means left by which sufficient evidence could be obtained. The bill specifically states that there is not sufficient evidence to be had without resort to a bill of discovery. To this bill a demurrer was interposed, and the questions raised by the demurrer are now pending before the Supreme Court.

"In the bill filed for discovery, the plaintiff avers that for the years 1862 and 1863 the defendant made returns of his income, but that the same were not true returns; and that for the years 1864, 1865, 1866,1867, 1868, 1869, 1870, and 1871 the defendant neglected to make any returns, and that in default of such returns the proper officers ' estimated the amount of the defendant's income for said years, and assessed the tax thereon, together with the additional penalties prescribed by law, which tax, additions, and penalties prescribed by law, which tax, additions and penalties so assessed, the defendant paid to the officers authorized, etc.'

"The Act of 1864, as amended by the Act of March 3, 1865 (13 Statues at Large, 480), provides, 'That it shall be the duty of all persons of lawful age to make and render a list or return of the amount of their income, gains, etc.

. . . and in case any person shall neglect or refuse to make and render such list or return, or shall render a false or fraudulent list or return, it shall be the duty of the assessor to make such list, according to the best information he can obtain, *by examination of such person, and his books and accounts, or any other evidence,* and to add twenty-five per cent *as a penalty* to the amount of the duty on such list, in all cases of willful neglect, or refusal to make and render a list or return; and all cases of a false of fraudulent return, to add one hundred per cent *as a penalty.'*

"The penalty for neglect to make returns was increased to fifty per cent by the Act of March 2, 1867 (14 U.S. Statues at Large, page 479).

"There is no charge that the returns made were false and fraudulent for the years 1862 and 1863, when under oath the returns were made, and I find no evidence that they were not correct; and if the case tested on those years alone, I am clearly of opinion that the government would dismiss the suit. I, therefore, consider the question only which relate to the years 1864, 1865, 1866,1867, 1868, 1869, 1870, and 1871, when the plaintiff alleges that the defendant *'neglected to make returns;* and *'paid the tax and penalties prescribed by the statues.'*

"The above cited prescribes in definite terms 'the duty' of citizen relating to returns of income; and in case of neglect imposes a penalty, and specifically directs how the assessor shall make a list for return and imposition of the penalties.

"The defendant denies all the material allegations contained in the various counts of the complaint, and (as a specimen) add: 'And for a further and separate defence to the seventh, eighth, tenth, eleventh, and twelfth causes of action contained in the complaint, the defendant alleges that he neglected to make a list or return, and that after said neglect for each of said years the assessor made a list of defendant's annual income, and did assess the duty thereon, and did add fifty per cent, as a penalty, all of which tax and penalties the defendant paid to the collector.'

To these pleas the plaintiff demurred, and Judge Blatchford, in a very elaborate opinion, sustained the demurrer, thus holding that the payment of the tax assessed, and the penalties imposed, did not discharge the defendant from further liabilities, notwithstanding the lapse of time and the absence of any charge that the assessor had been deceived or misled by any concealment or other act on the part of the defendant.

"I am not aware that his direct question had ever been decided by the Supreme Court of the United States, and until it is thus passed upon, there is likely to be much difference of opinion as to the law of this case.

"The question will of course arise on the trial, and its discussion in presence of the jury will (however irregular it may be) tend to bias their minds in favor of the defendant, on the ground that when the citizen had paid all the tax that the law seemed to require, with heavy penalties for his neglect, added exactly as the statute directed, and no charge of fraud, deception, or concealment is made, and the money is received and the receipt given, and years had been allowed to pass without any suggestion of the assessment or penalty being too low, it would not be equitable or just, so long after the repeal if the law, to impose a new burden. Of course, as this is a pure question of law, the jury would have no right to consider it, except as directed by the court; but I have had too much experience with juries not to be aware that they will consider it, and that it may be an excuse in some of their minds for refusing to find facts necessary to a recovery by the plaintiff.

"If it be decided that the payment of the tax and penalty is no bar to the action, then a legal question will arise as to the burden of proof.

"As a sample of the counts take the sixth. The complaint avers that the defendant in the year 1865 had gains, profits, and income from various sources, 'amounting to three hundred and thirty-two thousand dollars, in excess of the sum of six hundred dollars, and in excess of the sum which was subject by law to a duty at a lower rate than ten per centum, and also in excess of the sums which he was entitled by law to deduct from his said gains, profits, and income was estimating the amount thereof upon which he was required by law to pay a duty for said year, and also over and above the sum paid within the said year, by said defendant, for the national, State, county , and municipal taxes upon his property or other sources of income, and also above losses sustained by the defendant for the rent of the homestead used or occupied by himself or his family, and above losses sustained by the defendant upon the sales of real estate purchased by him within said "year."'

"The defendant takes issue. If the plaintiff must prove *the charge as laid* before we can get judgment, then the income of the defendant for a given year was fifty thousand dollars, and there rest, and the defendant says nothing, for what sum can we demand judgment? We sue for a sum over and above the statutory deductions, which is all that the law allows. We should be in difficulty unless the court held that the burden of proving deductions was thrown upon the defendant. Would the court so hold after the taxes and penalties imposed by the proper officers had all been paid?

"After this great lapse of time there is much difficulty in getting at such evidence as the court will receive. Every witness who knows anything of value is unwilling; some fear exposure of their own delinquencies, other profess forgetfulness, and the difficulty in reaching legal and reliable testimony is nearly insuperable, and it is quite certain that the tendency of the jury will be against overhauling stale claims for taxes when the defendant has paid all that assessors impose, with heavy penalties added, and especially as no charge is made of deceptive concealment; since the suit was not commenced, and no fault found until so many years after, when Mr. Tilden was nominated for President, political considerations will be likely to enter into the trial of the cause and may influence the verdict.

"The report of Mr. Webster, and officer of the internal revenue service, upon whom we rely to furnish the only valuable evidence, was strongly against risking a trial in April, 1880, as his report on file shows; and after a very careful examination of all the evidence which we can now produce, our case is in no respect stronger, but rather weaker that in 1880.

"The district attorney, General Woodford, in a late communication to the President, is of opinion, in which I concur, that the action ought to be dismissed; which communication of the district attorney to the President, and which is referred to the attorney-general, I ask leave to make a part of this report.

"We had hoped to elicit very valuable, though most unwilling, testimony from Mr. Lanier, a banker of New York, and on account of his infirm health we tried repeatedly to take his testimony conditionally, but we failed by reason of his feeble condition of health. Last July we obtained an order for his examination, but he was still too ill to be examined, and soon after he died. We had expected to obtain valuable evidence from a cross-examination of the defendant, but his physical condition makes success in that way quite improbable.

"If the action is to be tried, a laborious preparation is essential and should begin forthwith. The trial will take from six weeks to two months and will be attended with very large expenses to the government. If the case is to be dismissed, the terms of the dismissal will require your consideration.

"The defendant offers to reimburse the government its expenses. It has been suggested that the government should dismiss the action without costs. I should be of that mind if convinced that there was no reasonable ground for commencing it; but I do not entertain that view.

"I regard this as a case where for various causes we failed to obtain the legal evidence to maintain the action, and I think it would be just for the government to exact as a condition the payment of expenses incurred.

"In suit against Hazzard, in Rhode Island, the government claimed over $150,000, which with interest amounted to some $250,000. It was settled for just $1,000.

"So far as I can learn, this suit is the only one in the entire United States which has been prosecuted, except the above Hazzard suit mentioned.

"My opinion is that the suit ought to be dismissed on the terms proposed.

"I have the honor to remain, etc.,

"(Signed)   EDWARDS PIERREPONT,
                        "*Special Counsel for the United States.*

"NOTE: There seems to be evidence that for the year 1868 Mr. Tilden made returns, but neither the complaint, answer, or the bill of discovery so treat it."

United States District Attorney to the Commissioner of Internal Revenue.

"OFFICE OF THE UNITED STATES ATTORNEY
FOR THE SOUTHERN DISTRICT OF NEW YORK.
"NEW YORK, Dec. 10, 1881.

"GENERAL: Enclosed please find (1) original proposition by Mr. Vanderpoel, of counsel for Mr. Tilden, for settlement of the income-tax suit against the latter on payment of the expenses which the United States have incurred or become liable for in bringing and preparing this case, and (2) copy of letter from Mr. Pierrepont enclosing such proposition to me for transmittal to you.

"In Mr. Pierrepont's report to the acting attorney-general, dated November 27 ultimo, and referred to in the enclosed letter from him to me, Mr. Pierrepont advised that this action be dismissed on condition of payment of expenses incurred. I suppose that a copy of that report has been or will be sent to you from the attorney-generals office, with copy of my letter to the President, of November 19 ultimo, in which I agreed with Mr. Pierrepont in advising discontinuance of this suit.

"I advise the acceptance of this proposition of settlement, and beg to accompany this recommendation with the following statement:

"On Jan. 24, 1877, I entered on the duties of this office. On Jan. 22, 1877, two days before that date, the *capias* was issued by my predecessor, and this suit was then formally commenced. The complaint was subsequently drawn. Then the defendant answered, both denying any indebtedness and setting up as an affirmative defence that as to all the years during, which income taxes were due, except 1862 and 1863, he had made no returns, but had been assessed and had paid the taxes so found due by the United States assessors, with added penalties, and claiming that such assessment and payment satisfied the claim of the government. To that defence I demurred. That demurrer was argued and sustained. This left the cause at issue on the allegations of the complaint and the denials of the answer. Subsequently, after full examination of what details of evidence were then within my reach, and after full consultation with the then attorney-general, I filed a bill of discovery in May, 1879. To that Mr. Tilden demurred. He was again unsuccessful and appealed to the Supreme Court. That appeal is now pending unheard.

"Meanwhile the spring of 1880 had come. Special Agent E. D. Webster had, about Aug. 1, 1879, been assigned by you to ascertain as far as possible the real facts in the case and to assist in preparing for trial. Although sufficient evidence was not in our possession when we filed the bill of discovery in May, 1879, I thought in the spring of 1880, with the additional help of being then able to put Mr. Tilden on the stand and examine him in person, we could try the case as well as we ever could. Mr. Webster, who had worked with great energy and skill, and to whom I owed most that I really knew about the probable facts, did not think the government ready for trial on the facts, and strongly advised against trial at that time. On my application for special counsel to assist in preparing the case and in the trial, Mr. Pierrepont and Mr. Arnoux were retained for the government.[1]

"There seemed to me then an additional reason for the trial of the case then. Mr. Tilden had been a candidate of one of the greatest political parties of the country for the presidency in 1876. During that canvass the allegations were made, out of which this suit grew. In January, 1877, after that election had occurred, the suit was commenced.

"In the spring of 1880 his name was again frequently mentioned in connection with a presidential nomination in the following summer. It seemed to me that the case should then be tried and Mr. Tilden relieved from it imputations, or the claim of the government established in court. Mr. Tilden, however, himself applied for the postponement until autumn.

"That postponement was granted by direction of the government, communicated to me through Mr. Pierrepont on the 29th day of March, 1880, on which day I accordingly consented to the adjournment for which Mr. Tilden had applied.

"Since then there has been no term of the court at which this case could be tried consistently with the engagement of our judges and the condition of our calendars.

"It can now be put on the calendar for the next February term of the District Court, and possibly can then be tried.

"Its trial will occupy from four to eight weeks.

"Mr. Lanier, who was living in spring of 1880, and whom we thought a valuable witness for the government, is dead. Others, and important

---

1 Note: I was assured by Mr. Tilden that the letter containing what is here designated as a proposition originating with Mr. Vanderpoel, of counsel for Mr. Tilden, for settling the income-tax suit, by his paying the expenses incurred in prosecuting the suit to date, so far from originating with him, as actually propounded to Mr. Vanderpoel by the government's counsel. When the proposition was submitted to Mr. Tilden he said, "I can afford to settle this suit upon these terms, but Mr. Folger (the Secretary of the Treasury) cannot. He cannot afford to make me pay the expense of instituting the suit for which he admits that he has no cause of action." - J.B.

witnesses, whom I then thought willing and available, now remember nothing and are not available.

"The appeal at Washington on the bill of discovery is still pending unheard. Whether Mr. Tilden's health is such as to enable him now to be examined for continuous days, and in matters going into minute details running over many years long past, I do not know. I am told he is not. At all events, I doubt our practical ability to secure or compel his attendance for such examination I seriously doubt our ability to succeed.

"As to all the years except 1862, 1863, and 1868, we must confront the fact that our assessors fixed what tax Mr. Tilden should pay, and he paid it. As to 1862 and 1863 and 1868, he made returns. As to 1862 and 1863 we have no proof. As to 1868, we can perhaps show that his taxable income exceeded what he stated it to be in his return, by $48,405.59. Tax on this is $2,420.26.

"If Mr. Tilden is right in his view of the law, shared by many, and even accepted, I think, by your bureau in 1877, as to the years when he made no returns, but allowed the assessors to fix his income and then paid his tax as fixed by them, then the year 1868 is the only one on which we can recover. If the view as argued by me and sustained by the opinion of Judge Blatchford is the correct one, then we are left to prove his income for the years 1864,1865,1866,1867,1869,1870, and 1871. Of course, on the trial in the District Court here, Judge Blatchford's decision will control, but I fully agree with Judge Pierrepont in thinking that arguments and references in the presence of the jury to the assessments by government officers, and payments thereon by the defendant, will affect the opinion and the verdict of the jury.

"Our case is not as strong as it was in the spring of 1880. The passage of time steadily weakens it. It should be dismissed or tried.

"I believe that the pecuniary interests of the government will be best served by accepting the offer of Mr. Tilden's counsel to have the case dismissed, on repayment to the government of all expenses incurred, or for which the government is liable in bringing and preparing the case for trial.

"Very respectfully, etc.

(Signed)   S.L. WOODFORD,
                                           "*United States Attorney.*

"(Two enclosures.)"

Green B. Raum, United States Commissioner of Internal Revenue, to
Stewart L. Woodford, United States District Attorney.

> TREASURY DEPARTMENT,
> "OFFICE OF INTERNAL REVENUE,
> "WASHINGTON, DEC. 23, 1881.

"HONARABLE STEWART L. WOODFORD, United States Attorney,
New York:

"SIR: I acknowledge the receipt of your letter of the 10th instant,
enclosing copy of letter of Hon. Edwards Pierrepont, of December 6th,
and the letter of A.J. Vanderpoel, Esq., of December 3rd, in regard to the
case of the United States against Samuel J. Tilden.

"The suit against Mr. Tilden was instituted because of a belief
founded upon the recognized fact of his great wealth, much of which
was understood to have been accumulated during the tax period; that
he was largely indebted to the United States for taxes upon income.
This suit was not instituted until after one of the justices of the Supreme
Court of the United States had held in a similar case that the United
States had held in a similar case that the United States had a right to
sue for the recovery of unpaid income tax.

"If an investigation into this case has developed the fact to the attorneys of the government that there is no cause of action against Mr.
Tilden, then the suit should be dismissed at the cost of the United
States. If the attorneys for the United States are satisfied that a good
cause of action exists, but in consequence of the death of some of the
witnesses and the difficulty of establishing the facts in the case, are of
opinion that the government cannot recover, then a compromise for
costs and expenses would seem admissible. If, upon the other hand,
the district attorney and his associates are satisfied that Mr. Tilden is
indebted to the United States, and if put upon the witness stand by the
government that he would disclose such facts as would secure to the
government a verdict, then, in my opinion, if a compromise is effected,

it should be upon the basis of the payment of a considerable sum of money in satisfaction of the claim for taxes.[1]

"If the case could be brought to trial, it seems to me that Mr. Tilden should be made the first witness, and if his testimony failed to make out a case for the government I would dismiss the suit. I respectfully submit whether this would not be the best plan to pursue. It certainly would be no hardship to Mr. Tilden to have him spend two or three hours in the witness box to testify, in regard to his income for which the government claims. He could be given ample notice of your intention to call him as a witness, so that he could prepare the necessary memoranda in advance, My impression is that should you pursue this course you could get through with Mr. Tilden as a witness in thirty minutes, and test before the court and the country the question as to his liability for taxes.

"Very respectfully,

"(Signed)   Green B. Raum,
"Commissioner."

Edwards Pierrepont, Special Counsel of the United States, to the District Attorney of the United States.

"156 BROADWAY,
"NEW YORK, Jan. 28, 1882.

GEN. STEWART L. WOODFORD, *United States Attorney, etc.:*

"SIR: I returned from Washington a week ago this day, having seen General Raum the day before I left. I promptly saw Mr. Vanderpoel, Mr. Tilden's counsel, and he assured me that Mr. Tilden is in a *very feeble* condition of health; but at Mr. Tilden's house Mr. Vanderpoel

---

1 NOTE: Here we have an official admission that the most prominent individual in the nation had been summoned by its government to answer to charges of perjury and fraudulent accounting, not upon any evidence in it possession of any such specific crime having been committed, but solely, "upon the recognized fact of his great wealth, much of which was understood to have been accumulated during the tax period."

By whom was the fact of his great wealth recognized in 1867? By whom was much of it understood to have been accumulated during the tax period? And how much? On these crucial matters not a ray of light for court or country.

It is shocking to think that the vast inquisitorial powers of the judiciary of such a nation as ours should by any possibility ever lapse into the hands of men who ought to be cutting stone or picking oakum with felons.

had discussed that matter thoroughly, as he last night at my house assured me.

"Mr. Tilden asserts, and will swear, if he is ever able to take the stand, that it is utterly impossible for him, or for any one else, to find out whether of not he paid all the tax which the law might have exacted; that he had no partners, and was not obliged to, and did not, keep regular books; that when he was regularly assessed, and paid, with full penalty, all that the officers of the government demanded, for which they gave receipts, he supposed that he has paid all that any law could require, and gave himself no further trouble about it; that his first return was twenty years ago, and that lapse of time, if nothing else, would make it impossible, without books, for any human ingenuity to discover what gains, profits, and income he had, in the three years mentioned in the complaint, 'in excess of the sum of six hundred dollars, and in excess of the sum which was subject by law to a duty at a lower rate than ten per cent., and also in excess of the sum which he was entitled by law to deduct from his gains, profits, and income in estimating the amount thereof, upon which he was required by law to pay a duty; and also in excess of the amount of gain, profits, and income upon which he paid a duty for those years, and also over and above the sum paid within said year, by said defendant, for national, State and country, and municipal taxes upon his property or other sources of income, and also above the sum paid by said defendant for the rent of the homestead used or occupied by himself or his family, and above losses sustained by the defendant upon sales of real estate purchased by him within said years.'

"He further states 'that he did not make returns, because it was impossible from the nature of his transactions to make such returns as he could swear to, and because (like many others) he was not willing to disclose his affairs to all persons, some of whom would be likely to make unreasonable claims upon his bounty; that he cannot tell whether, even under the decision of Judge Blatchford, he would be liable for anything or not, if all the facts could be ascertained but that he is willing to pay, as proposed, if that will end the matter. '

"I append a copy of an elaborate report which I made to the attorney-general, in which I fully discussed the difficulties of the case, which report I beg that you will send to General Raum.

"I wrote that report after full consideration of the question whether the case ought to be dismissed without costs.

"I think that the commissioner of internal revenue will feel it due to us, either to take the responsibility himself if ordering the case to be dismissed without costs, or to accept the compromise offered, or to direct the cause to be tried, or to throw the responsibility upon us.

"I am very truly yours,

"(Signed)   EDWARDS PIERRPONT,
"Special Counsel for the United States."

The Secretary of the Treasury to the Commissioner of Internal Revenue.

"(Copy.)

"TREASURY DEPARTMENT,
"WASHINGTON D.C., May 23, 1882.

HON. GREEN B. RAUM, *Commissioner of Internal Revenue:*

"SIR: You have place before me a letter from Hon. Edwards Pierre-pont, and one from the United States attorney at New York city, in the matter of the suit of the United States v. Samuel J. Tilden. It is a case that should not be brought to trial without a reasonable prospect of success. It is one also in which, if there is no reasonable prospect of success, there should be no attempt to try it; nor should any terms be insisted upon, or sought, upon throwing it up. Of course I intend to place upon the counsel for the government the responsibility of advising as to the prospect of success, or rather, I intend to leave that responsibility upon them, as of right if belongs there. I suppose that you have given to counsel all the facts that you are able to supply. It is for counsel to determine and advise whether they are enough to warrant the trial of the suit. If they furnish a fair prospect of success on a trial, it should be had at once. If they do not, the case should be discontinued. It is due to the citizen that he be brought to trail, or that he be freed from the expectation of it. And if there is not enough in the facts to refuse him the latter, it does not seem to me just or worthy of the government that it exact or take from him a price for the privilege.

"Respectfully, etc.,

"(Signed)   CHARLES L. FOLGER,
"Secretary Treasury."

The Attorney- General to the Secretary of the Treasury."

"(Copy.)

'DEPARTMENT OF JUSTICE,
Washington. July 21, 1882.

"SIR: On the 21st of June were sent to me the papers pertaining to the suit of the United States against Samuel J. Tilden for my further examination. With this I return those papers to you, having given the subject my consideration. Among the papers I found your letter of May 23, 1882, to Hon. Green B. Raum, Commissioner of Internal Revenue. I will not undertake to review the subject, as I cannot express in more plain and direct terms the convictions that I entertain and the conclusions I have arrived at than you have expressed them in that letter. I concur in all you say. You explain the true policy and principle that should regulate the proceedings on behalf of the government against Mr. Tilden. The last sentence of your letter propounds the rule by which the case should be regulated. You say, 'It is due to the citizens that he be brought to trial, or that he be freed from the expectation of it. And if there is not enough in the facts to make it proper to refuse him that letter, it does not seem to me just of worthy of the government that it exact or take from him a price for the privilege.'

"I am positively opposed, as a point of principle and integrity of governmental action, in cases like these, to have them pursued when they should not be, and to surrender them only on condition of receiving from the defendant compensation to pay the counsel of the government. It is beneath the dignity of the government to stoop to such a settlement of any such case. It would result in corrupt practices of the most frightful kind if the legal officers of the government could institute suits which they could not maintain, and then compound them by exacting large sums of money from the defendants; selling their peace to them as a purchasable commodity. The mere thought of such things is odious.

"Your letter is addressed to Mr. Raum. As the district attorney is directly under my control, is it your desire that I shall communicate these views to him? Mr. Raum may hesitate to do so. It seems there have been private counsel employed upon behalf of the government.

To that gentleman Mr. Raum may have conveyed your ideas. If he has not, I will do it if you so instruct me.

"I have the honor to be, with great respect, your obedient servant,

"BENJAMIN HARRIS BREWSTER,

"*Attorney-General.*

"HON. CHAS J. FOLGER,
Secretary of the Treasury."

Secretary of the Treasury to the Attorney-General.

"TREASURY DEPARTMENT, July 25, 1882.

"HON. BENJAMIN HARRIS BREWSTER, *Attorney General,*
Department of Justice:

"SIR: I have the honor to acknowledge the receipt of you letter of the 21st instant, in which you are please to express your concurrence in all that was said in my letter of the 23rd of May last to Commissioner Raum, in regard to 'the true policy and principle that should regulate the proceedings on behalf of the government,' in the suit pending against Samuel J. Tilden.

"In reply to your inquiry as to communicating those views to the United States attorney, and to the private counsel employed by the government in this case, I have the honor to say that my letter to Commissioner Raum has been made known to Judge Pierrepont; and, therefore, all that is now needed, in my judgment, is for the attorney-general to inform the United States attorney at New York, and Judge Pierrepont, that the Department of Justice and the Treasury Department concur in the views put forth in my letter to Commissioner Raum, and that it is for counsel and the court to say what shall be done with the case, according to the rules and practice of the court.

"Very respectfully,

"(Signed)   CHAS. J. FOLGER.
                                              Secretary.

United States Attorney Stuart L. Woodford to Green B. Raum, the Commissioner of Internal Revenue.

OFFICE OF THE UNITED STATES ATTORNEY
FOR THE SOUTHERN DISTRICT OF NEW YORK,

"NEW YORK, OCT. 7, 1882.

THE HON. GREEN B. RAUM, *Commissioner of Internal Revenue:*
"GENERAL: Having determined as to the final disposition of the income-tax case against Mr. Tilden, I beg to present this report of the case.

"It was commenced by my immediate predecessor in office, the Hon. George Bliss, by filing a *præcipe* in our District Court on Jan. 22, 1877, two days before he went out of office.

"The case continued through various stages of intricate litigation until Aug. 1, 1879, when Revenue Agent E. D. Webster reported to me by your direction to investigate the facts and procure necessary evidence.

"He was engaged on this duty until the spring of 1880, when I came to the conclusion that the case was as well prepared as was within our then power, and should be tried at the April term, 1880. Witnesses were subpoenaed and arrangements made for the trial.

"There seemed to me an additional reason for the trial then.

"Mr. Tilden had been candidate for the presidency in 1876. During that canvas the allegations were made out, of which grew this suit. In January, 1877, after that canvass had closed, the suit was begun.

"In the spring of 1880 his name was again frequently mentioned for a like candidacy. I thought the case should be tried then and decided. This seemed to me most dignified for the government, and most just to Mr. Tilden.

"Mr. Webster, however, reported that we were not then ready on the facts. Of the special counsel for the government, Judge Pierrepont did think we could safely go to trial, while our other associated, Judge Arnoux, advised trial. The then attorney-general, Mr. Devens, agreed with Judge Pierrepont.

"Meanwhile, Mr. Tilden's counsel applied for postponement on the ground of his poor health. Then, against my judgment, and on the direction of the attorney-general, communicated through Judge Pierrepont, the case was postponed, on March 29, 1880, to the November term of that year.

"Since then there has been no term of our District Court at which this case could be tried, consistently with the engagements of our judges and the condition of the calendar, until February, 1882.

"In September, 1881, President Garfield died.

"In the preceding July, after he had been shot, and while the entire country was forgetting old differences and uniting in sympathy, I felt and advised Judge Pierrepont that I would be wise for President Garfield, on his expected recovery, to stop this suit himself.

"On the accession of President Arthur it seemed to me still more wise, as matter of public policy, to discontinue this litigation, and to do this without exacting any costs or conditions, but simply as an act of grace from the government to a citizen.

"After full consideration with Judge Pierrepont, he came to the further decision, that owing to lapse of time, death of witnesses, payment by Mr. Tilden of such taxes as the government officers had assessed against him, and for other reasons fully set forth in his subsequent report to the attorney-general, dated Nov. 27, 1881, it would be unwise to try the case.

"These two methods of discontinuance were open. One was to discontinue without costs. This I then advised. The other was to accept an offer which was about that time made by Mr. Vanderpoel to Judge Pierrepont, that Mr. Tilden would pay all the costs and expenses incurred by the government in bringing and preparing the suit for trial. Judge Pierrepont favored accepting the proposition because he feared that if we dismissed the case without taking the costs which were voluntarily offered to be paid, we should run the risk of rendering Mr. Bliss and the government, which he represented, liable to the suspicion of having threatened a groundless action against Mr. Tilden during the canvass of 1876, and which suit was in fact commenced two days before Mr. Bliss left office. Both Judge Pierrepont and I thought, as lawyers, that there had been probable cause for bringing the suit, and were unwilling to do so, to allow anything to be done that should be in any manner professionally unjust to Mr. Bliss who began, or myself who had continued, the case which I had found in the office so begun.

"But I did not share in this fear. The case was here. I was responsible for its conduct, and was willing to face whatever just criticism my management of it might involve.

"Thus differing in opinion as to what we should advise, and feeling that at the outset of a new administration the President should be himself consulted (as Mr. MacVeagh had resigned as attorney-general), I wrote the President, on Nov. 19, 1881, stating that for reasons fully discussed between Judge Pierrepont and myself, and which he would fully present to the President, I agreed in advising the discontinuance of the suit against Mr. Tilden in such manner and on such terms as the President might think wisest.

"Judge Pierrepont presented that letter to the President, had full consultation with him, and was by him referred to the then acting attorney-general, Mr. Phillips. The latter considered the entire subject, having before him the full report made by Judge Pierrepont on Nov. 27, 1881, and then, under date of Nov. 29, 1881, he wrote me officially that the case should be submitted to the commissioner of internal revenue with my opinion and that of Mr. Pierrepont as to the chances of recovery, and also with any proposition of arrangement suggested by the defendant. The acting, attorney-general added that this was a suit for money, the recovery of which had been obstructed by accident, and that the preponderance of reasons appeared to favor such arrangement as should be attended with least pecuniary loss.

"Such were my instructions from my official chief.

"The case and the desired opinions, with Mr. Tilden's propositions to pay the expenses of the suit, were subsequently submitted to you. You expressed your disinclination to exact costs or terms if the case was to be discontinued.

"The papers subsequently went to the Secretary of the Treasury. He returned them to you with a note dated May 2, 1882, of which you sent me a copy on May 18, 1882.

"This note stated that the proposition was to pay the costs and expenses of the suit and have it discontinued; that the government recovers nothing; that if there is any proof on which the government has an expectation of recovering, it ought to go on with the suit; that in either case it seemed to the secretary solely a question for the counsel for the government that they should decide whether to go on or whether to discontinue or ask leave of the court to discontinue; that there is nothing for the Treasury Department to pass upon in such a proposition as this.

"On May 20' 1882, I wrote you, acknowledging receipt of the foregoing and asking whether I was to understand that if after consultation with Mr. Pierrepont we both agree that this action cannot now be prosecuted with any reasonable prospect of success, we are authorized to discontinue it without costs. I added that as we construe the secretary's note this was his decision. I wrote you thus, because under the printed regulations of your bureau I could not legally discontinue this suit without your express instructions.

"On May 23, 1882, you again wrote me, enclosing copy of a second letter from the secretary, in which you gave me the express authority required. This letter of the secretary also stated that the case should not be tried without a reasonable prospect of success.

"These letters were received on May 24, 1882. They were submitted to Judge Pierrepont at once. Almost immediately afterward, on the same day, I received a telegram from you directing me to take no action upon your letter of the day before in the Tilden case until I should hear further from your office and asking me to answer. Accordingly I telegraphed you in reply that day, acknowledging receipt of your order and promising to obey your instructions and take no action until I heard further from your office.

"The next day, May 25th, I received a letter from Secretary Folger, dated May 20th, but evidently written May 24th, stating that he would probably be in New York city the next week, when he would try to see me on the matter of the Tilden case. He added that there were considerations which had come to him since writing his letter of the day before to General Raum which he desired to confer with me upon. He also stated that you (General Raum) had just shown him my telegraphic message in answer to your message sent to me that morning, which latter was sent at his suggestion.

"Although Secretary Folger came to New York soon afterward, we did not meet. He never stated to me that considerations on which he had ordered me, through you, to take no further action on your letter of May 23d, in regard to the Tilden case until I should hear further from your office. Nor have I ever had the advantage of the conference with him that he so considerately suggested.

"After the receipt of your telegram of May 24, and the secretary's said letter, I did not hear further from your office until July 27th last, when I received your letter of July 26th, covering copies of letters from Attorney-General Brewster to Secretary Folger, dated July 21, 1882, and from the secretary to the attorney general, dated July 25, 1882. These letters were of the same general tenor as the secretary's letter of May 23rd last, and left the matter to my final decision after consultation with him as to this case since that date.

"As the secretary arrested the operation of his instructions of May 23rd last from May 24th to July 25th, for considerations that must have seemed to him serious and weighty, I feel that I ought to reexamine the case carefully, and I asked Judge Pierrepont to do the same.

"Yesterday I received his carefully reconsidered opinion, in which he adheres to his former advice that the case ought now to be discontinued.

"After thinking the whole matter over I have decided that there is not a sufficient prospect of success to justify that long, expensive, and difficult trial which will be necessary to present this complicated case fully to the court. The trial would necessarily occupy from four to eight weeks, and the result would be very doubtful.

"I accordingly have this day sent to Mr. Tilden's counsel a consent to discontinue without costs.

"Very respectfully,

"(Signed)   STEWART. L. WOODFORD,
"United States Attorney."

"At a stated term of the Circuit Court of the United States for the Southern District of New York, held at the United States Court Rooms in the Post-Office Building, on the twenty-third day of October, 1882.

"Present:
"HON. CHARLES L. BENEDICT,
"Judge.

ORDER

"THE UNITED STATES OF AMERICA

AGAINST

SAMUEL J. TILDEN

"The original action of the District Court of the Untied States for the Southern District of New York between the same parties having been discontinued, and the appeal heretofore taken from the decree entered in this action having been dismissed and the proceedings remitted to this court, now, on reading and filing the consent of the United States attorney, it is

"*Ordered,* That this action be and the same is hereby discontinued without costs to either party as against the other.

"(Signed)   CHARLES L. BENEDICT."

Thus ended a vexatious litigation instituted solely for the purpose of defaming and discrediting the most eminent statesman in the country; instituted, too, without any evidence, at the instigation of a painfully notorious public officer, "because of a belief founded upon the recognized fact of Mr. Tilden's great wealth, much of which was understood to have been accumulated during the tax period."

For six long years Mr. Tilden was subjected to the expense of employing counsel and holding himself constantly ready for a trial of a suit, on the admission of its own officers, the government never had any evidence upon with it could prosecuted with any prospect of success.

A Republican form of government has always the power, and sometimes the disposition, to be despotic and oppressive. Of this a more flagrant illustration than the one just recited had rarely occurred.

Graystone (now St. John's Hospital), Yonkers, NY.

CHAPTER VIII

The purchase of Graystone – Dinner to J.S. Morgan – Mr. Tilden rebukes third-term candidates for the presidency – Withdraws from public life – Letter to Mr. Manning declaring the presidential nomination in 1880 – The Cincinnati convention – Urged for a renomination in 1884 – Second letter of declension.

In the summer of 1879 Mr. Tilden thought to benefit his health by establishing a home, for at least a portion of the year, in the country. He leased for the summer, and before the expiration of the lease purchased, the noble estate since widely known as Graystone at Yonkers, on the Hudson, then about three miles beyond the northernmost limit of New York city. The property consisted of sixty-three and one-third acres of land, and a palatial stone dwelling which had been recently finished, on the highest ground on the river's bank south of Highlands. To this estate he subsequently added forty-eight adjoining acres. The structure, the view, the air, the facilities of access to the city, everything about the place, was suited to his taste and his needs. If he had not by this time abandoned all thought of returning to public life, he had ceased to regard such a prospect with pleasure. He found all the employment and recreation he required in improving and stocking his new home. Thither he transported a portion of his library, in the seclusion of which he now enjoyed a welcome exemption from the incessant interruptions to which he was exposed in Gramercy Park. Graystone soon became, to a far greater extent than he had anticipated, his home. Here he received his friends with a generous hospitality. Though ceasing to take any responsibility for the leadership of the party, his views of public matters continued to be sought and his judgment deferred to as much as ever. He appeared rarely before the public, though scarcely an editor in the land ventured to send his paper to press without some allusion to him.

In the fall of 1877 he consented to preside at a dinner given to the late J.S. Morgan, then head of the banking house of J.S. Morgan and Company, of London. In the course of the speech, in which he proposed the health of Mr. Morgan, he referred, in a humorous way, to the very small share that the proprietors of colossal fortunes can appropriate to their personal use. It is the only instance, I believe, of his ever alluding in a public discourse or paper to the burdens or perquisites of wealth.

"I remember, when I was quite a young man, being sent for by one of the ablest men I have ever known, - a great statesman and a great thinker, - Martin Van Buren, who wanted to consult me about his will. Well, I walked with him all over his farm one afternoon, and I heard what he had to say, with the previous knowledge (not from him) that I was trustee under his will. The next morning, as I stood before his broad and large wood-fire, I stated that result of my reflections. I said: 'It is not well to be wiser than events; to attempt to control the far future, which no man can foresee; to trust one's grandchildren, whom one does not know, out of distrust, without special cause, of one's children, whom one does know.' I came home, and after a week I received a letter from him stating that he had thought much about the suggestion as to attempting to be wiser than events, and had abandoned all the complicated trusts by which he had proposed tying up his property; and he submitted to me a simple form according to the laws of the land and the laws of nature, which was approved and adopted.

"I went down to Roehampton last summer to see the beautiful country home of my friend Mr. Morgan, a few miles out of London. He was well pleased to show me about everywhere. No man could help being delighted with what I saw, and he was curious to know what were my impressions. Well, I had, while inspecting with pleasure the appliances of comfort and luxury, been thinking how much, after all, he got for himself out of his great wealth and great business; how much he was able to apply to his own use; what sort of wages he got for managing the great establishment at No. 22 Old Broad street, in London; and I said to him: "I don't see but what you are trustee here: you get only your food, your clothing, your shelter." Of course a man may have some delight in a sense of power, in a sense of consequence; but I rather thought his coachman beat him in that particular. And, on the whole, I thought aloud – I could not help it. I told him he was a trustee with a very handsome salary, doing very well; but I could not see that he got much more than any of the rest of the people about the place. Well, I did hear, when, soon after, I went down to 22 Old Broad street, that he was rather late to business the next morning. But I will do him the justice to say that he faithfully applied himself to his duties as trustee, and that he was diligent as though he had some personal interest in the great affairs he is managing.

Mr. Tilden was invited to dine with the Democratic Association of Massachusetts, on the anniversary of Washington's birthday in 1880. General Grant was still a candidate for the presidency for a third term, and was warmly supported by the Republicans of Massachusetts. In his letter excusing his absence, Mr. Tilden took an opportunity of repeating his views of third-term candidates for the presidency. He said:

"Nothing could be more fit at the present time than to commemorate that day. It was the Father of his Country, 'first in war, first in peace, and first in the hearts of his countrymen,' who set the original example against a third term in presidential office. He made that memorable precedent as a guide to all his successors, and as an unwritten law of the American people. He did so in the light of a prevalent fear in the minds of the most ardent of the patriots who have achieved our national independence, and created our system of free government, that indefinite re-eligibility would degenerate into a practical life-tenure.

"The vast power acquired by the federal government over the elections by its office-holders, its patronage, the money it levies, and its various forms of corrupt influence, have developed this danger, until it darkens the whole future of our country.

"In the choice between the republic and the empire, we must believe that the people will be true to their ancestry and to mankind.

Mr. Tilden continued to be regarded as the necessary and inevitable candidate of his party for the presidency in 1880. The name of no other candidate was seriously discussed. He was persecuted with unrelenting virulence by the administration, and the Republicans press neglected no opportunity of refreshing the memory of its readers in regard to his imputed capacities for wickedness, and the wholly imaginary value of his public services. The Democratic press and politicians, on the other hand, continued to speak of his nomination as a matter of course, though without any authority from Mr. Tilden that he desired, or even would accept, a renomination if tendered. They knew, of course, that he would accept, a renomination if his health would permit; and the evidence of unimpaired mental power and political resource he was constantly displaying caused his health to be regarded by the public as a very insignificant factor in the case. It was not so with Mr. Tilden, however. He wished a renomination and an opportunity of proving, by his re-election, that the country had been fraudulently deprived of its choice for the presidency in 1876. He was slow in making up his mind that he was unequal to the worries of a candidate, or for the more serious responsibilities of a chief magistrate. But however blind his partisans and friends were or pretended to be about his health, he had no longer any illusions upon the subject himself. He was fully conscious, in the winter of 1879 – 80, that his health had been steadily failing since 1876, and that the most his medical advisers had done or hoped to do was to retard a little the ravages of the disease which was held by the profession generally to be an incurable thought usually a lingering one.

I had been trying to assist him one day, early in the spring of 1880, in one of his vexatious litigations. I observed that he did not seem to have the full command of his resources. At last he rose from his seat, and with an air of discouragement on his face as well as in the tone of his voice, said, "Let us go and take a ride." As we rode up the avenue and after a protracted silence he spoke of the decline of force and intellectual endurance, of which he had just experienced such unequivocal evidence, and then added in a rather querulous tone, as if responding to some unwelcome pressure from without, "If I am no longer fit to prepare a case for trial, I am not fit to be President of the United States." He then turned and looked at me to tell him what I had to say in my defence. "Governor, "I replied, "I am the last person in the world to urge you to run for the presidency. No one has a right to ask you to accept such a burden at the risk of your life, and there is no use in trying to disguise the fact that there is nothing which would more imperil your health that the inevitable excitement of a canvass for the presidency and the first six months' service to which an election would expose you."

I think from this day forth he had satisfied himself that he did not wish to be a candidate for the presidency, and was determined not to be a party to any proceedings designed to make him President. He said to me on another occasion, "It takes all my time to live," so numerous were the hygienic precautions he found it necessary to take to meet the inevitable demands upon his strength even as a private citizen. His farm and his library were now to him what the muse was to Pope, - his chief reliance in helping him through "that long disease, his life."

Though conscious that it was as much as his life was worth to accept a renomination, the consequences to the party of refusing to run put on every day a more serious and perplexing aspect. Friends from every part of the country were telling him that he was the only one who could keep the party together. The Democratic press, with practical unanimity, refused to consider the chances of any other candidate; while the defeat of Robinson for governor in New York, at the fall election, had made the success of any new candidate extremely doubtful. But what at that time weighed more, perhaps, that any of these considerations with Mr. Tilden was the apprehension that if he withdrew, the friends of Mr. Hendricks might profit by the *vis inertia* of the old ticket, and insist upon his being placed at its head, which could only have resulted in disaster if the electoral vote of New York State should prove necessary to success, and that it would prove necessary at that time no practical politician entertained a doubt. It was a profounder sense of the difficulties of either course – running or withdrawing – than was possessed, perhaps, by any other statesman in the country that led him to defer until the meeting of the convention in June the promulgation of his desire not to be regarded as a candidate for a renomination. His letter, addressed to the delegates of New York on this occasion, is in some respects one of the most impressive papers that ever came from the pen of any American statesman.

MR. TILDEN'S LETTER DECLINING
A RENOMINATION TO THE PRESIDENCY.

"To the Delegates for the State of New York to the Democratic National Convention:

"Your first assembling is an occasion on which it is proper for me to state to you my relations to the nomination for the presidency, which you and your associates are commissioned to make in behalf of the Democratic party of the United States.

"Having passed my early years in an atmosphere filled with traditions of the war which secured our national independence, and of the struggles which made our constitutional system of government for the people, by the people, I learned to idealize the institutions of my country, and was educated to believe it the duty of a citizen of the Republic to take his fair allotment of care and trouble in public affairs. I fulfilled that duty to the best of my ability for forty years as a private citizen. Although during all my life, giving at least as much thought and effort to public affairs as to all other objects, I have never accepted official service except for a brief period, for a special purpose, and only when the occasion seemed to require of me that sacrifice of private preferences to public interests. My life has been substantially that of a private citizen.

"It was, I presume, the success of efforts, in which as a private citizen I had shared, to overthrow a corrupt combination then holding dominion in our metropolis, and to purify the judiciary which had become its tool, that induced the Democracy of the State of 1874 to nominate me for governor. This was done in spite of the protests of a minority, that the part I had borne in those reforms had created antagonisms fatal to me as a candidate. I felt constrained to accept the nomination as the most certain means of putting the power of the gubernatorial office on the side of reform, and of removing the impression, wherever it prevailed, that the faithful discharge of one's duty as a citizen is fatal to his usefulness as a public servant.

"The breaking up of the canal ring, the better management of our public works, the large reduction of taxes, and other reforms accomplished during my administration, doubtless occasioned my nomination for the presidency by the Democracy of the Union, in the hope that similar processes would be applied to the federal government. From the responsibilities of such and undertaking, appalling as it seemed to me, I did not feel at liberty to shrink.

"In the canvass which ensued, the Democratic party represented reform in the administration of the federal government, and a restoration of our complex political system to the pure ideals of its founders. Upon these issues the people of the United States, by a majority of more than a quarter of a million, chose a majority of the electors to cast their votes for the Democratic candidates for President and Vice President. It is my right and privilege here to say that I was nominated and elected to the presidency absolutely free from any engagement in respect to the exercise and of its powers or the disposal of its patronage. Through the whole period of my relation to the presidency I did everything in my power to elevate and nothing to lower moral standards in the competition of parties.

By what nefarious means the basis of a false count was laid in several of the States, I need not recite. These are now matters of history, about which, whatever diversity of opinion may have existed in either of the great parties of the country at the time of their consummation, has since practically disappeared.

"I refused to ransom from the Returning Boards of Southern States the documentary evidence, by the suppression of which and by the substitution of fraudulent and forged papers, a pretext was made for the perpetration of a false count.

"The constitutional duty of the two Houses of Congress to count the electoral votes as cast, and give effect to the will of the people as expressed by their suffrages, was never fulfilled. An Electoral Commission, for the existence of which I have no responsibility was formed, and to it the two Houses of Congress abdicated their duty to make the count, by a law enacting that the count of the commission should stand as lawful unless overruled by the concurrent action of the two Houses. Its false count was not overruled, owing the complicity of a Republican Senate with the Republican majority of the commission.

"Controlled by its Republican majority of eight to seven, the Electoral Commission counted out the men elected by the people.

"That subversion of the election created a new issue for the decision of the people of the United States, transcending in importance all questions of administration. It involved the vital principle of self-government through elections by the people.

"The immense growth of the means of corruption influence over the ballot-box, which is at the disposal of the party having possession of the executive administration, had already become a present evil and a great danger, tending to make elections irresponsive to public opinion, hampering the power of the people to change their rulers, and enabling the men holding the machinery of government to continue and perpetuate their power. It was my opinion in 1876 that the opposition attempting to change the administration needed to include at least two-thirds of the votes at the opening of the canvass in order to retain a majority at the election.

"If after such obstacles had been overcome, and a majority of the people had voted to change the administration of their government, the men in office could still procure a false count founded upon frauds, perjuries, and forgeries, furnishing a pretext of documentary evidence on which to base that false count, and if such a transaction were not only successful, but if, after allotment of its benefits were made to its contrivers, abettors, and apologist by the chief beneficiary of the transaction, it were condoned by the people, a practical destruction of elections by the people would have been accomplished.

"The failure to install the candidates chosen by the people, a contingency consequent upon no act or omission of mine, and beyond my control, has left me for the last three years, and until now, when the Democratic party by its delegates in national convention assembled shall choose a new leader, the involuntary but necessary representative of this momentous issue.

"As such, denied the immunities of private life, without the powers conferred by public station, subject to unceasing falsehoods and calumnies from the partisans of an administration laboring in vain to justify its existence, I have, nevertheless, steadfastly endeavored to preserve to the Democratic party of the United States the supreme issue before the people for their decision next November, whether this shall be a government by the sovereign people through elections, or a government by discarded servants holding over by force and fraud. And I have withheld no sacrifice and neglected no opportunity to uphold, organize, and consolidate against the enemies of representative institutions, the great party which alone under God can effectually resist their overthrow.

"Having now borne faithfully my full share of labor and care in the public service, and wearing the marks of its burdens, I desire nothing so much as an honorable discharge. I wish to lay down the honors and toils of even *quasi* party leadership, and to seek the repose of private life.

"In renouncing renomination for the presidency, I do so with no doubt in my mind as to the vote of the State of New York, or of the United States, but because I believe that it is a renunciation of re-election to the presidency.

"To those who think my renomination and re-election indispensable to an effectual vindication of the right of the people to elect their rulers – violated in my person – I have accorded as long as a reserve of my decision as possible, but I cannot overcome my repugnance to enter into a new engagement which involves four years of ceaseless toil.

"The dignity of the presidential office is above a merely personal ambition, but it creates in me no illusion. Its value is as great a power for good to the country. I said four years ago in accepting the nomination:

"'Knowing as I do, therefore, from fresh experience, how great the difference is between gliding through an official routine and working out a reform of systems and policies, it is impossible for me to contemplate what needs to be done in the federal administration without an anxious sense of the difficulties of the undertaking. If summoned by the suffrages of my countrymen to attempt this work, I shall endeavor, with God's help, to be the efficient instrument of their will.'

"Such a work of renovation after many years of misrule, such a reform of systems and policies, to which I would cheerfully have sacrificed all that remained to me of health and life, is now, I fear, beyond my strength.

"With unfeigned thanks for the honors bestowed upon me; with a heart swelling with emotions of gratitude to the Democratic masses for the support which they have given to the cause I represented, and for their steadfast confidence in every emergency, I remain,

"Your fellow-citizen,

"SAMUEL J. TILDEN."

This was not such a letter as Mr. Tilden would probably have written had he desired to render his renomination impossible. He was too accomplished a politician not to know that it was not only the true, but the only wise, policy for the Democratic party to renominate the old ticket and to give the loyal men of all parties an opportunity of administering a national rebuke to those who had participated in or connived at the usurpation of the chief magistracy. Failure to renominate the old ticket was to deprive the party of a vital issue which had already been made, which could not be shirked; which, not bravely to meet, was equivalent to a capitulation, and would in all probability prove fatal to any other candidate that could be nominated.

That Mr. Tilden would have accepted the nomination if tendered to him, no one is competent to affirm or deny. He probably did not know himself. I was under the impression, derived rather from anything he disclosed of his, that he wished the nomination to be offered him to save the "fraud" issue for his party, intending, if offered, to decline it – a course which, had I been consulted, I should certainly have advised. As I was driving with him one day near the close of December in 1879, he said to me, "I must talk with some one, but what I am going to say you must not allow to influence your conduct." He then said, referring to the condition of his health, that he did not see how it was possible for him to go through the excitement of another political canvass.

I felt that the idea then in his mind was, that for the sake of the party he must not act as though he were not to run, but he did not wish me to labor under false impression in regard to his purposes or expectations.

Had the convention nominated him it would probably have paid no attention to his declension, presuming from his character that he would do nothing unnecessarily embarrassing to his party. Had he promptly declined a renomination, as I believe he would have done, there is little doubt that the gallant soldier who was nominated, had he in the emergency been called to take his place on the ticket, would have been elected by a larger majority than Tilden himself had in 1876.

"There were too many candidates for the presidency among the members of the convention, however, and too little time for reflection, to permit this, which was so obviously the true policy, to prevail. For this, Mr. Manning, the chairman of the delegation, was partly responsible. He telegraphed Mr. Tilden to know if he might yield to the pressure for his renomination which had been stimulated by the publication of his letter. To this Mr. Tilden could make but one reply, and unless such a reply was desired, it was very indiscreet to ask the question. It ran as follows:

June 24, 1880.

"HON. DANIEL MANNING, *Grand Hotel, Cincinnati, O.:*

"Received your telegram and many others containing like information. My action was well considered and is irrevocable. No friends must be allowed to cast a doubt on my motives or my sincerity.

"T."

This, of course, rendered his renomination, impossible. The convention finally, and after much confusion, united upon Major-General Hancock, who, in point of fact, was the preference or first choice of but a very small proportion of the convention.

The committee appointed to wait upon and notify the candidates of their nomination called upon Mr. Tilden to present to him an engrossed copy of the resolutions adopted by the convention. On this occasion Governor Stevenson, of Virginia, the chairman of the committee, read to him the ninth, which ran as follows:

"*Resolved,* That the resolution of Samuel J. Tilden not again to be a candidate for the exalted position to which he was elected by a majority of his countrymen, and from which he was excluded by the leaders of the Republican party, is received by the Democracy of the United States with deep sensibility, and they declare their confidence in his wisdom, patriotism, and integrity unshaken by the assaults of the common enemy; and we further assure him he is followed into the retirement he has chosen for himself by the sympathy and respect of his fellow-country-men, who regard him as one who, by elevating the standard of public morality, and adorning and purifying the public service, merits the lasting gratitude of his country and his party."

Then, handing a copy of the resolution to Mr. Tilden, Governor Stevenson continued:

"That resolution embodies the true sentiment toward you of every Democrat in our land. Take it, as a memorial of their affectionate regard and confidence in your wisdom, statesmanship, and unsullied purity. In conclusion, I bet you, Mr. Tilden, to accept the best wishes of the committee and of myself for your future happiness and prosperity."

Mr. Tilden's was neither elaborate nor effusive. He could not have added a word that would have made it a more significant commentary upon the blunder of the convention. He said:

"MR. STEVENSON, PRESIDENT OF THE DEMOCRATIC NATIONAL CONVENTION: I thank you for the kind terms in which you have expressed the communication you make to me. A solution which enables the Democratic party of the United States to vindicate effectively the right of the people to choose their chief magistrate – a right violated in 1876 – and, at the same time, relieves me from the burden of a canvass and four years of administration, is most agreeable to me. My sincere good wishes and cordial cooperation as a private citizen attend the illustrious soldier whom the Democracy have designated as their standard-bearer in the presidential canvass. I congratulate you on the favorable prospects with which that canvass has been commenced, and the promise it affords of complete and final success."

In the winter of 1881 Mr. Tilden received from Mr. Hammers, of Gettysburg, a letter announcing the decease of the Hon. Isaac Hereter, a member of the State Senate of Pennsylvania, and a devoted friend of Mr. Tilden, whom, during the presidential canvass, Mr. Hammers represents as going with him from house to house in the mountain district canvassing for the Tilden and Hendricks ticket, and bursting into tears when the decision of the Electoral Commission reached him.

To this touching letter Mr. Tilden sent the following reply:

MR. TILDEN TO MR. S. S. W. HAMMERS.

GRAYSTONE, JUNE 23, 1882.

"DEAR SIR: It was not because I was not interested by your letter advising me of the decease of your lamented friend, the Hon. Isaac Hereter, that I have not sooner answered it; for the purpose has been all the while in my mind to write to you soon as other more pressing duties would permit.

"The incidents you relate are very touching.

"The cause which triumphed by the votes of the people in the great national contest of 1876, but which was foully lost in the count of those votes, was the cause of the sons of toil, who, on their farms and in their workshops, expect no special advantages from government, and only ask that the sunshine of its favor may fall equally upon all. These isolated atoms of human society are not easily combined, and not often truly represented; while the more selfish, active, and intriguing classes are all the while wrestling the government from its true functions, and making it a machine to enrich the few at the expense of the many, and then corrupting the administrative services, the legislation, and the elections, in order to hold and enlarge their unjust advantage.

"The meaning of the people in the election of 1876 was to restore the government to the pure, simple, and just system which the founders of the Republic intended, and which Jefferson exemplified in practice.

"How deeply the best interests and the most sacred rights of humanity were involved, I doubt not your deceased friend realized, when with you he went from 'house to house' through the mountains of Pennsylvania during the canvass, and when he wept over the destruction, by frauds, perjuries, and the forgery of electoral votes, of the fruits of the victory he had helped to achieve.

"With my best wishes for you health, prosperity, and happiness, I remain,

"Very truly yours,
S. J. Tilden."

"S. S. W. HAMMERS, ESQ.,
    "Gettysburg, PA."

"The results of the election in the defeat of Hancock and the triumph of the Republican candidate revealed to the party the mistake it had made, and revived the clamor for the renomination of Mr. Tilden in 1884, a clamor which, despite the private and public protestations of Mr. Tilden and of several of his most intimate friends, practically excluded the consideration of any other candidates. With the abundant

evidence which from time to time reached the public from his seclusion at Graystone, of the unimpaired mental force and sagacity of its
proprietor, the zeal of the party for his renomination seemed to have
received a new and accumulative impulse from the defeat in 1880.
Conflicting reports of the condition of his health, adapted to the uses
of the respective parties, were eagerly sought for and published, and he
continued to be treated by the Republican press as the only formidable
candidate of his party up to the very day that another candidate was
renominated.

Reports were put in circulation by the Republican press, in 1881, that
Mr. Tilden proposed to be a candidate for governor again the following
year. Ex-Governor Seymour, who had not been able to contemplate
with entire satisfaction the precedence which the party had been giving
of late years to Mr. Tilden, seems to have not indisposed to countenance these rumors. In reply to a letter from Seymour, Mr. Tilden sent
the following reply:

"GRAYSTONE, Oct. 3, 1881.

"MY DEAR SIR: I have received your letter stating you intended to call
on me, and your inability to do so.

"I should have written to you earlier, except for an illness and the
pressure of claims upon my attention during my convalescence.

"It would have been agreeable to me to have seen you and to have
treated you with that frankness and courtesy you have always experienced from me.

"In respect to your assurance that you would not be a candidate for
nomination, if your nomination, 'would be disagreeable to me, and be
discountenanced by me,' I have to say that I cannot assume any such
position. I have neither the right nor the wish to exclude you from a
legitimate and honorable competition for any public trust. My practice,
when I was at the head of the party organization, was not to become
a partisan of any particular candidate, but to confine myself to such
advisory suggestions as might seem fit and useful during the deliberations of the convention; to defer largely to the judgment of the best
men of the counties found at the convention, in view of the immediate
action on the complex considerations which enter into the formation
of a collective ticket. I need not say that I have not undertaken any such

function on the present occasion, and have not possessed myself of the information to make me competent to such a work. I assume that you have not given credit to the idle fictions of Republican and other newspapers, which ascribe to me a desire to control the nominations and canvass for the present year, with a view to becoming a candidate for the governor next year. The truth is I ran for governor in 1874, simply for the purpose of sustaining the reform movement to which I had given the three preceding years; *and I should not have continued in the office for a second term in any possible event, nor would I now entertain the idea of returning to it, even if I flattered myself that I would receive a unanimous vote of the people.*

"All I desire for the Democratic party in the coming canvass is that it shall make the best possible choice of candidates, and do everything to advance the principles of administration, to which I have devoted so many efforts and sacrifices. With cordial good wishes,

"Very truly yours,

"S. J. TILDEN."

Faithful to the declaration made in this letter, Mr. Tilden took no active part in the election of the candidate for governor, though his preference may have been inferred by his friends who were in control of the nominating convention, from the fact that one of his nephews, and his namesake, who was a delegate from Columbia county, at a critical moment voted for Grover Cleveland. This vote, supposed to reflect Mr. Tilden's preferences, no doubt exerted a controlling influence over the convention and secured Mr. Cleveland's nomination. A few days before the election Mr. Tilden's addressed to Mr. Manning, the chairman of the State committee, the following letter commending the nomination:

GRAYSTONE, Oct. 20, 1882.

"MY DEAR SIR: I have received your letter and in reply I hasten to say that, in my opinion, the excellent ticket nominated at Syracuse is auspicious of a reform administration in the executive government of the State. The large classes of independent voters who, during my administration as governor, honored me with their support included many citizens who were then first attracted to take an interest in public affairs; many others who had not been before classified as partisans, and a large number who broke away from their party ties and gave their adhesion to a system of politics which promised to purify administration and to elevate the standard of official morality. They were numerous enough and powerful enough to hold the balance of power in every successive contest. They can now much more easily determine the result in the approaching election. To all these classes, as well as to all others who are in general accord with me as to the principles on which the State ought to be governed, I cordially commend the support of Grover Cleveland and his associate candidates.

"Very truly yours,

"S. J. TILDEN.

"TO DANIEL MANNNING, ESQ."

The following letter to Mr. Henry Adams, in acknowledgment of his admirable biographies of John Randolph and of Albert Gallatin, betrays the change of interest and occupation to which Mr. Tilden was gradually habituating himself in his new home:

"GRAYSTONE, Jan. 12, 1883.

"DEAR MR. ADAMS: I was lately reading your very interesting book concerning John Randolph, and it suggested a desire to look over your work on the 'New England Federalists.' I sent to my library in the city for that book. When I came to look at it, I noticed that it was a presentation copy sent by you to me.

"I have no recollection of ever before having seen that entry, or having ever acknowledged your courtesy.

"I write now to repair the seeming want of attention, and to beg you to accept my thanks, not only for the volume you were so kind to send me, but for the great services which you have rendered to the history of our country.

"I consider your 'Life of Albert Gallatin' as the most valuable contribution which has been made to this department of our literature. I agree with your very high estimated of Mr. Gallatin as a practical statesman.

"There is a story told of Mr. Choate. It is that at a dinner party in Pennsylvania, where his wit was ruffled by a competition in the exhibition of great men, he gave as a toast, 'The two really great men of

Pennsylvania: Albert Gallatin, of Geneva, and Benjamin Franklin, of Boston.'

"John Randolph's epigrams, which were famous in their day, were as laboriously wrought as the impromptus of Sheridan are shown by Moore to have been.

"Mr. Van Buren told me that Randolph said to him, 'When I get a good think, I boil it down, and boil it down, until I can put it into the apple of my eye, and then I lay it away for use.'

"I hope your father's health has improved.

"With my best wishes for the health, prosperity, and happiness of yourself and the other members of your father's family, I remain,

Very truly yours,
"S. J. TILDEN.

"HENRY ADAMS, ESQ.
"Boston, Mass."

As the time approached for the nomination of a candidate for President in 1884 the purpose of his party to nominate Mr. Tilden threatened to be irresistible. He alone of all the prominent statesmen of his party had seemed, day by day, to expand and to assume continually enlarging proportions in popular estimation. The conviction that he alone could assure the party's success made them deaf to the protestations of Tilden or of his friends that he would not accept the nomination.

This feeling was instinctive and universal. It may have been in part founded on the knowledge of the special devotion to him of the working-classes, to whose interests he had been faithful for fifty years; the confidence of the business men, who trusted, to his wise and safe policy; and to the peculiar support which the adopted citizens of German origin had uniformly given to him, including large numbers of Republicans as well as Democrats.

But still more potential influence was the fact, at length conceded substantially by all parties, that he had been elected in 1876, but fraudulently deprived of office.

Each one of the four millions of voters who had given him their suffrages felt a sense of personal injury, and an intense desire to punish and to rectify that wrong. This feeling converted each man from being a comparatively indifferent voter, into a proselyting canvasser.

In behalf of the man who had been the victim of a great public crime, there was also a widespread disposition among many Republicans who loved fair play, to give their votes on the first opportunity in such a manner as to redress the wrong of 1876. Instances of this kind came within the knowledge of almost every Democratic voter, and the purpose was communicated, in many cases, to Mr. Tilden and to his friends, Accessions from this cause were believed to be very numerous, and were estimated to count by many thousands.[1]

So strong was the popular sentiment in favor of Mr. Tilden's renomination in his own State that when the time arrived for the selection of delegates to the State convention which was to choose the delegation to the national convention those Democrats who were hostile to Governor Cleveland's nomination to the presidency, and who knew that Mr. Tilden did not mean to accept a nomination, began to intrigue for the election of delegates whose first choice was understood to be Mr. Tilden, but were secretly opposed to Cleveland. Several delegates had been elected in this shape, when Mr. Manning called upon me one day early in June, 1884, and expressed the wish that I would accompany him to Graystone. After briefly referring to the political situation, he said that on the Sunday previous he had called upon Governor Cleveland, laid the whole case before him; pressed upon his attention the necessity of doing something at once, to prevent the friends of Mr. Tilden getting heedlessly pledged to other candidates as their second choice, a danger which was imminent so long as a hope of Mr. Tilden's yielding to the wishes of the party was indulged; and finally, that the only way of defeating such a scheme was for Mr. Tilden to signify, before the election of any more delegates, most of whom were to be chosen within the next eight or ten days, that he would not be a candidate. Mr. Manning then went on to say that Governor Cleveland promptly expressed the desire that Mr. Manning would go down to Graystone, represent the situation to Mr. Tilden, and consider himself authorized to give Mr. Tilden any assurances he required in regard to the naming of Mr. Cleveland's cabinet should he be elected, and in regard to the conduct of his administration upon the lines of reform which had been traced by Mr. Tilden during and since his election as governor. Mr. Manning said his object in coming to me was to ask

1 Note: For important evidence on this subject, the reader is referred to Appendix B.

me to accompany him to Graystone and assist him in persuading Mr. Tilden – if persuasion should be necessary – to no longer delay a formal announcement of his intentions, already well known to Mr. Manning and myself, not to accept a renomination.

I said that I approved entirely of an early publication by Mr. Tilden of his intention not to accept a renomination; that some two weeks previous I had written to him at length, urging upon him the inconveniences of permitting the delegates to be elected to the nominating convention in the expectations of making him their candidate; that such a letter had already been written, but the utterance of it had been delayed, partly out of deference to the wishes of friends in Washington, and partly for what seemed the more obvious and appropriate occasion for such a communication – the meeting of the State convention that was to choose the delegates to the national convention.

I accompanied Mr. Manning to Graystone, where he stated his errand to Mr. Tilden.

Mr. Tilden hesitated a little, partly perhaps, from a natural reluctance to pursue a course which might be construed into an unbecoming interference in behalf of a particular candidate, partly from delicacy about declining a nomination before the State convention had furnished him a suitable pretext for such a step, and partly from a profound sense of the risk the people would run in selecting a man of such limited administrative experience to conduct the government of sixty millions of people. He finally, however, gave Mr. Manning to understand that the State committee would probably hear from him in a day or two. A letter of declension was sent to Mr. Manning the following day, and appeared in the morning papers of the 12th of June, 1884.

After referring briefly to the terms in which he declined a renomination in 1880, he said that nothing had occurred in the four years which had since elapsed to weaken, but every thing to strengthen, the considerations which then induced him to withdraw from public life; that the occasion now to consider the question was an event for which he had no responsibility; that he had never accepted official service except for a brief period, for a special purpose, and only when the occasion seemed to require of him that sacrifice of his personal preferences for the public welfare; that he accepted the nomination for the presidency in 1876 because of the general conviction that his candidacy would best present the issue of reform which the Democratic majority of the people desired to have worked out in the federal government as it had been in that of the State of New York; that the canvass he was desired to undertake would embrace a period of nearly five years, the burden of which admitted of no illusions. The close of his letter was conspicuous for its eloquence, pathos, and dignity.

"At the present time the considerations which induced my action in 1880 have become imperative. I ought not to assume a task which I have not the physical strength to carry through. To reform the administration of the federal government, to realize my own ideal, and to fulfil the just expectations of the people, would indeed warrant, as they could alone compensate, the sacrifices which the undertaking would involve. But, in my condition of advancing years and declining strength, I feel no assurance of my ability to accomplish those objects. I am, therefore, constrained to say, definitely that I cannot now assume the labors of an administration or of a canvass.

"Undervaluing in nowise that best gift of heaven, the occasion and the power sometimes bestowed upon a mere individual to communicate an impulse for good; grateful beyond all words to my fellow-countrymen who would assign such a beneficent function to me – I am consoled by the reflection that neither the Democratic party, nor the Republic for whose future that party is the best guarantee, is now or ever can be dependent upon any one man for their successful progress in the path or a noble destiny.

"Having given to their welfare whatever of health and strength I possessed, or could borrow from the future, and having reached the term of my capacity for such labors as their welfare now demands, I but submit to the will of God in deeming my public career forever closed."

This letter was like a rainbow set in the political horizon, the harbinger of comparative peace for Mr. Tilden. It served nobody's purpose longer to assail him, and those who had assailed him most virulently seemed disposed to profit by the appearance of this letter to do what they could, and as fast as possible, to assist the public in forgetting their past injustice. Even the "New York Times," which for the previous eight years had blinded itself to all of Mr. Tilden's virtues in it intemperate search for pretexts to revile him, resumed at once the tone of decorous respect to which it had been habituated while laboring with Mr. Tilden some dozen years before municipal reform.

Said the "Times" of the 12th, in which Mr. Tilden's letter appeared:

"The vital point in what Mr. Tilden writes is his assertion that he cannot now 'assume the labors of an administration or of a canvass.'

"The assertion is made, it is fair to say, in full knowledge of the fact that in many States of the Union the Democratic party, without preliminary inquiry as to Mr. Tilden's wishes of Mr. Tilden's strength, had spoken almost without a dissenting voice in favor of his nomination at Chicago. He puts away a presidential nomination he might have had, an act which has few precedents in the history of parties in this country. That act is extremely creditable to the good sense and to the clear perception of Mr. Tilden. He is the best judge of his own strength, and his judgment is blinded by none of those dazzling illusions to which so many men are subject whenever and as often as the presidency comes even remotely within the range of their vision. Nor has his decision been in any way influenced by recent Republican action, for it is now more than a year since Mr. Tilden gave an intimation, in a quarter which left no doubt or question as to his entire earnestness; of his fixed purpose to adhere to the conclusion stated in his letter of June 18, 1880.

"It would be but a slight recognition of Mr. Tilden's motives and of the circumstances under which his letter is written to say that his act is an unselfish one. It is more than unselfish. In the present divided condition of the Republican party it is an act of great moment and promise."

It is a curious illustration of the extraordinary hold which Tilden's name had upon his party that but for the belief that the time chosen for the publication of his letter signified a desire for the nomination of Mr. Cleveland, the chances were even that he would have been nominated in spite of it. Of twenty-two States which held their conventions before the publication of the letter, twenty either instructed their delegates to vote for him, or by resolution declared him to be their preference, or appointed delegates known to favor his nomination. One of the remaining two, although nominally favoring a State candidate in the belief that Mr. Tilden did not mean to run, was really favorable to his nomination. Of fourteen States which held their conventions after the appearance of the letter, five either declared for his nomination or expressed their continued preference for him, while nine other appointed delegates, of whom he was their first choice.

"New York State held its convention on the 18th of June, six days after publication of his letter, and after delegates had been appointed from all the counties favorable to his renomination. The remaining one of the thirty-eight States then composing the Union, and which held it convention on the 17th of June, accepted Mr. Tilden's letter as final, and appointed delegates favorable to its State candidates.

I think Mr. Tilden resisted the importunities of his friends as much through fear of the consequences of a canvass to himself as to the party. His health would have become the controlling issue in the contest.[1]

His feebleness would have been exaggerated by his opponents. This would have compelled his appearances in public places, and his exposure at inconvenient times and to imprudent fatigues, the results of which might have left the party in the midst of the battle without a leader. Only a few months after the election he told me that he thought he should live about two years longer. He overestimated his longevity by a few months.

It was there from no selfish consideration, from no lack of deference for the judgment of others, from no mistrust of his popularity in the country, that he did not allow himself to be moved by the importunities of his partisans. He knew better that any one else the risks that would be incurred by his renomination, and he was too wise a man to assume that his party was lacking men abundantly competent to lead it with success.

Mr. Blaine had already been nominated for the presidency by the Republican party, and Governor Cleveland was finally nominated by the Democratic party, and elected.

The convention which nominated Mr. Cleveland signalized its deliberations by inserting in its declaration of principles the following tribute to its retired leader:

---

1 Note: Shortly after Mr. Cleveland's nomination I was assured by one of the more prominent delegates to the national convention from a Southern State that but for the impressions prevailing in the convention that Mr. Cleveland was Mr. Tilden's choice for the nomination; he would not have received a single vote.

See Appendix B.

"With profound regret we have been apprised by the venerable statesman, through whose person was struck that blow at the vital principle of republics (acquiescence in the will of the majority), that he cannot permit us again to place in his hands the leadership of the Democratic hosts, for the reason that the achievement of reform in the administration of the federal government is an undertaking now too heavy for his age and failing strength. Rejoicing that his life has been prolonged until the general judgment of our fellow-countrymen is united in the wish that that wrong were righted in his person, for the Democracy of the United States, we offer to him in his withdrawal from public cares not only our respectful sympathy and esteem, but also that best homage of freemen, the pledge of our devotion to the principles and the cause now inseparable in the history of this Republic from the labors and the name of Samuel J. Tilden."

The convention also unanimously adopted the following resolutions:

"*Resolved*, That this convention has read with profound regret and intense admiration the statesmanlike and patriotic letter of Samuel J. Tilden expressing the overpowering and providential necessity which constrains him to decline a nomination for the highest office in the gift of the American people.

"*Resolved*, That though fraud, force, and violence deprived Samuel J. Tilden and Thomas A. Hendricks of the offices conferred upon them by the Democratic party of the nation in 1876, they yet lived, and ever will, first in the hearts of Democracy of the country.

"*Resolved*, That this convention expresses a nation's regret that this same lofty patriotism and splendid executive and administrative ability which cleansed and purified the city and State governments of the great Empire State cannot now be turned upon the Augean stable of national fraud and corruption so long and successfully maintained by the Republican party at the national capital.

"*Resolved*, That copies of these resolutions be suitably engrossed, and that the chairman of the convention appoint a committee whose duty it shall be, in the name of the convention, to forward or present the same to the Hon. Samuel J. Tilden and the Hon. Thomas A. Hendricks."

The chairman of the convention in compliance with its instructions appointed a committee consisting of one delegate from each State to wait upon Mr. Tilden and present him with an engrossed copy of these resolutions.

The committee assembled in New York on the third day of September, whence they were conveyed to Yonkers in Mr. Tilden's steam-yacht, the "Viking," which had been place at their disposal.

The resolutions were communicated to Mr. Tilden, with a few appropriate remarks by the Hon. R. R. Henry, of Mississippi, chairman of the committee. Mr. Tilden briefly expressed his thanks, and said that the state of his health compelled him to ask of the committee the indulgence of a few days for a more formal reply.

On the 6th of October he addressed the committee a letter the burden of which was the characteristics by which the Democratic party had been distinguished from the Republican party from their foundations respectively. Of the latter his view is substantially presented in the following paragraphs:

"The Democratic party had its origin in the efforts of the more advanced patriots of the Revolution to resist the perversion of our government from the ideal contemplated by the people. Among its conspicuous founders are Benjamin Frankin and Thomas Jefferson, Samuel Adams and John Hancock, of Massachusetts; George Wythe and James Madison, of Virginia. From the election of Mr. Jefferson as President in 1800, for sixty years the Democratic party mainly directed our national policy. It extended the boundaries of the Republic, and laid the foundations of all our national greatness, while it preserved the limitations imposed by the Constitution and maintained a simple and pure system of domestic administration.

"On the other hand, the Republican party has always been dominated by principles which favor legislation for the benefit of particular classes at the expense of the body of the people. It has become deeply tainted with the abuses which naturally grow up during a long possession of unchecked power, especially in a period of civil war and false finance. The patriotic and virtuous in it are now unable to emancipate it from the sway of selfish interests which subordinate public duty to personal gain. The most hopeful of the best citizens it contains, despair of its amendment except through its temporary expulsion from power.

"It has been boastingly asserted by a modern Massachusetts statesman, struggling to reconcile himself and his followers to their presidential candidate, that the Republican party contains a disproportionate share of the wealth, the culture, and the intelligence of the country. The unprincipled Grafton, when taunted by James the Second with his personal want of conscience, answered, *'That is true, but I belong to a party that has a great deal of conscience.'*

"Such reasoners forget that the same claim has been made in all ages and countries by the defenders of old wrongs against new reforms. It was alleged by the Tories of the American Revolution against the Patriots of that day. It was repeated against Jefferson and afterwards against Jackson. It is alleged by the Conservatives against those who, in England, are now endeavoring to enlarge the popular suffrage.

"All history shows that reforms in government must not be expected from those who sit serenely on the social mountain- tops enjoying the benefits of the existing order of things. Even the Divine Author of our religion found his followers, not among the self-complacent Pharisees, but among the lowly minded fisherman.

Of all American statesmen who have risen to eminence Mr. Tilden was probably the least given to sarcastic or personally offensive allusions of any kind to a political opponent. I am not aware that in all his long public life he ever had an unpleasant personal controversy about any words that fell from his lips or pen. No one knew him better than he, nor acted more uniformly upon the knowledge, that "whoso keepeth his mouth and tongue, keepeth his soul from troubles." He would not, therefore, have made the reflections upon some of the unfortunate events in the congressional career of the Republican candidate which is disguised in this paragraph had not Mr. Blaine stimulated the malicious persecutions with which the administration had pursued him so relentlessly from the dawn to the close of his candidature for the presidency, and merely, as Mr. Tilden believed, because Mr. Blaine regarded him as his most formidable rival.

CHAPTER IX

Tilden's relations to the new President - Senator Garland a suitor - Letters to Manning - Tilden's and Jefferson's views of civil service - Harbor defences - Letter to Carlisle - Tilden's friends proscribed at Washington - Letter to Watterson - George W. Julian - Tilden discourages his nephew and namesake from embarking in politics - R.B. Minturn - Manning's illness and retirement from the treasury - History of the Monroe Doctrine - The Broadway railroad - Advice to Governor Hill against the proposed enlargement of the Erie canal - Favors the bill for and international park and for the protection of the Adirondack forests.

MR. CLEVLAND'S election was generally and very naturally regarded as a continuation of the Tilden dynasty, and as a consequence his supposed influence with the new President was very extensively solicited by candidates for place under the new administration from all parts of the country. Among the earlier applications of this character was one from Senator Garland, of Arkansas, who desired the position of attorney-general. To him, Mr. Tilden sent a letter evidently intended not entirely to conceal his mistrust that whatever value Mr. Cleveland had professed to attach to his advice in the previous June, the election had seriously impaired. It would have been fortunate for Mr. Garland had he followed the advice which Mr. Tilden, with so much delicacy, tried to convey to him. He left a place where his manifold limitations escaped observation, for one in which they alone were conspicuous.

TILDEN TO GARLAND.

"(Confidential.)

GRAYSTONE, Dec, 5, 1884.

"DEAR SENATOR GARLAND: I have received your letter. I appreciate all the consideration which it so frankly suggests. Although I have had less personal acquaintance with you since 1868 than I could have wished, I have not been left without the means to form a just estimate of your acquirements as a lawyer, your rank as a Senator, and your high personal character.

"I do not know to what extent, or in what cases, if any, I shall be consulted by Mr. Cleveland in respect to the constitution of his cabinet. I do not intend to intrude upon him any advice unasked, or to volunteer any recommendations or requests. If consulted, I shall not act as a partisan of any of my numerous friends who would like to enter his cabinet, but shall endeavor, with judicial impartiality, to canvass the personal merits and other considerations which ought to influence the choice. I am anxious that he should do the best thing possible for the country and for his administration, and shall desire rather to help him in his difficult task than to add to his embarrassments.

"The formation of a cabinet is a piece of mosaic in which each element may be affected by the size, texture, and color of the others entering into the combination; and it is impossible to foresee how much an individual element may be affected by the cast of the whole.

"Impressed as I am with your adaptation to the trust which you indicated as most agreeable to you, I should feel some regret at your leaving the Senate, both on account of the public interest and the personal distinction and growth which you would surrender. An intelligent and judicious friend, who reads all the reported debates, tells me that you appear to great advantage in the senatorial discussions. The role as the confidential representative of the administration in the Senate is greater than any cabinet office. I remember how Thomas H. Benton and Silas Wright felt on that subject. While occupying that relation, Mr. Wright grew to greater prominence than any other Democrat in the country. In 1844 he was nominated against his will for the vice-presidency, and, I happen to know, was informally offered the presidential nomination before it was conferred on Mr. Polk. His transcendent hold upon the country carried the presidential election for the Democracy.

"If it should fall to the lot of Mr. Cleveland to fill several appointments in the Supreme Court, I hope that he will select men, not only of eminent legal capacities and of pure personal character, and of sounder constitutional ideas that have lately been found in that body, but have something more to give to the country than the dregs of life. Most of the great judges have been taken young, and their character formed on the bench.

"Very truly yours,

"S. J. TILDEN.

"HON. A. H. GARLAND,
"Washington, D.C."

In point of fact Mr. Tilden was not consulted about his cabinet by President Cleveland until nearly or quite every place but one had been filled, when his advice about a secretary of the treasury was invited. He recommended Mr. Daniel Manning, of New York. Mr. Manning was reluctantly appointed to that position, but never welcomed to it nor in it.

Whether Mr. Cleveland underrated the value of Mr. Tilden's judgment, or overrated his own, it is quite certain that Mr. Manning did neither, for he appears to have rarely, if ever, taken any important step while he continued in the cabinet without trying to secure Mr. Tilden's approval of it. Some of Mr. Tilden's letters on public questions submitted to him for his views have not yet lost their value. On the 1st of March, and only three days before Manning was to take office, Mr. Tilden wrote to him:

TILDEN TO MANNING.

"GRAYSTONE, YONKERS, N.Y., March 1, 1885.

"DEAR MR. MANNING: The first thing to be done in the treasury is to ascertain how far the redemption fund, as it is called, which is the stock of gold kept in reserve to redeem the greenbacks, has been impaired. I suspect the deficiency is not less than thirty or forty millions. The construction of the laws adopted by Mr. Sherman, late secretary; by Mr. McCulloch, present secretary; and by Mr. Weyman, treasurer – is there is express legal authority to make good, by sale of the United States bonds, such deficiency as may be found from time to time to assist in the redemption fund. Mr. McCulloch in his letter to me claimed the right to check out, in the discretion of the secretary, from the existing mass of gold in the treasury, if thereby a deficiency was created in the redemption fund, and then to make good that deficiency by the sale of bonds.

"If the government pay the interest on the public debt in gold, as it ought, it will take somewhat over four millions a month, beside payments for the sinking-fund and for called bonds, and besides payments and beside keeping the reserve for the redemption of the greenbacks. If there is no financial alarm, and no export demand for gold, the sale of bonds of twenty to forty millions might, as many think, maintain the gold basis for all the government payments, and lose two millions a month through the rest of the year. That is to say, it would make good deterioration in the financial condition of the government consequent upon paying two millions a month for silver bullion.

"If the government should be compelled to use silver in its payments, it would have to be considered whether it should not pay the interest on the bonds, the sinking-fund, and the called bonds in gold, and maintain the gold fund for the redemption of greenbacks, and use the silver in common with such surplus of gold as may remain, in the payment of the other expenditures of the government. This would perfectly protect the public honor and faith, but you might have some clamor against two currencies. It could scarcely be said that that made one currency for the government and another for the people, because the greenbacks are really the people's currency. I write in great haste, because there is no time, and can but make imperfect suggestions.

"Mr. Jordon has submitted this morning four statements, of which I send one, as containing some suggestions of detail which might be useful.

"Yours truly,
"S. J. T."

The financial crisis of 1883, which compelled an extra session of Congress, and the repeal of the law requiring large monthly purchases of silver by the treasury, lend a special interest to the following prescient letter to Mr. Manning:

"GRAYSTONE, YONKERS, N.Y., March 14, 1885.

"DEAR MR. MANNING: I enclose a small pamphlet written by Mr. Coe. His theory is to depend upon the policy of not calling in any bonds, as a means for carrying the additional quantity of silver which the law compels you to buy, until some time after the next session of Congress to suspend the silver purchases. If the making or withholding of calls is in the discretion of the secretary, which I am inclined to think it is, having as yet found no compulsory mandate, I think it will be highly inexpedient to exhaust the treasury, if you mean to continue all the gold payments on the gold basis.

"Mr. Jordon has sent me a series of statements which show that about $33,000,000 of the gold fund reserved for the redemption of the legal tenders have been consumed in the ordinary payments of the treasury. According to the construction adopted by your predecessors, Untied States 4 per cent, bonds can lawfully be sold to make good that deficiency. Mr. Jordon's figures cover some other topics. Having partially examined them, I have given them to Mr. Marble for a few days, as he can verify the references to the authorities more conveniently than I can.

"I think that between these two resources you can tide yourself along until the opportunity arises to make the issue in Congress, without resorting to any silver payments.

"I expect to write to you again within a few days.

"Very truly yours,
"S. J. TILDEN

"HON. DAN'L MANNING,
"Secretary of the Treasury."

Mr. Jordon, to whom the following letter was addressed, had been selected by Mr. Manning for the position of treasurer of the United States. It is quoted here partly for its intrinsic value and partly to show the active interest which Mr. Tilden took in the administration of the national finances at a time when the roar of the breakers towards which the ship of state was drifting seemed more audible at Graystone than elsewhere.

TILDEN TO JORDAN.

"(Confidential.)

"GRAYSTONE, YONKER, N.Y., May, 15, 1885.

"DEAR MR. JORDON: The memorandum for the solution of the silver question enclosed in your letter appears to me to have elements from which to devise a measure. It would need some modification and require to be perfected. The law will put the proposition in more definite shape and will be a better basis to act on than so brief and general a proposition. When General Warner shall have written it out please send me a copy. The advantage of bringing up the coin in fineness and weight to the market value of the silver it contains is very great. It would widen the market for silver and so benefit the producers. It should apply to the half and quarter dollars. Can you inform me what per cent the cost of coinage is on the dollar? Also on the halves and quarters taken together? You will remember that when it was proposed to resume specie payment nearly everybody thought that the preliminary step was to contract the currency. I maintained the opposite views. I said that nobody could tell how much currency the wants of business would require; that to assume an arbitrary amount was the height of quackery; that the only true way was to leave that matter to adjust itself under a free system. I apply the same principle to silver. I am willing to take all that the business of the country can absorb; it is impossible to do anything more. To force the quantity of the currency above its natural level is as idle an attempt as was Dame Partington's effort with her mop to keep back the Atlantic ocean. The measure should be carefully guarded to avoid any such folly. It would be necessary to invest the treasury with a discretion which would enable it to follow and not to force nature.

"It will give me pleasure to see General Warner at Graystone. I know him very well and think well of him.

"Very truly yours,
"S. J. TILDEN."

Application having been made to Mr. Tilden for his views of a draught of some resolutions designed to be presented for the adoption of the State convention of the Democratic party of New York State in the fall of 1885, he sent the following reply:

"Sect. VI., relating to the silver question, is well enough in substance.

"Sect. I., relating to the civil service, is free from objections.

"Sect. II. Is right and well expressed.

"Sect. III., proposing a repeal of certain laws of 1869 relating to the tenure of office. That is right. It restores to the President his power of appointment, which by those laws has been in part usurped by the Senate. But a question arises as to the expediency of making this declaration at the present time. That question will be considered in connection with Sect. IV.

Sect. IV. Proposes a repeal of the laws of May 15, 1820, which fixes the term of four years to a large number of important offices. Without deciding the question whether if that stood alone the extinction of fixed terms for these offices is expedient, which is not free from doubt, in practice at the present time the proposition involves insurmountable mischiefs.

"The Senate will not consent to a repeal of the laws of 1867 and 1869. The Senate will be glad to obtain the repeal of the law of May 15, 1820. If the President and the House of Representatives make a Democratic party question in favor of repealing the law of May 15, 1820, the measure will be passed. The practical effect will be to put all the offices which now have fixed tenures under the laws of 1867 and 1869. That result would strip the President of the only independent power of appointment which he now has, and place him completely under the tutelage of the Senate. It would sweep away from the Democrats any chance of obtaining any participation in the government of the country. If a declaration in favor of repealing the laws of 1867 and 1869, which declaration will be wholly nugatory and useless, involves also the declaration in favor of the repeal of the law of May 15, 1820, which would be effectual, both ought to be omitted.

"The repeal of the law of May 15, 1820, even if proper, as part of the system in which the repeal of the laws of 1867 and 1869 should be also a part, it should never be done separately or in advance. The effect on the Democratic party of such a piece of Democratic insanity it is easy to foresee. It probably would be a collapse of the Democratic party, and of the present Democratic administration.

"On the whole, in my judgment Sections III and IV are too abstruse, and involve topics which not one man in fifty in the convention will have any knowledge of.

"They are unfit for planks in the platform. They had better be omitted, even apart from the objection above stated.

"Sec. V. The authority of Washington, cited in this section, involves a doubt. Washington language seems to imply that all office-holders should be in political accord with the President. That means a clean sweep. That greatly exceeded the claim of Mr. Jefferson for his party. He only asked that they should have a fair participation in the public trusts of the country. He said, when he came into the presidency, if he had found the Democrats in possession of even a moderate share, he would have waited for time and circumstances to have remedied the injustice; but, having found a complete monopoly of the offices in the hands of the minority, who had been discarded by the people, he was compelled to apply a prompter corrective.

"You can study Mr. Jefferson's principals and views of this subject with great advantage."

In March of the year in which this criticism was dispatched to Mr. Manning, Mr. Tilden made a careful analysis of President Jefferson's views of the tenure of office of the civil officers of the federal government, with a commentary thereon which reflected his own views, and the principals upon which, if clothed with the responsibilities of a chief magistrate, he would have endeavored to regulate that service. It will be found to illustrate the difference in the ways this problem is dealt with by statesmen and by cranks.

JEFFERSON AND THE CIVIL SERVICE.

"Thomas Jefferson was one of the greatest reformers that this country has produced – perhaps the greatest. When he became President the country was first divided politically according to the two fundamental interpretations of the Constitution – the Federalist and the Democratic. Under the presidency of John Adams, as it had been previously under Washington, the tendency of the administration was strongly toward the establishment of an overmastering Federal government and the whole government machinery was solidly organized in the harmony with that tendency. None but Federalist were in office. The Federalist idea had gained a great hold upon the people. If such weapons as the alien and sedition laws had not been furnished to the Democrats by the administration, it is scarcely possible that they could have beaten their opponents; and, instead of the establishment of the Democracy in power at that time, the Federalist might have retained their control of the country, and so strengthened it that the complexion of our politics might now have been materially different, and perhaps lacking in some features that we to-day regard as essential to Republicanism. It was Jefferson's mission to arrest the inclination toward a more highly centralized system of Federal control, and formally to lay the foundation on which our Democracy has rested since his time, and must continue to rest so long as the Democratic idea shall endure.

"Upon Jefferson's accession to office he found all national posts filled by members of the Federal party. Men of Democratic views of politics had been entirely proscribed. There was scarcely a Republican – so the Democrats were then called – enjoying a place of honor or trust under the government. In short, the party that had just carried the election and demonstrated its supremacy among the people had absolutely no participation whatsoever in the government beyond its representations on the national ticket and its members of Congress. The votes of the majority had changed the elective officers only. That was all they could change. What remained to be done in order to carry out their wishes was to be done by the executive. To do this, to correct the existing abuses, and to restore a political equilibrium, was regarded by the new President as kindred in importance to the firm establishment of Democratic principles. Indeed, such a reform was implied and rendered necessary by those principles, not only for the sake of a more equal and Democratic distribution of responsibility, but because the spirit of Democracy is opposed to the endless continuation of one party in power, and to the institution of a class of bureaucrats.

"Not withstanding the immensity of labor, and in spite of vigorous remonstrances from the Federalist, as well as the feeble and petulant protests of impartial idlers who were remote from politics, and whose souls revolted at any form of upheaval or of progress, Mr. Jefferson began his task and carried it to a successful completion. But it was not done without appreciation of the disadvantages and imperfections attached to the work. An occasion for the expression of Mr. Jefferson's views upon the subject of official changes, and of the principles and motives under which he exercised the power conferred upon him for making them, came but a few months after his inauguration. It was brought about by a protest of Elias Shipman and others, a committee of the merchants of New Haven, against two appointments of the President; and his views on the subject are explained in the following letter:

WASHINGTON, July 12, 1801.

"GENTLEMEN: I have received the remonstrance you were pleased to address to me on the appointment of Samuel Bishop to the office of collector of New Haven, lately vacated by the deal of David Austin. The right of our fellow-citizens to represent to the public functionaries their opinion on proceedings interesting to them is unquestionably a constitutional right, often useful, sometimes necessary, and will always be respectfully acknowledged by me.

"Of the various executive duties, no one excites more anxious concern than that of placing the interests of four fellow-citizens in the hands of honest men, with understandings sufficient for their stations. No duty at the same time, is more difficult to fulfil. The knowledge of character possessed by a single individual is, of necessity, limited. To seek out the best through the whole Union, we must resort to other information, which, from the best of men, acting disinterestedly and with the purest of motives, is sometimes incorrect. In the case of Samuel Bishop, however, the subject of your remonstrance, time was taken, information was sought, and such obtained as could leave no room for doubt of his fitness. From private sources it was learned that his understanding was sound, his integrity pure, his character unstained. And the offices confided to him within his own State are public evidence of the estimation in which he is held by the State in general and the city and township particularly in which he lives. He is said to be the town clerk, a justice of the peace, mayor of the city of New Haven, and office held at the will of the Legislature; chief judge of the Court of Common Pleas for New Haven county, a court of high criminal and civil jurisdiction, wherein most causes are decided without the right of appeal or review; and sole judge of the Court of Probates. Wherein he singly decided all questions of wills, settlement of estates, testate and intestate, appoints guardians, settles their accounts, and, in fact, has under his jurisdiction and care all the property, real and personal of persons dying. The two last offices in the annual gift of the Legislature were given to him in May last. It is possible that the man to whom the Legislature of Connecticut has so recently committed trusts of such difficulty and magnitude is 'unfit to be the Collector of the District of New Haven,' though acknowledged in the same writing to have obtained all this confidence 'by long life of usefulness'? It is objected, indeed, in the remonstrance, that he is seventy-seven years of age; but at a much more advanced age our Franklin was the ornament of human nature. He may not be able to perform in person all the details of his office; but if he gives us the benefit of his understanding, his integrity, his watchfulness, and takes care that all the details are well performed by himself or his necessary assistants, all public purposes will be answered. The remonstrance, indeed, does not allege that the office *has been* illy conducted, but only apprehends that it *will be so*. Should this happen, in an event, be assured I will do in it what shall be just and necessary for the public service. In the meantime, he should be tried without being, 'prejudged.

"The removal, as it is called, of Mr. Goodrich forms another subject of complaint. Declarations by myself in favor of *political tolerance,* exhortations to *harmony* and affection in social intercourse, and to respect for the *equal rights* of the minority, have, on certain occasions, been quoted and misconstrued into assurances that the tenure of offices was to be undisturbed. But could candor apply to such a construction? It is not, indeed, in the remonstrance that we find it; but it leads to the explanation which that calls for. When it is considered that during the late administration those who were not of a political sect of politics were excluded from all office; when, by a steady pursuit of this measure, nearly the whole offices of the United States were monopolized by that sect; when the public sentiment at length declared itself, and burst open the doors of honor and confidence to those whose opinions they more approved – was it to be imagined that this monopoly of office was still to be continued in the hands of the minority? Does it violate their *equal rights* to assert some rights in the majority also? Is it *political intolerance* to claim a proportionate share in the direction of public affairs? Can they not *harmonize* in society unless they have everything in their own hands? If the will of the nation, manifested by their various elections, calls for an administration of government according with the opinions of those elected; if, for, the fulfillment of that will, displacements are necessary, with whom can they so justly begin as with persons appointed in the last moments of an administration, not for its own aid, but to begin a career at the same time with their successors, by whom they had never been approved, and who could scarcely expect from them a cordial cooperation? Mr. Goodrich was one of these. Was it proper for him to place himself in office without knowing whether those whose agent he was to be would have confidence in his agency? Can the preference of another as the successor to Mr. Austin be candidly called a removal of Mr. Goodrich? If a due participation of office is a matter of right, how are vacancies to be obtained? Those by death are few; by resignation, none.

"Can any other mode than that of removal be proposed? This is a painful office; but it is made my duty, and I meet it as such. I proceed in the operation with deliberation and inquiry, that it may injure the best men least, and effect the purposes of justice and public utility with the least private distress; that it may be thrown, as much as possible, on delinquency, on oppression, on intolerance, on ante-revolutionary adherence to our enemies.

"The remonstrance laments 'that a change in administration must produce a change in the subordinate officers;' in other words, that it should be deemed necessary for all officers to think with their principal. But on whom does this imputation bear? On those who have excluded from the office every shade of opinion which was not theirs? Or on those who have been so excluded? I lament sincerely that unessential differences of opinion should ever have been deemed sufficient to interdict half the society from the rights and the blessings of self government; to proscribe them as unworthy of every trust. It would have been to me a circumstance of great relief had I found a moderate participation of office in the hands of the majority. I would gladly have left to time and accident to raise them to their just share. But their total exclusion calls for prompter corrections. I shall correct the procedure; but that done, return with joy to that state of things when the only questions concerning a candidate shall be, Is he honest? Is he capable? Is he faithful to the Constitution?

"I tender you the homage of my high respect.

"THOMAS JEFFERSON.

"This was not all of Mr. Jefferson's correspondence on this matter. On August 26, a little more than one month after the letter to the New Haven merchants, the President wrote as follows from Monticello to Mr. Levi Lincoln, of Massachusetts, the attorney-general in his cabinet:

"DEAR SIR: . . . I am glad to learn from you that the answer to New Haven had a good effect in Massachusetts on the Republicans, and no ill-effects on the sincere Federalists. I had foreseen, years ago, that the first Republican President who should come into office after all the places in the government had become exclusively occupied by Federalists, would have a dreadful operation to perform. That the Republicans would consent to a continuation of everything in Federal hands was not to be expected, because neither just nor polite. On him, then, was to devolve the office of an executioner, that of lopping off. I cannot say that it has worked harder than I expected. You know the moderations of our views in this business, and that we all concurred in them. We determined to proceed with deliberation. This produced impatience in the Republicans, and a belief we meant to do nothing. Some occasion of public explanation was eagerly desired, when the New Haven remonstrance offered up that occasion. The answer was meant as an explanation to our friends. It has had on them, everywhere, the most wholesome effect. Appearances of schismatizing from us have been entirely done away.

"It will be particularly interesting to those who now expect changed in offices with anxiety, to read such high testimony as that of Mr. Jefferson and Mr. Lincoln, that such changes can be accomplished with benefit to the public service and with the acquiescence of such of the withdrawing party as have a right to be heard in the political world, those who take part in its contest, and understand its obligations. The action of Mr. Jefferson in these instances had 'a good effect on the Republicans, and no ill effects on the sincere Federalists.' But a third letter from the President to Mr. Lincoln, dated at Washington on Oct. 25, 1802, gives a still clearer education of the ideas which guided him in his administration, with some additional comments, which are peculiarly pertinent to the situation of to-day:

"DEAR SIR: . . . I still think our original idea as to office is best; this is to depend, for the obtaining a just participation, on deaths, resignations and delinquencies. This will least affect the tranquility of the people, and prevent their giving in to the suggestions of our enemies, that ours had been a contest for office, not for principle. This is rather a slow operation, but it sure if we pursue it steadily, which however, has not been done with the undeviating resolution I could have wished. To these means of obtaining a just share in the transaction of the public business shall be added one other, to wit removal for electioneering activity, or open and industrious opposition to the principles of the present government, legislative and executive. Every officer of the government may vote at elections according to his conscience; but we should betray the cause committed to our care were we to permit the influence of official patronage to be used to overthrow that cause.

"Here, then, in these three short epistles of the founder of the Democracy, is his theory upon which a party succeeding to the management of the national machinery after it has been under the hostile control of an uncompromising partisan organization, should address itself to the task of obliterating the most objectionable elements of partisan rule, and instituting in their stead a purer and more Democratic system.

"But these arguments of Mr. Jefferson are concerned merely with the principle that when a party succeeds to the management of federal affairs, and finds the government functions wholly in the hands of its opponents, it has the right, and it is its duty, to establish it won power by turning its opponents out of office; even if for no other reason than that it wants to put its own adherents in their places. Other cases, where changes are confessedly necessary, are not referred to by Mr. Jefferson.

"Confidential offices, which powerfully affect the action of the chief executive, must be filled by persons in cordial harmony with the executive. Under any other supposition the election of a partisan President would be a farce, and government party would be impossible. More over, offices that have been filled in violation of modern civil service principles may be changed without violating those principles. So, also, offices conferred on the spoils system, without reference to the competency or fitness of the incumbents, are not required by civil service principles to remain with the abuses uncorrected.

"Besides, experience has shown that all trusts where the abuse is not restrained by the vigilant and firm supervision of the superior, directly interested in maintaining economy, there is a tendency to the useless multiplication of assistants. Every officer, after a little while, wants a waiter, and by and by that waiter himself wants a waiter. Everybody disputes his duties to a subordinate, and withdraws himself into a mere superintendence of the underling. Moreover, while subordinates are appointed to oblige members of Congress or other prominent persons, the whole drift is to a creation of more offices. The distention to which the public service had now grown from these and other causes is enormous and incredible. A glance at the Blue Book will amaze any one who is not acquainted with that astonishing record. Removals may therefore be necessary, not only on the other grounds we have mentioned, but also for the purpose of promoting economy in the public service.

"The state of the government is now worse by many fold – more in need of a change, more in need of regeneration, by retrenchment as well as by removals – than it was when the Democracy began its career in 1801. The defeated party retires after a term of power twice as long as that which the Federalists had enjoyed when they were overthrown. The perversion of the government from the standard to which government in this country should conform is proportionately far greater than it had been when Mr. Jefferson's administration began. By just so much is the present work of reform more arduous and its necessity more imperative.

"Thus the principles enunciated by President Jefferson eighty-four years ago are as true-today as they were then, and they will operate as beneficially now as they did when first brought into practice by that great Democratic statesman."

In the following letter we have an opportunity of seeing something of the directions in which he helped to shape Mr. Manning's first report to Congress:

TILDEN TO MANNING

"(Confidential.)

Nov. 14, 1885.

"DEAR MR. MANNING: I have been so much troubled by a derangement of my digestion that I could not find an opportunity to put in shape suggestions for you. But yesterday having noticed from Mr. Marble that he would call in the afternoon for consultation I dictated, notwithstanding the suffering I was undergoing, the paper which I now send.

"I notice that you make the surplus for the present year to be $70,000,000. Mr. Jordon told me a few days ago it would not exceed $40,000,000, of which $24,000,000 would be consumed by purchasers of silver, leaving only $16,000,000 of real surplus. I ought to know the true amount. In my judgment the passage of the harbor defences ought to precede all other discussions about the surplus revenue. What Mr. Marble is preparing relates to the silver question.

"If anything is said about revenue reform or the tariff, that topic should come third. I incline to doubt whether you can discuss the latter topic with any advantage. Certainly you cannot submit a specific plan in your annual report. The subject is too complicated and extensive to be disposed of incidentally in the general finance report.

"I am clear that the discussion about harbor defence properly belongs to your department. The reason is stated in the beginning of the paper I send you. No doubt either the War of the Navy Department would be glad to occupy that ground. But not to them, but to you alone, belong the general survey of the financial policy of the government.

"Very truly yours,

"S.J. Tilden."

The defence of our sea-coast, to which allusions are made in the foregoing paper, had been occupying no inconsiderable portion of Mr. Tilden's thought and study during the greater part of the year 1885, and he was anxious that the subject should be pressed upon the attention of Congress and of the country with all the authority of a new administration. Having no encouragement to submit his opinions upon this or any other subject to the President directly, and anxious to give Mr. Manning something for his report calculated, as he correctly believed, to produce upon the country a favorable impression of their new and inexperienced minister of finance, Mr. Tilden sent him a letter setting forth in a general way the results of his reflections upon the subject of harbor defences. In due time he received from the secretary the following humiliating reply – humiliating to Mr. Tilden only because it disclosed a situation so humiliating to Mr. Manning:

MANNING TO TILDEN.

"WASHINGTON, D.C., Dec. 1, 1885.

"MY DEAR GOVERNOR: I find that I cannot do what I wish to do with the Sea-Coast Defences' paper, and I am in great distress about it. I had intended to begin my first report with that paper, but I am now reluctantly forced to the conclusion that it will be impracticable. My report has not been read or discussed by any of the people here, but during the past few days I have been called upon to listen to several public documents, and the conclusion I have been driven to is, that if I were to submit my report (as I must, sooner or later) to like reading and criticism, with the Sea-Coast Defences,' paragraphs therein could not be retained.

"I am certain that if I were to publish the report without conference with any one, it would immediately and seriously embroil my personal relations in two or three cases. Moreover as I now know what recommendations are to be made, I should put myself in a most invidious position. Such publication would be fatal to carrying through the plan. If there is no publication, I can be of much service in pressing forward the policy so powerfully recommended in the paper, and I judge that you will prefer that to any form of stating it. I have arrived at this decision after deliberate thought, and I regret that I cannot give you my reasons more fully; but I have talked them over with Mr. Marble, and I hope to hear, after he has explained the case to you in all its bearings, that you approve my judgment.

"Anxiously hoping that this may not carry disappointment, I am,

"Sincerely your friend,
"DANIEL MANNING."

By return mail Mr. Manning received the following reply from Mr. Tilden:

TILDEN TO MANNING.

GRAYSTONE, YONKERS, N.Y., Dec 3, 1885.

"DEAR MR. MANNING: You need not concern yourself for the omission to use the discussion on our 'Sea-Coast Defences' which I sent you. My purpose was to advance a public object, and to help you to take a position not only wise and patriotic, but embracing many elements of public satisfaction and popularity.

"If it would excite the jealousy of any one of your colleagues, or be regarded by them as trenching upon their peculiar domain, although I should not agree that they would have any cause for discontent, it may be best to sacrifice something to appease them. No explanation to me is necessary. Perhaps, to save the waste of a morning's dictation at a time when I was not fit to work, I may think it expedient to use the material some other way.

"Very truly yours,
"S. J. TILDEN

It had by this time become manifest to Mr. Tilden, not only that he was not a *persona grata* to the President, which he more than suspected before, but that it was anything but a recommendation in the President's eyes to be a friend of his. It was no doubt a conviction of this sort which impelled Mr. Tilden to address a copy of his rejected views about sea-coast defences in the following letter to the Speaker of the House of Representatives, by whom it was immediately given to the press:

TILDEN TO CARLISLE.

"GRAYSTONE, YONKERS, N.Y., Dec. 1, 1885.

"DEAR MR. CARLISLE: As public opinion point to you as the Speaker of the House of Representatives, I desire to submit a suggestion as to one of the public objects for which an appropriation ought to be prompt and liberal.

In considering the state and management of the public revenues, the subject involves the questions whether we shall extinguish the surplus by reducing the revenue, or whether we shall apply the surplus to payments on the public debt, or whether we shall seize the occasion to provide for our sea-coast defences, which have been long neglected. I am of the opinion that the latter is a paramount necessity which ought to proceed the reduction of the revenue, and ought also to precede an excessive rapidity in the payment of the public debt.

The property exposed to destruction in the twelve seaports – Portland, Portsmouth, Boston, Newport, New York, Philadelphia, Baltimore, Charleston, Savannah, New Orleans, Galveston, and San Francisco – cannot be less in value than five thousand million of dollars. To this must be added a vast amount of property dependent for its use on these seaports. Nor does this statement afford a true measure of the damage which might be caused to the property and business of the country by a failure to protect these seaports from hostile naval attacks.

They are the centres, not only of foreign commerce, but of most of the internal trade and exchanges of domestic productions. To this state of things the machinery of transportation of the whole country has become adapted. The interruption of the currents of traffic by the occupation of one or more of our principal seaports by a foreign enemy, or the destruction of them by bombardment, or holding over them the menace of destruction for the purpose of exacting contribution or ransom, would inflict upon the property and business of the country and injury which can neither be foreseen nor measured. The elaborate and costly fortifications which were constructed with the greatest engineering skill, are now practically useless. They are not capable of resisting the attacks of modern artillery.

A still greater defect exists in our coast defences. The range of the best modern artillery has become so extended that our present fortifications, designed to protect the harbor of New York, where two thirds of the import trade and more than one-half of the export trade of the whole United States is carried on, and are too near the great populations of New York city and Jersey City, and Brooklyn to be of any value as protection.

To provide effectual defences would be the work of years. It would take much time to construct permanent fortifications. A small provision of the best modern guns would take several years. Neither of these works can be extemporized in presence of emergent danger. A million of soldiers, with the best equipments, on the heights surrounding the harbor of New York, in our present state of preparation, or rather in our total want of preparation, would be powerless to resist a small squadron of war steamers. This state of things is discreditable to our foresight and to our prudence. The best guarantee against aggression, the best assurance that our diplomacy will be successful and pacific, and that our rights and honor will be respected by other nations, is in their knowledge that we are in a situation to vindicate our reputation and interests. While we may afford to be deficient in the means of offence, we can not afford to be defenceless. The notoriety of the fact that we have neglected the ordinary precautions of defence invites want to consideration in our diplomacy, injustice, arrogance, and insult at the hand of nations. It is now more than sixty years since we announced to the world that we should resist any attempts, from whatever quarter they might come, to make any new colonizations on any part of the American continent; that while we should respect the *status quo* we should protect the people of different nations inhabiting this continent from every attempt to subject them to the dominion of any European power, or to interfere with their undisturbed exercise of the rights of self-government. This announcement was formally made by President Monroe, after consultation with Mr. Madison and Mr. Jefferson. It was formulated by John Quincy Adams. Our government has firmly adhered to the Monroe Doctrine, and even so late as 1865 it warned Napoleon III out of Mexico. It is impossible to foresee, in the recent scramble of the European powers for acquisition of colonies, how soon an occasion may arise for our putting in practice the Monroe Doctrine. It is clear that there ought to be some relation between our assertion of that doctrine and our preparation to maintain it. It is not intended to recommend any attempt to rival the great European powers in the creation of a powerful navy. The changes which have rapidly occurred by the diminution of relative resisting power of the defensive armor of ironclads, and by the increased efficiency of modern artillery, which on a whole has gained in the competition, suggest we should not at present enter largely into the creation of armored vessels. In the questions that beset this subject until they have reached a solution, we can content ourselves with adding but sparingly to our navy. But what we do add should be the very best that science and experience can indicate. This prudential view is reinforced by the consideration that the annual charge of maintaining war vessel bears an important proportion to the original cost of construction.

In constructing permanent fortifications, and in providing an ample supply of the best modern artillery, the annual cost of maintenance is inconsiderable. Nearly the whole expenditure is in the original outlay for construction. If we do not make the expenditure necessary to provide for our sea-coast defences when we have a surplus, and have no need to levy new taxes, we certainly will not make those expenditures when we have no longer a surplus in the treasury. To leave our vast interests defenceless in order to reduce the cost of whiskey to its consumers would be solecism. The present time is peculiarly favorable for providing for this great national necessity too long neglected. Not only does the surplus in the treasury supply ample means to meet this great public want without laying new burdens upon the people, but the work can now be done at a much lower cost than has ever before been possible. The defensive works would consist almost entirely of steel and iron. These materials can now be had at unprecedentedly low price. A vast supply of machinery and of labor called into existence by a great vicissitude in the steel and iron industries offers itself to our service. We should have the satisfaction of knowing that while we were availing ourselves of the supplies which would ordinarily be unattainable, we were setting in motion important industries and giving employment to labor in a period of depression. With encouragement by the guarantee of work, or perhaps by the government itself furnishing the plant, the inventive genius of our people would be applied to the creation of new means and improved machinery, and establishments would spring into existence capable of supplying all of the national wants, and rendering us completely independent of all other countries in respect to the means of national defence. I endeavor to impress these ideas upon Mr. Randall the last time I had the pleasure of seeing him.

With my highest regards to Mrs. Carlisle and yourself,

I remain,

Very truly yours,

S.J. Tilden

"HON. JOHN G. CARLISLE."

The appearance of this communication a few days before the submission of the President's first annual message to Congress was regarded with anything but satisfaction at the White House, and all the less because the recommendations it contained received not only more attention from the public than any made by the President in his message. The liberal appropriations for our "wooden walls" during the succeeding five or six years were, I believe, in a large degree attributable to the impression left upon Congress and the country by this communication.

When announcing Mr. Tilden's death, the "New York World" said:

"Only eight months ago to-day Mr. Tilden wrote his letter to Mr. Carlisle on the subject of coast defences. The letter had more weight with the people than a presidential message. It was recognized as the thoughtful plea of a patriotic citizen and statesman for what he believed was for the safety and honor of the nation. Later still, less than two months ago, this impressive document was followed by a letter to Senator Hawley regretting the apathy of Congress on the subject, and stating that seven hundred papers from all parts of the country and representing all political parties had been sent to the writer endorsing his suggestions for strengthening our sea-coast defences. Mr. Tilden may be truly said to have died at the post of duty."

Mr. Tilden's communication would probably not have appeared just when it did, had he not been willing to undeceive all who were under the impression that he was in any respect responsible for the acts or omissions of the President; and this had become important for his own peace, so general was the impression that his voice was potential at the White House.

Governor Tilden and Mayor Wickham opening the promenade at the Martha Washington Reception, Academy of Music.

Mr. Tilden was reluctant to believe that Mr. Cleveland had deliberately determined to proscribe his friends, and in spite of the apparent
discrepancy between his reported declarations to Mr. Manning in the
fall of 1884, and his action in the construction of his cabinet in 1885,
had, till now, affected to believe that the novelty of Mr. Cleveland's
position, his inexperience his extremely limited acquaintance with the
prominent figures in the arena of federal politics, and the intoxica-
tions of an unexpected and inexplicable elevation, were all transient
conditions, and might safely be left to the remedial influences of time.
To his friend Watterson, who had inferred that he or his friends were
not sharing in fair proportions the results of Mr. Tilden's presumed
influence with the President, he wrote the following letter, designed
apparently to apologize for or extenuate the conduct of the President.
It will be observed that this letter was written within a month after the
inauguration, and eight months before the appearance of his letter to
Mr. Carlisle, and that it reveals to some extent the change which his
relations with the President were already undergoing:

TILDEN TO WATTERSON.

"GRAYSTONE, YONKERS, N.Y., March 26, 1885.

"DEAR MR. WATTERSON: Your vision of the triumphant set you mention
is an illusion. Mr. Green is less jubilant than you. Mr. Weed expects
nothing and desires nothing. Neither of them is excited with a sense
of influence. Mr. Manning was *coerced into the treasury*. Mr. Whitney
alone, of all your New York friends whom you imagine in power and
forgetting you, can be considered as successful; others who might be
regarded as more particular friends of yours have sought nothing, and
no search-warrant has been issued to find them out and install them in
illustrious positions. On the whole, your momentary sense of neglect
by old friends passed away because it had no basis in fact.

"As to your conduct at the convention in respect to the formation
of the platform, my information is that it was as meritorious as you
state it to have been.

"I do not doubt that practical men tending to the views of both
sides could sit down in a corner and agree upon a reasonable measure

for revenue reform which would satisfy you, and in which you would especially aid in the concoction.

"The administration has a difficult, if not an impossible, task in respect to appointments. Mr. Cleveland cannot be expected to know men in all parts of the country. He ought to try to deal impartially and equitably by every class. I do not doubt that he is desirous to do so. It is a very different matter to stand before the country as the responsible author of an appointment, or to ask that appointment under the dictation of personal or local feeling. Some allowance ought, therefore, to be made for disappointments. And the appointing power, when asked to do what it cannot, should soften a refusal by patient hearing, by frank and friendly explanation, and by seeking occasion to do some equivalent act denoting a disposition to be considerate of the interest disappointed. It is not every hand that has the sleight, even if the requisite knowledge of men and access to the best sources of information be possessed. It is related of two famous New York governors that a man applied to Governor Tompkins for an executive favor, who in his own gracious manner refused it, and afterwards to Governor Clinton, who granted it, and that he came away much better pleased with Tompkins than with Clinton.

"Besides, it must be recollected that the Democratic party has now been twenty-four years out of power, and has had no means of educating trained party leaders.

"In England the government is carried on by parliamentary leaders, and the oratorical or debating faculty is of great consequence. In this country the government must be carried on by popular leaders, and a capacity for party leadership is essential. In both, government has to be carried on through by human beings, a fact too often forgotten by theorists.

"I depended on ideas as a political force more liberally and less on party machinery than anybody else has done. What is called patronage I never had to any appreciable extent, and yet I held my ascendancy with the Democratic masses of this State when I had to confront the adverse influence of the executive, of the heads of departments, of the judiciary, and of the majority of the voters of this State against at least twenty thousand office holders. I carried politics upon a plane which approached to the impracticable. I do not exact of anybody else to encounter the risks I ran, or to imitate so adventurous a policy. For there was no moment in which I was not willing to be consigned to private life. It seems to me sometimes remarkable to hear men called great leaders who, while swaying all the patronage of the country – federal, State, and local – failed to hold their own party, or to hold a majority of the people.

"The Republican mischief-makers of the press must be expected to try to array the Democratic party into contending factions, as, for instance, the friends of Carlisle and the friends of Randall, and they sometimes classify me in these divisions. I am sure you know me too well to think that there is any truth in such representations so far as concerns me.

"If I were really exercising the power of the government, I would dispel such fables. I do not think the administration means to give any occasion for such gossip. For my part, I substantially pursue the policy of non-interference in the distribution of appointments by the national administration. Aside from other considerations which require this reserve from me, the totally unfounded gossip of the journals, that Mr. Tilden's hand is seen in this or in that, already swells my mail to dimensions impossible to answer or even to read. If I were really to take an active part in appointments, it would impose upon me a burden of correspondence which I could not endure.

"I began to write you a short letter, but have been thinking aloud until my letter has outgrown my intention.

"Very truly yours,

"S.J. Tilden."

Soon after Mr. Cleveland's inauguration Mr. Tilden had written Mr. Manning advising the appointment of Hon. George W. Julian, of Indiana, as Commissioner of the General Land Office, and suggesting that his letter be shown to the President and to Mr. Lamar, the Secretary of the Interior. After enumerating the evidences of his abundant qualifications for this office, he said:

"I think it would be a most admirable appointment. Considering that he was an original anti-slavery man, it would be a graceful act in Mr. Lamar to favor him. It would show how completely the lion and the lamb had laid down together, and would tend to conciliate a powerful class in the Northern States."

If the lion had laid down with the lamb, it appeared, in this case, that one had laid down inside of the other, for Mr. Julian did not get the appointment. In reply to a letter from Mr. Julian, thanking Mr. Tilden for his effort, and announcing his own disappointment, Mr. Tilden said:

TILDEN TO GEORGE W. JULIAN.

"GRAYSTONE, YONKERS, N.Y., March 24, 1885.

"DEAR MR. JULIAN: I am extremely sorry to learn that you are not to be Commissioner of the Land Office. My letter presented your case as strongly as possible, and I presume was communicated according to the request it contained; although I have not heard from Mr. Manning since. But I do not ascribe so much potentially to it as you seem inclined to do. Men in power generally have their plans, and take their views which they prefer to the wishes of those who have ceased to have power. I hope that there may something else be opened to you in respect to which you may have better success.

"Very truly yours,

"S.J. Tilden."

In point of fact, no one who had taken any active interest in establishing Mr. Tilden's claims to the presidency before the Electoral Commission, or in securing the testimony establishing the fraudulent character of the votes which were made the pretext for electing Hayes, ever received any recognition from Mr. Cleveland; not even those in whose fortunes Mr. Tilden took the trouble, which ought to have been unnecessary, to express to the President his personal interest. And as if to leave the friends of Mr. Tilden in no doubt as to the significance of this policy, he appointed to an important office Mr. E.H. Noyes, of Ohio, who had been one of the visiting statesmen selected by Chandler to "hold Florida," and whose defence of the Alachua fraud was of so gross and scandalous a character that nothing less than the mission to France was deemed by the principle beneficiary of that fraud a sufficient compensation.

In the fall of this year the rumor reached Mr. Tilden that one of his nephews was talked of for a place on the State ticket in New York. The following letter which he addressed to his nephew shows that, as early as September, 1885, he was no longer under any illusions in regard to the attitude of the administration towards him:

TILDEN TO HIS NEPHEW.

"GRAYSTONE, YONKERS, N.Y., Sept, 1, 1885.

"MY DEAR NEPHEW: In my judgment you should not entertain the slightest doubt in respect to going on the State ticket this fall, if that is within your power. Both your interest and your duty require that you should refuse any opportunity if it should open to you. I should look upon your embarking upon a political career as total ruin to your business interests, to your independence, and to your whole future. You cannot afford the expense of such a career. You cannot afford to pay even the first assessment. You cannot afford to withdraw your attention from your business – to do so would be unjust to your brother and to your creditors.

"I have felt much concern in respect to your growing taste for politics. You have now reached a fork in the road when you must choose whether you will aim at pecuniary independence, safety, and comfort; or whether you will consent to become a mere hanger-on to the uncertain chances of politics. Besides, if you were to enter upon a political career, you could not select a worse time in which to do it than this fall. The elements were never more uncertain. You would be foolish to take the chances now, even if you should do it hereafter.

"I write strongly, because I see clearly the complications which your becoming a candidate now would involve. If you wish to see me on the subject, *I can tell you things which I cannot write.*

"Very truly yours,

"S.J. TILDEN"

Nor where the relations between Mr. Manning and the President much less, if at all less, strained before the close of their first official year than with Mr. Tilden. In reply to some complimentary lines from the latter about the secretary's first report, and congratulations upon

the manner in which it had been received by the public, Mr. Manning
wrote:

MANNING TO TILDEN

"WASHINGTON D.C., Dec. 21, 1885.

"MY DEAR GOVERNOR: Your note of the 19th instant came to me
yesterday.

"Words of commendation from you have always been most welcome,
but are more so now than ever, feeling, as I do, that I am living in an
atmosphere that is full of mischief, and where the whirl is so great
that one is inclined sometimes to doubt whether he comprehends his
associates, or fully understands anything of what he is about.

"I think of you every day and of your delicate health, and often wish
that you were here to guide us with your advice.

"Faithfully yours,

DANIEL MANNING.

HON. SAM. J. TILDEN,
"Graystone."

From this time forth Mr. Tilden refused to compromise the chances
of any candidates for public employment under the federal government
by yielding to their appeals for his recommendation. To his friend, the
late Robert B. Minturn, he wrote:

TILDEN TO ROBERT B. MINTURN.

"YONKERS, N.Y., Jan. 2, 1885.

"DEAR MR. MINTURN: It would be at any time a pleasure to see you; but
I am not in communication with Governor Cleveland in respect to his
appointments, and think it would be better for you to say what you
wish directly to him or through Mr. Manning.

"Very truly yours,

"S.J. TILDEN

"R.B. MINTURN, ESQ."

Mr. Manning, the only member of the executive branch of the government with whom Mr. Tilden was in correspondence, was prostrated by apoplexy as he was returning to his office from a cabinet meeting in the following May, and as soon as he was well enough to do so, left Washington never to revisit again. After a few months' vacation in search of health, on the 26th of July he wrote Mr. Tilden from Watch Hill, where he was staying at the time:

"I want to see you very much to talk about my proposed communication to the President. I feel more and more, daily, that I need your assistance. Have you thought over the matter? Have you prepared a form for me? . . . I do not know when I can get to see you. It occupies a day to go from Watch Hill to New York or Yonkers, and for me the trip will be a long one. Kindly clear my mind on this point. I do so want to decide on my action before the occasion closes. That done, I should feel comparatively free. My health is improving daily. My physician talks encouragingly, and I feel that I am better and stronger than when I left Graystone."

To this letter Mr. Tilden sent the following reply:

TILDEN TO MANNING.

"GRAYSTONE, July 27, 1886.

"DEAR MR. MANNING: Your letter of the 26th is received. I have thought much of the nature of the communication which you wish to make, but have written nothing. Do you wish to say anything further than to announce your final purpose and your reasons for it? The letter, it seems to me, will be short.

"I will try my hand on a draft and send it you.

"No further intelligence has been received from our friends in Europe.

"I have been busy all the morning answering a letter from Mr. Fairchild.

"Yours truly,
"S.J. TILDEN."

The Hon. Charles S. Fairchild, who had been assistant secretary of the treasury, was at this time acting secretary of the treasury. The letter referred to here and Mr. Tilden's reply seem to have closed his relations with the administration at Washington.

ACTING SECRETARY FAIRCHILD TO TILDEN.

"TREASURY DEPARTMENT, July 24, 1886.

"MY DEAR MR. TILDEN: You have by this time received a little pamphlet containing a copy of Mr. Morrison's surplus resolutions, a few remarks upon it by myself, and a number of tables prepared by Mr. Jordan. I wish to ask a favor of you, and that is to give me your views as to the probable effect of that resolution if it becomes law; if the effects may, in your judgment, be evil, the nature of the evil, and how it will manifest itself. If it causes silver mono-metallism in this county, what will be the evil of that? When is this likely to be felt? Would all the gold be driven from use, and, if not, what will be the difference in value between a gold and silver dollar? Etc.

"I wish to get all the information that I can upon this subject for immediate use. I do not wish to take an exaggerated view of the evils which may come, but, on the contrary, prefer for present purposes to under rather than over state them. I know that you will be glad to help me in this, and hope that it may not be too much trouble to you to do so.

"Very respectfully yours,
"CHARLES S. FAIRCHILD.

"HON. SAMUEL J. TILDEN."

TILDEN TO ACTING SECRETARY FAIRCHILD.

"*(Personal and confidential.)*

"GRAYSTONE, YONKERS, N.Y., July 27, 1886.

"DEAR MR. FAIRCHILD: Your letter of July 24th reached me yesterday afternoon. I hastened to acknowledge and answer it. You are right supposing that I would be glad to help you in your difficult and responsible duty.

"You mention that you desire to get all the information you can upon the subject of your letter, for 'immediate use.' Congress is stated by the public journals as likely to adjourn within a few days. These circumstances do not allow room for much discussion of the complicated topics adverted to in your letter.

"It cannot be doubted that the resolution adopted by the House, if it should become law, would embarrass the effort of the Treasury Department to maintain the equality in the market value of the different elements which compose our circulating medium. The United States notes, or legal-tenders, as they are commonly called, and the silver certificates are kept par with gold simply because they are received and paid out by the treasury as equal to gold coin; because the known policy of the treasury is to maintain that equality; and because the treasury is kept in possession, at all times, of a sufficient amount of gold to pay off any surplus of legal tenders and silver certificates beyond the amount which the uses of business can absorb; and because the public confidence that the treasury has the ability to carry out its declared policy is thereby assured. Of course every measure which impairs the resources of the treasury or its discretion in the use of those resources weakens its power to maintain the equality between the various elements of our present currency. But as the House resolution seems likely to be materially altered by the Senate, it is not useful to discuss hypothetical measures.

"The present fallacy which infests the minds of many members of Congress is in counting large amounts of purely trust funds and large amounts of other unavailable funds as if they were resources of the treasury.

"As to what would be the premium on gold if the treasury should come to a silver basis in its receipts and payments, that is a matter of conjecture. In present market value, gold measured by silver is thirty-five per cent higher than silver. I do not think that if gold and silver were to 'part company' the premium on gold would at once be nearly as large as that. Much would depend on the general opinion as to when the equity in market value between the two metals could or would be restored, and something upon the future cost of producing silver. Of course, gold would cease to circulate as currency and would take its place among commodities, and be bought and sold like iron and wheat. The deficiency in the currency would probably be supplied by paper issues. But these questions are too speculative to be discussed or even stated with exactness in this hasty letter.

"It would be very desirable to bring both silver and gold into use as reserves for the basis of the currency, and as means of international exchanges, thereby doubling the quantity of the precious metals available for those purposes; but that object cannot be effected by the action of the United States alone.

"Very Truly Yours,

"S. J. TILDEN.

HON. CHARLES S. FAIRCHILD,
"Acting Secretary of the Treasury."

Though Mr. Tilden had no occasion to waste any more advice upon the administration at Washington, he continued to take an undiminished interest in public affairs, of which to the close of his private as well as public correspondence bears testimony. His physical disabilities were gradually multiplying, and engrossed a corresponding proportion of his thought and time. His own appreciation of this progressive decay is given in the following letters:

TILDEN TO SEYMOUR.

GRAYSTONE, YONKERS, N.Y. Sept. 22, 1885.

"DEAR SIR: I have received your letter of September, 1885, enclosing a slip cut from the 'Rochester Post Express,' criticizing Mr. Bigelow's republication of my speeches, and 'speaking of my action in regard to canal matters;' and also saying that you had 'written to him to correct the errors.'

"I am much obliged to you for the trouble you have taken in the matter. I apprehend, however, that it may be safely left to the public or posterity to discredit or confute the writer's misrepresentations.

"I regret to hear that your health is so unsatisfactory. You have my cordial sympathies and my best wishes for the comfort and happiness of your declining years.

"I am myself, although somewhat your junior, subject to some infirmities which annoy me and create inconvenient disabilities. My eyes, happily, are strong, and enable me to read as much as ever; and my hearing, also is very acute in both ears; but I have trouble of my vocal cords which makes my voice weak and sometimes reduces me to a whisper. Some of my nerves of motion, too, are tremulous. Fatigue aggravates this so much that I do not travel, which I believe you are generally able to do.

"I should hope to see you if you should be able to visit me, were it not, as I understand, your hearing is impaired, and if we met social intercourse would be very imperfect between a dumb man and a deaf one.

"With my earnest good wishes,

"Very Truly Yours,

"S. J. TILDEN.

"HON. HORATIO SEYMOUR."

A few weeks later he gives some further and more interesting particulars about his physical condition in a letter to an old friend in Rochester.

MR. TILDEN TO MARK SIBLEY.

"GRAYSTONE, Feb. 27, 1886.

"DEAR MR. SIBLEY: I have received your interesting letter. The newspapers are correct in saying that the 9th of February is my birthday, but some of them are quite astray in saying that I am seventy-nine years old. I was born the 9th of February, 1814, and was seventy-two years old on my last birthday. Although seven years younger that you are, I can readily believe that you are practically younger than I. You have not done so much as I to exhaust the vital powers, and have not so large a debt to pay for strength borrowed and consumed in advance. My eyes are extremely good and enable me to pass most of my time in reading; my ears are both of them much more acute than those of most people. The doctors tell me that every vital organ is in strong and sound condition. But I have been for some years greatly annoyed by a mysterious malady of some of the nerves of motion, which imparts a tremor to my hands and impairs my voice so that I lose most of the pleasure of conversation.

"I have also read the brief biography of your life and doings which you were kind enough to send me. It illustrates an example of an active, useful, and successful career.

"Wishing you every blessing of continued health, and prolonged years of happiness and prosperity,

"I am very truly yours,

"S.J. TILDEN."[1]

---

1 NOTE: A few months only prior to the date of this letter, and while engaged in a revision of his will, Mr. Tilden held a consultation with an eminent physician not in regular attendance upon him, at which I was invited to be present. I deemed the occasion of sufficient importance to warrant me in making a note of the diagnosis as it transpired. I quote the principal features of it.

"Troubled all his life with a delicate stomach. If he went out to dine and the dinner was served a little later than usual, he suffered from it.

"Used to surmount this trouble by horseback riding. Used to ride in Albany in '75 when the thermometer was fourteen degrees below zero.

"Now cannot ride a horse, can only walk around the house and ride in a carriage.

"The shaking commenced two or three years ago.

"Some shaking in legs, aggravated by fatigue or excitement, with pulsations in back of head.

"Feels that he is growing more feeble and his grip less firm. Has had a cold about three weeks. Not usually susceptible to colds. Has not had one for two years before.

"It began with a slight cough and catarrh. Drinking makes him cough sometimes. He wakes occasionally during the night.

"Sleeps about an hour and half, three or four times a night – say, five hours at night and two in the daytime.

"Never had a pain in his head in his life.

""Eats four times a day. Takes a great deal of mutton broth, beef bread, and a little, but not much, vegetables.

"Inclined to be costive.

"Uses enema of tepid water.

"About once a week he takes a cathartic of Carlsbad water, sprudel, or rhubarb and aloes. Takes stewed prunes meantime.

"Takes now four grains of quinine three times a day – twelve grains a day. This is his regular habit.

"The doctors advised more, but he held off, but was afraid to leave off altogether. Is not conscious of any effect of it except more strength; no effect on his head and chest.

"Had been taking, until a few weeks back, hyoscyamus, one table of 1/200 of a grain. Four times a day. Sometimes of 1/100. The highest he ever took less strength since and more tremor. Took quinine at the same time that he took hyoscyamus. Thinks he was worse when he left it off than when he commenced taking it. While he took it, was troubled with dryness of the mouth and corrugated tongue. Less of that discontinuance. Sometimes feels that he must resume it as a palliative.

"Has twice stopped the use of quinine altogether, when he was living in the country. Resumed it in consequence of a cold and painless diarrhea which weakened him very much.

"The doctors report his liver and lungs all right. Four years ago, when he went to live in the country, could ride six hours. The next year he trembled, but could walk a good deal. The first winter he tried electricity, but it did him no good – he thought harm, rather."

Mr. Tilden neglected no suitable opportunity for pressing upon his friends in Congress his views of the importance of strengthening our coast defences. In a letter to the Hon. Samuel Randall, of March 2, 1886, he dwelt upon the expediency of the government's purchasing Captain Erickson's "Destroyer" as a means of testing the efficiency of his theory of submarine guns.

"It is a special measure of economy," he wrote, "for if it should turn out that a machine costing about a hundred thousand dollars should be capable of destroying a first class ironclad costing from three to five millions, the result would be to cheapen some of the necessary defences.

"I wish you would send me the names of the gentlemen composing the committee or sub-committee whose province it will be to investigate and decide upon the appropriation necessary to purchase the 'Destroyer.'"

The gravity of the principle involved in what is popularly known as the Monroe Doctrine, in consequence of the increasing complication of the relations of our sister republics with foreign nations, furnished a special motive for strengthening our sea-coast defences which was not receiving the attention from the authorities at Washington, still less from the public, which Mr. Tilden thought is deserved. To assist in arousing a livelier sensibility to the dangers which were to be apprehended from this quarter of the horizon, Mr. Tilden prepared a compact history of the origin of the Monroe Doctrine, and some of the responsibilities involved in maintaining it, to reinforce his plea for strengthening our sea-coast defences. I give here the material portions of it as it appeared in the columns of the "New York Sun."

"THE MONROE DOCTRINE AND ITS ORIGIN.

"After the final fall of Napoleon and his second abdication, the Emperor Alexander I of Russia, the Emperor Francis of Austria, and King William III of Prussia, formed a league. Alexander drew up the agreement, which was signed at Paris by these monarchs, Sept. 26, 1815; they christened the league the Holy Alliance. It professed purpose was to regulate the States of Christendom on principles of Christian amity. Its real aim was to maintain existing dynasties and to suppress all revolutionary or popular movements. To secure the cooperation of the people, some of these sovereigns, especially Frederick William III., had promised to give to their subjects a liberal charter, allowing them practical self-government. But all such promises were violated. To this alliance most of the European powers except the Holy See and England acceded.

"The Holy Alliance held frequent congresses, and its policy was to intervene with military force in the internal affairs of any country which should attempt to establish less despotic government. At its instance the revolutionary movements in Naples and in Piedmont were suppressed in 1821. At its instance, in 1823, France marched an army, nominally of 100,000 men, into Spain, and restored absolutism in that country. Alexander of Russia assured France of his support, offering to march an army to the Rhine.

"It was known that the Holy Alliance mediated enabling Spain to reconquer the States of South America and Mexico. It was arranged that the Holy Alliance should have a consultation on the subject. The policy was avowed to Mr. Canning by Prince Polignac, Ambassador of France to England, of ensuring, by concert between the European powers, the establishment of monarchical governments over the revolted colonies of Spain.

"Under Castlereagh England had refused to be a party to the engagements of the Holy Alliance. Under the lead of his successor as Secretary of State of Foreign Affairs. George Canning, she took a position of more pronounced dissent and opposition. She threw her moral weight in the scale of condemnation of the intervention of France in the domestic affairs of Spain.

"In the meantime the United States had recognized the independence of the revolted colonies of Spain. President Monroe, by his special message of March 8.1822, recommended the measure. Congress, by an act approved May 4, 1822, made an appropriation to defray the expenses of such missions as the President might institute to the independent nations on the American continents.

"In 1823 Mr. Canning proposed to Mr. Rush, the American Minister to Great Britain, that the United States should unite with England in a joint declaration condemning any attempt of the Holy Alliance to help Spain to reconquer its revolted colonies in South America and Mexico. In reply Mr. Rush urged the immediate recognition by England of the independence of the South American States. If that were done he offered to unite in the joint declaration proposed by Mr. Canning. The correspondence was transmitted to John Quincy Adams, Secretary of State. President Monroe submitted that correspondence to Mr. Jefferson and through him to Mr. Madison.

"President Monroe, after consulting Mr. Jefferson and Mr. Madison, availed himself of his annual message of Dec. 2, 1823, to state the position of the American government upon the subject. The two passages of the message relating to this subject are here given in full:

I.

"At the proposal of the Russian imperial government, made through the Minister of the Emperor residing here, a full power and instructions have been transmitted to the Minister of the United States at St. Petersburg to arrange, by amicable negotiation, the respective rights and interests of the two nations on the north-west coast of this continent. A similar proposal had been made by His Imperial Majesty to the government of Great Britain, which has likewise been acceded to. The government of the United States has been desirous, by this friendly proceeding, of manifesting the great value which they have invariably attached to the friendship of the Emperor, and their solicitude to cultivate the best understanding with his government. In the discussions to which this interest has given rise, and in the arrangements by which they may terminate, the occasion has been judged proper for asserting, as a principle in which the rights and interests of the United States are involved, that *the American continents, by the free and independent condition which they have assumed and maintained, are henceforth not to be considered as subjects for future colonization by any European powers.*

"It was stated at the commencement of the last session that a great effort was then making in Spain and Portugal to improve the condition of the people of those countries, and that it appears to be conducted with extraordinary moderation. It need scarcely be remarked that the result has been so far very different from what was then anticipated. Of events in that quarter of the globe, with which we have so much intercourse, and from which we derive our origin, we have always been anxious and interested spectators. The citizens of the United States cherish sentiments the most friendly in favor of the liberty and happiness of their fellow-men on that side of the Atlantic. In the wars of the European powers, in matters relating to themselves, we have never taken any part, nor does it comfort with our policy so to do. It is only when our rights are invaded or seriously menaced that we resent injuries or make preparation for our defence. With the movements in this hemisphere we are of necessity more immediately connected, and by causes which must be obvious to all enlightened and impartial observers.

"The political system of the allied powers is essentially in this respect from that of America. This difference proceeds from that which exists in their respective governments. And to the defence of our own, which has been achieved by the loss of so much blood and treasure, and matured by the wisdom of their most enlightened citizens, and under which we have enjoyed unexampled felicity, this whole nation is devoted. We owe it, therefore, to candor and to the amicable relations existing between the United States and those powers to declare that we should consider any attempt on their part to extend their system to any portion of this hemisphere as dangerous to our peace and safety. With the existing colonies or dependencies of any European power we have not interfered, and shall not interfere. But with the governments who have declared their independence and maintained it, and whose independence we have, on great consideration and on just principles, acknowledge, we could not view any interposition for the purpose of oppressing them, or controlling in any other manner their destiny, by any European power, in any other light that as the manifestation of an unfriendly disposition toward the United States. In the war between those new governments and Spain we declared our neutrality at the time of their recognition, and to this we have adhered, and shall continue to adhere, provided no change shall occur which, in the judgment of the competent authorities of this government, shall make a correspondence change on the part of the United States indispensable to their security.

"The late events in Spain and Portugal show that Europe is still unsettled. Of this important fact no stronger proof can be adduced than that the allied powers should have thought it proper, on a principle satisfactory to themselves, to have interposed by force in the internal concerns of Spain. To what extent such interposition may be carried on the same principle is a question to which all independent powers whose governments differ from theirs are interested, even those most remote, and surely none more so than the United States. Our policy in regard to Europe, which was adopted at an early stage of the wars which have so long agitated that quarter of the globe, nevertheless remains the same, which is, not to interfere in the internal concerns of any of its powers; to consider the government *de facto* as the legitimate government for us; to cultivate friendly relations with it, and to preserve those relations by a frank, firm, and manly policy; meeting, in all instances, the just claims of every power, submitting to injuries from none. But in regard to these continents, circumstances are eminently and conspicuously different. It is impossible that the allied powers should extend their political system to any portion of either continent without endangering our peace and happiness; nor can any one believe that our Southern brethren, if left to themselves would adopt it of their own accord. It is equally impossible, therefore, that we should behold such interposition, in any form, with indifference. If we look to the comparative strength and resources of Spain and those new governments, and their distance from each other, it must be obvious that she can never subdue them. It is still the true policy of the United States to leave the parties to themselves, in the hope that other powers will pursue the same course.

"These passages were undoubtedly written by John Quincy Adams, and assented to and adopted by President Monroe.

"President Monroe had previously written to Mr. Jefferson asking his advice upon the subject, and requesting him to consult Mr. Madison. He had also sent to Mr. Jefferson a correspondence between Richard Rush, United States Minister at London, and George Canning, Foreign Secretary of State for Great Britain.

"Mr. Jefferson's reply was as follows:

"Monticello, Oct. 24, 1823.

"Dear Sir: The question presented by the letters you have sent me is the most momentous which has ever been offered to my contemplation since that of independence. That made us a nation; this sets our compass and points the course which we are to steer through the ocean of time opening on us. And never could we embark upon it under any circumstances more auspicious. Our first and fundamental maxim should be, never to tangle ourselves in the broils of Europe. Our second, never to suffer Europe to intermeddle with cis-Atlantic affairs. America, North and South, has a set of interests distinct from those of Europe, and peculiarly her own. She should, therefore, have a system of her own, separate and apart from that of Europe. While the last is laboring to become the domicile of despotism, our endeavor should surely be to make our hemisphere that of freedom.

"One nation, most of all, could disturb us in this pursuit; she now offers to lead, aid, and accompany us in it. By acceding to her proposition we detach her from the bands, bring her mighty weight into the scale of free government, and emancipate a continent at one stroke, which might otherwise linger long in doubt and difficulty. Great Britain is the nation which can do us the most harm of any one of all on earth, and with her on our side we need not fear the whole world. With her, then, we should sedulously cherish a cordial friendship, and nothing would tend more to knit our affections than to be fighting once more side by side in the same cause. Not that I would purchase even her amity at the price of taking part in her wars.

"But the war in which the present proposition might engage us, should that be its consequence, is not her war, but ours. Its object is to introduce and establish the American system of keeping out of our land all foreign powers, of never permitting those of Europe to intermeddle with the affairs of our nations. It is to maintain our own principle, not to depart from it. And if, to facilitate this, we can effect a division in the body of the European powers, and draw over to our side its most powerful member, surely we should do it. But I am clearly of Mr. Canning's opinion that it will prevent instead of provoke war. With Great Britain withdrawn from their scale and shifted into that of our two continents, all Europe combined would not undertake such a war. For how would they propose to get at either enemy without superior fleets? Nor is the occasion to be slighted which this proposition offers, of declaring our protest against the atrocious violations of the rights of nations, by the interference of any one in the internal affairs of another, so flagitiously begun by Bonaparte, and now continued by the equally lawless alliance, calling itself holy.

"But we have first to ask ourselves a question: Do we wish to acquire to our own confederacy any one or more of the Spanish provinces? I candidly confess that I have ever looked on Cuba as the most interesting addition which could ever be made to our systems of States. The control which, with Florida Point, this island would give us over the Gulf of Mexico and the countries and isthmus bordering on it, as well as those whose waters flow into it, would fill up the measure of our political well-being. Yet, as I am sensible that this can never be obtained, even with her own consent, but by war, and its independence which is our second interests (and especially its independence of England), can be secured without it, I have no hesitation in abandoning my first wish to future chances, and accepting its independence, with peace and the friendship of England, rather than its association at the expense of war and her enmity.

"I could honestly, therefore, join in the declaration proposed, that we aim not at the acquisition of any of those possessions, that we will not stand in the way of any amicable arrangement between them and the mother country; but that we will oppose with all our means the forcible interposition of any other power, as auxiliary, stipendiary, or under any other form or pretext, and most especially their transfer to any power by conquest, cession, or acquisition in any other way. I should think it, therefore, advisable that the Executive should encourage the British government to a continuance in the dispositions expressed in these letters by an assurance of his concurrence with them as far as his authority goes; and that it may lead to war, the declaration of which requires an act of Congress, the case shall be laid before them for consideration at their first meeting and under the reasonable aspect in which it is seen by himself.

"I have so long weaned from political subjects, and have so long ceased to take any interest in them, that I am sensible. I am not qualified to offer opinions on them worthy of any attention. But the question now proposed involves consequences so lasting and effects so decisive of our future destinies as to rekindle all the interest I have heretofore felt on such occasions, and to induce me to the hazard of opinions which will prove only my wish to contribute still my mite toward anything which may be useful to our country. And, praying you to accept it at only what it is worth, I add the assurance of my constant and affectionate friendship and respect.

"The general idea of keeping ourselves disentangled from the controversies and wars of European States was also contained in Washington's Farwell Address.

"The germ of the Monroe Doctrine will be found in several letters of Jefferson – one to Thomas Paine, dated March 18, 1801; another to William Short, dated Oct. 3, 1801.

"Still later, a letter of Jefferson, dated Oct. 29, 1808, said: 'We consider their interests and ours as the same, and that the object of both must be to exclude all European influence in this hemisphere.'

"Mr. Gallatin, the American Minister to France, wrote to J.Q. Adams, Secretary of State, June 24, 1823, that before leaving Paris he had said to M. Chateaubriand, the French Minister of Foreign Affairs, on May 13: 'The United States would undoubtedly preserve their neutrality, provided it were respected, and avoid every interference with the politics of Europe.... On the other hand, they would not suffer others to interfere against the emancipation of America.'

"Mr. John Quincy Adams, Secretary of State, in his diary, under date of July 17, 1823, says that, in a conversation, with Baron Tuyl, the Russian Minister, he told him that 'we should contest the right of Russia to any territorial establishment on this continent, and that we should assume distinctly the principle that the American continents are no longer subjects for any new European colonial establishments.'

"The reply of Mr. Madison was as follows:

"DEAR SIR: I have just received from Mr. Jefferson your letter to him, with the correspondence between Mr. Canning and Mr. Rush, sent for his and my perusal, and our opinions on the subject of it.

"From the disclosures of Mr. Canning it appears, as otherwise to be inferred, that the success of France against Spain would be followed by an attempt of the holy allies to reduce the revolutionized colonies of the latter to their former dependence.

"The professions we have made to these neighbors, our sympathies with their liberties and independence, the deep interest we have in the most friendly relations with them, and the consequences threatened by a command of their resources by the great powers, confederated against the rights and reforms of which we have given so conspicuous and persuasive an example, all unite in calling for our efforts to defeat the mediated crusade. It is particularly fortunate that the policy of Great Britain, though guarded by calculations different from ours, has presented cooperation for an object the same with ours. With the cooperation we have nothing to fear from the rest of Europe, and with it the best assurance of success to our laudable views. There ought not, therefore, to be any backwardness, I think, in meeting her in the way she has proposed; keeping in view, of course, the spirit and forms of the Constitution in every step taken in the road to war, which must be the last step if those short of war should be without avail.

"It cannot be doubted that Mr. Canning's proposal, though made with the air of consultation as well as concert, was founded on a predetermination to take the course marked out, whatever might be the reception given here to his invitation. But this consideration ought not to divert us from what is just and proper in itself. Our cooperation is due to ourselves and to the world, and while it must ensure success in the event of an appeal to force, it doubles the chance of success without that appeal. It is not improbable that Great Britain would like best to have the merit of being the sole champion of her new friends, notwithstanding the greater difficulty to be encountered, but for the dilemma in which she would be placed. She must, in that case, either leave us as neutrals, to extend our commerce and navigation at the expense of her, or make us enemies by renewing her paper blockades and other arbitrary proceedings on the ocean. It may be hoped that such a dilemma with not be without a permanent tendency to check her proneness to unnecessary wars.

"Why the British cabinet should have scrupled to arrest the calamity it now apprehends, by applying to the threats of France against Spain the small effort which it scruples not to employ in behalf of Spanish America, is best known to itself. It is difficult to find any other explanation that that interest in the one case has more weight in its casuistry than principle had in the other.

"Will it not be honorable to our country, and possibly not altogether in vain, to invite the British government to extend the 'avowed disapprobation' of the project against the Spanish colonies to the enterprise of France against Spain herself, and even to join in some declaratory act in behalf of the Greeks? On the supposition that no form could be given to the act clearing it of a pledge to follow it up by war, we ought to compare the good to be done with the little injury to be apprehended to the United States, shielded as their interests would be by the power and the fleets of Great Britain united with their own. These are questions, however, which may require more information that I possess, and more reflection than I can now give them.

"What is the extent of Mr. Canning's disclaimer as to 'the remaining possessions of Spain in America?' Does it exclude future views of acquiring Porto Rico, etc., as well as Cuba? It leaves Great Britain free, as I understand it, in relation to other quarters of the globe.

"I return the correspondence of Mr. Rush and Mr. Canning, with assurances, etc.

"J. M.

"To Thomas Jefferson.
MONTPELIER, Nov. 1, 1823

"DEAR SIR: I return the letter of the President. The correspondence from abroad has gone back to him as you desired. I have expressed to him my concurrence in the policy of meeting the advances of the British government, having an eye to the forms of our Constitution in every step in the road to war. With the British power and navy combined with our own, we have nothing to fear from the rest of the world, and in the great struggle of the epoch between liberty and despotism, we owe it to ourselves to sustain the former, in this hemisphere at least. I have even suggested an invitation to the British government to join in applying the 'small effort for so much good' to the French invasion of Spain, and to make Greece an object of some such favorable attention. Why Mr. Canning and his colleague did not sooner interpose against the calamity, which could not have escaped foresight, cannot be otherwise explained but by the different aspect of the question when it related to liberty in Spain, and to the extension of British commerce to her former colonies.

"Mr. Canning was glad of the cooperation of the United States, but was too much devoted to the aggrandizement of England to accept President Monroe's declaration against the colonization of any portion of America by any European power. France and Russia likewise objected to that principle.

"The position taken by England, and especially the announcement by Mr. Canning that any attempt by France to aid Spain in the reconquest of her revolted colonies would be followed by the immediate acknowledgment by England of their independence, undoubtedly had great effect in defeating the plans of the Holy Alliance, and, indeed, of all schemes by European powers to appropriate to themselves any part of the former colonial dominions of Spain.

"But it was not until January, 1825, that England formally acknowledged the independence of the South American States. In announcing that event Mr. Canning gave way to his celebrated burst of oratory: 'I sought materials for compensation in another hemisphere. Contemplating Spain such as our ancestors had known her, I resolve that, if France had Spain, it should not be Spain with the Indies. I called the New World into existence to redress the balance of the Old.' Thus the English statesman claimed credit for a result largely due to the assertion by the United States of the principle which has become so well known as the Monroe Doctrine."

"In the year 1884 Jacob Sharp, of New York city, succeeded in procuring from the Legislature a charter for the construction of a surface railway through Broadway, then the most considerable and popular thoroughfare in New York city. It soon became notorious that the charter was obtained by the rankest corruption, and that the aldermen of New York city who gave effect to the charter were, with a few exceptions, paid largely for their votes. Mr. Tilden, through the press and through his private correspondence, urged upon the Legislature its duty to repeal the charter at once. It was largely due to his exertions that the railroad committee of the Senate, early in March, reported that unanimously that the charter was obtained by fraud; that the organization was a sham, and concealed a scheme to appropriate to the personal benefit of a few desperate speculators "the most valuable street railroad in the world without legal authority, without the consent of the property-holders on Broadway, and without any adequate compensation to the city." Most of the articles which appeared in the leading New York journals during the latter days of the session of the Legislature in 1886, urging the repeal of this charter, were dictated by Mr. Tilden. He also urged Governor Hill to support him in his efforts. The two letters which follow were written mainly to press this duty upon the Governor.

TILDEN TO GOVERNOR HILL.

"(Personal and confidential)

"GRAYSTONE, YONKERS, N.Y., March 20, 1886.
"DEAR GOVERNOR HILL: I send you a series of papers.

"1. The first is on the accountability of corporations, which shows the authority for a legislative repeal of the Broadway Railroad charter. It is the same which I handed to you when you were at Graystone. I send it in connection with the papers which are now added.

"2. The second paper is an authority from the Supreme Court of the United States showing the repealability of a street-railroad charter, and its effect not only to vacate the charter, but also to vacate the franchise in a public street.

"3. Papers 3, 4, 5, and 6 elicited by Mr. Carter's argument in behalf of the Seventh Avenue Railroad Company, showing how the great organs of public opinion deal with the pretext of those who claim to be innocent holders, and as such entitled to indulgence and protection.

"The truth is, that on the facts as now disclosed there are no innocent holders, nor any holders who had not sufficient information to put them on their guard against the stock and bonds tainted with fraud and corruption.

"Least of all can the Seventh Avenue Company set up any such preference.

"In the first place, the notoriety of the grounds of suspicion and fraud and corruption which has attended the transaction from its beginning, and which carried moral conviction to the whole public, is sufficient to deprive any purchaser of the character of an innocent investor, and to convict him of engaging in the transaction at his voluntary risk.

"In the second place, the omission of a compliance with the legal conditions necessary to a valid organization of the Broadway Railroad Company; and the legal conditions necessary to the existence of the right to construct the railroad; the failure to give adequate notice of the meeting of the aldermen at which the grant was carried over the Mayor's veto, which rendered the action of the Board of Aldermen giving their consent totally void, and other legal irregularities – were all things which the purchaser of stock and bonds was bound to inquire into.

"The Seventh Avenue Company, so far from being an innocent holder, was the active principal in the whole transaction. It controlled the disposal of the stock and bonds, and leased in perpetuity the Broadway Railroad. If any other party afterwards bought stock or bonds, he would acquire no better title than Seventh Avenue Railroad Company had, and could communicate. If he has been cheated, his remedy lies on the guarantee of the Seventh Avenue Railroad Company, or otherwise against that company. He has no equity against the defrauded city to indemnify him against his own laches.

"The interests of public morality require that the holders of the booty, whether at first or second hand, should not be allowed to carry it off triumphantly.

"You are the representative of the Democratic party of the State of New York. It is necessary that the purpose to defeat this conspiracy of fraud, corruption, and public robbery should be conspicuously manifested by you.

"The more effectual and the more swift the measures of redress are, the greater will be the popular approval. An accessory measure would be to take away from the aldermen the power to pass any grant over a Mayor's veto. A single man standing up before the face of the community would never make such a grant. The Cantor bill, as amended, ought to pass; but it is imperfect, and the additional legislation ought to be applied. It can be added to, or its operation limited, hereafter.

"Very truly yours,
"S. J. TILDEN."

TILDEN TO GOVERNOR HILL.

"(Personal and confidential.)

"GRAYSTONE, YONKERS, N.Y., March 24, 1886.

"DEAR GOVERNOR HILL: Your special message is admirable. Such action is the best answer to those who depreciated you in the last canvass. I was not mistaken in thinking it would be received with general popular applause. But you have now to follow up the issue which you have so well made, and, if possible, conduct your side of it to complete success.

I have always regarded President Cleveland's advertisement that he did not desire to influence the action of Congress as a great mistake. A public man must show not only that he is individually (though impotently) right, but that he *can* lead his party-followers and make them, and be himself, to the largest practicable extent, a power for good. Otherwise, when he comes to be judged it will be said that he is better than his party, by must be discarded because he cannot effect results. I hope, therefore, you will exert all the moral influence you possess to induce the Legislature to pass such legislation as you recommend. I think a law ought to be enacted that the consent of the local authorities of the city of New York to the laying down of a railroad track in any street of the said city shall not be made effectual by the vote of any aldermen if the resolution giving such consent shall have been vetoed by the Mayor of the said city, or without the assent of a majority in interest of owners of property abutting on the said street. The streets in the city of New York are already well provided with north and south railroads, so that a man need walk but one block, and generally but half a block, in order to reach one of these railroads, and very little room is left for the convenience of vehicles other than railroad cars. Additional lines should only be granted after great deliberation and the fullest public discussion. The Fifth avenue should be kept clear as an access to the Central Park. On the east side of it, Madison, Fourth, Third, and Second avenues have each a horse railroad, and the Third and Second have elevated railroads. On the west side the Sixth, Seventh, Eighth, and Ninth Avenues and Broadway have each a horse railroad; and Sixth and Ninth avenues have each elevated railroad. Nothing is left except Fifth avenue, most of Lexington avenue and Broadway below Fourteenth street.

"The cable railroad would take Lexington avenue, cutting through Gramercy park, which is maintained by the adjacent owners without cost to the city.

"These facts are sufficient to show that no harm can come from imposing the restraints suggested. The abuse of the power of the aldermen to give the consent of the local authorities against the veto of the Mayor shows that such power ought to be taken away. The improvidence attending the appointment of commissioners by General Term empowered to dispense with the consent of the abutting property-owners shows that such authority ought to be taken away.

"But, of course, the great measure is to repeal the Broadway Railroad charter and the franchise of that company, if it has in reality acquired that franchise to run a street railroad in Broadway. I do not know that you will be able to accomplish all that is desirable, but there is no harm in submitting the foregoing suggestions for your considerations.

"Since writing the above, I have received the printed copy of the message.

"Very truly yours,

"SAMUEL J. TILDEN."

Learning that I was expecting to meet Mr. Roscoe Conkling, then acting as counsel for the Broadway property-holders for the repeal of the charter, Mr. Tilden addressed me the following letter:

TILDEN TO BIGELOW

(Personal and Confidential)

GRAYSTONE, YONKERS, N.Y., March 21, 1886.

"DEAR MR. BIGELOW: If you see Mr. Conkling I wish you would suggest to him, in case he frames remedial bills for the Senate committee, the high expediency of a bill taking away the power of the Board of Aldermen to pass an act over the Mayor's veto, giving the consent of the local authorities to the laying down of railroad tracks in any street in the city of New York. The bill should also impose the condition requiring the consent of a majority in interests of the owners of property abutting on every street in which such tracks are proposed to be laid down.

"The bill should also require that the franchise of running such railroad should be sold at auction, for a gross sum, to be paid in cash for the benefit of the sinking-fund of the city of New York.

"The necessity of the provision taking away the power of the Board of Aldermen to pass a grant over the Mayor's veto is quite obvious. Then requiring the separate consent of the Mayor will be effectual. No Mayor will defy the general public opinion, or consent to an improvident or corrupt act.

"The propriety of taking away the power of the General Term by appointing commissioners and confirming their action, to overcome the restraint created by the disapproval or antagonism of the property-owners, is shown by the evidence taken by the Senate committee, illustrating the improvidence, favoritism, or collusion which attended the recent appointment or improper persons as commissioners.

"The sale of the franchise for a gross sum instead of a percentage on the gross or net income of the railroad will be alone effectual to secure the city a just compensation. In one contest the city may triumph; but in a continuing contest for annual payments, to be annually ascertained and collected, the city will sooner or later be beaten.

"If any credit should be given, that should be only on first-mortgage bonds deposited in the sinking-fund. Even that is not altogether safe. If the grant is valuable, the grantee may as well raise the money and pay it into the sinking-fund. That system will be free from after-claps.

"One word in respect to the Broadway Railroad grant. The interest of public morality and official fidelity and honor cannot afford to have Mr. Conkling beaten in his present professional crusade. It is of great importance that the present case should be an example of public justice, and not of successful villainy.

"Mr. Conkling's professional reputation will be greatly enhanced by his success in defeating the conspiracy of plunder. This cannot be done by paltering in half measures. The exercise of the indubitable power of the Legislature to repeal the Broadway charter (which would carry with it the annulment of the franchise to run the road, but which had better be expressed in the bill) is the only proper measure.

"Public opinion strongly and unanimously demands this remedy. The sham of pretended innocent holders deceives nobody.

"Very truly yours,

"S.J. TILDEN.

"HON. JOHN BIGELOW."

Mr. Tilden shared the sympathy generally felt in this country for the cause of Home Rule, which in 1886 was passing into one of its most discouraging phases. He had, however, more faith that was then generally felt in Gladstone as the Moses to whom the task of leading the people of Ireland out of bondage seemed to have been confided.

In reply to an invitation to address a mass meeting of the friends of the cause in New York city, Mr. Tilden sent the following reply:

"GRAYSTONE, YONKERS, N.Y., May 6, 1886.

"DEAR SIR: I am honored by your invitation to attend and address the grand mass meeting at the Academy of Music, on Friday evening, May 7th.

"The delicate state of my health will prevent me from complying with your invitation.

"I cordially and earnestly concur with you in desiring to give the most imposing expression of the approval, admiration, and applause with which America regards the magnificent effort of the Premier of Great Britain to consummate and crown his career of illustrious services to mankind, by giving the blessings of Home Rule to the long misgoverned people of Ireland.

"The voice of America speaks in the place of the voice of posterity. It is inspired by the best hopes of a genuine human progress which may redeem past errors of England towards Ireland, and the false policy towards other peoples which has cost England so dear.

"Next to the renowned Gladstone the need of gratitude is due to Parnell for so signal an advance of the cause of local self-government among mankind.

"Your fellow-citizen,
"Samuel J. Tilden.

"Hon. John Fox,
    "Chairman Sub-Committee."

"There were two bills being pressed on the Legislature in the interest of rogues at the session of 1885-1886, both of which Mr. Tilden exerted all his influence, and with success, to defeat. Their character and his view of them will appear in the following letter to the Governor:

"(Confidential.)
"GRAYSTONE, June 16, 1886.

"DEAR GOVERNOR HILL: I infer from what Mr. Green tells me that you feel the burden of resisting the pressure of the advocates of the bill pretending to complete the abolition of imprisonment for debt, and of the bill appropriating two hundred thousand dollars for doubling the length of the locks on the Eric canal.

"In respect to the first of these bills, in my judgment, the clamor in its favor is confined to a very few persons who have been imposed upon by scoundrels seeking to get a legislative pardon for their offenses. It is superficial and will not endure discussion. The bill is artfully worded so as to destroy what Mr. O'Conor and myself thought to be the most valuable instrument which the laws afford for the punishment of great acts of public robbery. If the existing law needs to be made more lenient in some cases, that should be done by a carefully framed bill which should do no general mischief. If you veto this bill you will be success-fully defended, and will add to your reputation as a watchful guardian of the public interests.

"In respect to the other bill, its immediate effect will be the waste of two hundred thousand dollars of the public money; but its ultimate effect will be to enter upon an immense expenditure and the creation of new canal rings. You will have, sooner or later, to arrest the system or discredit your administration.

"I think a pitched battle on the subject would in the long run do you good instead of harm; but I admit that a considerable ....public opinion has been artificially created in its favor.

"I have twice destroyed a similar scheme. But if you think it expe-dient to defer the contest until the public mind can be better educated (though if were my case I should make it now), you can let this bill pass with less permanent harm that the first-mentioned bill would produce.

"If the State has already borrowed or authorized the borrowing of a million of dollars for the Niagara Falls park, or for that and other purposes, amounting in the aggregate to a million of dollars, this act would be a violation of Section 10 of Article 7 of the Constitution.

"Perhaps a simple statement of this objection, if it exist, would be the easiest way to dispose of this bill and of adjourning the discus-sion.

"I would not trouble myself if I had not sincere and deep solicitude for the welfare of your administration.

"Very truly yours,

"S.J. TILDEN."

Among Mr. Tilden's papers was found a document endorsed "Copy of Notes on the Canals, written by Mr. Tilden on Sept. 4 and 5, 1885, in answer to queries addressed to him." I presume the original was sent to some one in the Legislature who was conducting the war upon the canal-enlarging scheme referred to in the preceding letter. There is probably no American now living who knows as much about the New York canal system or interior water-way economics of all kinds as Mr. Tilden did. The questions to which these notes reply are as vital to-day as they ever were, for the constitutional convention of New York in 1894 rashly broke down the barriers wisely erected by the Convention of 1846, and successfully guarded by Tilden as legislator, governor, and counselor for forty years, and has placed the people once more at the mercy of a new canal ring, which is rapidly taking shape again under its auspices.

I may here remark incidentally that I have reason to believe that it was largely in deference to Mr. Tilden's advice that Governor Hill gave his approval also to the bill for the protection of the Adirondack forests and the International Park bill.

"NOTES ON THE CANALS, 1884-5.

"I. *Would not the expense of deepening the canal, so as to add two feet to the depth of water, be very great? I understand that now for a great part of its course the bottom of the canal is composed for about a foot of clay and hydraulic cement, packed closely, so as to prevent breakage, and would not expense of taking this up, and replacing it after the bottom was dug up, and replacing it after the bottom was dug up, be more serious than any calculation has yet allowed?*

"The idea of increasing the depth of the canal two feet is a gross exaggeration of what is possible or proper to do.

"To build up the banks two feet would necessitate building up the locks. To excavate the bottom two feet would be impracticable.[1]

Note: The following is the provision which opens the door of the public treasury to the new canal ring:

Art. Vii. Section 10. The canals may be improved in such manner as the Legislature shall provide by law. A debt may be authorized for that purpose in the mode prescribed be section four of this article, or the cost of such improvement may be defrayed *by the appropriation of funds from the State treasury, or by equitable annual tax.*

"At page 23 of my message for 1875, It was stated: 'The water-way was practically never excavated in every part to its proper dimensions. Time, the action of the elements, and neglect of administration, all tend to fill it by deposits.'

"There is no doubt that the sides of the water-way have been changed and the slope filled in with silt, narrowing the bottom of the canal so that it is only in the middle that the proper depth is approached, and inconvenience is felt in one boat passing another.

"My suggestion was to bring up the canal to an honest seven feet. All the structures of the canal were adapted to that. Bring it up to seven feet – honest seven feet – and on all levels, wherever you can, bottom it out; throw the excavation upon the banks; increase that seven feet toward eight feet, as you can do so progressively and economically; you may take out the bench walls. This suggestion looked to gaining on the long levels, when it was found practicable, some inches increasing seven feet toward eight feet. The suggestion was carefully limited, because in many places you cannot change the bottom without interfering with culverts or carrying the excavation below the mitre sills of the locks.

"As to the capacity of the Erie.

"The lockages at Frankfort during the season of 1884 were 20,800.

"The lockages in 1873 were stated, on page 22 of my message of 1875, to have been 24,960.

"The theoretical capacity of the canal will be three or four times the largest tonnage it has reached. There is no doubt it can conveniently and easily do double the business which has ever existed, even though the locks be not manned and worked with the highest efficiency.'

"If that was true was true when the lockages were 25,000, how much more so is it when the lockages have fallen to 20,800, as in 1884?

"II. *How far does the fact that the lake transportation has almost entirely passed into the hands of railroad people effect the probability of increasing the business of the canal, in case it should be deepened?*

"III. Can *the canal be maintained in the face of the increasing railroad competition?*

"Total tons of each class of articles which came to the Hudson river from Eric and Champlain canal:

"(*Annual Re port of the Superintendent of Public Works upon the Trade and Tonnage of the Canals for the Year 1884, page 100.*)

	1874	1884
Products of the forest	1,192,681	1,097,450
Agriculture	1,470,872	1,054,041
Manufacture	49,426	56,899
Merchandise	12,905	45,538
Other Articles	497,228	377,259
Total	3,223,112	2,631,190

"Tonnage of the canal and of the Central and Erie Railroads:

"(*From the Annual Report of the Superintendent of Public Works upon Trade and Tonnage of the Canals for the Year 1880, pages 94 – 95.*)

	1874	1884
New York canals	5,804,588	5,009,488
New York Central Railroad	6,114,678	10,212,418
Erie Railway	6,364,276	16,219,598
Total	18,283,542	31,441,504

"The railroads have competed successfully with the Erie canal and have carried off all the increase in the tonnage. Notwithstanding the State has ceased to charge tolls, and has imposed an annual tax of $700,000 upon the taxpayers to maintain the canals, the Erie canal has failed to keep up its business. It holds on to a portion of the lumber and of the grain.

"There seems to be no probability that the Erie canal will regain any portion of the business it has lost.

"None of the grand schemes by which it is proposed to enlarge or improve it can to any appreciable extent cheapen the transportation.

They will simply waste the money of the taxpayer and revive the system of contracting, jobbery, and fraud.

"The advantage of lengthening the locks so as to pass two boats at once, where there is plenty of time to pass four times the boats which the tonnage requires, is doubtful and is at best inconsiderable. It can only pretend to save five minutes in a lockage – if in fact, it will save any time. [1]

"Unless some effectual expedient be adopted to prevent the waste of water in locking through a single boat, it would consume three times as much water in the long lock as in the short lock. I understand that the superintendent thinks that ruinous mischief can be avoided, but I have had no means of testing how the thing would work in practice.

"In 1867, when I examined the subject, I found that on the Delaware and Raritan they used boats of about the same dimensions as the boats in use on the Erie, notwithstanding the locks were capable of passing two boats at a time.

"I send my message of 1875, my speech in the constitutional convention of 1867, which contains a fuller discussion of the subject.

"I send also the last report of the Superintendent of Public Works on the canals.

"The statistical tables are so changed from the ancient forms that it is difficult to get the materials for a satisfactory comparison of the present with the former business. A certain portion of the business naturally belongs to the railroads. The principles which govern this division are set forth in the beginning of my speech in 1867.

"The business would naturally be divided and the share of the railroads would be increased as the net-work of the railroads is perfected and more and more points are touched. Besides, the railroads will compete for additional business at less that cost, charging the loss upon the paying portion of their traffic.

"On the whole it must be observed within the last ten years the cost of transportation by railroads has been reduced one-half. All the improvements tending to cheapen transportation are made by the railroads.

---

1 Note: Of this amount 5,147,660 tons is the tonnage for twelve months of the Ny.Y., P., & O. R.R. Co. leased by the Erie.

"As to the clamor about diverting traffic to the Canadian lines, it is senseless. The great mass of grain brought from the West is for local consumption. Two millions and a half of people residing in the city of New York and its suburbs are not going to bring the grain for their own consumption by way of Montreal. A large share of the flour and grain carried by the New York Central is for local consumption in New England. Formerly it came to New York city and was distributed from that point. It is now carried direct. For instance, flour grain for consumption at Springfield and Worcester are carried from the point of shipment in the West direct to those places without change of cars. They cannot be diverted.

"The Eric canal still has a certain utility. It should be nursed along, but without any expectation of regaining the place it once occupied in the transportation of the country.

"The taxpayer of this State will not always consent to pay a bonus of seven hundred thousand dollars per year in order to get tonnage for the Erie canal."

"In the year 1886 the "Albany Argus" proposed to celebrate its bi-centennial birthday. Mr. James H. Manning, the son of his old friend the late Secretary of the Treasury and representative of his interest in the paper, asked Mr. Tilden to make a contribution to its bi-centen-nial number. In response to this appeal Mr. Tilden sent the following letter:

GRAYSTONE, June 30, 1886

"DEAR MR. JAMES H. MANNING: I have received your note asking me to contribute to the bi-centennial number of the 'Argus.' You are about to publish something concerning 'the old city of Albany and the days I spent there.'

"I was in Albany between nine and ten months of the year 1846 as a member of the Assembly, and member of the constitutional conven-tion held in that year; and again most of the summer of 1867 as a member of the constitutional convention held in that year; and again most of the winter of 1872 as a member of the Assembly; and again the two years of 1875 and 1876 as Governor. On all these occasions life in Albany was characterized by the polite and liberal hospitality which

I have sometimes heard ascribed to inheritance from the good old Dutch customs and manners. I was occasionally in Albany during the ten years preceding 1846, so that I have some recollections extending back at least fifty years.

"The city has greatly changed during that time. I used often to walk through the part of Albany called "The Colonie" to see the Old Dutch houses, of which many specimens then existed. Their gables fronted on the street, the edges of their roofs ascending by notches like saw-teeth, and their entrances being in the corner through doors horizontally cut into two parts.

"My father lived in New Lebanon, about twenty-three miles east of Albany, and was in frequent communication and correspondence with the political notabilities of Albany on the Democratic side from the days of Governor Tompkins to more recent times.

"In my youth, at my father's house I saw most of the leaders of the Democratic party of the State and some of the leaders of the nation.

"But as I am contributing to the bi-centennial number of the 'Argus,' I must not forget the journalists.

"I distinctly remember seeing at my father's house Solomon Southwick, Jesse Buel, and often Edwin Crosswell, all famous journalists in their day.

"As I am dictating on the last day when you can receive the contribution you ask, and doing it in great haste, I will conclude with a reminiscence touching a part of Albany county, which went for independence before July 4, 1776.

"The locality in which I was born, now in the town New Lebanon, Columbia county, New York, was at the time of my birth embraced was in the town of Canaan, which until 1788 was a part of 'Kings District,' – a subdivision created in 1772 – of the county of Albany.

"The people of Kings District before and during the Revolution acted as a little republic. The town meeting was its organ.

"The records of the town contain the following proceedings: 'At a meeting of the inhabitants of the county of Albany, legally warned by the committee of said county at the house of William Warner, innkeeper, in said district, on Monday the 24th day of June, 1776, for the purpose of electing twelve delegates to represent said county in the Provincial Congress, be voted: First, that Daniel Buck be moderator of this meeting; second, that the present committee's clerk be clerk of this meeting; third, that the district's books be delivered to the care of said committee's clerk until the next district meeting; fourth, that a committee be chosen by this meeting for the purpose of drawing up instructions for a new form of government to be introduced by said delegates.

"*The question being put, whether the said district chooses to have the United American colonies independent of Great Britain, voted unanimously in the affirmative.*' (History of Columbia County,' p. 322.)

"Kings District was mainly settled by emigrants from Connecticut, and its settlers fought for their country during the Revolution by levies *en masse.*

"Signed)   S. J. TILDEN

CHAPTER X

During the winter and spring of 1886 Mr. Tilden's infirmities had been gaining so rapidly upon him that when the warm weather arrived he was capable of scarcely more physical exertion that an infant. He could not endure the jar of the carriage which bore him to his yacht, and even went so far as to have plans drawn for a railway from his house to the river that he might reach his yacht without exertion. He had a carriage made expressly with extra springs and cushions in which to take the air with the least possible fatigue. He had not been to his city home for many months, and had abandoned all expectation of seeing it or the city again. He spent most of his waking hours and many of nearly every night – after vainly courtly sleep – extended upon a couch reading, or rather in being read to, for his hands had long ceased to retain sufficient prehensile power to hold a volume, nor could he, without great difficulty, even turn its leaves. The luxury of conversation was practically denied to him, for his articulation, for many months never rising above a whisper, had become so indistinct that none but those in pretty constant attendance upon him could understand much, if anything, he said. He felt this privation intensely, for it compelled him to refuse himself to many visitors whose conversation he would have greatly enjoyed, and destroyed much of the pleasure he felt entitled to from those he did receive. This cut off from intercourse with the living, he indemnified himself as well as he could by cultivating a more familiar intercourse with the dead. In the earlier and active portions of his life he had not been a wide reader. He had been in the habit of educating himself and fixing his opinions more from conversations than from books. He devoured books by the hecatomb, as much to distract his attention from his physical troubles as to increase his stock of knowledge. The books he most affected were of a biographical and historical character. He did not care for poetry, nor much for fiction, still less for books of metaphysics or natural science. During the last six or seven years of his live, when not otherwise engaged, it was his habit to have John Cahill, one of his clerks, or Miss Gould, a sister of his brother Henry's widow, who had become a member of his family, to read to him more or less every day, and not unfrequently at night after he retired. Miss Gould, who kept a careful list, informed me that she herself had read to him during the last four years of his life the contents of eight hundred volumes, besides magazines and newspapers.

Though not a book collector in the ordinary sense, Mr. Tilden had a very fastidious taste for books, which he indulged without much regard to expense. His library numbered some fifteen thousand volumes. Though the larger part of them were of the class "which no gentlemen's library is complete without," There were also among them a very considerable number of the most rare and costly publications of the world, now in commerce. He bought books for his immediate use and enjoyment, and apparently with no thought of collection a library that should be complete in any department – always excepting his law library, which was one of the most complete in the country up to the time of his withdrawal from the active practice of his profession.

His illustrated and extra-illustrated books, upon which he lavished money without stint, would add distinction to any private library in this country, perhaps in any other. He was for many years one of the most valuable clients of M. J. W. Bouton and accomplished bibliopole of New York, through whom he purchased the greater part of his more rare and costly works.

Note: I am indebted to Miss Gould for a list of these books and a note accompanying it, which will be found in Appendix C. Mr. Cahill informs me that he read to Mr. Tilden a number of books not noted on Miss Gould's list, among which he remembers Burn's' "Prose Writings," Irving's "Life of Washington," which greatly interested him, and Gibbon's "Decline and Fall of the Roman Empire," for the style of which he frequently expressed admiration.

The titles of some of these acquisitions will give the reader an idea of the value and character of the collection.

1. Baron Taylor's "Voyages Pittoresquess et Romantiques dans l'Ancienne France." The copy is complete and perfect in every respect, and comprised 27 large folio volumes, containing about 5,000 plates executed in lithography after original sketches by the best artists of France. All the great buildings and monuments of the different departments of France are represented here, with details and sections. Much of the text is printed with elaborate ornamental borders adorned with medallion portraits of celebrated personages, arms and armor, figures, views, etc. Baron Taylor, who projected this work, was the man who brought the obelisk of Luxor from Egypt to Paris and erected it on the Place de la Concorde. He was also for many years at the head of the Theatre Francais. The publication was commenced in 1820, and continued through the ensuing years till its completion in 1878. It was issued to subscribers in parts, of which there were in all 1,000, at twelve and a half franc apiece, making the price of the whole 12,500 francs. The complete sets of this work in this country can be counted on one man's fingers, very few of the original subscribers having outlived the six decades taken for its publication, and but a few of the original subscription sets have ever been offered for sale.

2. Piranesi's works illustrating the antiquities, monuments, architecture. Etc., of the Romans. This splendid set, comprising 35 volumes. Is bound in 23 large folio volumes, containing nearly a thousand large etched plates. Some of the folding plates open ten feet in length.

3. Gillray's "Drawing and Caricatures," nearly if not quite the only complete collection in existence. It comprises a series of 831 caricatures, all original issues and the larger portion in colors, 156 original drawings, 19 miscellaneous engravings, and 4 autographed letters; the whole in 8 folio volumes, sumptuously bound in crimson morocco by Riviere. Upwards of 250 of the subjects have never been catalogued or indexed in any work. The collection was formed by an English gentleman who spent five years in its formation. In 1866 he obtained the collection of Gillray's belonging to the Marquis of Bath, and subsequently added to it that of Lord Farnham and another private collection. To these three collections were added from time to time, as opportunity offered, many other rare prints. Gillray's are among the scarcest of autographs. There are four in this collection.

4. Audubon's "Bird," the great folio edition. This was bought of Mr. Bouton from the family of one of the original subscribers, in the original parts, unbound. It contains 435 very large copper-plates, colored by hand, including about 1,000 figures of birds, from drawings made by Audubon from nature during many years' sojourn in the wilds of America. The set was then bound to order for Mr. Tilden in half morocco, uncut edges, and is unquestionable one of the finest copies in existence. The plate depicting the turkey, which Dr. Franklin recommended instead of the eagle as our national emblem, one of the largest in the work, and usually found with half the head cut off, is in this copy perfect.

5. Audubon's "Quadrupeds," 3 volumes, folio, also an original subscriber's copy, and bound to order for Mr. Tilden from the original parts. This is almost equal in rarity to the "Birds." It consists of 150 very large and beautifully colored engravings, depicting the animals mostly in their natural sizes, male and female, with their very young, prey, and views of their favorite haunts and localities. This collection also contains a copy of the original octavo edition of Audubon's "Birds," in seven volumes, together with the three volumes octavo of "Quadrupeds" issued by Audubon in conjunction with Dr. Bachman.

6. The first folio "Shakespeare" (London, 1623,) bound in full red morocco extra by De Coverley.

7. The second folio, "Shakespeare" (London, 1632, also bound in full morocco by De Coverley.

8. A find copy of the third folio "Shakespeare" (London, 1664), handsomely bound in full red morocco extra by Francis Bedford.

9. A set of Ashbee's "Facsimiles" of the Shakespeare quartos, traced letter by letter from original copies to ensure accuracy – something which it is asserted has not been altogether secured in the Grigg's "photolithographic Facsimiles" more recently published. Of this series there were but 50 sets, and of these sets 19 were destroyed, only 31 sets being preserved as satisfactory in every respect. Each copy is certified to by the signatures of E. W. Ashbee and J.O. Halliwell.

10. A copy of Halliwell's "Shakespeare" in 16 folio volumes, containing in addition to the great playwright's works the literary sources to which the great dramatist was supposed to be under obligation, each play being accompanied by used literary and antiquarian illustrations, copious philological notes, complete reprints of all novels, tales, or dramas on which it is founded, including many other documents of a strictly illustrative character. There are besides numerous wood engravings and facsimiles. But 150 copies were printed.

11. Purchas' "Pilgrims," 5 volumes, folio; a fine tall copy of this old collection of voyages, dated 1625, the best edition, clean and perfect, with a fine impression of the rare frontispiece, and good margins. Mr. Tilden had also previously

obtained a copy of the second edition of the first volume of Purchas, printed in 1614.

12. An early copy of Dr. Robertson's "Historical Works," large paper, 12 volumes, quarto, in contemporary old red morocco, with a large number of rare old prints inserted, and most of which at this day it would be difficult, if not impossible, to duplicate. This is one of the earliest specimens of extra illustrations.

13. "Hudibras," the best edition, edited by Dr. Nash, 3 volumes, quarto, large paper, with Indian proof of the plates, numerous extra plates inserted, substantially bound in full red morocco.

14. A magnificent copy of "Cromwelliana," the folio volume extended and inlaid to 5 volumes, imperial folio, and about 1,000 extra portraits and engravings inserted, many of which are of extreme rarity, including, among others, an extraordinary assemblage of portraits of Cromwell, of his family, of Charles I., and of James I and James II.

15. A sumptuous copy of Mrs. Bray's "Life of Thomas Stothard, R.A." (her father), the little quarto inlaid to folio size and extended to 3 volumes by the insertion of several hundred plates, handsomely bound in full red morocco extra.

16. A copy of Thompson's "Seasons," Bentley's fine edition in large type, imperial folio, with exquisite engravings by Bertolozzi, full green morocco. This copy has a large number of extra plates inserted.

17. A collection of caricatures got together by Horace Walpole, comprising 137 plates of Gillray and others, relating to Walpole and his times, bound in full blue morocco, elephant folio in size.

18. A select collection of humorous caricatures of a miscellaneous character collected by Thomas McLean, comprising several hundred large plates colored by hand; unique. Elephant folio, bound in full morocco.

19. A copy of the first edition of Milton's "Paradise Lost," small quarto, calf, gilt, London, 1669. It is a perfect copy, with what Lowndes terms a seventh title page. This copy formerly belonged to Blakeway, the historian of Shrewsbury, and bears his autograph.

20. A copy of the third edition (1678) of "Paradise Lost," bound up with a copy of the first edition of "Paradise Regained." (1680).

21. A small quarto volume of Milton's "Plagiarisms," a highly interesting volume, containing Lauder's two tracts on Milton's "Plagiarisms," 1650 – 51; Dr. Douglass' "Expo of Lauder," 1756; Lauder's "Recantation and Confession" (drawn up by Dr. Johnson), with an original autograph letter of Lauder to Dr. Mead (never published), two original autograph letters of Salmasius, portraits, etc. The

volume came from the library of Mr. Dillon. An account of this controversy is to be found in Boswell's "Johnson."

22. The Milton "Memorial," consisting of a collection of early tracts, proof portraits of Milton, with autograph letters of his various editions. Etc.

23. An elaborately illustrated copy of Keysler's "Travels through Germany," etc., the 4 volumes, quarto, extended to 8 thick volumes, royal folio, 2,000 rare and curious plates, portraits, views, maps, etc., and bound in half Russia, uncut edges.

24. A superb set of the Abbotsford edition of the Waverley novels, the 12 royal octavo volumes extended to 44 by the insertion of several thousand find plates illustrative of these works, and several autograph letters of Scott, Lockhart, and other contemporary notabilities. The copy was illustrated by a gentleman of wealth and taste for his own amusement, and occupied his leisure hours for many years. Sudden business reverses forced him to sell, and Mr. Bouton became its purchaser. From him it passed into Mr. Tilden's collection. The set is probably the richest and finest ever made. The 44 volumes are handsomely bound in dark-blue crushed levant morocco, elegantly tooled, by Mathews.

25. The Boydell edition of Milton's works, 3 volumes, folio, extended to 8 volumes by the addition of several thousand engravings, handsomely bound in morocco extra by R. W. Smith. This set is without doubt the most elaborately extra-illustrated copy of Milton's works in the world.

26. Doran's "Annals of the Stage," a larger-paper copy of Middleton's handsome edition in 2 volumes, imperial octavo, extended to 4 volumes by the addition of portraits of celebrated actors and actresses. The volumes are handsomely bound in dark-blue morocco by Mathews.

27. Moore's "Life Letters, and Journals of Lord Byron," 2 volumes, quarto, extended to 4 by the insertion of choice plates.

28. Boswell's "Johnson," Murray's royal octavo edition, extended to 6 volumes by the addition of a profusion of beautiful engravings illustrating the life and time of famous lexicographer.

29. "Walpoliana," in 5 volumes, folio, bound in half red morocco, with a large number of portraits, views, facsimiles, etc., relating to Horace Walpole and his contemporaries.

30. The old quarto edition of "Hudibras," edited by Dr. Nash, of which but 200 copies were printed, extended from 3 to 6 volumes by the addition of a host of fine engravings extracted from other editions.

31. Duyckinck's "Cyclopædia of American Literature," the large-paper edition printed on a hand press by William Alvord, with special view to the needs of extra

illustrators, and increased in thickness as much again by the insertion of portraits, view, etc., of celebrated authors, and localities connected with them.

32. The New Testament (in French), issued by Hachette & Co., of Paris, illustrated by a series of beautiful etchings done by Bida after sketches made by himself in the Holy Land, in 2 volumes folio.

33. "Musée Napoleon," in 11 volumes, quarto, a large-paper copy, with proofs before letters, with the scarce supplementary volume, which is uniform in size, and not inlaid as is usually the case. This fine work is the only one containing reproductions of all the pictures selected and appropriated by Napoleon from the principal art galleries of Europe, and transferred to Paris, where they were engraved by his command.

34. Layard's "Monuments of Nineveh," comprising 170 large and curious outlines, tinted plates, on large paper, both series, in 2 imperial folio volumes, bound in half morocco.

35. "Il Vaticano, by Pistolesi, 8 volumes, large folio, containing over 800 fine outline engravings.

36. "Rejected Addresses," fourth edition, inlaid, folio size, and extra illustrated, and bound in maroon morocco.

37. Mathias' "Pursuits of Literature," 1812, a copy on largest paper, with about 100 fine portraits of celebrities inserted, folio, half morocco.

38. Ticknor's "Life of Prescott," quarto, 1866, large paper, extended to 3 volumes by the addition of engravings.

39. Parton's "Life of Franklin," 2 volumes, imperial octavo, large paper, extended to 4 by the insertion of plates, bound in green morocco.

40. Hogarth's "Engravings," in 3 volumes, folio, containing a fine early impression of the plates.

41. A choice collection of "Cruikshankiana," formed by a friend of Cruikshank who enjoyed unusual opportunities for collecting in this line. It forms 6 volumes, folio, bound in morocco.

42. A large-paper copy of a beautiful edition of "Don Quixote," printed throughout on Whatman paper, with etchings by Lalauze, in three states, of which but 50 copies were printed, published by William Patterson, of Edinburgh, in 1879. This is the handsomest edition of this celebrated book yet published.

43. Charles Le Blanc's "Catalogue of Rembrandt's Etchings," last edition; one of the 20 copies printed on Whatman paper, with the plates in three states.

44. Maximilian's "Travels in the Interior of North America," a folio volume, containing 80 fine tinted plates after original drawings, with a quarto volume of text in English.

45. A proof edition of "L'Art, printed on Holland paper, with duplicate proofs on Japanese paper, from its commencement in 1875, the etchings being of the best French artists. There were 4 volumes to the year, folio size, each year containing 52 full-page etchings. Thanks to Mr. Bouton, Mr. Tilden was one of the early subscribers to this precious publication.

46. A proof copy of the "Musée Francaise," in 5 volumes, folio, with about 400 fine, large copper-plate engravings of the masterpieces of the great painters, the finest collection of pictures ever got together; a presentation copy to one of Napoleon's marshals.

47. The "Musée Borbonico," in 16 quarto volumes, containing about 1,000 beautiful engravings of ancient art unearthed at Pompeii, Herculaneum, etc.

48. "Dramatic Biographies," 24 volumes, octavo, with numerous plates inserted.

49. "Oratory and Gesture," by J. Sheridan Knowles, privately printed for the late James McHenry, by whom it was presented to Mr. Tilden. It is an imperial quarto, bound in red crimped morocco by Riviere. The date is 1873.

50. "Actors and Actresses," a magnificent volume, enriched with the choicest portraits in the finest possible state, nearly all open-letter of India-proof impressions, collected, without regard to expense, by Sir Charles Price. The volume is superbly bound in full morocco by Riviere. The date is 1873.

51. The Pilkington's "Dictionary of Engravers," old edition, 805, a unique copy, copiously illustrated with many hundred fine and rare prints, etchings, original drawings, etc., bound in pale old Russia, the 2 volumes, quarto, extended to 4.

52. A remarkable collection of books of scenery, 33 volumes, quarto, 1816 – 1835, issued in parts by subscription, illustrated with fine engravings on steel.

53. A large-paper copy of Lodge's "Portraits," 12 volumes bound in 6, quarto, India proofs of the portraits, bound in full morocco.

54. Pickering's beautiful edition of "Isaac Walton," 1836, edited by Sir Harris Nicholas, with fine steel engravings, India-proof copy; also a copy of Zouch's "Life of Walton," 1823, large paper, with some extra plates inserted mostly India proof, quarto, bound in green morocco extra Châselin.

55. A remarkable collection of works on "Folk Lore," 46 volumes in all, including many works now rare.

56. Speeches of celebrated parliamentary orators, in all 49 volumes.

57. Jesse's works, in 23 volumes, handsomely bound in tree calf.

58. The works of Charles Dickens, printed at the Riverside press, large paper, the handsomest edition ever printed in this country.

59. Large-paper copies of Massinger's "Dramatic Works," in 4 volumes, 1813; of Middleton's "Dramatic Work's, in 5 volumes, 1840; and of Ford's "Dramatic Works," in 3 volumes, 1869.

60. Owen Jones' "Grammar of Ornament," the fine folio edition of 1856, containing 100 superb colored plates.

61. A large-paper set of the "Galerie de Versailles," in 19 imperial folio volumes, illustrating the history of France to the time of Louis Philippe.

62. The "Florence Gallery," 4 volumes, folio, 1739; proofs before letters of the superb plates.

63. The "Galerie du Palais Royal," 3 volumes, folio, half morocco containing 355 copper-plate engravings of the pictures of the celebrated collection of the Duke of Orleans.

64. A colored copy of the "Stafford Gallery," 4 volumes, imperial folio, bound in full red morocco.

65. Finden's "Royal Gallery," India proofs of the plates, folio, full morocco.

66. A large-paper copy of the "Turner Gallery," containing 60 exquisite engravings on steel of the masterpiece of England's greatest painter.

67. A proof copy of the "Logia of Raphael," imperial folio, Meulomester, half red morocco.

68. "Tableaux Historiques," original issue, 3 volumes, royal folio, red morocco.

69. One volume of the personal-expense accounts of President Jefferson, a detailed description of which appeared in the "Century Magazine" a few years prior to Mr. Tilden's death.

One of his few subsidiary diversions during the winter of 1885 – 86 was the compilation of the genealogical notes of the Tilden family, to which reference is made in the early part of this work. It was the fruit of considerable labor, covering, as it did, the history of a family life on two continents, and a period of over three centuries. It was finished during the week in which he died. Not to speak of the considerable expense necessarily incurred for the printed and manuscript records which had to be acquired and consulted, these notes are another striking illustration of the thoroughness with which he executed everything he undertook, and which no degree of physical weakness could ever make him relax. He now rarely saw strangers. He had long ceased to join his family at the table, taking his meals alone in his library. Requiring to be fed by an attendant, he naturally was averse to having witnesses to the ceremony. He had lost almost entirely the use of one arm; he rarely walked alone more than four or five rods at a time, and then with a shuffling gate which betrayed an impaired control of his lower limbs.

I visited Graystone on the 17th of July, 1886, and spent the Sabbath with him. We rode out together in the afternoon. I had to do most of the talking, for the effort to make himself intelligible was painful and rarely successful. He frequently called my attention to the scenery, for he had a lively sensibility for the beauties of nature. I had recently returned from Philadelphia, where I had been inspecting the collection of Franklin manuscripts in the Pennsylvania Historical Society for a new edition of the works of Franklin, which I was engaged. We discussed a scheme, to which he had already given some attention, for procuring copies of valuable manuscripts for his library. Before we separated Monday he said that if I would organize such a work he would not mind the expense of it. I promised him when I returned to town with my family to discuss the matter further with him.

On Monday morning before I left he read me the following letter which he had been writing in reply to an invitation to attend the celebration of the two hundredth anniversary of the granting of a charter to the city of Albany:

TILDEN TO THE ALBANY RECEPTION COMMITTEE.

GRAYSTONE, YONKERS, N.Y., July 19, 1886.

"GENTLEMEN: I have to thank you for your invitation to assist in commemorating the two hundredth anniversary of the granting of a charter to the city of Albany.

"I regret that I cannot be personally present at the ceremonies so worthy of your ancient and renowned municipality.

"Albany is a historic city, and has long occupied a prominent place in the annals of the State and nation. It was the scene of the early struggles which determined where the colonization of the vast country tributary to it should be of a Dutch or English type.

"Albany formed a centre of the great natural highways, connecting on the south by the majestic and placid Hudson with the Atlantic ocean; on the north by Lake Champlain with the waters of the St. Lawrence; and on the west by the great plateau that stretches to Lake Erie. It thus became the objective point in military operations during the protracted contests for supremacy upon this continent between England and France, and afterwards between England and the rising Republic of the United States.

"The same geographical configuration which caused it to be a strategical point of such importance made it afterwards the gateway of a continental commerce.

"It was Albany which, twenty years before the Declaration of Independence, was the seat of the first conference looking to the formation of a union between what afterwards became the independent States of America.

"It is eminently fit that by such a celebration as you propose, the momentous events with which Albany has been associated should be kept in the memory of the present generation and of posterity.

"S. J. TILDEN.

"To Robert Lenox Banks, James H. Manning, John C. Nott, Lewis Boss, Archibald McClure, Samuel B. Towner, William Bayard Van Rensselaer, Augustus Whitman, John Zimmerman, James Otis Woodward,
    "*Reception Committee.*"

When I took leave of him he showed unusual emotion, and expressed some disappointment. He spoke of several things of which he would like to talk with me when I returned. Had not my duty to my family imperatively required it, I should not then have left him.

Just two weeks and two days from the day we parted at Graystone, and on the 4th of August, I received the following telegram from Mr. G. W. Smith, his secretary:

"Mr. Tilden died this morning at 8."

In spite of the fact that Mr. Tilden had been an invalid for many years, and his death at any moment not improbable, the intelligence was a surprise and shock to the nation. So long a time had elapsed since his physical infirmities had become notorious, that they had come to be regarded as one of the conditions of life with him. Besides, his feebleness, which was physical only, was not apparent to the public, while his unimpaired intellectual activity and his active solicitude about public affairs gave no premonitions of decay.

His death was equally unexpected by his physicians, two of whom were present at his bedside when his great spirit went its way. As soon as the news reached the city, the flags on all the public buildings and most of the newspaper offices were displayed at half-mast. Governor Hill proclamation in which, among other things, he said;

"The country loses one of it ablest statesmen and the State of New York one of its foremost citizens. He was twice a representative in the State Legislature, a member of two constitutional conventions, Governor of the State for two years, and in 1876 was the candidate of one of the greater parties of the country for the presidency, and received therefore the electoral vote of his native State, and upon the popular votes as declared the choice of a majority of the voters of the United States. As a private citizen and in every public station he was pure and upright, and discharged every trust with conspicuous fidelity. His last public utterance, which attracted universal attention, exhibited the same spirit of unselfish patriotism which characterized his whole career, and was in behalf of strengthening the defences of his country that he loved so well."

The Governor then ordered the flags upon the capitol and upon all the public buildings of the State, including arsenals of the National Guard, to be displayed at half-mast until and including the day of the funeral, and the citizens of the State, for a like period, were requested to unite in appropriate tokens of respect.

President Cleveland telegraphed to the family his, "individual sorrow in an event by which the State of New York had lost her most distinguished son, and the nation one of its wisest and most patriotic counselors."

The funeral was solemnized at Graystone, on the 7th of August, and the same day the remains of the deceased statesman were conveyed to New Lebanon, where, after a supplementary funeral service in the Presbyterian church of that village, they were interred near those of his deceased kindred.

Whittier, the poet, found in Mr. Tilden's death a theme for the following noble lines:

> "Once more, O all-adjusting Death,
> The nation's Pantheon opens wide;
> Once more a common sorrow saith,
>   'A strong, wise man has died.'

"Faults doubtless had he. Had we not
Our own, to question and asperse
The worth we doubled or forgot
Until we stood beside his hearse?

"Ambitious, cautious, yet the man
To strike down fraud with resolute hand;
A patriot, if a partisan
He loved his native land.

"So let the mourning bells be rung,
The banner droop its folds half way,
And let the public pen and tongue
Their fitting tribute pay.

"Then let us vow above is bier
To set our feet on party lies,
And wound no more a living ear
With words that death denies."

On the Monday following the funeral Mr. Tilden's will, which had been executed on the 23rd of April, 1884, was opened and read in the presence of the heirs and the executors, by James C. Carter, Esq., of the law firm of Carter and Ledyard, and it was admitted to probate by the Surrogate of Westchester country, in October of the year 1886.

The testator, never having married, had no direct descendants. His surviving next of kin consisted of his sister, Mrs. Mary B. Pelton, and the two sons and four daughters of his brother Henry. His estate consisted chiefly of personal property; about one-tenth in houses and lands, and another tenth in iron mines in New York and Michigan. The estate was appraised by experts at a little over five millions. Of this about one million was appropriated to legacies and to the constitution of trust funds for relatives and other beneficiaries. His will provided for the establishment of free libraries at New Lebanon and Yonkers, at the cost of somewhat beyond $100,000; and set apart $10,000 for "keeping repairs, improving, and adorning the cemetery in the town of New Lebanon."

"The substantial residue of his estate, amounting to about $4,000,000.00 he disposed of as follows:

"**XXXV.** I request my said Executors and Trustees to obtain as speedily as possible from the Legislator an Act of Incorporation of an institution to be know as the Tilden Trust, with capacity to establish and maintain a Free Library and Reading Room in the city of New York, and to promote such scientific and educational objects as my said Executors and Trustees may more particularly designate. Such corporation shall have not less than five Trustees, with power to fill vacancies in their number, and in case said institution shall be incorporated in a form and manner satisfactory to my said Executors and Trustees during the lifetime of the survivor of the two lives in being upon which the Trust of my general estate herein created is limited to, to wit: the lives of Ruby S. Tilden and Susan Whittlesey, I hereby authorize my said Executors and Trustees to organize the said corporation, designate the first Trustees thereof, and to convey to or apply to the use of the same, the rest, residue, and remainder of all my real and personal estate not specifically disposed of by this instrument, or so much thereof as they may deem expedient, but subject, nevertheless, to the special Trusts herein directed to be constituted for particular persons, and to the obligations to make and keep good the said special Trusts, provided that the said corporation shall be authorized by law to assume such obligation. But in case such institution shall not be so incorporated, during the lifetime of the survivor of the said Ruby S. Tilden and Susan Whittlesey, or if for any cause or reason my said Executors and Trustees shall deem it inexpedient to convey said rest, residue, and remainder or any part thereof or to apply the same or any part thereof to the said institution, I authorize my said Executors and Trustees to apply the rest , residue, and remainder of my property , real and personal, after making good the said special Trusts herein directed to be constituted, or such portions thereof as they may not deem it expedient to apply to its use, to such charitable educational and scientific purposes as in the judgment of my said Executors and Trustees will render the said rest, residue, and remainder of my property most widely and substantially beneficial to the interests of mankind.

The executors and trustees named in the will were John Bigelow, Andrew H. Green, and George W. Smith. In pursuance of the directions contained in the foregoing clause the executors applied to the Legislature of the State of New York for an act of incorporation of an institution to be known as the Tilden Trust, and on the 26th day of March, 1877, the Legislature passed "an act to incorporate the Tilden Trust for the establishment and maintenance of a Free Library and Reading-Room in the city of New York.

In pursuance of the terms of their charter the executors "designated and appointed in writing" Alexander E. Orr and Stephen A. Walker as the two other trustees of such corporation, on the 26th days of April, 1887.

The establishment of a free library in the city of New York, with an endowment of between three and four millions of dollars, was regarded as a most becoming crown to a life of which so large a portion had been consecrated to public uses.

The hopes, however, which had been awakened throughout the nation by the publication of the will, were destined to be only partially realized. The nephews of Mr. Tilden, who were largely in debt, were pressed by their creditors to contest the validity of the above cited thirty-fifth clause of the will, and proceedings were instituted for that purpose in the Supreme Court of New York on the very day the will was admitted to probate. The ground taken by Messrs. Vanderpool, Green, and Cuming, of counsel for the heirs, was that the thirty-fifth clause was invalid for indefiniteness of subject, in failing to specify with sufficient precision the portions of that residency estate to be appropriated to the several objects of his bounty. The case came on for trial before Justice Lawrence at special term – Joseph H. Choate and Delos McCurdy, of counsel for the heirs; and James C. Carter, Lewis Cass Ledyard, and Daniel Rollins, of counsel for the executors – in November, 1888.[1]

At the January special term of the Supreme Court in 1889 Mr. Justice Lawrence rendered a decision sustaining the validity of the contested clause. The plaintiffs appealed to the general term of the Supreme Court, where Chief-Justice Van Brunt and Associate-Justices Brady and Daniels reversed the decision of Judge Lawrence by a vote of two to one: Jude Daniels voting and writing an opinion in defence of it, and Judges Van Brunt and Brady writing opinions for reversal. Judge Brady's opinion is so unique a specimen of juridical literature, that no one will think the space it will occupy in these pages disproportioned to its value.

---

1 Note: Appendix E.

On the 25th day of April, 1893, Lewis Cass Ledyard was elected as a trustee of the Tilden Trust, to fill the vacancy occasioned by the decease of Mr. Walker.

"The questions discussed by the presiding justice and Justice Daniels are not free from difficulty or doubt, but I think, on authority and proper judicial interpretation, the solution of them by the presiding justice is the most acceptable. I concur with him, therefore. [1]

The case was taken to the Court of Appeals, where it came on for argument before the second division, consisting of seven judges of the Supreme Court temporarily designated by Governor Hill, to assist the appellate court in disposing of business in arrear. It was argued by Carter and Rollins for the appellants and by Choate and McCurdy for the heirs, at the June term in 1891.

Mr. Carter's argument closed with the following impressive appeal:

"Now then, if your Honors please, I have gone over, so far as I have had strength, the principle grounds upon which the validity of this devise has been contested. They are, to my mind, unsubstantial in the extreme. Nothing but the circumstance, that is seems to be impossible nowadays for a man to make any considerable disposition of property outside of the range of those who claim to be kindred by blood; nothing but the disposition to question bequests given to public objects, to take the chances of litigation, because so many of those contests have been successful; nothing, I say, but this practice, which has become too universal, would have ever induced any one to question the simple provisions of this will. If I could persuade myself that this munificent bequest of Governor Tilden, this beneficent design so constantly associated with his thoughts in the closing years of his life – stood in any sort of hazard, I should be affected with the deepest anxiety. The idea that a man cannot, when it comes to step from this mortal scene, or make his preparations for stepping from it, look about him and see what he can do with his wealth which fortune has been pleased to grant him; that he cannot do that

---

1 Note: The opinion of Judge Van Brunt, who at this time had become chief justice, lends a melancholy interest to the circumstance that it was a special instance and request of Aaron J. Vanderpool, Green, & Cumming, the counsel for the contestants of the will, that Judge Van Brunt, while a judge of the Court of Common Pleas, was detailed by Governor Tilden to act as a supplementary judge of the Supreme Court in 1874, a detail which was continued for six out of the eight succeeding years, when he was elected one of the justices of that court.

It was in his opinion, perhaps, which inspired the wags of the bar to exclaim, when Judge Brady entered the court-room.

"Lo, the con-curring hero comes!"

without apprehension that somebody who has some connection with him, near or remote, by blood, will come into a court of justice and defeat all his beneficent intentions, is to me a circumstance of a most melancholy nature. And that these people who contest this will, of all others, should be permitted to grasp this property; no near relations of the testator; with no near ties, either of blood or affection; living upon his bounty while he was alive; taking a million from him when he died; and all without a word of gratitude. And even then they would not let him rear that monument to his name, which was the dearest wish of his closing hours. I take it that there is to be no decision here which will prevent, I am glad to believe that there is no doctrine of law which prevents the full accomplishment of his benevolent purpose. I rejoice to believe that he will be permitted to crown a life of usefulness, although a life of contention which excited many animosities, with an act of beneficence as to which none of his fellow-citizens would feel any other sentiment than praise and applause."

On the 28th of October the Court of Appeals sustained the decision of the Supreme Court *in banc*, holding that the thirty-fifth clause of the will was invalid, and that all the residuary estate covered by that clause vested in the heirs-at-law on the death of the testator, Judge Brown writing the opinion of the court, in which Chief-Judge Follet and Judges Haight and Parker concurred. Judge Bradley wrote an opinion sustaining the validity of the thirty-fifth clause, in which Judges Potter and Vann concurred.

In his opinion Judge Brown rested the decision of the court upon a point which had not been taken by counsel for the heirs, and which, therefore, the counsel for the appellants had had no occasion to discuss. As that ground was deemed entirely indefensible by Mr. Carter; as the case had been decided, not by the regular judges of the Court of Appeals, but by judges of the Supreme Court set apart by the Governor temporarily to hear appeals; as two of the judges in the courts below were for sustaining the will to four against it; in other words, as the case in the three hearings had been heard only by Supreme Court judges, five of which were for sustaining the will and only six opposed, Mr. Carter felt that he was entitled to an opportunity of rearguing the case for the purpose of discussing the new point raised by Mr. Justice Brown. In this view the executors and the trustees of the Tilden Trust concurred.

This motion, that which none could have been more reasonable, if a reargument is ever reasonable in any case – and though not frequent there is no lack of precedents for them – the court promptly denied, the same members voting against the reargument as had voted to invalidate the thirty-fifth clause, and those two had voted to sustain the will, with the exception of Judge Potter, who had ceased to be a member of the court, voting in favor of a reargument.

Whatever may be the merits or the demerits of the decision of the court of the opinion of Judge Brown, the majority of that body laid itself open to just criticism for refusing the application of Mr. Carter. It may be reasonably questioned whether any decision of a bench of seven judges ought to stand that is reached by a majority of only one. There are only two conditions upon which such a result can occur: either the members of the court do not equally comprehend the questions upon which their opinions are divided, or some members of the court are yielding to influences which are extra-judicial. For centuries the English-speaking people have required a unanimous verdict from their juries of twelve men sitting in judgment on questions of fact; and when the twelve do not agree, the presiding judge may, in his discretion, send them back to the jury-room for further deliberation to secure unanimity. It is assumed that with further discussion and reflection their comprehension of the question at issue will be equalized. If this policy, so venerable and so cherished wherever it has prevailed, is a sound one, why should it not have its weight with a bench of judges? why should not the majority be required to convince at least a considerable proportion of the minority, or be convinced by them? Can any case be deemed to have been fully discussed by counsel or adequately considered by a court of seven judges, all having precisely the same law to apply, precisely the same state of facts to apply the law to, and presumably the same degree of concern to interpret that law correctly, when three members of the court, after only a single hearing of counsel, take views precisely the opposite of those entertained by the other four? There is no attribute or function of the judiciary more important than its ability to inspire the public with respect for its decisions. But it is idle to expect that a court of seven judges can retain the respect of the public which declines an application to review a decision reached by the meager majority of one upon grounds not raised, and therefore, of course, not discussed, by counsel on either side.

To those who are skilled in interpreting the mystic properties of numbers, I commend the problem presented by the prominent part which the number one has played in the career of Mr. Tilden.

At the election of 1876 it was conceded that he lacked but one disputed electoral vote to make him President.

When the Electoral Commission was appointed to count the electoral vote, every vital question raised during the deliberations of the commission was decided by a vote of eight to seven, or one majority.

When the count of the electoral vote was made final, Rutherford B. Hayes was declared elected, and as a consequence Samuel J. Tilden declared elected to have been defeated on an electoral vote of 185 to 184, or by a majority of one.

At the special term of the Supreme Court, the clause of the will by which he disposed of about a third of his large estate was sustained by one judge. On appeal to the Supreme Court *in banc*, that disposition was declared invalid by a majority of one. On the appeal to the court of last resort, their decision was confirmed again by a majority of one; and finally a reargument was refused by the same vote as that which had pronounced the thirty-fifth clause invalid; and all these decisions in the face of a provision in the will revoking any devise or legacy made in it to any one who should institute any proceedings to invalidate its provisions.

Though by the decision of the Court of Appeals none of Mr. Tilden's estate could be claimed by his trustees for the great library which he had so much at heart, measures were taken by the trustees of the Tilden Trust, by which they may reasonably expect to accomplish in a satisfactory way, if not to the extent contemplated by Mr. Tilden, the munificent purpose to which he had to consecrate the bulk of his fortune. In view the uncertainties, expense, and delays incident to litigation of this character, the executors of Mr. Tilden and the trustees of the Tilden Trust deems it prudent, shortly before the final argument in the Court of Appeals, and about six months before its decision was rendered, to accept the terms of a settlement proffered by Mrs. Laura P. Hazard, a grand-niece of Mr. Tilden's sister, and under her will became entitled to one-half of all that part of the estate that been intended for the Tilden Trust.

During the five and half years occupied by this litigation, the executors, by judicious investments and reinvestments, and by careful attention to doubtful assets, were fortunate enough, not only to protect the estate from any losses, but to add to it about two millions in income and profit, so that at the time of the settlement with the heirs in March, 1892, the general estate, apart from the special trusts, legacies, etc., already referred to, had increased from four millions to six millions of dollars, one-half of which, under the arrangement with Mrs. Hazard, came to the Tilden Trust, less the sum of $975,000, which she received for her interest while it was yet subject to the risks of litigation. Of the personal estate something over five and a half millions were distributed in March, 1892. The real estate is still undivided.

On the 16th of November, 1886, a few weeks after the probate of the will, Mr. L. V. F. Randolph, who had been for many years a director and treasurer of the Illinois Central Railroad, was appointed secretary of the executors and trustees under the will, to the duties of which position were subsequently added those of secretary to the Tilden Trust.

On the 23rd day of January, 1893, the trustees of the Tilden Trust, learning that it was contemplated by the municipal government of New York city to remove the old city hall to make place for a larger and more commodious edifice on its site, address the following communication to the Municipal Building Committee:

"THE TILDEN TRUST.

"15 GRAMERCY PARK, Jan. 23, 1893.

"GENTLEMEN: On the 22nd day of October last I had the honor to submit to the Mayor and commonalty of the city of New York, on behalf of the trustees of the Tilden Trust, a communication, of which the annexed is a copy and to which tour attention is respectfully invited.

"It is now rumored that legislation is in contemplation for the removal of the reservoir from Bryant park, and also for the removal of the old city hall to make place for more spacious and adequate accommodations for the municipal offices. Much as we regret the necessity of disturbing a structure consecrated to us like our city hall by so many precious historical and forensic associations, should such a necessity be found to exist, we respectfully suggest that that admirable structure be transferred to the site now occupied by the reservoir in Bryant park and appropriated to the uses of the Tilden Trust upon the conditions set forth in the annexed communication.

"By order of the Trustees of the Tilden Trust,

John Bigelow,

"President."[1]

The following is a copy of the letter of October 22, referred to in the foregoing communication:

"OFFICE OF THE TILDEN TRUST
15 GRAMERCY PARK, NY., OCTOBER 22, 1893"

"To the Mayor, Alderman, and Commonalty of the City of New York:

The trustees of the Tilden Trust, incorporated by chapter 85 of the Laws of the State of New York, passed the 21st of March, 1877, respectfully represent,

That the late Samuel J. Tilden having in his will, a copy of which is hereunto annexed, made provisions for his heirs-at-law and certain legatees, sought, by the thirty-fifth article of said instrument, to consecrate the remainder of his estate to the creation of an institution to be know as the Tilden Trust, with capacity to establish and maintain a free library and reading room in the city of New York, and to 'promote such scientific and educational objects as his executors and trustees might more particularly designate.'

That the validity of the thirty-fifth clause of said will was successfully contested by the heirs-at law of the testator and pronounce invalid. Pending such litigation, and in view of the uncertainties, expense, and delays incident to litigation of this character, the trustees of the Tilden Trust deemed it prudent, prior to the argument of the case in the Court of Appeals, to accept the terms of a settlement proffered by one of the parties contesting said will, in virtue of which the Tilden Trust became possessed of about one third of that part of the estate that had been intended by the testator for such trust, from which they expect to realize

---

Note: I feel it to be a duty, as it certainly is a pleasure, for me to make a public acknowledgement of his invaluable services in both capacities, and formally to recognize the very substantial obligations under which his varied accomplishments as a business manager, his indefatigable assiduity, and his high personal character have placed all who are or may hereafter be in any way interested in this estate.

from two to two and a quarter million dollars, the annual income from which may be moderately estimated at $80,000.

That the trustees of the Tilden Trust are anxious to apply this fund in the way that shall prove most advantageous to the people of the city of New York, and at the same time most strictly conform to the wishes and expectations of the testator as manifested in his will.

That the income of this trust is insufficient to provide suitable buildings for the accommodation of such a library as was contemplated by the testator, and in addition to equip and operate it if suitable accommodations for its installation are provided from other sources.

In view of these facts, and in view of the fact that the city of New York is not only more destitute of library accommodation than any other city of its size in the world, but more destitute than many cities in our own country of far less wealth and population, the undersigned trustees of the Tilden Trust, respectfully invite your honorable bodies to consider the propriety of availing yourselves of this opportunity of establishing a library commensurate with the magnitude and importance of our commercial metropolis, and taking measure to provide for it the requisite accommodations, with the understanding, to which the trustees of the Tilden Trust hereby avow their readiness to become parties, that they will equip and operate such library so soon as such accommodations can be provided.

By order of the Trustees of the Tilden Trust,
John Bigelow, *President*

"Oct 22, 1892."

On the 2nd of May, 1893, Governor Flower approved an act passed by Legislature authorizing the Commissioners of Public Works, on the request of the Commissioners of Public Buildings, to cause the old city hall 'to be removed, re-erected, furnished, and equipped elsewhere upon the property therein, belonging to the Mayor, Aldermen, and Commonality of the city of New York, with the consent of the Department of Public Parks, if such property shall be subject to the jurisdiction of such department. If said building shall be removed and re-erected, the same shall be done in such manner as said Board of Commissioners shall determine, with alterations as may in their judgment be rendered necessary by the site selected and the purpose to which such re-erected building shall be devoted, and as may be in harmony with the present general architectural features of the exterior of said building.

On the same day the Governor approved of an act authorizing the Department of Public Works, with the sanction of the Board of Estimate and Apportionment, to remove the reservoir from Bryant Park.

On the same day the Governor also approved of an act which authorized the Department of Public Parks, to contract with the Tilden Trust for its use and occupation of any building that may be hereafter erected in pursuance of law upon land belonging to the Mayor, Aldermen, and Commonalty of the city of New York between Fortieth and Forty-second streets and between Fifth and Sixth Avenues in said city, and establishing and maintaining therein a free library, and carrying out the objects and purposes of said corporation.

It was hoped and expected that these measures would result in soon giving to the commercial metropolis of the United States a library commensurate with its magnitude, needs and resources, and thus fitly commemorate its obligations to one of its most eminent citizens and generous benefactors. That prospect, unhappily, has been indefinitely postponed by the repeal of the act authorizing the removal of the old city hall. In what way, if any, the municipal government will give effect to the disposition it manifested in 1893 to provide a suitable structure for the Tilden library neither the Trustees nor the public have as yet any intimation.

CHAPTER XI

I HAVE said that Mr. Tilden never married. I may say further of him what Milton wrote on the decease of his most cherished friend Diodati:

> "Thy blush was maiden, and thy youth, the taste
> Of wedded bliss knew never; pure and chaste
> The honors, therefore, by divine decree
> The lot of virgin worth, are giving to thee."

On two separate occasions I received from Mr. Tilden the assurance that he had never had any acquaintance of relations with the female sex, of which he would have hesitated, from motives of delicacy, to speak with his mother or sisters. As Jules Simon said of an illustrious French *célibartaire*.

> "Il n'y a pas de femmes dans sa vie.
> Il reste cette grand lacune dans son Coeur et dans son talent."

That Mr. Tilden's life would have been more peaceful and fuller of joys had he married, that the affectionate side of his nature would have been more developed and his personality more generally attractive, there is a reason to presume; but that he would have been so great a force in the world as he ultimately became, or that his life would have been so prolonged, may be doubted.

The ancients, not without reason made Venus not only their god of love, but their presiding deity at funerals also, under the name of Libertina. The exceptional longevity of some of the famous anchorites had been attributed in a large degree, and no doubt correctly, to their continence, "whereby their whole vigor was concentrated to self maintenance instead of being expended in two directions." The pigeon, say Lord Bacon, lives only eight years. The mule is much longer-lived than the horse or the ass. The nightingale that has young annually, rarely lives more than six or eight years, while the *célibartaires* live on for twenty more. It is a well-ascertained fact that hybrid plants live longer that their parents. To be sure

> "It is not all of life to live
> Nor all of death to die;"

but a nature so keenly sensible to any genuine tenderness, and physically so dependent from infancy upon others, could have well afforded to surrender a few of the later years of his life – during three of which he once told me that he did not remember to have had a single pleasurable emotion – for the love of a sensible woman and the soothing influences of a cheerful domestic fireside.

The following distich inscribed over a statue of Love is as full of wisdom as of wit:

> "Qui que tu sois, voici ton maitre
> Il l'est, le fut ou le doit etre."

Tilden's vital forces, which, in spite of his unrelenting valetudinarianism, were prodigious which should have been perpetuated in a family, were husbanded to the last, and as in the case of the poet Pope, Sir Isaac Newton, the philosopher, and especially of some of the famous ascetics of the Christian church, like St. Anthony, Theodosius the cenobite, and St. Paul the anchorite, who lived over a century, seemed all to have been derived to the brain and to have induced a cerebral activity and vigor of which the Tilden family tree, so far as it is now possible to trace it, had produced no other example. That he often thought of marrying, that he no aversion to matrimony, and that he never had any relations with the other sex which might interfere with the most solemn engagements which a man can contract with it, no one who knew him well could entertain a doubt.

> "Whoe'er you are, your master see -
> Who is, has been, or ought to be."

Nor was he in the least degree shy or lacking of ease in the presence of the fair sex. Though reared in an obscure village among plain people, he never at any period of his life betrayed any of that awkward shyness so common with persons unaccustomed to the usages of polite society, nor was there ever a time since he was of age that he would have felt the least embarrassment in the presence of any man or woman, whatever their rank.

Like England's great cardinal,
> "Though from humble stock, undoubtedly
> He was fashioned to honor from the cradle."

Tilden never married, only because he never felt the need of a wife. His health was always so uncertain; his mind from youth upward was so constantly absorbed with large affairs, public or private, most of the time with both; his temperament was so purely nervous, and women were, so far as he could see, so unimportant to his success in any of the enterprises upon which his heart was set, that marriage never became the subject of leading interest, as it does, for a time at least, with most men whether they marry of not. In fact, he never knew any woman intimately enough to fall completely under the influence of sexual charms. He seemed to have been betrothed in early life to his country, and the Democratic party occupied with him the place offspring, until it was too late to think of having any other.

He was far as possible from sharing the cynical notion of woman proclaimed by St. Chrysostom, that she was a "necessary evil, a natural temptation, a desirable calamity, a domestic peril, a deadly fascination, and a painted devil;" though he might perhaps have agreed with the lover of Eve, that she, as the type of her sex was

> "Fair no doubt and worthy well
> His cherishing, his honoring, and his love,
> Not his subjection."[1]

Had he been elected to the presidency in 1876, Mr. Tilden would probably have contracted a matrimonial alliance, more, however, for the better discharge of the duties of his station than to fill any void in his own scheme of life. Had he in prime married a sensible woman, capable of appreciating his refinement of nature, he would have made a devoted husband and father, though he would have laid a very different and probably much less costly sacrifice upon the altar of his country.

Mr. Tilden had no pronounced taste for any of the fine arts, nor did it appear that they ever exerted much influence upon his work or life. He never appeared to care much for music; he never learned to dance; when his fortune permitted him to indulge in luxuries he went occasionally to the play and the opera, but rather to gratify others than for the pleasure he expected to derive from the entertainment. Even in his school-days his pleasures were all intellectual. He never participated in the athletic games in which his comrades delighted. I doubt if he was ever seen to walk or run very fast. As an antidote to dyspepsia in middle life he got in the way of riding on horseback, but he never learned how to ride or drive, and those who drove with him, while he held the reins, were apt to breathe more freely when they found themselves, if they did, safely set down again at their homes. He liked to get his exercise by riding or driving because his horses did most of the work. He always had fine horses. For one span he paid $10,000; for one of his saddle-horses he paid $1,500 and $1,000 for another. He was but partially acquainted with the uses of which hands were capable and for which they were provided. He probably never whittled a stick, tossed a ball, climbed a tree, ran a race, or pulled an oar, nor even carried a cane, except for a few days in Paris under the advice of his physicians as a check to certain arthritic tendencies. He could not be prevailed upon,

---

1   Note: In this respect Tilden's experience is not without illustrious precedents. Dalembert, in his eulogy of Bossuet, the Bishop of Meaux, discountenances the rumor that prelated had been secretly married, on the ground that he had been too much occupied with controversies, absorbed with theological speculations, etc., to be forced to have recourse to such consolations as are to be fund in a mutual union of tender and peaceful souls. *Il avait plus besoin du combat que de societe domestique, et de gloire que d'attachments.*

however, to continue its use. He enjoyed massage because it gave him exercise with exertion.

When he established himself at Graystone he surprised his friends by the interest he exhibited and the money he lavished in adding to its attractions. He expended some $75,000 in the construction of glass houses, which he stocked with rare and the costliest growths of many climes, besides compelling them to supply his table with the choicest fruits without much reference to season or climate. He expended about $13,000 in stocking these houses alone. For a single plant indigenous to Mexico he paid $600. He was very proud of a grand old palm reputed to have once belonged to Washington's collection at Mt. Vernon. It was between two and three centuries old. His grapevine plants cost him between thirteen and fourteen hundred dollars. In the spring of the year immediately preceding his death, he expended over $5,000 in addition to his greenhouse varieties. He also took great pride in his herd of cows and his poultry, upon which he spared no expense to secure the finest breeds to be purchased in his own or any other country. Two superb St. Bernard dogs were his constant companions in his strolls about his place so long as his limbs allowed him that luxury. To accompany him on his visits to his numerous brute pets was one of the usual privileges, occasionally one of the penalties, attached to his hospitality.

While from early youth so economical of his physical functions, he exercised no such economy of his intellectual forces. He seemed to have transferred to his brain all the vitality which he spared his muscles, and to have been as lavish, not to say intemperate, in the use of the one as parsimonious of the other. Whatever he undertook to do he did with all his might. Thoroughness with him amounted to genius. He labored only with his intellect, but with that instrument he never did anything slovenly or by halves. Whether preparing an argument for the courts, reorganizing a corporation, planning a financial operation or a political campaign, he took nothing for granted. He was sometimes accused of being bold to rashness in some of his financial operations; but in point of fact, few men took less risk. Indeed, he took none which study, labor, or expense could avoid. He could not slur work of any kind. The condition of his health often prevented his embarking in enterprises, but it never made him less fastidious about the perfection of those in which he did engage. No matter how feeble he was, he spared neither time, money, nor strength in mastering every detail, in providing for every emergency, in anticipating ever contingency. Reference has already been made to this trait in his character, in his preparation for his war upon the canal ring, and in some of his important triumphs at the bar. It was equally conspicuous in things of comparatively trivial importance, If he had any responsibility for the decisions, he could not be induced to accept any conclusion but that which he had satisfied himself was the very best, even in matters of trifling moment. I remember when we were crossing over from England to France, in 1877, he asked me at what hotel we should alight in Paris. I named three or four, of which it seemed to me to be a matter of perfect indifference which we chose. This did not suit him. The constitution of his mind compelled him to believe that for some reason or another, one of the hotels must have some advantages for our purposes over either of the others. He ordered his valet to bring him one of his boxes, out of which he took a small library of guide books and maps, and he spent most of the time of our journey between Dover and Paris in ascertaining which of the several dozen first-class hotels in the French metropolis would incontestibly answer our purposes best for the three or four weeks of our proposal sojourn there. Once when I was present he was waited upon by a gentleman who wished to commend to him a pretty important financial enterprise. The promoter had not been trained in his school. Mr. Tilden asked him a few crucial questions, none of which he could answer with precision. Mr. Tilden dismissed him summarily, and showed considerable irritation at being asked to associate himself in a scheme with a man who knew none of the facts which were necessary to establish even a presumption as to its merits or its demerits.

It was this extraordinary crucible to which he subjected everything upon which he passed his judgment which made him always from his youth up, in whatever circle he was placed, whether in the councils of a corporation or in the councils of statesmen, sooner or later the leader and the man to whose guidance his associates found themselves compelled to defer. It is no disparagement to others to say that our country had hitherto produced no one man who appeared to have combined in himself, in the same degree, the essential qualities of a statesman and a politician, nor one so admirable equipped for the most exalted function of both.

It was this quality of thoroughness, of always doing his best, to which he was indebted for his ample fortune. His talents justified his ambition from early youth to be a ruler of men, to mature and execute plans for the greatest good of the greatest number. When he found the political career upon which he had embarked interrupted by the schism which divided both the great parties in 1848, he determined to try another mode of acquiring authority among his countrymen. He set his remarkable energies his pecuniary independence, without which he realized that the time had come when the politician was the slave rather than the master. For this the times proved eminently propitious to those who, like Tilden, had the genius to read them aright. But even those advantages without his indefatigable thoroughness would not have enabled him to amass the largest fortune ever acquired by any lawyer in the practice of his profession in this or, so far as I know, in any other country in so brief a period.

"The malice of political opponents," says Mr. Carter, "was wont to ascribe his success in money-getting to schemes for obtaining interests in the property of insolvent railway companies at less than their value. They stigmatized him as a 'railroad wrecker." Never was there less foundation for a charge. He was a railroad preserver. His skill in the management of difficult and complicated affairs, combined with his profound knowledge of the fundamental principles of equity, made his services invaluable to parties interested in the properties and securities of railroad companies which by bad management, or in consequence of over-sanguine expectations, had fallen into difficulties. His capacious mind was just fitted for the survey of such situations. He was among the first, if not the first , to perceive that a ruthless attempt to foreclose the first mortgage, and thus to crush out all subordinate liens and interests was ill suited to such cases; that the just and true method was to ascertain the real capacities of the business, and to reorganize the enterprise upon a scheme which would indulge the hope of saving to the junior securities a large part of their supposed original value. More than one of the great railroads of the country have, at his skillful touch, risen from absolute bankruptcy into prosperity, and repaid all or the larger part of the original investment."

When the making of money was Mr. Tilden's object he concentrated all his energies upon any money making enterprise in which he embarked, as completely as when he engaged with the Tweed ring and with the canal ring. He did not give a few hours a day to business and the rest to pleasure, after the manner of most unsuccessful business men. He took his recreation, if at all, when his work was done and his ends had been achieved. He was so thorough in everything he undertook while in the active practice of his profession, that his services were always in demand and his accumulations rapid. In seeking investments for his earnings he was equally careful and thorough, and was rewarded with corresponding success.

Not infrequently he extended to others the benefit of his judgment and enlightened foresight. The results in one of these cases, to which my colleague, Mr. Smith, has called my attention, were quite remarkable. Between the years 1849 and 1868, Miss Catherine Pierson, a maiden lady of Massachusetts and an old friend of the Tilden family, placed in Mr. Tilden's hands at intervals, or authorized him to collect for her, divers sums of money amounting in the aggregate to a little over $74,000. Mr. Tilden attended to the collection and investment of her money without charge even for his expenses, and in September, 1880, when he resigned his stewardship, delivered to her representative registered four per cent. United States bonds of the par value of $250,000. and of the market value of about $270,000.

To a woman from Michigan, who had asked him near the close of his life to invest some money for her, he, in a few words, gives some pregnant advice which it would be well if women especially would lay to heart. He directed his secretary to say:

"Mr. Tilden cannot undertake the charge of the investment you wish to make. He has gradually retired from every such engagement. His advice in respect to the $2,000 is not to lose it by bad investment or to consume it. At six percent it will give you $120 a year, which will keep you from absolute want. You should be careful *not to lend it or deposit it with any relation or friend*; but should invest it and keep the principle intact."

He was no speculator, in the common acceptation of that term. He resented the imputation sometimes made by his political opponents, that he had acquired his large estate by speculations instead of earning it by hard work. He testified a legitimate sensibility upon this point in a letter to Mr. Dorsheimer, who, in his "Life of Grover Cleveland," had given currency to this reproach.

Dorsheimer had been recommended by Mr. Tilden for the office of Lieutenant-Governor, when he himself was elected Governor in 1874.

When, in 1876, Mr. Tilden was nominated for the Presidency, Mr. Dorsheimer wished to succeed him as Governor, and very unwisely, as well as unjustly, held Mr. Tilden responsible for his failure to get the nomination. He was never constituted to be popular with his party, and powerful as Mr. Tilden was in those days, it is extremely doubtful if he could have secured Dorsheimer's nomination had he put forth all his strength to accomplish it, while there is no doubt that it would have been extremely imprudent in him to have done so, even had success been probable. Dorsheimer was weak enough to resent this, and thenceforth walked no more with him, but made an alliance with the anti-Tilden factions in New York city, where, on leaving office, he took up his residence. Some eight years later, and a few days after Mr. Tilden had written his second letter in June, 1884, declining a renomination to the presidency, which secured the nomination of Mr. Cleveland, Dorsheimer, who had written a campaign life of Mr. Cleveland and was a candidate for favors at his hands, was indiscreet enough to suppose the moment a propitious one to seek a revival of former relations with Mr. Tilden. The following correspondence was the result of it:

DORSHEIMER TO TILDEN

WASHINGTON, June 29, 1884.

"MY DEAR SIR: At the time of your brother Henry's death I was on the point of writing to you, but was restrained by some considerations which I do not think necessary to mention.

"The announcement of your final retirement from public life has again awakened in me a strong desire that our long estrangement should end, and therefore I write to tell you so. And if the memory of our former friendship shall be vivid and pleasing to you as it is to me, I shall not need to make any excuse for intruding upon you.

"With sincere regards,
"I am your servant,
"WILLIAM DORSHEIMER.

"To the HON. SAMUEL J. TILDEN

In Mr. Tilden's reply we see, among other things, how he resented the imputation of having accumulated his wealth, by "speculation."

TILDEN TO DORCHEIMER.

"GRAYSTONE, YONKERS, N.Y. Oct. 8, 1884.

"DEAR SIR: I received with pleasure your letter written after the publication of mine declining renomination for the presidency, and referring to your purpose to have written an earlier one after my brother Henry's death. It should have been answered sooner but for some causes not affecting you or the nature of my reply and which have now passed away.

"If your reference to an estrangement were designed to imply that any occasion for the same had been given by me, or to imply that any time during the seven years that have passed I have ever manifested or felt any resentment or any disposition to do you harm, I should be justified in affirming to you the contrary, and even in mentioning that my conduct towards you ought, in a singular degree, to have inspired the opposite sentiments on your part.

"But I do not doubt that the reference was but another form of words for saying, "Let bygones be bygones," and so I accept your letter and respond to it in the same spirit in which I believe it to have been written.

"I have been better able to perceive how much of your time in the interval must have been misspent, since my attention was called to a statement in your biography of Governor Cleveland, that at the time I became interested in the New York Elevated Railroad my fortune had been made by speculation.

"I could not suppose, with your letter at hand, that in this you designed to say anything disagreeable or unfriendly to me, but it so happens that the statement is an almost total error. My fortune, such as it was, was the result of professional earnings: of growth of investments intended to be permanent; and of profits of regular business which had been carried on for many years under my personal administration.

"Very truly yours,

"S.J. TILDEN

"HON. WILLIAM DORSHEIMER,
"115 Broadway, New York City."

It is but just to Dorsheimer to give his reply which closed their correspondence. Dorsheimer's motives for seeking a reconciliation with Mr. Tilden were not such as to prevent his dancing over the Governor's grave when he was no longer an object to be courted or feared, thus furnishing a post-mortem justification for the chilly reception which the Governor gave to the professions of friendship with which he had covered his advances.

DORSHEIMER TO TILDEN

"NEW YORK, NOVE. 25, 1884.

"HON. SAMUEL J. TILDEN, Graystone Yonkers, N.Y.:

"MY DEAR SIR: I have not made an earlier reply to your letter, because I could not give the assurance with reference to an allusion to you in my sketch of Mr. Cleveland's life, which circumstances now enable me to give.

"The publishers propose a new and extended edition of the biography, which will give me an opportunity to correct a phrase referring to you which was used without due consideration.

"I think it, however, proper to say that had you consulted as familiar an authority as Webster's Dictionary, you would have found that I had some justification for the use of the word 'speculation,' even in view of your own criticism upon it.

"But I admit that the word has come to have a popular meaning which refers it to such operations as are carried on in Wall street, that it is not appropriate to apply it to you.

"The carefully considered passage, which begins on page one hundred and thirty-one of the biography, should, I think, have satisfied you that there could have been no purpose to annoy you by the observation of which you complain.

"Believe me very respectfully,
"Your servant,
"WILLIAM DORSHEIMER."

Mr. Tilden acquired a large fortune, but he earned it by very hard labor and by the exercise of those qualities which commonly ensure success. He was always frugal in his expenditures and simple in his habits; he contracted no obligations which he was not always perfectly competent and ready to meet, and he was extremely cautious to make no promises nor to authorize any expectations which he did not loyally respect. During the fifteen or sixteen years which were pretty exclusively devoted to his profession he was justly proud of being able to say that he never accepted a contingent fee; that he never made a bargain in advance for the price of his services; that he never had any controversy with a client about the value of his services, which were rendered, on his client's own estimate and as we have already shown, usually for less that an ordinary broker's commission, but in a single instance, and in that the justice of his claim was eventually admitted. The money thus honorably and judiciously invested placed him in a condition of pecuniary independence which rendered him entirely inaccessible to those influences which not infrequently impair the usefulness of the most gifted men.

Though as far as possible from indulging that spirit of self-righteousness on which there is a class of politicians more or less numerous always trading, **Tilden never gave his confidence to men engaged in politics "for what there was in it,"** albeit as a party leader sometimes obliged to cooperated with them, and it would be easy to name many prominent men who he quietly assisted in dropping from pubic life, because of their tendency to sacrifice the interests of their party or country to their personal greed, vanity, or ambition. The predatory habits which this tendency fostered among politicians he regarded, and no doubt correctly, as one of the most deplorable results of our Civil war. At the public dinner at Delmonico's, on the 8th of February, 1869, Charles O'Conor in the chair, Mr. Tilden expressed himself with much feeling upon this subject.

"I may in early life have been disposed to censure extreme ambition; if so, I have unlearned the sentiment when I behold how much worse, in all its influences and all its consequences, is the spirit of venality in public affairs. [Immense applause.] I have often felt, of late years, that I would thank God if there would arise men with a generous devotion to the pursuit of ambition in the public councils, so that thus politics would cease to be the theatre of the votaries of gain, and that human nature, even in its selfishness, would be present its more generous and more useful forms. [Applause.] I think the time will speedily come when among good citizens of all parties and all classes this will be

urged as the great need of the time and when we may meet together
and discuss our differences of opinion, our differences of sentiment,
and entertain charity for those vagaries which it is impossible for us not
to have, remembering that this human society of which we form a part
can only get on when our public servants are faithful, single-minded,
and pure in their public trusts. And to them we all, of all classes, of all
parties, and of all degrees, must unite in rendering one homage.

In early life Mr. Tilden was a very careful student of the history of
the first Napoleon, and I have heard him say that nothing would have
suited him so well as a military career. That he was a born general, and
at the head of an army would have made a place for himself among the
great soldiers of the world, had the opportunity been afforded him, I
have no difficulty believing. He was sometimes accused of indecision
and of wasting opportunities in deliberation. I think this a superficial
criticism. He decided promptly enough when all the elements for a
decision were in his possession or under his control, or when more was
to be accomplished by decision than delay. He was not constitutionally
a Fabian general, but he was a Fabius when the war he was prosecuting
required Fabian generalship. He sometimes disappointed his political
partisans by declining to adopt their views, but events generally proved
that it was because he saw much farther than they. Political forces are
not all under the control of a party leader in the same degree that the
forces of an army are under the control of its general, and what seemed
indecision in him was often, if not always, prudence, good judgment,
and an uncommonly correct appreciation of the value of time as an
ally. When he said, "Not yet," it always meant that he was waiting for
the reserves which time was bringing to his aid.

"His confidences," says Mr. Carter, very truly, "were not effusive, nor
their subjects numerous; his deliberation was unfailing, and sometimes
carried the idea of indecision, not to say of an actual love of procrastination; but in my experience with him I found that he invariably ended
where he began, and it was never difficult for those to whom he gave
his trust to divine at once the bias of his mind when he thought it best
to reserve its conclusions. I do not think that in any great affair he ever
hesitated longer than the gravity of the case required of a prudent man,
or that he had a preference for delays, or that he clung over-tenaciously
to both horns of the dilemma, as his professional training and instincts

might lead him to do, and did certainly expose him to the suspicion of doing."

"I accompanied Mr. Tilden to the theatre one evening in the spring on 1877. He had been delving at his leisure for some weeks in "Carlyle's Letters and Speeches of Cromwell," prompted thereto originally, perhaps, by the traditional kinship of his ancestry with that of the "Great Usurper." When we returned I made the following memoranda of his conversation upon the theme which just then seem to interest him far more than the play"

"Tilden's has been reading Carlyle's 'Cromwell,' and in connection various biographies of C. in his library, and monographs. He says he does not remember to have had his views of any eminent man more seriously modified by reading about him that his about Cromwell. He is specially impressed with the man's moderation, sagacity, and general superiority. He seems to have considered and provided everything that was required for the success of the revolution he conducted. He recurred to the subject repeatedly in the course of the evening and after we returned from the theatre. He was constantly viewing Cromwell from his own standpoint. He remarked that Cromwell had a religious fanaticism to aid him in controlling his partisans, which had far more cohesive power than any of the ordinary political discontents which operate upon parties now. He also noticed that Cromwell began his revolution with money raised exclusively by subscription; a thought suggested no doubt by the excuses assigned by some of his friends for not insisting upon our rights in Washington at all hazards, because the State Legislatures in all the Northern and Middle States were Republican. Knowing, as I did, the situation which attracted Tilden's attention to the study of Cromwell's career at this period, I could not help thinking that if Tilden were as badly disposed a man as the Republican press represented him during the late canvass, how dangerous he might have been."

It was the thoroughness with which he mastered every detail, forecast every contingency, and by his precautions, as it were, defied the Fates, that made him always and *everywhere primus inter pares,* that impressed Mr. Carter "with his prodigious superiority to other men." And which, *mutatis mutandis,* might have made him as famous a leader in the field as in the council chamber, for he had few adventitious advantages. He had no particular charm of person, he always looked the invalid he was; he had no special graces of manner, nor was he eloquent of speech. The effect of his oratory was due exclusively to the things he said, not to the way he said them. He had a feeble voice, his elocution was utterly ineffective, and but for the fact that he never spoke without having something to say which no other speaker was likely to say with equal authority, he would have passed for a dull and tedious speaker.

Though his public papers, especially those which were written after he had reached maturity, are models of pure and idiomatic English, and some of them in many respects superior to anything to be found in our political literature, Mr. Tilden wrote with great difficulty. He always wrote for the purpose of commending his opinions to his readers, little occupied with what they were going to think of him as a writer. He shrank from no amount of labor to make his statement exhaustive and irresistible. He would spend more days over a paper designed for the public eye than most men would spend hours. It mattered not how many other things were pressing upon his attention, nor what the condition of his health at the time, he would never permit a paper to go out of his hands until he had made its positions as nearly impregnable as it was possible for him to make them. Though perfectly just toward an adversary, he never neglected a fair advantage. His logic was sure to be irresistible, and every statement of fact susceptible of verification. He never made public use of rumors or presumptions or suspicions. He left them on the tree where they grew till they ripened or rotted. He was not fluent; his first draft of paper was to its ultimate appearance but as clay to porcelain. He was indefatigable in altering and perfecting. He rarely – I think it would be safe to say that he never – sent a paper to the press that he did not submit to two or three or more friends as a sort of jury of his countrymen for the purpose of gathering from their criticism whether what he had written was likely to leave upon the public mind the impression he intended to leave. He had not the least pride of authorship, and was as ready to avail himself of the suggestions of others as to adhere to his own; indeed rather more, for it was the public which they represented, not himself, who he wished to impress. His judgment of words or forms of expression that weaken or strengthen a sentence was infallible. He never allowed himself the use of expressions not idiomatic or which the plainest people would stumble over.

As a negotiator Mr. Tilden was a marvel. He always began by making himself acquainted with the merits and strength of both sides, and he fought only for the margin. He never lost his temper – though he sometimes affected to do so – nor the control of his tongue. I have rarely known a man of eminence in public life who was less censorious, or whose judgments were at once more inflexible towards the sin and at the same time so charitable towards the sinner. Whether systematically or unconsciously, he always dealt with his friends as if they might some day become his enemies, and with his enemies as if they might become his friends, the results of both which he had frequent experience.

As a consequence, it was never embarrassing for him to enter into correspondence and relations with his adversaries whenever any adequate object for doing so presented itself. Thought holding more or less familiar relations with Mr. Tilden for a period of more than fifty years, I should find it very difficult to recall a half-dozen instances in which he allowed himself to apply an opprobrious epithet to or speak of any one in terms which, if repeated, would have disturbed their relations with each other. Were any one the object of denunciations in his presence, he was apt to make some remark which disqualified their author for assuming from his silence that he acquiesced in their justice. It was also a rare thing for any one to leave him without feeling that in one way or another his acquaintance was an important asset.

As the leader of a great party, he was compelled to enter into relations with all sorts and conditions of men. Many people eschew cooperation with those of low degree and of questionable character, as frequently from selfish as from virtuous motives. Mr. Tilden appropriated force wherever he found it, for he had no fear of being over-reached by any one. He used men of low standards for his purposes when they could be made useful, but never exhibited contempt for those who did not choose to follow him. This gave him a prodigious influence for good with the classes most dangerous to society when not properly led. He usually managed to divide those he could not control, so that they should waste their energies upon each other, leaving him the comparatively easy task of holding and wielding the balance of power between them. It was in this way that he rendered Tammany Hall practically powerless, when under leadership factions it as bent upon mischief.

There were two principles of leadership upon which he often dwelt in conversation and which were peculiarly his own. One was a generous recognition of the part which the imagination exercises upon the tidal ebbs and flows of public opinion, and the other was the importance of keeping his party constantly in the presence of the enemy. He regarded the imagination of a nation as of an individual, much as the furnace to a steamer. It must be carefully fed, and the force it generates wisely directed. Disaster is sure to follow the neglect of either of these conditions. There was something dramatic, appealing directly to the imagination, in everything he did, upon which his fame either as a lawyer or as a statesman rests. For example, the manner in which he reconstructed the tallies fraudulently destroyed in the Flagg case, and won it without calling a single witness or having a witness to call; the manner in which he proved in the Burdell case that the clergyman had actually married another woman than the one he supposed and swore he had married; the manner in which he possessed himself of the evidence by which he overthrew the Tweed ring at the moment when it seemed most securely entrenched, and sent Tweed and his confederates into exile or prison; the manner in which – no one suspecting what he was about – he procured the evidence upon which he trailed his guns upon the canal ring, morally and politically the most important of all his victories; and finally, the triumphant manner in which he used the hold he had already acquired upon the popular imagination to carry off the presidential nomination from the numerous and impatient aspirants in and out of Congress, in 1876; in all these cases the part he played was more or less unique, and so managed as to appeal, as no other Democratic statesman since Jackson's time had done, strongly to the imagination, not only of his own State, but of the whole nation.

He believed also in keeping his party always under arms, and in or ready for a fight, upon the same principle that a good general always keeps his troops, or the captain of an ocean steamer his sailors, fully employed. An army has no reason for existing without an enemy. He held the same to be true with a party. The very name implies an adversary and hostility. The duty of the leader is to keep the hostile energy distinctly in view of his followers, and in leading his followers to expect every moment, and to be always prepared to profit by, an advantageous opportunity of assailing it. A party thus led does not clamor for bipartisan commission, and the voice of the dealer is not heard in its camp.

He liked praise, but it never seemed to mislead him, for he judged his own achievements most impartially. He liked praise when he felt himself entitled to it, but he did not purchase it for more than it was worth. Flattery is the homage consciously or unconsciously paid to some kind of superiority. Of that he received an abundance; but no one better than he knew the difference between flattery and honest commendation.

He was intensely pleased with what O'Conor said of his part in the Flagg case, and was fond of repeating it, as he might be, for though a junior counsel to the two most eminent lawyers then at the New York bar, to him belonged the entire credit of winning a case of almost national importance, which, but for his ingenious defence, would unquestionably have been lost.

Though he conducted his business on business principles, and never allowed it to be confounded with his charities, he was a liberal giver. Aside from his contributions to party purposes, which after he became chairman of the State central committee were usually as large and often larger than those of any other person to the end of his days, no one was ever allowed to go empty away, who represented a cause or an object which commended itself to his judgment.

Mr. Tilden "experienced religion" at the age of nineteen, when he and his sister Mary were simultaneously admitted as members of the Presbyterian church in New Lebanon. He owned a pew in the Madison-square Presbyterian church in New York city for many years, and up to the time of his death, where he was in the habit of attending service until he took up his residence, as Governor, in Albany. There he attended the church of which Chancellor Upson was pastor, pretty regularly. When he resumed his residence in New York, in 1877, his infirmities rendered it first embarrassing and afterwards painful to submit to the constraints of a house of worship during the ordinary Sabbath exercises. He rarely, if ever, attended divine service in any church after that year. Mr. Tilden used to quote a remark of Bryant, who I suspect borrowed it from Chesterfield, that a gentleman never talks of his love affairs or his religion. Tilden at least lived up to this principle. He had no love affairs to talk of, and while he often encouraged others to unfold their opinions upon religious subjects to him, I doubt if at any time during the last half of his life he exposed his own views to any one. The Bible could hardly be regarded as a lamp to his feet and a light to his path.

If it was, it must have been by virtue of the lessons he received from it in early youth, when he undoubtedly acquired as thorough a familiarity with its contents as he was qualified to receive. But the Bible is a fountain, not a reservoir, and though one may carry the words, he can no more carry all the lessons of the Bible in his memory, than he can warm himself in winter with the summer's heat. When devoutly read, it is a new book every day, for the import of those lessons to every one changes with every change of his spiritual condition. Had Mr. Tilden studied it as he studied the other subjects which engrossed his attention in later life, he might perhaps have found shorter and easier ways out of many of his troubles, and have experienced many more pleasurable emotions in his declining years. But though apparently little occupied with the dogmas for which the different religious sects find pretext in the Bible, Mr. Tilden was profoundly penetrated and permeated by its ethics, and in many ways betrayed the tenacity of his early faith in their divine origin and authority.

Whatever may be the judgment which history is to pass upon the career of a hero of this imperfect narrative, it will search in vain to find in the political annals of this Republic the names of many who ever rendered it such effective and enduring service, nor of those, any whose service costs it so little.

APPENDIX A

DRAFT OF THE ADDRESS PREPARED FOR THE MINORITY OF THE ELECTORAL COMMISSION OF 1877 - In this instance the minority was the Democratic Party even though the Democratic Party controlled the House of Representative. There were seven Democrats and eight Republicans; which gave the deciding vote to Hayes to steal the election from Samuel Tilden by one electoral vote.

Address of and BY THE HONORABLE JOSIAH G. ABBOTT, L.L.D. – Massachusetts – House of Representatives and a member of the Electoral Commission.

To the People of the United States:

The minority of the joint commission established by the act of Congress of January 27, 1877, to decide questions arising in the count of the electoral votes, desire to address the people of the whole country on the subjects submitted to and decided by that commission.

No more important questions can ever come before any tribunal or people for consideration and determination. Upon their determination depends who shall be President of this country, whether he shall owe that great office to the free, honest choice of the people, or to bribery, forgery, and gross fraud.

The minority of that commission, by the law establishing it, had no opportunity of reporting the reasons for their action to the two Houses of Congress. The presence of a stenographer at these consultations was denied, so that record thereof exists. No way is open to those who did not join in, but on the contrary protested against, the decisions of the commission, to make public their protest except by this address. The returns of the electoral vote of four States – Florida, Louisiana, Oregon, and South Carolina – were submitted to and decided upon by the commission.

FLORIDA

In the case of Florida there were three certificates. The first, signed by the Governor, certified that the four Hayes electors were elected according to the law of Florida and the acts of Congress. The second was signed by the Attorney-General, and the third by the Governor elected on the seventh of November last; both certified the election of the Tilden electors. The Attorney General was one of the three persons first canvassing the votes.

To the third certificate were attached certified copies of all the returns of votes from every precinct in the State, which were originally made to the Secretary of the State, together with an act of the Legislature providing for a new canvass of the vote according to the law as it had been decided by the Supreme Court, and the result of the new canvass thus ordered.

It was offered to be proved, and it was not denied that such was the fact that by counting all the votes returned to the Secretary of State, according to law of Florida as expounded by the Supreme Court, the Tilden electors had been duly elected.

It was offered to be proved, and was not denied, that the Tilden electors commenced proceedings in *quo warranto* (noun : a hearing to determine by what authority someone has an office or franchise or liberty) against the Hayes electors in the court of that State having jurisdiction by its constitution, notice of which was served on the latter before they gave their votes, and as soon as they were declared elected, and which was prosecuted to this judgment – that the Hayes electors had not been elected and had no title to the office, but that the Tilden electors had legally elected and were entitled to the office.

It was offered to be proved, and was not denied, that the two canvassers who had made the certificate of election of the Hayes electors, which by the law of Florida was made on *prima facie (adv. - At first sight; before closer inspection) evidence, had erred in their construction of the law and exceeded their jurisdiction by so doing, in their canvass of votes on which the certificate was based.

Thus if was offered to be proved, and the facts were not denied, that the Governor's certificate given to the Hayes electors was false, and that the determination and certificate of two of the three who made the Board of Canvassers was false in fact and in violation of the laws of Florida, and that in making it the two had exceeded their jurisdiction. It was offered to be proved that the Supreme Court of Florida had, in effect, decided that the two canvassers had made a false certificate and exceeded their jurisdiction, and that the Circuit Court had so decided. It was offered to be proved that both the Legislation and the executive of the State had so determined, and had attempted by all means in their power to prevent the State being defrauded of its true and real vote.

The majority of the commission decided that the determination and certificate of two of a board of three canvassers, with ministerial powers only, and which by law was prima facie, not conclusive, evidence must stand and decide the great question of the presidency, although it could clearly be proved to be false in fact, and that in making it the two canvassers had exceeded their jurisdiction and authority, as held by the Supreme Court of the State, and although the Legislature and Governor had both declared it false , and that by giving effect to it the State would be defrauded of its true and real vote; and although the electors, in whose favor it was made, had been declared by the courts not to have been elected. The injustice of the decision was the more marked and flagrant by contrast. All the State officers, from the Governor down, who were voted for on the same ticket with the Tilden electors, and been counted out by the same two canvassers, at the same time, and by the same canvass by which the latter were counted out, had been declared elected by the action of the highest court of the State, and are now and have been holding their several offices to the general contentment of the citizens of Florida. But the Hayes electors alone are permitted by this decision to consummate the wrong, and act in offices to which they were never elected.

Against this decision of the commission the undersigned protested and now protest as wrong in law, bad in morals, and worse in the consequences which it entails on a great country.

It gives absolute power to two inferior ministerial (_Law._ Of, relating to, or being a mandatory act or duty admitting of no personal discretion or judgment in its performance officers) officers to withhold their determination till the day when the electoral vote is cast, as was done in this case, and then give the vote of a State to a candidate who has never received it, as was done in this case, and tells the people there is no redress (To set right; remedy or rectify) for such an outrage.

It is the decision admirably calculated to encourage fraud, and ensure its being perpetrated with success and impunity (Exemption from punishment, penalty, or harm).

It is a decision by which the people of a State may be defrauded and robbed of their dearest rights by a few unprincipled wretches, and be then compelled to acquiesce in the great wrong.

It is a decision claimed to be based on the doctrine of State rights, but, in fact, is in direct conflict with that great doctrine, for by it States and the people of States can be stripped of their rights and liberties, with no power to resist.

We protest against the decision finally because by it the people of the whole United States are defrauded and cheated; because by it a person is put into it the great office of President, who has never been chosen according to the Constitution and law, and whose only title depends on the false and fraudulent certificate of two men in the State of Florida, instead of a majority of legal voices of the whole people, declared through and by their electoral college.

LOUISIANA

In the case of Louisiana, the decision of a majority of the commission is a stupendous wrong to the people of that State, and all the other States, and in defiance of all right, justice, law, and fair dealing among men.

The law of that State establishes a Returning Board to consist of five persons of different parties, with power to fill vacancies, and to canvass and compile returns of votes from the different parishes and precincts, and declare the result. The board is given power and jurisdiction – provided affidavits are annexed to and received with the return from any precinct or parish – to inquire whether intimidation has existed, and if it is established to throw out the return for such parish;

but this jurisdiction is carefully confined to cases where affidavits are attached to and returned with the returns with the returns of the votes; in no other case whatsoever is the power to reject votes given.

It was offered to be proved, and was not denied, that the board giving the certificate to the Hayes electors consisted of four persons – all of the Republican party – instead of the five persons of different parties, as required by law; that these four members had been requested by Democrats to fill the vacancy with a Democrat, but had uniformly refused to do so.

It was offered to be proved, also, that this board of four persons- all of the Republican party- in order to perpetrate the frauds with ease and impunity, employed five disreputable persons as clerks and assistants, all of whom had been convicted, or were under indictment, for various offences, ranging from subornation of perjury up to murder. Indictment, at least, if not conviction, seemed the only admitted qualification of employment by that extraordinary board.

It was offered to be proved, and was not denied, that this board, in order to give the certificate of election to the Hayes electors, had rejected ten thousand votes, and this was done, although not a return thrown out had been accompanied by the requisite affidavit to give jurisdiction to act at all.

It was offered to be proved that the members of this Returning Board, in order to give the certificate to Hayes electors had resorted to and used affidavits known by them to be false and forged, had themselves been guilty of forgery, and had been paid for making their determination, thus adding bribery to the catalogue of their crimes.

Numerous other corrupt and fraudulent practices were offered to be proved against the members of this Returning Board, among the least of which was a wicked conspiracy to rob the people of Louisiana of their rights and liberties.

The decision of a majority of the commission rejected all this evidence and held that the certificate of election given to the Hayes electors must stand, and could not be inquired into, if all such offers of proof could be substantiated.

By that decision the people of the United States are told that the certificate of a board constituted in direct defiance of the law establishing it, and made by grasping a jurisdiction never granted to it, arrived at by forgery, perjury, wicked conspiracy, and the grossest frauds, and finally bought and paid for, must stand, and cannot be set aside; although steeped in sin and iniquity, it must make the chief magistrate of a great, free, and intelligent people.

The undersigned protest against this decision, also, as bad law, worse in morals, and absolutely ruinous in its consequences.

They denounce it in the presence of the people of the United States, and in the face of the world, because if intended and designed for such a purpose, it could not have been more cunningly contrived than it is to encourage the grossest frauds, conspiracies, and corruptions in the election of a President.

They denounce it, because it will debase the national character, deaden the public conscience, and encourage fraud and corruption in all public and private transactions and business of the people.

They denounce it, because for the first time it declares to the people by their organic law, the Constitution, it is ordained that a man may seek for, obtain, and hold this great office of chief magistrate of two and forty millions of freemen by fraud and cheating.

Nay, more , that he may openly buy the votes to elect himself, and pay down the price when the purchase is consummated by the count by the two Houses of Congress, and call them to witness the payment; and that there is no help for it but revolution.

They denounce it, because, in effect, it puts up the great office of President at auction, and says to the whole world that it may be bought in safety, and that there is no way known to man by which the title by purchase can be disputed or gainsaid (to declare false; deny).

OREGON

In the Oregon case, a certificate signed by the Governor and Secretary of State, and under the great seal of the State, certified to the election of two Hayes and one Tilden elector. The three Hayes electors produced no certificate of election signed by any person – only a certificate of certain results – from which it was claimed that it could be inferred who were elected. The law of Oregon required a list of the persons elected to be signed by the Governor and Secretary of State, under the great seal, and this requirement, as well as that of the acts of Congress, was fully met and satisfied by the first certificate. There was no certificate in the second case in any manner complying with the laws of Oregon or the acts of Congress. Yet by the decision of the commission the first certificate was rejected and the second taken, although clearly neither in conformity with State or Federal law.

The undersigned voted against counting the vote of the Tilden elector, because, notwithstanding the certificate of the Governor and Secretary of State, they were satisfied he had not been elected by the people of Oregon, and that his vote would not have been the true vote of that State.

The majority of the commission decided to set aside and reject the certificate and return, precisely the same in character that they had holden to be conclusive against all evidence in the Florida and Louisiana cases. They adopted and acted on a certificate insufficient if they regarded their former rulings, under any law, State or National.

The undersigned denounce the Oregon decision as utterly at war with and reversing the rule established in the former two cases, and because it changes the law to meet the wants of the case, establishing different rules applicable to the same facts to bring about a desired result.

In the Florida case, where the evidence failed to establish the fact, the majority of the commission voted to receive evidence to prove one elector held an office of profit and trust under the United States when appointed.

In the Louisiana case, where there was no doubt that the two electors held such office when appointed, it was voted not to receive evidence of the fact, because it was not offered to be proved that they continued to hold such offices where they voted.

Apparently, the rules change as the requirements of the case change.

SOUTH CAROLINA

In South Carolina, the undersigned voted against the Tilden electors being declared elected, because they had not received a majority of the votes of the people.

In that case it was offered to be proved, in substance, that the United States troops in large numbers were sent to the State before the election, for the purpose of influencing and controlling the votes to be given thereat (Adv - At that place, there), by interfering with and overawing the people, and that the militia of the State was used for the same purpose; that the polls were surrounded by armed bands, who by violence and force prevented any exercise of the right of suffrage (Noun-The right or privilege of voting; franchise) except on one side; in fact, that the election was controlled by the armed forces of the State and Nation, and a resort to all manner of brutality, violence, and cruelty, and was not free.

The majority of the commission refuse to admit the evidence, on grounds that would fairly warrant a President of the United States in using the whole army to take possession of all the ballot-boxes in any State, and allow no voting except for himself if he was a candidate for re-election, or for his party, and which would require both Houses of Congress to recount the vote so obtained, and to give him the fruits of such a willful and wicked violation of all constitutional law and right.

If any decision better calculated to destroy the liberty of a free people, to destroy all faith in a Republican form of government, a government of the people by the people, could be devised and contrived, the undersigned have not been able to discover it.

They denounced the decision as an outrage upon the rights of all the people, and, if sustained, and acted on, as the utter ruin of our institutions and government.

The foregoing is a brief statement of the action of the commission. To defeat that action the undersigned have done all in their power. They protest against it before it was accomplished, and they protest against it now.

They know the commission was established to receive the evidence, not to shut it out.

They know the conscience of this great people was troubled by fear that any one should obtain the high office of President by fraud, cheating, and conspiracy, and that it demanded that the charges and counter-charges of corrupt practices in reference to the election in three States should be honestly investigated and inquired into, not established and sanctified, by refusing all inquiry and examination.

They know the conscience of the whole people approved the law establishing the commission, nay, hailed it with joy, because it established, as all believed, a fair tribunal, to examine, to inquire into, and determine the charges of fraud and corruption in the election of three States; and they believe that this conscience has been terribly disappointed and shocked by the action of the commission, which establishes fraud and legalizes it perpetration, instead of inquiring into and condemning it.

The undersigned believe the action of the majority of the commission to be wrong, dangerous, nay, ruinous in its consequences and effects.

It tends to destroy the rights and liberties of the States and United States and the people thereof; because by it States may be robbed of their votes for President with impunity, and the people of the United States have foisted upon them a chief magistrate, not by their own free choice honestly expressed, but by practices too foul to be tolerated in a gambling hell.

By the action of the commission the American people are commanded to submit to one as their chief magistrate one who was never elected by their votes, whose only title depends on fraud, corruption, and conspiracy.

A person so holding that great office is a *usurper* (noun - one who seizes and holds (the power or rights of another, for example) by force and without legal authority) and should not be and will be so held by the people. As much as a usurper as if he had signed and held it by military force; in either case, he equally holds against the consent of the people.

Let the people rebuke and overrule the action of the commission. The only hope of the country rests on this being done, and done speedily and effectually, so it may never become a precedent to sustain wrong and fraud in the future.

It is the first and highest duty of all good citizens who love their country to right this foul wrong, as soon as it may be done under the Constitution and laws.

Let it be done so thoroughly, so signally, so effectually, that no encouragement shall be given to put a second time so foul a blot on our nation escutcheon (Noun - A shield or shield-shaped emblem bearing a coat of arms).

APPENDIX B

PARTY SENTIMENT IN FAVOR OF TILDEN'S RENOMINATION FOR THE PRESIDENCY IN 1884.

CLAMOR FOR TILDEN'S RENOMINATION

The following are a few specimens of the many letters addressed to Mr. Tilden and others, urging that he should accept a renomination.

Lyman Trumbull to S. J. Tilden
CHICAGO, June 7, 1884.

MY DEAR SIR: The Republicans have now made nominations for President and Vice-President, of men who are fair representatives of the Republican organization. Their election means a continuance of the partisanship, abuses, corruptions, and centralizing tendencies of the last twenty years, which you and I both believe dangerous, and if continued, in the end destructive of Republican liberty. It seems to me the patriotic duty of all men so believing to sacrifice all personal considerations for their country's good.

The Democracy all over the land are looking to you as the one person above all others to lead them in the coming political contest. The only question seems to be, Will you consent to be the candidate? I know nothing of your determination except what may be gathered from the conflicting statements of the press, and I do not expect or ask a reply to my letter. My only object in writing is to urge upon you the *duty* of yielding to the united demand of the Democracy. There are times when patriots must not hesitate, if necessary, to take their lives in their hands for liberty's sake. I know not your physical condition, but mentally you are all that your friends require, and even at the hazard of your life, I believe it your duty to listen to the united voice of the friends of constitutional liberty. I *know* that you were once fairly elected President. I feel confident that you can be again. Whether any other Democrat can be is uncertain. I fear not. It was a great mistake not to have nominated you four years ago. I felt it at the time. The country now sees it.

With the highest regard for you personally, I beg of you to let us make you President in fact.

W. S. Groesbeck to S.J. Tilden.

MY DEAR SIR: I have felt an inclination for some time to write you a letter about the approaching presidential election.

Moreover, with you as a candidate, the campaign of 1884 will take it complexion and character from yourself, and would be mainly a repetition of the campaign of 1876. "Tilden and Reform" would be again the battle cry, and the fraud of '76 would unite and arouse the Democracy as nothing else would, You hold this great card in your hand, No one else has it, nor can you transfer it to any else.

Some of the papers are saying you do not feel equal to a renewal of the contest. This brings me to what I desire especially to submit to your consideration. It is this: The contest is already prepared. We will fight again the battle of '76. With you as the candidate, the preparations for '84 are complete. The people will ask no more of you- only your name and battle-cry. Don't you see it? The campaign of '76 required great labor. You performed it well and satisfactorily. That same preparation is at hand and suitable for the campaign of '84.

Your work is already done; you may rest, as it were, and the Democracy will fight. So it seems to me.

If you are a candidate, you will be elected. Were I in your place, I would rather be President a single day and die, than live ten years without this vindication. It is true that every hour adds to the number of those who feel that you were wronged, and your right to the presidency will be affirmed in authentic and accepted history; but all this is incomplete and unsatisfactory compared with a triumphant reelection and inauguration into the office. Mr. Tilden, that would be a big day throughout the Untied States, and enough to quicken you into a new life.

John A. McClernand to S.J. Tilden.

SPRINGFIELD, ILL, JUNE 5, 1884.

TO HIS EXCELLENCY SAMUEL J. TILDEN, President-elect:

DEAR SIR: The crime which defeated the will of the people in 1876, and kept you from exercising the presidential office, needs to be avenged.

Time, and your example, have subdued and conciliated all factious opposition to you in the Democratic party. The opponents of former years are now your most noisy partisans. Your nomination in July will follow as a spontaneous and consentaneous act unless you prevent it.

Preventing it, calamitous consequences must ensue. The Democratic party will be left to fall into strife, anarchy, an impotency. The old guard and your old friends – what will become of them? The barriers to latitudinous construction will be broken down, and license given to public extravagance, official corruption, and the greed of unscrupulous and powerful monopolies.

Your declination in inadmissible. Accept the nomination, even if death should overcome you during or after the fight. If I know myself, I would, in the present extremity of country and party, suffer the martyrdom for you, vicariously, if it was possible to do so.

Excuse the freedom and energy of these remarks. They proceed from a sense of duty. I have done.

Mary P. Hoadly to S.J. Tilden.
(Personal.)

MY DEAR GOVERNOR TILDEN: Will you pardon me for taking a few moments of your time with a plea for our country?

The nomination of Blaine, with his great popularity, renders it necessary for the Democratic party to put forth as his antagonist its strongest man – its one strong man.

Never before was a political party so perfectly unanimous in its expressions of confidence and fealty as the Democratic party now gives to you and your consent to take the office of President would make your nomination and election sure. Of no other Democrat can this be said.

I know it is said that you dread the fatigue and excitement of the campaign. It will be a campaign that will run itself, for the voters will be inspired by the magic of your name, and will march to victory without your assuming any part of the necessary labor attending an election. Your friends will do all that for you and for the cause.

But even admitting that your health might suffer, and I trust that would not be the case, is not this a time, when like the soldier going to battle, a man ought to risk even his life for his country? With such a corrupt administration as Blaine would give us, and four years more of Republican party, getting itself still more firmly entrenched, what hope would there ever be of any change for the better if Samuel J. Tilden refuses to lead the hosts of his party ready to follow him to the death?

Pardon me if I have rushed in where angels fear to tread," but – do think and before positively saying, "No," try if it be not possible to say "Yes."

Very cordially your friend and admirer,

MARY P. HOADLY.

Columbus, June 7, 1884.

MY DEAR MR. TILDEN: To every word of my wife I say AMEN and AMEN.

Your friend,

GEO. HOADLY.

Hermann Lieb to S. J. Tilden.

CHICAGO, April 16, 1884.

DEAR SIR: Your letter to the Iroquois Club was the event of the evening, and forms the topic of conversation among Democrats throughout the city to-day. The sentiment for your renomination is growing into a popular demand. The party is hopelessly divided upon the tariff question, and you alone can unite it by substituting "Vindication" as battle-cry for the campaign.

Your nomination would give the signal to a resistless onslaught upon the enemy's entrenched positions upon the whole line, and it is questionable whether the Republicans could save the electoral vote of a single State. The uprising would be so spontaneous as to require no special effort on your part, and the drafting of the national platform would close the personal effort on your part. No anxiety, no trouble as to the final outcome of the struggle, need disturb your peace, as your election by a tremendous popular vote is conceded by the majority of Republicans.

Do not stifle this generous outburst of the American people by a refusal to allow your name to be used in the convention. You *may* save the Republic.

"La patrie est en danger!
Elle demande la sacrifice
De son fils bien aime!"

Hon. John Campbell to S. J. Tilden.

PITTSBURGH, PA., June 8, 1884.

DEAR SIR: There is a great deal of doubt, and I may say anxiety, on the part of the masses of the Democratic and Independent voters of the country, as to whether you will accept the Democratic nomination for President of the United States.

Without any desire to draw you out on this subject, I thought I would write to you and urge upon you the great importance of your acceptance of that nomination which will undoubtedly be unanimously tendered. In the year 1876, when you were the Democratic standard-bearer, I was chairman of the Republican City Central

Committee at Steubenville, Ohio, my home, and I did all I could to defeat you, and honestly believed that you were defeated; but later events satisfied me, and I say thousands of others, that you were cheated out of the presidency, and I have never since voted the Republican ticket. Thousands of Independent voters are waiting a chance to right the wrong that was done in 1876. But there is another reason why you should again consent to allow your name to be used. The people are tired of the Republican party and want a change, and knowing that it is almost beyond their power to dislodge the greedy hoard of office-holders, who have become so thoroughly entrenched that they cannot be routed unless they are opposed by a leader who is considered almost invincible – they, the people, demand that you again become their standard-bearer. In my capacity as late chief executive officer of the Brotherhood or Telegraphers, I have travelled all over the United States and know that I do not exaggerate when I say that the Democratic voters, are unanimous in their desire that you once more sacrifice your comfort and lead them to victory; and they *confidently* expect that you will not disappoint them.

Although I am not a public speaker, I flatter myself that I am a good organizer, and promise you that I will do all in my power to assist in the campaign, should you accept the nomination.

G. Albert Cutler to S. J. Tilden.

CHICAGO, JUNE 4, 1884.

DEAR SIR: As a Republican of thirty years' standing, and in behalf of thousands of Republicans who believe you were fairly elected President of the United States eight years ago. We earnestly beg of you to accept the nomination which will be unanimously tendered you by a convention of *white* men in July next. Should you do so, we promise you a "Tilden Club," not only in Chicago, but in every locality, composed exclusively of former Republicans who desire to see right and justice vindicated, and who will give you their earnest and most heartfelt support.

W. L. Scott to S.J. Tilden.

ERIE, PA., May 3, 1884.

If we cannot have you for a candidate, I give up all hopes of ever seeing a Democrat elected President of the United States.

Hon. Samuel J. Randall to S. J. Tilden.

HOUSE OF REPRESENTATIVES,

WASHINGTON, D.C. May 19, 1884.

The people of every part of our broad country are of one voice and opinion, that you must be our candidate. You will have to yield, and you ought to do so.

Hon. Geo. S. Converse to S. J. Tilden.

HOUSE OF REPRESENTATIVES,

WASHINGTON, D.C. June 10, 1884.

MY DEAR SIR: In confirmation of the suggestions I made to you a week ago, Saturday, that the masses of the people in the West are determined to make you our candidate for President, I wish to mention the fact that at all of the congressional conventions which have been held in Ohio, resolutions have been adopted in your favor. A more significant fact, however, is, that every county convention thus far held, with two exceptions, has passed such resolutions. The people in their primary conventions, without the consultation of politicians, are all moving in one direction. Your declination must not be thought of. A triumphant election will follow such spontaneous movement of the masses. Without you, divisions will arise in our party which are liable to result in defeat.

Cyrus McCormick to S. J. Tilden.

CHICAGO, ILL., March 27, 1884.

MY DEAR SIR: I venture to write a line to you upon a subject with which your name has been connected for some time past, with such comments as seem to make it questionable how such a letter as this may be received by you. From our past relations, however, I feel that, whatever others may say, you will allow me to express my sentiments upon this subject, not doubting their earnestness and patriotism. Permit me, then, to say, sir, that as matters now stand, Democratically considered, I have strong doubts whether your nomination by the Democratic convention is not a necessity to the success of the Democratic party, and hence that, whatever might be your personal feeling on that question, it becomes a duty you owe to the country, under such circumstances, to sacrifice private considerations for so momentous an object.

You have once been elected by the people to that high position, but were prevented from occupying it by a system of frauds disgraceful to the country, and which must yet recoil upon the heads of the party leaders responsible for the same; while the cry now is that "Tilden alone by being reinstated, can save the Democratic party," and the country.

Some have called for "the old ticket;" but my own humble impression is that "Tilden and McDonald" would be most acceptable to the Democratic party and to the whole people, East and West.

Unable, myself, for some time to take an active part in politics, while with an interest unabated in the prosperity of our great country, agitated as it now is through conflicting view of politicians on local issues, I have felt unable to restrain myself from giving expression to these sentiments towards one who, I feel, had the *ability* and the *patriotism* to steer the noble old Democratic ship through the breakers which again threaten her destruction.

Hon. J.R. Tucker to S.J. Tilden.

WASHINGTON, June 13, 1884.

MY DEAR MR. TILDEN: I have never sought to intrude myself upon your consideration during your eminent career, which by your late letter is declared to be closed forever. But I cannot forbear to express my sincere admiration of the dignity and magnanimity of the utterance with which you have made it known to your country.

No man in this era of our history has filled so distinguished a position in the eyes of his country as you have done and now do. In the comprehension of its needs, in the clear and analytic investigation of political truth, and in the formation of the statements of political philosophy, you stand, in my judgment, without a peer among our statesmen. But in practical administration, in the adaptation of sound political doctrines to the affairs of State, in shaping public policy according to the rules of political science, you have exhibited qualities which, had Providence called you, as the voice of your country did, to the presidency, would have made your term of service on of the most memorable and illustrious in our history.

Fate has denied to your country the benefit of your eminent abilities; but history will never fail to name you as the statesman who in our day best deserved the highest place to which American ambition aspires, and whose noble utterance in your act of voluntary retirement has kindled anew the admiration of the people, and moved the deepest sensibilities of their hearts.

My praise is unstinted, because bestowed on one who can offer me nothing but respect for its sincerity. You will do me the justice to believe it would not have been offered under other circumstances.

I can only hope that a kind Providence may continue your health and life to see and rejoice in the triumph of your principles and policy, though through other hands than your own, upon which alone can be based the security of our liberties and the promotion of good government and the prosperity and glory of our common country.

Note: Mr. McCormick dies shortly after this letter was written.

Hon. Thomas Ewing to S.J. Tilden
NEW YORK, June 13, 1884.

MY DEAR SIR: The statement in the enclosed slip from the "Tribune," That I have intimated that you would use your influence if favor of Cleveland, is absolutely unfounded. It is a matter of no consequence to you whether it be true or not, but it is to me, as I don't want to seem as unworthy of your uniform courtesy and consideration as such loose-tongued talk would make me appear.

The outburst of affection for you and regret at your retirement, which your letter evokes, reminds me, by contrast, of an interesting incident in the close of Mr. Webster's political career. The evening of the day on which he was beaten by Scott for the Whig nomination in 1852, myself and some other young gentlemen in Washington manifested our sympathy and respect by a serenade. In the course of a beautiful and touching response he said: Ah! My young friends, politicians are not sunflowers. They do not

"Turn on their god when he sets
The same look which they gave when he rose!"

What a contrast between your retirement from public life and that of Mr. Webster! He went out after seeking the presidency in vain, dejected and broken-hearted, while you voluntarily decline a unanimous nomination and an assured election.

With best wishes for your health and happiness, I am, etc.

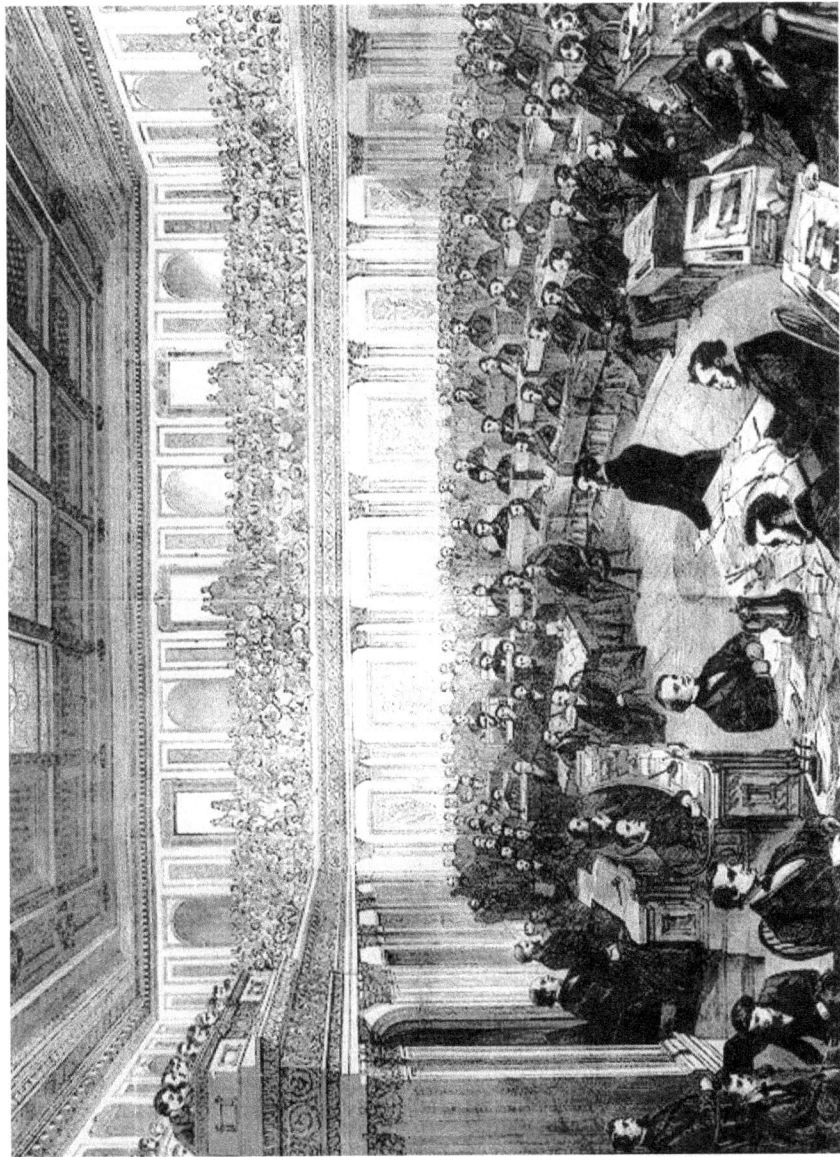

U.S. Senate Hearings

APPENDIX C

MISS GOULD'S LIST OF THE BOOKS READ TO MR. TILDEN DURING THE LAST FOUR YEARS OF HIS LIFE.

14 EAST FIFTY-THIRD STREET,
DEC. 12, 1893.

DEAR MR. BIGELOW: I enclose the copy of the list of books which I read at "Graystone." In addition to it were all the monthly and quarterly magazines. Often the entire number of an English quarterly magazines. Often the entire number of an English quarterly would take more time than a biography or novel. Then the encyclopedia was almost daily in hand. Certain of Macaulay's essays were read over and over again. Then guide-books had an important place, and were read over and over in connection with travels, etc.

One reason the number of books read in '86 was smaller than in '82 was that Mr. Tilden was working on his ancestral list, and much of the time went to reading and working on that subject.

Yours,

ANNA T. GOULD

April 1882	
Life of John Stuart Mill	Bain
Life of James Mill	Bain
Life of Jeremy Bentham	2 Vols. Bowring
Correspondence of McVey	Napier
Caroline Fox's Letters	2 Vols. Pym
A Good-Natured Man	Goldsmith
She Stoops to Conquer	Goldsmith
History of Russia	Part of Vol. 1
The Burgomaster's Wife	Ebers
Carlyle's Life	Froude
Carlyle's Reminiscences	Froude
Wicklif's Place in History	
English History	2 Vols. Green
Molinos	John Bigelow
May 1882	
Charles I., Fall of Monarchy	2 Vols. Gardiner
Autobiography of J.S. Mill	Mill
Three Years in Norway	
History of Champagne	Vizitelli
Hesperathon	2 Vols. W. H. Russell
Obelisks	Gorringe
Senior and Tocqueville Correspondence	2 Vols
Ballantyne's Experience	2 Vols
Life of George Grote	H. Grote
Conversations of Distinguished Men	2 Vols. Senior Simpson
Correspondence of Talleyrand and Louis XVIII	
Caroline von Linsingen and Wm. IV.	
Memoirs of A. de Tocqueville and Letters	2 Vols. Beaumont.
Metternich	Correspondence
Baron Stein	Correspondence
History of Constitution of United States	2 Vols. Bancroft
June 1882	
Writings of Albert Gallatin.	2 Vols. H. Adams
Life of Albert Gallatin	H. Adams
Writings of Madison	4 Vols.

The Old Regime	A. de Tocqueville
Life and Letters of Robertson	2 Vols. S. Brooke
Lives of Burke, Fox, etc.	
Conversations with Theirs, Guizot, etc.	2 Vols. Senior
July 1882	
Life of the Prince Consort	2 vols. Martin
History of England	2 Vols. Lecky
Bismarck's Letters	
The Story of Avis	E. Phelps
John Inglesant	Shorthouse
Milton, Life and Times	6 Vols. Masson
August 1882	
Ben Johnson's Works	
Life Of Lord Lyndhurst	Campbell
History of France	Vols. 1, 2, 4, 5, 6 - Guizot
Anne of Geirstein	Walter Scott
France under Richelieu and Colbert	Bridges
September 1882	
International Episode	H. James
Daisy Miller	H. James
Golden Rod	
Andrew Jackson, Life of	Sumner
Henry Erskine, Kinship and Times	Ferguson
Anne	C. F. Woolson
Gray, Life of.	Gosse
Recollections of Military Service and Society	2 Vols. Ramsay
History of My Time	4 Vols. Guizot
Embassy to Court of St. James	Guizot
Corneille and His Time	Guizot
Shakespeare and His Time	Guizot
Biographical and Critical Essays	3 Vols. A Hayward
A Chance Acquaintance	Howells
October 1882	
Fashionable Women	2 Vols. Davenport - Adams
Life of Alexander Hamilton	Lodge
English Party Leaders	2 Vols. Davenport-Adams
H. Martineau, Autobiography	2 Vols.

Journal and Correspondence of Miss Berry	3 Vols. Theresa Lewis
The Salon of Mme. Neckar	2 Vols. D'Hausonville
The Friendship of M.R. Mitford	2 Vols. L'Estrange
Outlines of Life of Shakespeare	Hallowell-Phillipps
November 1882	
Short History of French Literature	Saintsbury
Life of John Randolph	Adams
New England Federalism	Adams
Life of Gibbon	Morison
Rochefoucault's Travels	2 Vols. (1795 -6-7)
Marquis De Chastellux	2 Vols. (1780 – 1- 2
Letters of a Traveller	W. C. Bryant
What I saw in California	Vol. 1 E. Bryant
The French Court	2 Vols. Lady Jackson
Life of Samuel Johnson	Vols. 1, 4, 5, 6 - Boswell
December 1882	
German Life and Literature	2 Vols. Alex-Japp
Shelly and Mary Wollstonecraft	
French Men of Letters	Mauris
Quits	2 Vols. Baroness Tautphæus
Life of Macaulay	Morison
Initials	2 Vols. Baroness Tautphæus
Pepy's Life and World	Whateley
Life of Samuel Johnson	Leslie Stephen
The Reign of Queen Anne	Vol. 1 - Ashton
Macaulay's Essays	2 Vols.
Court Life Below Stairs	2 Vols. Fitzgerald Molloy
A Modern Instance	Howells
Dukes and Princesses in the Family of George III	2 Vols.
My Life of Writings	Arch. Allison
Reign of George II	Vol. 1 H. Walpole
Memoirs of H. Walpole	2 Vols. - Warburton
History of French Literature	Vol. 3 - Van Laun
French Society	2 Vols.
Mme. De Sévigné	2 Vols. – Countess Puliga
January 1883	

Mrs. Fletcher, Autobiography	
Heart of Steel	C. Reid
Dumont's Recollections of Mirabeau	
Valerie Aylmer	C. Reid
London to John o' Groats	E. Burritt
Confidence	H. James
Macaulay's History of England	Vol. 3
Tom Moore, Mem., Jour., and Cor.	Vols. 2, 3, 5, 6, 6 - J. Russell
Tom Moore, Mem., Jour., and Cor.	Vols. 1,2,4,8 – J. Russell
Dr. Faustus	
Lalla Rookh, etc.	T. Moore
Washington Irving, Life and Letters	Vols. 1, 2, 3, 4 - Irving
February 1883	
Hawthorne's English Note-Book	2 Vols.
Newstead Abbey, Abbotsford, etc.	Vol. 1 - Irving
Pioneer	Cooper
Doctor Zay	E. Phelps
Margravine of Baireuth, Autobiography	2 Vols.
Columbus and Friends	Vols. 1 & 2
Health Resorts	Burney Yeo
Mr. Issacs	F.M. Crawford
Lady Cowper's Diary	
Rheinsberg	Vols. 1, 2 - Hamilton
Men and Times of the Revolution	Elk Watson
Life of James Monroe	Gilman
Elective Affinities, Werther, etc.	Goethe
Life of James Mackintosh	Vol. 2.
Memoirs of Mrs. Schuyler	Mrs. Grant
March 1883	
Rush's Residence at the Court of London	Rush
Souvenirs of Mme. Vigée Le Brun	
Diary of Court Life, George IV.	3 Vols. – Lady Bury
Letters of G.C. Lewis	
An American Lady	Mrs. Gray
The People of the United States	Vol. 1 - McMasters
Hawthorne's Italian Note-Books	
Dangeau's Court France	2 Vols.

Life of J. Fenimore Cooper	Lounsbury
Red Rover	J.F. Cooper
Figures of the Past	Josiah Quincy
Life of Wadsworth	Myers
Siege of London, etc.	H. James
Eras and Characters of History	Williams
A Gentle Savage	Edw. King
Life of Sir Walter Scott	Hutton
April 1883	
Life of Wm. C. Bryant	Vol. 2 P. Godwin
Life of Charles Lamb	Ainger
Louis XIV and Court of France	Vols. 1, 2, 3 - Ms. Pardoe
Letters of Jane Carlyle	2 Vols. Froude
Secret Memories of Louis XIV	Duchess of Orleans
Reminiscences of Lord John Russell	
Walpole's Letters	Vol. 1
Memories of Louis XVIII's Court	2 Vols. 4, 5, 6 – Miss Pardoe
Mme. Recamier's Memoirs	Luyster
Louis XIV and Court of France	Vols. 4, 5, 6 – Miss Pardoe
Mme. Swetchine	
Theirs' Consulate and the Empire	Vols. 1, 2 - Theirs
The Youth of Mme. De Longueville	Victor Cousin
The Friendship of Women	W. R. Alger
Life of Thomas Jefferson	J.I. Morse
May 1883	
Life of Napoleon	Vols. 1, 2, 3, 4 - Las Casas
Napoleon in Exile	2 Vols.
Last Days of Napoleon	2 Vols. Automachi
Life of Audubon	2 Vols. Buchanan
Adams, John, Letters	
Memoirs of Napoleon	2 Vols. D'Abrantes
June 1883	
Recollections of Dean Stanley	Bradley
Life of Mme. de Staël.	2 Vols. Stevens
Duchess of Marlborough	
Accounts of Conduct of Duchess of Marlborough	
Gray Studies	J.R. Green

Four Georges and English Humorist	Thackeray
July 1883	
Memoir of S.R. Steele	Vol. 1 – Montgomery
Lord Holland's Foreign Reminiscences	
H. Walpole's Letters	Vols. 5, 6, 7
Life of Charles J. Fox	Trevelyan
Three Criticisms of Life of Wilberforce	
Two Criticisms of on J.R. Green	
Life of Lord Lawrence	2 Vols. B. Smith
Three Criticisms on Lord Lawrence	
Life of Lord Lawrence Shelburne	Vol. 3 – Fitz Maurice
Reminiscences of Ronald Gower	2 Vols. Gower
Life and Mission of Swedenborg	Worchester
August 1883	
Court of the Regency	2 Vols. Buckingham
Life of Francis Horner	
Life of Samuel Romilly	2 Vols. His Sons
History of Reign of Queen Anne	Stanhope
History of England	Mahon
Leaves from H. Greville's Journal	
Life of Lord Broughham	Campbell
Diary of Court of George IV.	Vols. 3,4 – Galt, editor
Historical Study of Edmund Burke	Morley
Life of Prince Consort	Vols. 1, 2 - Martin
September 1883	
Life of Prince Consort	Vols. 3, 4, 5 - Martin
Baron Stockmar, Memoir of	2 Vols – Max Miller
Life of Bismarck	Tr. Hezekiel Mackenzie
Life of Lord Palmerston	2 Vols – Evelyn Ashley
Life of Adolphe Thiers	LeGoff
Consulate and Empire	Vols. 6, 7 - Theirs
October 1883	
Court of James I	Lucy Aiken
Court of Charles II	Lucy Aiken
The Pilot	J.F. Cooper
History of American Navy	Vol. 1 - J.F. Cooper
Memoirs of Baroness Bunsen	A. Hare

Royal and Republican France	2. Vols – H. Reeve
Mrs. Piozzi	Vols. 1
Mrs. Adams, Journal and Correspondence	
J. Adams and Wife, Familiar Letters	
November 1883	
George Selwyn and His Contemporaries	4 Vols. - Jesse
Roger's Table Talk	
Life of Cranmer	Gilpin
Life of John Quincy Adams	12 Vols. – C.F. Adams
Nooks and Corners in England	Timbs
Life of John Huss	Gilpin
John Adams, Life and Works	Vol. 3 – C. F. Adams
December 1883	
Wraxhall's Memoirs	2 Vols.
Life of B. Franklin	Parton
Memoirs of Geo. III	Vols. 3 - Jesse
Memoirs of George III	Vol. 3 - Buckingham
Life of Andrew Jackson	Vols. 1, 3 - poarton
January 1884	
Works of Brougham	Vol. 3 5 - Brougham
Life and Correspondence of John Adams	Vols. 9, 10, 11 - Adams
Huguenots	Smiles
Life of Lord Lyndhurst	Martin
Court and Diplomatic Life	Lady Bloomfield
Life of E. Bulwer-Lytton	2 Vols. – "Son"
Marie Antoinette	2 Vols.- Campan
February 1884	
Royal Windsor	4 Vols. - Dixon
Portraits of Places	H. James
The Mohicans	J.F. Cooper
Memoirs of House of Orleans	3 Vols. - Taylor
Early Years of My Life	Albemarle
Court of the Tuileries	2 Vols. - Jackson
Revolt of the Netherlands	Schiller
Diaries of a Lady of Quality	
March 1884	
More Leaves from the Highlands	Queen Victoria

But Yet a Woman	Hardy
Berlin Society	
A Woman's Memories of World-Known Men	Houston
Address before Vermont Historical Society on Taking of Ticonderoga MS	Chittenden
Diary of William Tylden, 1815 MS	Tylden
Travels in Greece, Poland, Russia etc.	2 Vols. Stephens
Regency of Anne of Austria	2 Vols. Frere
Gil Blas	3 Vols. – LeSage – Tr., Malkin
History of the United States	Vols. 3, 4, 5, 6, 7 - Bancroft
April 1884	
Life of Philip Schuyler	2 Vols. - Lossing
Life and Times of General Lamb	Leake
Annals of Tryon County	William Campbell
Memoirs of William Wirt	2 Vols. - Kennedy
Tancred, or New Crusade	Disraeli
Charles Townsend, Wit and Statesman	Fitzgerald
Old Merchants of New York	Vols. 1, 3 - Barrett
Life of Cowper	Southey
Grays's Letters	Vols. 1, 3 - Pickering
Life of John Adams	Vol. 1 – C.F. Adams
Treason of Charles Lee	Moore
May 1884	
Her Dearest Foe	Mrs. Alexander
Life of Edward Livingston	Hart
Historical Studies	Cabot Lodge
Life of Rufus Choate	E.G. Parker
Henry V.	Towle
Curwen's Journal and Letters	Ward
Reminiscences of George Washington	Custis
Choate	Vol. 1 – S.G. Brown
Germany	De Staël
Roderick Hudson	Henry James
Old Ma'mselle's Secret	Marlitt
Life of James Otis	Tudor
American Biography,	Vol. 1 – Stark, Montgomery, Allen, Edited by Sparks

American Biography. Allen and Putnam	Vol 7 – J. Sparks
American Biography Steuben	Vol. 9 – J. Sparks
American Biography, Wayne and Vane	Vol. 4 - Sparks
American Biography - Boone	Sparks
American Biography - Oglethorpe	Sparks
American Biography - Pulaski	Sparks
June 1884	
American Biography Decatur and R. Williams	Sparks
American Biography La Selle	Sparks
Deerslayer	J.F. Cooper
Republican Court	
American Biography Charles Lee	Sparks
Pathfinder	J.F. Cooper
American Biography John Ledyard	Sparks
American Biography Jacob Leisler	Sparks
Through Belgium and France in the Ytene	Moens
In the Ardennes	K. Macquiod
Quentin Durward	W. Scott
Old Merchants of New York	Vol. 2 - Barrett
July 1884	
Vanity Fair	Thackeray
Ivanhoe	2 Vols. W. Scott
Waverley	2 Vols. W. Scott
Old Mortality	W. Scott
Peveril of the Peak	2 Vols. W. Scott
Life and Times of William IV	2 Vols. P. Fitzgerald
Northern Heights of London	Hewitt
History of the City of New York	Vols. 1, 2 – M. Lamb
A Voyage in the "Sunbeam"	Brassey
August 1884	
The Dutchman's Fireside	2 Vols. F.K. Paulding
The Fate of Mansfield Humphreys	R.G. White
History of New York City	Vol. 3 – M. Lamb
Our Chancellor	Busch
Life of Chaucer	Vols. 2, 3, 4 - Godwin
History of New York City	Vol. 4 - M. Lamb
History of New York City	2 Vols. Jones

Wilhelm Meister	Goethe
Georgina's Reasons and Pandora	H. James
Life of Sir Water Raleigh	2 Vols. – St. John
Letters of Princess Alice	Helena
Bolingbroke, Political Study and Criticism	R. Harrop
Sept 1884	
General Hull's Civil and Military Life	Campbell Clark
Reign of Henry VIII	2 Vols. - Brewer
German Tales	Auerbach
History of England	Vols. 1, 2 - Macaulay
History of England	Vols. 1, 2, 3 - J.R. Green
The Greatest of Plantagenets	
Men and the Events of My Time (India)	Sir R. Temple
Cardinal Wolsey and His Time	Howard
History of England	Vol. 4 - Green
History of Philadelphia	Scharf and Westcott
Lord Hubert, Autobiography	
Life of Mounstuart Elphinstone	Vol. 2 - Colebrook
Thirty Years' War	J.R. Greene
October 1884	
Biographical Studies	W. Bagehot
History of England	Vols. 1to 12 - Froude
Oriental Experience	Sir R. Temple
Princesses of England	A. Strickland
Queens of England – Wives of Henry VIII	A. Strickland
Queen Elizabeth	A. Strickland
The Real Lord Byron	Jeafferson
Carlyle	Vols. 3 & 4 - Froude
Life of Walter Scott	T. Carlyle
Varnhagen von Ense.	T. Carlyle
Boswell's Life of Johnson	T. Carlyle
Voltaire	T. Carlyle
November 1884	
French Revolution	2 Vols. - T. Carlyle
Posthumous Memoirs of Karoline Bauer	Vol. 2
French Revolution	Vol. 1 - Thiers
History of France	Vols. 1 & 2 - Martin

Old World Questions and New World Answers	Pidgeon
Fifty Years' Observation of Men and Events	Keyes
Leaves from Diary of H. Greville	Enfield
Retrospect of a Long Life	S.C. Hall
The Young Duke	Disraeli
Life of S. T. Coleridge	Traill
Vivian Grey	Disraeli
Crocker's Correspondence and Diaries	Vols. 1, 2 - Jennings
December 1884	
Tales of Three Cities	H. James
Napoleon I Letters and Despatches	3 Vols. - Bingham
Montcalm and Wolfe	2 Vols. - Parkman
Croker's Correspondence and Diaries	Vol. 3 - Jennings
Historical Characters	H. Bulwer
France, Social Literary, and Political	H. Bulwer
Coningsby	Disraeli
Lothair	Disraeli
Endymion	Disraeli
Marcus Aurelius	Watson
January 1885	
Life of Bolingbroke	Campbell
Life of Lord Brougham	Campbell
Life and Times of Lord Brougham	Vol. 1 - Brougham
Life of Lord Eldon	Campbell
Memoirs of Lord Abinger	Scarlett
Denman	2 Vols. J. Arnold
Life of Lord Camden	Campbell
Life of Charles Yorke	Campbell
Life of Thurlow	Campbell
Life of Lord Erskine	Campbell
Life and Times of Thos. Jefferson	Vol. 1 - Randall
February 1885	
Life and Times of T. Jefferson	Vols. 2, 3 - Randall
Speech on Lafayette	J. Q. Adams
Sandwich Islands	Cheever
Paradise in the Pacific	Wm. R. Bliss
The Solitary of Juan Fernandez	Sanitine

Jamaica	John Bigelow
Lincoln and Seward	Gideon Wells
Lord George Bentwick , Political Biography	Disraeli
Polynesian Researches	Vol. 1 - Ellis
March 1885	
Life of George Eliot	3 Vols. – J.W. Cross
Trades, Tropics, etc.	Lady Brassey
Edgar Allan Poe	Geo. E. Woodbury
Memoirs of an Ex-Minister	Malmsbury
Life of Abraham Lincoln	I.N. Arnold
Storm and Sunshine in the East	Lady Brassey
George Cabot, Life and Letters	H.C. Lodge
A Voyage in the "Sunbeam"	Lady Brassey
Hayti, or the Black Republic	Sir Spencer St. John
Jefferson's Complete Works	Vols. 4, 5 – H.A. Washington
April 1885	
Mill on the Floss	George Eliot
Jefferson's Works	Vols. 6, 7
Bloomfield at Court of Sweden	2 Vols. Lady Bloomfield
Magazine of American History, 1884	2 Vols. M. Lamb
Henry Taylor, Autobiography	2 Vols.
India Men and Times	Sir R. Temple
The Russians at the Gate of Herat	Chas. Marvin
American Political Ideas	John Fiske
Magazine of American History, 1883	2 Vols. – M. Lamb
Afghanistan and Anglo-Russian Disputes	Theo. Rodenburgh
May 1885	
Life of N.P. Willis	Henry A. Beers
Life of Samuel Adams	Vol. II – 27 - James K. Hosmer
Life of R. Waldo Emerson	O.W. Holmes
Magazine of American History,1879 – 80-81	3 Vols. – M. Lamb, editor
Russia under the Tzars	Stepniak
New York during the American Revolution	
Type	Herman Melville
Magazine American History, 1878	1 Vol. – M. Lamb
South Sea Bubbles	
The Earl and Doctor (Earl of Pemberton)	

Journal of A Cruise in the Pacific Oceans	Vol. 2 – David Porter
June 1885	
Sandwich Islands	Cheever
Stewart's Visit to the South Seas	Stewart
Jacob Barker, Incidents of Life of New Zealand and South Seas Islands.	Meade
Six Months in the Sandwich Islands	I. Bird
A Faggot of French Sticks, or Paris in 1851	Sir Thomas Head
Home Letters, 1830-1831	Disraeli
Personal Recollections of Lord Cloncurry	
Antiquities of Long Island	Furman
The Pattern on the Mount	C. II. Parkhurst
Bubbles – Brunnen of Nassau	Sir Thomas Head
Incidents of Travel in Egypt, Arabia. Petræa, and the Holy Land	2 Vols. John Loyd Stephens
July 1885	
Lafayette. Memoirs	2 Vols. – B. Sauans
Mlle. Rachel. Memoirs	2 Vols.- Mme. de B.
Incidents of Travel In Central America	2 Vols. – J.L. Stephens
Compendium of Geography and Travel, Central Asia, etc.	H.W. Bates
Compendium of Geography and Travel, Europe	Sir A. C. Ramsay
Biblical Researches	Vol. 1 – Edw. Robinson
History of the People of the United States	Vol. 2 – J.B. McMasters
Magazines of American History, 1877	1 Vol. - Lamb
History of the American Navy	2 Vols. – J.F. Cooper
Magazine of American History, 1878	1 Vol. - Lamb
Eothen	Kinglake
August 1885	
Zoraster	F.M. Crawford
Harry Marline	Admiral Porter
Aulnay Tower	Blanche Howard
Aspasia	1st Vol. Robert Hamerling
Silas Lapham	Howells
Debates, New York, etc.	
Diary of Two Parliaments	Lucy
The World of London	Paul Vasili
Society of London	Foreign Resident

Strange Adventures of a Phaeton	Black
A Pair of Blue Eyes	Hardy
Holland and Scandinavia	A.C. Hare
Addison	W.G. Courthope
Sheridan	Mrs. Oliphant
Adventures and Sufferings in Nootha Sound	John Jewett
September 1885	
Fielding	Austin Dobson
Bacon	Church
Life of Jonathan Trumbull	J.W. Stewart
Spain and the Spaniards	De Amicis
Letters from High Latitudes	Lord Dufferin
Studies of Paris	De Amicis
Oregon	Barrows
Kentucky	N.H. Shaler
Virginia	J. Esten Cooke
Michigan	Thom. McIntyre
Journey to the Hebrides	Boswell
Journey to the Hebrides	Johnson
White Wings	Black
Swallow Barn	J.P. Kennedy
The Lindwoods	2 Vols. – C. Sedgwick
Due South	M.M. Ballou
An Inland Voyage	R.L. Stevenson
October 1885	
Hope Leslie	2 Vols. – C. Sedgwick
The Redwoods	C. Sedgwick
Due West	M.M. Ballou
Wm. Wirt, Life and Times	2 Vols. – J.P. Kennedy
Constantinople	De Amicis
Around the World in Eighty Days	Jules Verne
Maryland	Wm. H. Browne
Life of Agassiz	2 Vols. – Mrs. Agassiz
Gustave Doré, Life and Reminiscences	Blanch Roosevelt
One Summer	Blanch Howard
Pride and Prejudice	Jane Austen
Bryant and His Friends	James G. Wilson

Greville, Journal 1827 – 1852	Vols. 1,2 – H. Reeve
November 1885	
Greville's Journal	Vol. 3 – H. Reeve
Gleanings in Europe - England	2 Vols. – J.F. Cooper
Souvenirs of A Diplomat	Bacourt
Gleanings in Europe - France	2 Vols. – J.F. Cooper
Gleanings in Europe - Italy	2 Vols. – J.F. Cooper
A Larger History of the United States	T. Wentworth Higginson
Life of James Monroe	D. C. Gilman
A Merry Monarch– England under Charles II	2 Vols. – W.H. Davenport
Royalty Restored	2 Vols. – J. Fitzgerald Molloy
Life of James Madison	Gay
Life and Letters of Hallock	J.G. Wilson
December 1885	
Thos. Hutchinson, Diary and Letters	P.O. Hutchinson
Colonial History of New York	Vol. 1 – Geo. W. Schuyler
Lionel Lincoln	J.F. Cooper
Rush's Court Life in London 1815-1819	Rush
Rush's Court Life	1819 - 1825
John Quincy Adams. Works	Vol. 3 – C.F. Adams
January 1886	
John Quincy Adams	Vols. 4, 5, 6, 7, 8,9 – C.F. Adams
The Cruise of the "Brooklyn"	Lt. Buhler
House of Stuart	Jesse
Lives of Engineers	Smiles
Life of Pickering	
February 1886	
John Quincy Adams	Vol. 10 – C.F. Adams
Random Recollections	H.B. Stanton
Pilgrim Fathers	
Mme. Mohl, Her Salon and Friends	K. O'Meara
Salisbury Cathedral	
Oceana	Froude
History of Tryon County	
Old Merchants of New York	Vol. 5 – Scoville Barrett
History of Wyoming	
Beaconsfield's Letters to his Sister–1832-52	

Senior's Conversations in France and Italy, 1848 --52	Simpson
Senior's Conversations with Distinguished Men, 1860-63	2 Vols. - Simpson
March 1886	
Mme. de Maintenon – A Study	
Marlborough	Saintsbury
Letters of George Sand	3 Vols.
Literature	H. Grimm
The Age of Louis XIV	Voltaire
George Ticknor, Life and Letters	2 Vols.
History of the Three Judges	Ezra Stiles
April 1886	
Reminiscences, Ronald Gower.	Vol. 1
Letters of Mme. Rémusat – 1804-1813	
Biographical Sketches	N. Senior
Haphazard	Lauman
The last Days of the Consulate	Fauriel
May 1886	
California	Royce
Colorado	Vol. 1, 2 – Bayard Taylor
Tocqueville's Conversations	2 Vols. – N. Senior
Life of J.Q. Adams	Vol. 1 – C.F. Adams
The New Puritan	J.S. Pike
June 1886	
Shaftesbury	H.D. Trail
J. Q. Adams	Vols. 2, 3 – C.F. Adams
Triumphant Democracy	And. Carnegie
Joel Barlow	Chas. B. Todd
Prince Bismarck	2 Vols. – Chas. Lowe
July 1886	
At Home in Fiji	C.F. Gordon-Cumming
Peveril of the Peak	2 Vols. – Walter Scott
Henry Esmond	Vol. 1 - Thackeray
Taine's Notes pm England	Taine
Fireside Travels	J.R. Lowell
Life of Longfellow	2 Vols. – S. Longfellow

A Walk from London to Fulham	T. Crofton Croker
High Lights	
August 1886	
2. Diary and Letters of Hugh S. Legaré	Vol. 1
2. Essays of H.S. Legaré	Vol. 2
3. American Notes	Hawthorne

Appendix D

The Last Will and Testament

of Samuel Jones Tilden

Died August 4, 1886

Mindful of the uncertainty of life, and beginning now in the full possession of all the faculties of mind and memory, I, Samuel J. Tilden of Graystone, in the city of Yonkers, county of Westchester and State of New York, do hereby make, publish, and declare this my last Will and Testament, in the manner and form following, that is to say:

I.   I hereby expressly revoke and cancel any and all other wills heretofore made by me.

II.   I hereby nominate, constitute, and appoint John Bigelow, of Highland Falls, Andrew H. Greene, and George W. Smith, of the city of New York, Executors and Trustees under this my last Will and Testament.

III.   I direct that the compensation to be paid to and receive by my said Executors and Trustees shall be to each the yearly sum of Five-thousand dollars; but such annual compensation shall be in lieu of and a full satisfaction and discharge for any and all commissions and charges other than actual disbursements to which my Executors and Trustees might or would be entitled in capacity, under the laws of this State, in any and all trusts (including all services in the special Trusts to be constituted under this Will), if their compensation were not hereby fixed and agreed upon as aforesaid; that any sum which George W. Smith may receive as my private secretary or as an officer or servant of the York Mining Company or Delphic Iron Company be deducted from his compensation as Executor and Trustee. Such compensation of Five thousand dollars shall be so long as he shall be in performance of the duties of the special Trustee under this Will of my general estate, and as trustee, manager, or director of the corporation herein-after provided. Such compensation shall be paid out of my general estate so long as it shall remain in the custody of my Executors and Trustees, and by the corporation herein-after provided, after the residue of my general estate shall be vested in such corporation.

IV.   I will and direct that all the powers and authorities granted in and by this my last Will and Testament to my said Execu-tors and Trustees shall and may be exercised by a majority of the persons or by the person who shall for the time being lawfully hold and be in the exercise of teh the func-tions of an Executor and Trustee hereunder.

V.   I request and direct that no bond or security shall be required by any Surrogate, Probate Court, or judge from my Executors and Trustees on account of the non-residence of such Executor and Trustee, or either of them, within the jurisdiction of such Surrogate, Probate Court, or judge, or for any reason whatsoever.

VI.   In case of the death, resignation, or incapacity of either of my said Executors and Trustees, the survivors of them shall immediately appoint a successor by and instrument in writing under their hands and seals; and upon such appointment being made, the person so appointed shall thereupon become and be invested with all the powers, rights, and authorities conferred upon an Executor and Trustee hereby appointed.

VII.   I direct my said Executors and Trustees to pay and discharge all my just debts and liabilities out of my personal estate.

VIII.   My said Executors and Trustees are directed to constitute the Trusts for specific persons hereinafter more particularly described and defined. My said Executors and Trustees shall be Trustees of the special Trusts by them so constituted; but the said Trusts shall be distinct and separate from the general Trust under this instrument. In their capacity of Trustees of Trusts for specific persons, they shall have power to manage the several Trusts; to collect the income thereof, and to apply the same as herein directed; to sell in their discretion the securities and to reinvest the proceeds thereof.

IX.   I hereby direct my said Executors and Trustees to allow my sister, Mrs. Mary B. Pelton, during her natural life, the use of the house number thirty-eight West Thirty-eight Street in the city of New York. I also direct them to pay any mortgage to which the said premises may be now subject. I also direct my said Executors and Trustees to invest two several sums of Fifty thousand dollars each, in separate and distinct Trusts, and to apply the income of the said two Trusts to use of the said Mary B. Pelton during her natural life. Upon the decease of my said sister Mary B. Pelton, the house known as number thirty-eight West Thirty-eighth Street in the city of New York shall be applied to the use of my grand-niece Laura A. Pelton for the remainder of her natural life. Upon the decease of my sister Mary B. Pelton , one of the said Trusts of Fifty thousand dollars shall be applied to the use of my grand niece Laura B. Pelton, unless my said sister Mary B. Pelton shall by her last will and testament have made a different disposition of the same, which she is hereby empowered to do. Upon the decease of the said Laura A. Pelton, if she leave issue, the said house number thirty-eight-West Thirty-eighth Street designated as the first Trust, and the principal of the said second Trust, being Fifty thousand dollars, shall be paid over to the heirs of her body. If she leave no issue the principal of said first Trust, being of the said house number thirty-eight West Thirty-eighth Street, shall be paid over as she may by her last will and testament direct, and the principal of the said second Trust shall be paid over to the Tilden Trust here-inafter mentioned, if the same shall have been authorized and constituted; or, if the said Tilden Trust shall not be capable of receiving the same, the principal of the said two Trusts shall be applied to such charitable objects as the Trustees for the time being. Of the two said Trusts, may designate. Upon the decease of my sister Mary B. Pelton, the principal of the third Trust, being for Fifty thousand dollars, shall be applied to the use of my niece Caroline B. Whittlesey, during her natural life, and upon her decease shall be paid over to the heirs of her body, if she leave any. If she leave no such heir, the same shall be paid over by her last will and testament she may direct. In addition to the foregoing provisions herein made for the benefit of my sister Mary B. Pelton, my Executors and Trustees shall invest such sum not exceeding fifty thousand dollars as I may hereinafter in writing instruct them to do, and hold the same as a distinct and separate Trust. The Trustees of the said special Trust shall apply the income thereof to the use of the said Mary B. Pelton during her natural life, and after her decease shall pay over the principal sum to the Tilden Trust thereinafter mentioned, if the same shall have authorized and constituted; or if the said Tilden Trust shall not be capable of receiving the same, the principal of the said Trust shall be applied to such charitable objects as the Trustees for the time being of the said Trust may designate.

X.   I direct my said Executors and Trustees to invest Fifty thousand dollars in two special and separate Trusts of Twenty-five thousand dollars each, and apply the income to the said two Trusts to the use of Lucy F. Tilden, widow of my late brother Moses Y. Tilden, during her natural life. Upon her decease, the income of one of the two said Trusts shall be applied to the use of her adopted daughter

Adelaide E. Buchanan during her natural life, unless the said Lucy F. Tilden shall by her last will and testament have made a different disposition of the same, which she is hereby empowered to do. Upon the decease of the said Adelaide E. Buchanan, the principal of the said Trust of Twenty-five thousand dollars shall be paid over to the heirs of her body, if she leave any, unless the said Adelaide E. Buchanan shall by her last will and testament have made a different disposition of the same, where she is hereby empowered to do. If she leave no issue, the principal of the said Twenty-five thousand dollars shall be paid over to such person or persons as she may designate by her last will and testament. Upon the decease of the said Lucy F. Tilden, the principal of the other Trust of Twenty-five thousand dollars shall be disposed of as hereinafter directed. --My Executors and Trustees are directed to convey to Adelaide E. Buchanan the obligations of her husband for Five thousand dollars which I loaned to him some years ago. In addition to the other provisions made in this instrument for the benefit of the said Adelaide E. Buchanan, my Executors and Trustees are also directed to set apart Twenty thousand dollars in the First Mortgage bonds of the Oregon Short Line Railroad Company as a special Trust for the benefit of the said Adelaide E. Buchanan. The Trustees of said special Trust shall apply the income thereof to the use of the said Adelaide E. Buchanan during her natural life, and after her decease shall dispose of the same as in this instrument in hereafter directed.

XI.   I hereby direct my said Executors and Trustees to invest the sum of Fifty thousand dollars, to be known as the Sixth Trust, and to apply the income of the same to the use of Susan G. Tilden, the widow of my brother Henry A. Tilden, during her natural life. Upon her decease the income of the same shall be applied to the use of my niece Henrietta A. Swan, during her natural life, unless that the said Susan G. Tilden shall by her last will and testament have made a different disposition of the same, which she is hereby

empowered to do. Upon the decease of the said Henrietta A. Swan, the principal of the said Trust shall be paid
over to the heirs of her body, if she leave any, unless the
said Henrietta A. Swan shall by her last will and testament
have made a different disposition of the same, which she
is entitled to do. If she leave no issue, then the principal of
the said Trust of Fifty thousand dollars shall be paid over
as she may direct by her last will and testament, which she
is hereby empowered to do.

XII.   I direct that my said Executors and Trustees shall vest in a
special Trust for the benefit of my niece Caroline B. Whittlesey One hundred shares of the stock of the Cleveland
& Pittsburg Railroad Company standing in my name as
Trustee, but for which she holds the power of attorney from
me to collect the income thereof. The Trustees of the said
special Trust shall apply the income thereof to the use of
the said Caroline B. Whittlesey during her natural life; and
upon her decease they shall pay over the proceeds of the
said stock to the heirs of the body of my said niece Caroline B. Whittlesey, if she leave any, and if she no such heir
pay over or assign the same to such person as she may be
her last will and testament direct.

XIII.   I also direct my said Executors and Trustees to assign to the
said Caroline B. Whittlesey my interest in the Delphic Iron
Company, whether consisting of stock or loans, counting
the same at cost and interest, and also assign all sums her
husband William A. Whittlesey may be owing to me at
the time of my decease for loans or advances to him or
for which he may be liable. I also direct my said Executors
and Trustees to invest a sum sufficient to make with the
stock in and loans to the Delphic Iron Company and the
said loans and advances to the said William A. Whittlesey,
or for which he may be liable the sum of Fifty thousand
dollars in a special Trust for the benefit of the said Caroline
B. Whittlesey. The Trustees of the said special Trust shall
apply the income of the said special Trust to the use of the
said Caroline B. Whittlesey during her natural life, and after
her decease shall pay over the same to the heirs of her body,

if she leaves any. If she leaves no such heirs then they shall pay over the same as she may by her last will and testament direct.

XIV. I direct that my said Executors and Trustees shall vest in a special Trust for the benefit of my niece Henrietta A. Swan One hundred shares of the stock of the Cleveland & Pittsburg Railroad Company standing in my name as Trustee, but for which she holds the power of attorney from me to collect the income thereof. The Trustees of the said special Trust shall apply the income thereof to the use of the said Henrietta A. Swan during her natural life; and upon her decease they shall pay over the proceeds of the said stock to the heirs of the body of my said niece Henrietta A. Swan, if she leave any, and if she no such heir pay over or assign the same to such person as she may be her last will and testament direct.--I also direct my said Executors and Trustees to invest the sum of Fifty thousand dollars as a special Trust for the use of my said niece Henrietta A. Swan during her natural life, and after her decease shall pay over the same to the heirs of her body, unless she in her last will and testament shall otherwise direct, which she is hereby empowered to do. If she leaves no such heir the said principal shall be disposed of as hereinafter provided.

XV. I hereby request the heirs-at-law of my late brother Moses Y. Tilden to unite in conveying to Lucy F. Tilden his widow, for her use during her natural life, the dwelling house in which he formerly resided at New Lebanon, with about thirty acres of land adjacent thereto, and I direct my Executors and Trustees to join in such conveyance in my behalf.------ ------------------------------I hereby request the heirs of my late brother Moses Y. Tilden, and the heirs of my late brother Henry A. Tilden and my sister Mary B. Pelton or her heirs, to unite in conveying to my Executors and Trustees the residue of the lands formerly owned by my father, Elam Tilden, or subsequently acquired by my late brother Moses Y. Tilden other than the thirty acres, or acquired by my late brother Henry A. Tilden other than the lands adjacent to

his dwelling- house or used in connection with his manu-
factories, and excepting also the land upon which a stone
building heretofore uses as a school was erected by my
late brother Henry A. Tilden. I hereby direct my Executors
and Trustees to cause said conveyances to be executed as a
condition precedent to the payment of the legacies hereby
given. My object is to keep the landed property together
and in the family, and I direct my Executors and Trustees to
apply the same use of my nephews George H. Tilden and
Samuel J. Tilden, second, during their natural lives. After
their decease the same shall be disposed of as they or the
survivor of them in their last will and testament direct.

XVI.   I authorize my said Executors and Trustees, at such time as
they may deem judicious, to release to my said nephews
George H. Tilden and Samuel J. Tilden, second, a debt
which they owe to me for cash advances lately made by
me to them in their business now amounting with interest
to the sum of about Thirty-four thousand dollars, and also
a mortgage which I hold against them now amounting
with interest to about Thirty-three thousand dollars. ----
---------------I direct my said Executors and Trustees to pay
certain notes given many years ago by my late brothers
Moses Y. Tilden and Henry A. Tilden to Catherine H.
Pierson, the principal of which I afterwards guaranteed
to save my mother form endorsing the same, which said
notes have been assumed by my nephews George H. Tilden
and Samuel J. Tilden, second, who will be relieved by the
payment thereof.

XVII.   I direct my said Executors and Trustees to set apart the sum
of Seventy-five thousand dollars as a special Trust for the
benefit of my nephew George H. Tilden. The income of the
said special Trust shall be applied by the Trustees thereof to
the use of the said George H. Tilden during his natural life.
Upon his decease, the said Fund shall be paid over to the
heirs of the body of the said George H. Tilden, if he leave
any. If he leave no such heir, then my nephew Samuel J.
Tilden, second, him survive, the said Fund shall be applied
by the Trustees of the said Fund the use of the said Samuel

J. Tilden, second, and upon his decease the said Fund shall be paid over to the heirs of his body, if he leave any. If he leave no such heir the said Fund shall be paid over as he in his last will and testament may direct.

XVIII.   I direct my said Executors and Trustees to set apart the sum of Seventy-five dollars as a special Trust for the benefit of my nephew Samuel J. Tilden, second. The income of the said special Trust shall be applied by the Trustees thereof to the use of the said Samuel J. Tilden, second during his natural life. Upon his decease the said Fund shall be paid over to the heirs of his body, if he leave any. If he leave no such heir, then if my nephew George H. Tilden survive him, the said Fund shall be applied by the Trustees of the said Fund to the use of the said George H. Tilden, and upon his decease the said Fund shall be paid over to heirs of his body, if he leave any. If he leave no such heir the aid Fund shall be paid over as he is his last will and testament may direct.

XIX.   I direct my said Executors and Trustees to set apart the sum of One hundred and fifty thousand dollars as a special Trust for the benefit of my niece Ruby S. Tilden. The income of the said special Trust shall be applied by the Trustees thereof to the use of the said Ruby S. Tilden during her natural life. Upon her decease the said Fund shall be paid over to the heirs of her body, if she leave any. If she leave no such heir, then if my niece Susan G. Tilden her survive, the said Fund shall be applied by the Trustees of the said Fund to the use of Susan G. Tilden, and upon her decease the said Fund shall be paid over to the heirs of her body, if she leave any. If she leave no such heir the said Fund shall be paid over as she in her last will and testament may direct.

XX.   I direct my said Executors and Trustees to set apart the sum of One hundred fifty thousand dollars as a special Trust for the benefit of my niece Susan G. Tilden. The income of the said special Trust shall be applied by the Trustees thereof to the use of the said Susan G. Tilden during her natural life. Upon her decease the said Fund shall be paid over to the heirs of her body, if she leave any. If she leave no such heir, then my niece Ruby S. Tilden her survive, the said Fund to the use of the said Ruby S. Tilden, and up her decease the said Fund shall be paid over to the heirs of her body, if she leave any. If she leave no such heir the said Fund shall be paid over as she in her last will and testament may direct.

XXI.   I direct my said Executors and Trustees not to enforce against the estate of my brother, the late Henry A. Tilden, or against the estate of my late brother Moses Y. Tilden, loans which I heretofore made to them, amounting to about Three hundred thousand dollars; but to release and cancel the same wherever the said Executors and Trustees shall be requested in writing to do so by George H. Tilden and Samuel J. Tilden, the second sons of the late Henry A. Tilden, or by the survivor of them.

XXII.   I direct my said Executors and Trustees to set apart a separate Trust the sum of Twenty-five thousand dollars for the benefit of Anna J. Gould during her natural life. In case she shall be with me exercising care over me during the rest of my life, I direct that the said sum of Twenty-five thousand dollars be increased to One hundred thousand dollars. The income of the said special Trust shall be applied by the Trustees thereof to the use of the said Anna J. Gould during her natural life. Upon her decease one-half of the said Fund shall be paid over as the said Anna J. Gould may by her last will and testament direct. The other half shall be paid over as herein directed.

XXIII.   I direct my said Executors and Trustees to set apart Fifty thousand dollars of First Mortgage six per cent International and Great Northern Railroad Company bonds, and Fifty thousand dollars of the First Mortgage binds of the Oregon Short Line Railroad Company guaranteed by the Union Pacific Railway Company, as a special Trust fir the benefit if my friend Miss Marie Celeste Stauffer, daughter if Isaac Stauffer, Esquire, of New Orleans. The income of the said special Trust shall be applied by the Trustees thereof to the use of the said Marie Celeste Stauffer during her natural life; free form any interference or control of any

husband she may have; and upon the decease of the said
Marie Celeste Stauffer the Trustees of the said special Trust
shall pay over the principal of the said bonds, or assign
the same, to the devisees or heirs of the said Marie Celeste
Stauffer.

XXIV.   In all cases in which the special Trusts are herein directed
to be created for the benefit of particular persons and the
income directed to be applied by the Trustees of special
Trusts. It is hereby declared that the said income shall be
kept free form all pledges, incumberances, or anticipation
thereof, and every such pledge, incumberance, or anticipation shall be void. The Trustees of the said special Trusts
are hereby empowered and directed to suspend payment
of such income during the existence of any such pretended
pledge, incumberance, or anticipation. In all cases in which
such special Trust shall be for the benefit of any female, the
said income shall be kept free from the control or interference of any husband which the said female now has or may
hereafter have; such income being intended to be sacredly
devoted to the separate personal use of said female, and is
not to be pledged, incumbered, or anticipated by her.

XXV.   I direct my Executors and Trustees, in case any special Trust
hereby directed to be constituted shall fail in whole or in
whole or in part by depreciation of securities, to make the
same good out of my general estate, so long as the general
Trust to my Executors and Trustees shall continue; and in
the case the said Executors and Trustees shall convey any
portion of that estate to a corporation designated as the
Tilden Trust, or shall vest the same in any Trust or Trusts
for charitable purposes to do so on the express condition
that the said conveyance shall be subjected to obligations to make good the funds devoted to the said special
Trusts, and shall exact from the grantee in every such case
an acknowledgement of such obligation and agreement
to fulfil the same. This provision is made subject to the
condition that the corporation shall be duly authorized
by law, by a special act or otherwise, to accept the grant,
subject to the obligations herein directed to be imposed

upon or assumed by the said corporation. I also direct my said Executors and Trustees to obey such instructions as I may hereafter give them in respect to the allotment or selection of securities for the said special Trusts or any of them.

XXVI.   I hereby authorize and direct my Executors and Trustees during the continuance of the trust of my general estate to apply any surplus income to or towards the several special Trusts hereby directed to be constituted in the same manner as they might apply the principal of my said estate to the said purposes.

XXVII.   I direct my said Executors and Trustees to apply the use of Henrietta Jones, of Monticello, out of my general estate, a sum not exceeding Five hundred dollars per annum during her natural life, or so long as the Trust embracing my general estate shall continue.

XXVIII.   In case John J. Cahill shall remain in my service the residue of my life, I authorize and direct my Executors and Trustees to pay over to him the sum of Five thousand dollars.

XXIX.   The Trustees of the said special Trust are hereby authorized form time to time to change the investments hereby directed to be made for the use of specific persons, and to purchase other securities in lieu thereof, except in the cases where the securities are herein designated and appropriated to a specific purpose.

XXX.   I authorize my Executors and Trustees to contribute out of my estate to Mrs. Maria Sinnott, for the purpose and the education of the children of her late husband, James P. Sinnott, such sum as they may deem sufficient, not exceeding, however, the sum of Five hundred dollars per annum for five years.

XXXI.   I direct my said Executors and Trustees to pay over to such of the following persons as may be in my service at the time of my decease to wit, George Johansen, Henry Gilbert, Edward Riley, Catherine Burke, and Rosa Clark each the sum of One thousand dollars; and to John Lynch, Elizabeth Byrnes, Bridget Gettins, Dennis O'Hare, and Daniel Herr each the sum of Five hundred dollars.

XXXII.   I direct to my Executors and Trustees to apply Ten thousand dollars, or such part of it as may be necessary, according to such instruction as I may hereafter to them from time to time give in writing of verbally,

XXXIII.   I authorize my Executors and Trustees to cause the establishment of a Library and Free Reading-Room in my native town of New Lebanon in the manner following, that is to say; they shall obtain title to the land on which the building stands which was erected by my brother Henry A. Tilden, and which has been occupied by a school; buying in the mortgage on the same, amounting to Fifteen thousand dollars, and, if necessary, obtaining releases from the heirs of my brother Henry A. Tilden from my sister Mary B. Pelton or her heirs, and from Mrs. Lucy F. Tilden. They shall vest the title in a corporation, if a charter shall be granted on their application to the Legislature, or a corporation can be formed under any general law. My said Executors and Trustees are hereby authorized to require, if needful, proper conveyances to be executed by the heirs of the said Henry A. Tilden or Mary B. Pelton or her heirs and by Lucy F. Tilden as condition precedent to the payment of the legacies herein given to them respectively. They shall also convey to the corporation, if one need be created, any interest which I may have in the said premises. My Executors and Trustees are authorized to expend for the creation and equipment and to invest as a permanent fund to maintain the said Library and Reading-Room the sum of Sixty-five thousand dollars, and any further sum not exceeding Thirty-five thousand dollars which I may in writing instruct my said Executors and Trustees to apply to those objects. They are also authorized to use the said building and endowment hereby provided in part for a school for the training of girls, if they find the same expedient in connection with the Free Library and Reading-Room.

XXXIV.   I hereby authorize my said Executors and Trustees to appropriate out of my estate, in such manner as they may deem most expedient, the sum of Fifty thousand dollars towards the establishment of a Library and Free Reading Room in

the city of Yonkers, and such further sum not exceeding
Fifty thousand dollars as I may hereafter instruct my said
Executors and Trustees to apply to that object. My said
Executors and Trustees are requested to apply to the Legislature for a special charter to enable them to carry out this
provision or to form a corporation under any general law
which in their judgment shall be most desirable.

XXXV.   I request my said Executors and Trustees to obtain as
speedily as possible from the Legislator an Act of Incorporation of an institution to be know as the Tilden Trust,
with capacity to establish and maintain a Free Library and
Reading Room in the city of New York, and to promote
such scientific and educational objects as my said Executors
and Trustees may more particularly designate. Such corporation shall have not less than five Trustees, with power to
fill vacancies in their number, and in case said institution
shall be incorporated in a form and manner satisfactory
to my said Executors and Trustees during the lifetime of
the survivor of the two lives in being upon which the Trust
of my general estate herein created is limited to, to wit:
the lives of Ruby S. Tilden and Susan Whittlesey, I hereby
authorize my said Executors and Trustees to organize the
said corporation, designate the first Trustees thereof, and to
convey to or apply to the use of the same, the rest, residue,
and remainder of all my real and personal estate not specifically disposed of by this instrument, or so much thereof as
they may deem expedient, but subject, nevertheless, to the
special Trusts herein directed to be constituted for particular
persons, and to the obligations to make and keep good the
said special Trusts, provided that the said corporation shall
be authorized by law to assume such obligation. But in
case such institution shall not be so incorporated, during
the lifetime of the survivor of the said Ruby S. Tilden and
Susan Whittlesey, or if for any cause or reason my said
Executors and Trustees shall deem it inexpedient to convey
said Rest, residue, and remainder or any part thereof or to
apply the same or any part thereof to the said institution, I
authorize my said Executors and Trustees to apply the rest ,

residue, and remainder of my property , real and personal, after making good the said special Trusts herein directed to be constituted, or such portions thereof as they may not deem it expedient to apply to its use, to such charitable educational and scientific purposes as in the judgment of my said Executors and Trustees will render the said rest, residue, and remainder of my property most widely and substantially beneficial to the interests if mankind.

XXXVI.   I hereby authorize my said Executors and Trustees to reserve from any disposition made by this Will such of my books as they may deem expedient, and to dispose of the same in such manner as in their judgment would have been most agreeable to me; and in such case any of my illustrated books or books of art should be given to or to the care of the institution described in this Will, my said Executors and Trustees shall make suitable regulations to preserve the same from damage and to regulate access thereto. And such disposition shall be subject to such instructions as I may hereinafter in writing give to my said Executors and Trustees.

XXXVII.   In case at any time during the Trust embracing my general estate any interest in any special Trust hereby directed to be constituted shall lapse or no disposition of such interest contained in this instrument shall be effectual to finally dispose of the same, such interest shall go to my said Executors and Trustees to be disposed of under the provisions of this Will, or if the said general Trust shall have ceased, but a corporation designated as the Tilden Trust shall be in operation, such interest shall go to the said corporation.

XXXVIII. My said Executors and Trustees are hereby invested with the following powers: 1) To manage the funds herein directed to be invested in the Trusts for specific persons until such investments shall have been made, with like authorities as in cases of other portions of my estate. 2) To sell and dispose from time to time, in their discretion, of such parts and parcels of the real estate and other property hereby devised, given, and bequeathed to them as they shall deem advisable, and so sell and dispose of the same at public or private sale, at such price or prices, and upon such terms as to mode, time, and security of payment, as they shall deem proper, and to sign, seal, execute, and deliver all proper and necessary conveyances therefore. 3) From time to time to invest and reinvest all moneys belonging to my estate whether derived form sales of said devised and bequeathed property or otherwise in such manner as they may deem expedient, subject, however, to the same Trusts upon which moneys or property were originally held by my said Executors and Trustees.

XXXIX.   I hereby devise and bequeath to my said Executors and Trustees, and to their successors in the Trust hereby created, and to the survivors and survivor of them. All the rest and residue of all the property, real and personal, or whatever name or nature and wheresesoever situated, if which I may be seized or possessed, or to which I may be entitled at the time of my decease which may remain after instituting the several Trusts for the benefit of specific persons, and after making provisions for the specific bequests and objects as herein directed. To have and to hold the same unto my said Executors and Trustees and to their successors in the Trust hereby created and the survivors and survivor of them in trust to possess, hold, manage, and take care of the same during a period not exceeding tow lives in being, that is to say: the lives of my niece Ruby S. Tilden and my grand-niece Susie Whittlesey, and until the decease of the survivor of the said two persons, and after deducting all necessary and proper expenses, to apply the same and the proceeds thereof to the objects and purposes mentioned in this my Will.

XL.   I hereby authorize my Executors and Trustees to apply Ten Thousand dollars to the creation of a trust, the income of which shall be applied to keeping in repair, improving, and adorning the cemetery in the town of New Lebanon in which the most of my near relatives are buried. I request my Executors and Trustees to make available any lawful power which may exist or can be procured for vesting the said cemetery in a corporation, to the end that the appropriation hereby authorized shall be as permanent as possible.

XLI.   I authorize my said Executors and Trustees to cause to be erected a monument which in their judgment and discretion shall seem suitable to my memory, and to defray the expense thereof from my estate.

XLII.   I also authorize my said Executors and Trustees to collect and publish, in such form as they deem proper, my speeches and public documents, and other such writings and papers as they may think expedient to include with the same, which shall be done under their direction. The expenses thereof shall be paid out of my estate. My Trustees and Executors are authorized and empowered to burn and destroy any of my letters, papers, or other documents, whether printed or in manuscript, which in their judgment will answer no useful purpose to preserve.

XLIII.   Since I have made no disposition of my property according to my best judgment and since as most of the devisees of legatees under it are females, it is impossible to foresee under what influences some one or more of them might possibly come; and since it is desirable to avert unseemly or speculative litigations, I hereby declare it to be my will that in case any person, who if I had died intestate would be entitled to any share in my property or estate shall, under any pretence whatever, institute, take or share in any proceeding to oppose the probate of this my last Will and Testament, or to impeach or impair or to set aside or invalidate any of it provisions, any devise or legacy to or for the benefit of such person or persons under this will is hereby revoked, and such person shall be excluded form any participation in and shall not have any share or portion of my property or estate real or personal, and the portion to which such person might be entitled, if I had died intestate or might otherwise be entitled under the provisions of this instrument, shall be devoted to such charitable purposes as my said Executors and Trustees shall designate.

In witness whereof, I, the said Samuel J. Tilden, the above-name-
testator, have herein set my hand and seal this twenty-third day of April
in the year one thousand eight hundred and eighty-four.

SAMUEL J. TILDEN (seal)

APPENDIX E

**AN ACT TO INCORPORATE THE TILDEN TRUST,
FOR THE ESTABLISHMENT AND MAINTENANCE OF
A FREE LIBRARY AND READING ROOM
IN THE CITY OF NEW YORK**

Passed March 26, 1887; three-fifths being present.

WHEREAS, John Bigelow, Andrew H. Green, and George W. Smith, the Executors and Trustees of the last will and testament of Samuel J. Tilden, deceased, have, in pursuance of provisions of said will and testament, made application to the Legislature for the enactment of the following act; and,

WHEREAS, The said executors and trustees deem it inexpedient to designate any purpose of the corporation herein and hereby created other than the establishment and maintenance of a free library and reading-room in the city of New York, in accordance with the purpose and intention of said testator; therefore:

The People of the State of New York, represented in Senate and Assembly, do enact as follows:

SECTION 1. The said John Bigelow, of Highland Falls, in Orange county, and Andrew H. Green and George W. Smith, of the city of New York, and such other persons as they may associate with themselves, and their successors are hereby created a body corporation and politic under the name and title of the Tilden Trust.

SECTION 2. The said John Bigelow, Andrew H. Green, and George W. Smith shall be permanent trustees of such corporation in accordance with the intention of the said will in that behalf. Within ninety days from the passage of this act they shall designate and appoint, in writing, other trustees, so that the number of trustees shall not be less than five.

SECTION 3. One-half of the other trustees so designated and appointed shall hold office for the term of one year and the other half thereof for the term of two years. After such designation and appointment shall have been made, every trustee appointed to fill any vacancy in the board of trustees shall hold office for the term of two years. Any vacancy which may at any time occur in said board through death, resignation, incapacity, expiration of term, or otherwise, shall be filled by the remaining trustees.

SECTION 4. All the powers of the said corporation shall be vested in the trustees. They shall have the power to appoint a president and vice president, secretary and treasurer, of whom the secretary and treasurer need not be members of said board. Such officers shall hold their offices upon such tenure, and shall receive such compensation as the by-laws may prescribe. Said trustees shall also have power to appoint such other officers and agents as the proper conduct of the affairs of said corporation shall require, removable at the pleasure of the board, and to fix their compensation.

SECTION 5. The said corporation shall have, in addition to the powers now conferred by law upon all corporations as such, the capacity and power to establish and maintain a free library and reading room in the city of New York, for these purposes it shall have power to demand, recover, accept, and receive all such money and other property, real or personal, as is given to it by virtue of the will of Samuel J. Tilden, or shall be conveyed or transferred to , or in any manner bestowed upon, it by the aforesaid executors and trustees by virtue of the powers therein conferred upon them; and the said corporation shall have power to hold, manage, improve, dispose of, and convey all property at any time received or acquired by it in such manner as may be best calculated to carry out its objects and purposes.

SECTION 6. The said corporation shall accept and receive all such money or other property as is given to it by the said will of Samuel J. Tilden, or shall be conveyed or transferred to, or in may manner bestowed upon, it as aforesaid by the aforesaid executors and trustees, subject to the terms and conditions expressed in and imposed by the said will of Samuel J. Tilden, in respect to the gift or gifts therein and thereby made or provided for, to a corporation to be formed and to be known as the Tilden Trust, and the said corporation shall have power to make and enter into any obligation or obligations to secure due compliance with such terms and conditions.

SECTION 7. The said corporation shall possess the powers and, except as may be otherwise provided by this act, be subject to the provisions, liabilities, and restrictions contained in the third title of the eighteenth chapter of the first part of the Revised Statutes, but nothing herein contained shall affect the rights of any parties to any action now pending or of any heir-at-law of said Samuel J. Tilden, deceased.

SECTION 8. This act shall take effect immediately.

www.ingramcontent.com/pod-product-compliance
Lightning Source LLC
Chambersburg PA
CBHW060423100426
42812CB00030B/3288/J